KU-257-102

EDUCATING YOUNG CHILDREN WITH SPECIAL NEEDS

Louise Porter

P·C·P

Copyright © this collection Louise Porter, 2002
Copyright © individual chapters remains with their authors

First published in 2002 by
Allen & Unwin
83 Alexander Street
Crows Nest NSW 2065
Australia

Reprinted 2005

Apart from any fair dealing for the purposes of research or private study, or criticism
or review, as permitted under the Copyright, Designs and Patents Act, 1988, this
publication may be reproduced, stored or transmitted in any form, or by any means,
only with the prior permission in writing of the publishers, or in the case of
reprographic reproduction, in accordance with the terms of licences issued by the
Copyright Licensing Agency. Inquiries concerning reproduction outside those terms
should be sent to the publishers.

 Paul Chapman Publishing
A SAGE Publications Company
1 Oliver's Yard, 55 City Road
London EC1Y 1SP

SAGE Publications Inc
2455 Teller Road
Thousand Oaks, California 91320

SAGE Publications India Pvt Ltd
B-42, Panchsheel Enclave
PO Box 4109
New Delhi - 100 017

British Library Cataloguing in Publication data

A catalogue record for this book is available from the British Library

ISBN 0 7619 4125 8 (hbk)   ISBN- 13 978-0-7619-5128-5
ISBN 0 7619 4126 6 (pbk)   ISBN- 13 978-0-7619-4126-2 (pbk)

Typeset by Midland Typesetters, Maryborough, Victoria, Australia
Printed and bound in Great Britain by Athenaeum Press Ltd., Gateshead, Tyne & Wear.

CONTENTS

Figures and tables   viii

About the contributors   ix

PART I—FOUNDATIONS OF EARLY YEARS EDUCATION   1

1   FUNDAMENTALS OF EARLY EDUCATION   3
Louise Porter

Key points • Introduction • Terminology • Effects of early care and education • Core values of early years education • Recommended early education practices • Conclusion • Additional resources

2   COLLABORATING WITH PARENTS   19
Louise Porter

Key points • Introduction • Rationale for collaboration with parents • The evolving parent–professional relationship • A family-centred style of service delivery • Families' service needs in the early years • Communication issues • Conclusion • Additional resources

3   IDENTIFICATION AND ASSESSMENT   36
Louise Porter

Key points • Introduction • Definitions • Purposes of assessment • Principles of assessment • Assessment methods • Issues when testing children with atypical development • Parental involvement in assessment • Equating contradictory results • Some interpretive statistics • Setting priorities • A word about labelling • Conclusion • Additional resources

4   PRINCIPLES OF PROGRAM INDIVIDUALISATION   56
Louise Porter

Key points • Introduction • Program planning • Aims of early childhood programs • Program differentiation • Planning transitions • Program evaluation • Conclusion • Additional resources

PART II—PROGRAMMING FOR ATYPICAL DEVELOPMENTAL
NEEDS   79

5   **VISION**   81
    James D. Kenefick

    *Key points • Introduction • Developmental effects of impaired vision
    • Components of vision • Atypical vision • Identification of vision
    difficulties • Children with atypical development • Programming for
    children with vision difficulties • Conclusion • Additional resources*

6   **MOTOR SKILLS**   96
    Margaret Sullivan

    *Key points • Introduction • Factors influencing motor learning and
    performance • Conditions associated with atypical physical skills •
    Trends in the development of movement control • Promoting motor
    learning • Playground games that foster motor learning • Con-
    clusion • Additional resources*

7   **DAILY LIVING SKILLS**   117
    Zara Soden

    *Key points • Introduction • Sensory skills • Sensory processing •
    Hand function • Self-care activities • Conclusion • Additional
    resources*

8   **HEARING**   140
    Lindsay Burnip

    *Key points • Introduction • The importance of hearing • The nature
    of hearing loss • Causes of hearing impairment • Intervening with
    hearing impairment • Conclusion • Additional resources*

9   **COMMUNICATION SKILLS**   154
    Bernice Burnip

    *Key points • Introduction • The components of communication •
    Facilitators of language acquisition • Causes of atypical language
    development • Communication disorders • Language delay •
    Assessment • Intervention • Conclusion • Additional resources*

10 **COGNITIVE SKILLS**   174
    Louise Porter

    *Key points • Introduction • Early cognitive attainments • Knowl-
    edge acquisition skills • Metacognitive skills • Emotional learning
    style • Conclusion • Additional resources*

11   EMOTIONAL AND SOCIAL NEEDS   191
Louise Porter

*Key points • Introduction • The need for protection and safety •
Self-esteem • Autonomy • Social needs • Social skills interventions
• Conclusion • Additional resources*

12   GUIDING CHILDREN'S BEHAVIOUR   210
Louise Porter

*Key points • Introduction • Debates about discipline of young
children • Selecting disciplinary methods • Skills for guiding
children • Conclusion • Additional resources*

Appendix I—Common causes of atypical development   228
Appendix II—Typical developmental milestones   241
Appendix II—Indicators of advanced development in young children   260
Bibliography   264
Index   296

FIGURES AND TABLES

FIGURES

3.1	A proposed process for the identification of atypical needs in young children	46
3.2	Timing of two testings coinciding with a learning plateau	49
3.3	Timing of two testings measuring two growth spurts but only one plateau	50
3.4	Distribution of abilities within a population	53
4.1	Process of program evaluation	76
5.1	Structure of the eye	84
5.2	Refractive errors	87
6.1	Changes in proportion of the human body during growth	98
6.2	Typical changes in bony alignment during early childhood relative to the appearance of 'bow legs' and 'knock-knees'	99
6.3	Preschoolers' version of a jogger's wall stretch	111
7.1	Sequence of sensory processing	120
7.2	Mature grasp patterns	127
7.3	Handing an object to be grasped to encourage forearm supination and thumb opposition	129
7.4	Developmental progression of pencil grip	131
8.1	The ear in cross-section showing regions of conductive and sensorineural hearing loss	143
8.2	Comparison of the angle of the eustachian tube in children and adults	146
9.1	The components of communication	156
11.1	Diagram of self-esteem as the overlap between the self-concept and ideal self	196

TABLES

4.1	Common and differentiated features of programs for young children	61
4.2	Young children's mode of learning and corresponding modes of teaching	66
AI.1	Summary of common disabilities	238

ABOUT THE CONTRIBUTORS

Bernice Burnip, MSpecEd, BSpecEd (Hearing Impairment), BEd, is the author of chapter 9 and contributed to Appendix II. She has worked as a mainstream and special education teacher since 1972. For the past 20 years she has worked with children with additional needs, particularly those with hearing impairments. Her special interest is in early intervention for young children's language and speech difficulties. Since 1993 she has been employed as a lecturer in special education topics at Flinders University in South Australia and continues to provide speech and language therapy to children and their parents.

Lindsay Burnip, MEd, DipTch (Primary), DipTch (Ed of the Deaf), DipAud, is the author of chapter 8. He is an audiologist, having originally qualified and worked as a primary school teacher and subsequently as a teacher of the deaf. He is a senior lecturer in the School of Education at Flinders University in South Australia, formerly coordinating and teaching topics on hearing impairment and currently specialising in the area of information technology, particularly as applied to the delivery of distance education topics.

James D. Kenefick, BOpt, is the author of chapter 5. He is a behavioural optometrist and co-founder and director of Kenefick and Associates, which is a private practice specialising in children's vision and associated learning difficulties. He is a co-founder and fellow of the Australasian College of Behavioural Optometrists and is the current state director for this organisation for South Australia and the Northern Territory. He is a past president of the Optometric Association of Australia (SA Division).

Louise Porter, PhD, MA(Hons), MGiftedEd, DipEd, is the author of seven chapters and editor of this volume. She is a child psychologist and senior lecturer in special and gifted education topics in the School of Education at Flinders University in South Australia. Her specialty areas are disability and giftedness in early childhood, professional collaboration with parents, young children's social and emotional needs, and children's behavioural difficulties. She maintains a private practice, consulting with parents and educators about developmental and emotional issues of young children. She is the author of several books, including *Student behaviour: Theory and practice for teachers* (2nd edn, 2000, Allen & Unwin, Sydney); *Behaviour in schools* (2000, Open University Press, Buckingham, UK); *Gifted young children: A guide for teachers and parents* (1999, Allen

& Unwin, Sydney; also Open University Press, Buckingham, UK); *Young children's behaviour: Practical approaches for caregivers and teachers* (1999, MacLennan & Petty, Sydney); and, co-authored with Susan McKenzie, the text *Professional collaboration with parents of children with disabilities* (Whurr, London; also MacLennan & Petty, Sydney).

Zara Soden, BAppSci (OT), is the author of chapter 7 and contributed to Appendix II. She is a paediatric occupational therapist with a specialty focus on children's sensory processing difficulties and the autism spectrum disorders. She is currently principally employed by the Flinders Medical Centre, Adelaide, whose Occupational Therapy department supported her in writing her chapter. She has lectured at Flinders University in the Bachelor of Applied Science (Disability Studies) and Bachelor of Special Education awards on daily living skills in early childhood, and has conducted numerous inservice workshops for early childhood practitioners and parents on topics such as sensory integration and relaxation in children.

Margaret Sullivan, BPthy, MAppSci (Pthy), is the author of chapter 6, co-author of Appendix II and provided advice on physical disabilities for Appendix I. She is a paediatric physiotherapist in private practice, a frequent presenter of workshops for early childhood educators and parents, and is also employed at an Adelaide hospital offering paediatric physiotherapy services. She is a clinical educator and former lecturer in paediatric physiotherapy at the University of South Australia, and has taught at Flinders University in the Bachelor of Applied Science (Disability Studies) and Bachelor of Special Education awards on the motor development of young children.

ACKNOWLEDGMENT

The authors would like to acknowledge with gratitude the comprehensive and insightful review of the draft of this text provided by Dr Linda Newman of the University of Western Sydney.

PART I

FOUNDATIONS OF EARLY YEARS EDUCATION

In the first four chapters of this text, the principles and inherent values of early years education are discussed and applied to young children with additional educational needs. As described in chapter 1, this label refers to children with learning difficulties, those with recognised disabilities and those who are learning at an advanced level—that is, those whom we call 'gifted'. All these children are included under this umbrella term, as they might not automatically be having their needs met in regular educational programs and so are likely to need adjustments to facilitate their productive engagement.

As well as focusing on the needs of individual children, this text examines how practitioners can collaborate with the children's parents or other caregivers, engaging in a two-way sharing of information and thus enriching and expanding the knowledge of both parents and professionals. Given that their families are an integral part of children's lives, we cannot consider children's needs apart from their family context and cannot expect to advance children's interests unless we equally support their families.

Even though children who are developing atypically will have some needs in addition to the usual, not all aspects of their program will have to be modified. They have many characteristics in common with typically developing children and so will require many similar educational provisions; even so, aspects of their program will need to be individualised to take account of their additional needs. Any such curricular adjustments must be framed on the basis of detailed knowledge of the children's particular strengths and needs. This can be attained only through assessment, which is a comprehensive and systematic process of gathering educationally relevant information from a variety of sources.

The main criterion for adjusting programs for children with atypical development is that the regular program must not be disrupted in the process. This is most likely to be achieved when regular programs have processes in place to plan for and meet a diversity of needs in attending children and can equip practitioners with the knowledge, skills and support for extending their programs to children whose needs are atypical.

1

FUNDAMENTALS OF EARLY EDUCATION

LOUISE PORTER

KEY POINTS

- Education in the early years has been shown to benefit children with developmental disabilities, those experiencing educationally disadvantaging circumstances, and those with typical development.
- Across the spectrum of development, children have many needs in common, but children with atypical development have additional needs. Society has the obligation to cater for a range of typical and atypical requirements.
- Although the ideal components of early education programs for children with atypical needs have been difficult to identify through research, some core values of early education imply a range of recommended practices.

INTRODUCTION

In the United States, the types of educational services provided to young children with disabilities are specified by legislation (e.g. see Cook et al. 2000); in the United Kingdom (see Long 1996; Roffey 1999) and Australia (see Williams 1996) the legislation is less prescriptive for this population, although a general educational framework governs some practices. Elsewhere, services for these children are dictated only by local policy or are not yet established practice. As for children with advanced development, where services exist at all, these are typically recommended at policy level only, with no legislative backing. Regardless of the presence of a local legal imperative, however, the authors of this book concur with the special education rationale that society has a responsibility to provide all children with an education that meets their needs—however these are manifested—and to support their families through relevant service provision (Guralnick 1997).

3

This rationale applies equally to children with compromised and with advanced development. The needs of children with disabilities might seem self-evident; while a focus on gifted children might seem unnecessary, as these children are already advantaged in that they can learn more easily than most. Nevertheless, they are still children and still need to be taught how to learn; they cannot excel without support (Braggett 1994). Thus, a special education approach advocates modified provisions for all children with atypical needs.

TERMINOLOGY

Internationally, the early childhood period is considered to span from birth to 8 years of age. However, because of the programming differences between pre-school and school settings, this text will focus mainly on children who have not yet entered school.

Remedial programs provided in the early childhood period are often referred to as 'early intervention'. The adjective 'early' in this term implies the provision of supports and resources to children and families as soon as a developmental anomaly is detected, which might be at or even before birth (Bredekamp 1993). 'Intervention' can be characterised along a continuum, from typical educational experiences and informal social supports through to the more structured and systematic provision of remedial activities for children with atypical development (Dunst 2000; Simeonsson et al. 1982).

The aim of early intervention is to optimise children's learning by making use of their strengths and attempting to circumvent their difficulties to improve their daily functioning and wellbeing (Cook et al. 2000). It also aims at supporting families in their role of meeting their child's needs. It can achieve this at a number of levels: primary prevention comprises detecting a condition before it has any expression in the child's development, as with screening for PKU, for example (see Appendix I); secondary prevention seeks to prevent identified risk conditions from affecting children's functioning; while tertiary prevention seeks to restrict the impact of an impairment on development (Guralnick 1997; Meisels 1991).

In Australia, the term *intellectual disability* is used when children's cognitive development is significantly delayed or otherwise impaired in comparison with the typical milestones and timetable. In the early childhood years we tend to be cautious about making diagnoses so early in children's lives, and thus usually employ the term 'developmental delay'. While justifiably avoiding bestowing diagnoses based on a short history of development, this term can be unfortunate, in that the word 'delay' might imply that delayed children will catch up, which is unlikely when the delay is severe.

In the United Kingdom, the terms 'learning difficulty' and 'learning disability' are used synonymously with intellectual disability or developmental delay. However, elsewhere these same terms are used to refer to difficulties—usually manifested during the school years—with reading, writing, spelling or computation, perhaps the best known being dyslexia. These difficulties are both less severe and more domain-specific than intellectual disability and so, to avoid confusion, the UK terms will not be employed in this text.

In the USA, the term *mental retardation* is used synonymously with the two terms favoured in Australia. However, as well as the stigma which the US label attracts, it leaves the door open for two misunderstandings, particularly in the lay community. The first misconception arises from the fact that its root word 'tardy' implies that 'retarded' children are able to achieve normal development—merely later than usual. For children with severe disabilities this is not going to be the case: intellectually, some may never progress beyond dealing with concrete materials, having very limited capacity to reason in the abstract.

The second misconception leads to the opposite misinformation—namely, that children who are 'retarded' are unable to learn anything at all. This is clearly not the case.

> Having assessed a six year-old's developmental skills, I subsequently explained at length to her mother that her daughter had an intellectual disability. As I was preparing to leave, the mother declared that she was extremely relieved and, on enquiry, expressed the belief that 'retarded' children cannot learn anything and so she had been hoping that her daughter would not be retarded.

Another cluster of terms comprises the triumvirate of impairment, disability and handicap. To simplify the World Health Organization's classification (see Pope 1992), an *impairment* is a discrete loss of mental or physical functioning, such as brain damage; a *disability* refers to the effect of this on the individual, such as the movement difficulties associated with cerebral palsy; while a *handicap* is the social stigma and environmental restrictions that are often imposed on those with disabilities but which are not usually an inevitable feature of their condition.

At the other end of the spectrum of abilities is the equally numerous group of children with advanced development. In the UK these children are referred to as *highly able* but elsewhere they are usually known as *gifted*. The former term, while seeming preferable, has the limitation of focusing only on those children who are currently successful, rather than including children who have the potential for high performances but whose educational circumstances or accompanying disabilities impair the expression of their skills. The term 'gifted', however, is unfortunate as it implies getting something for nothing, and ignores the fact that even very bright children have to put in effort in order to succeed.

Notwithstanding the stigma associated with the term, in this text writers will use the term 'gifted' to mean children who have the *potential* to display significantly advanced skills in any developmental domain. This is distinguished from 'talented' (or highly able) children who are already *expressing* that potential in the form of advanced achievements (as a rough guide, those who are achieving around 30% ahead of age). This distinction between giftedness and talent is proposed by Gagné (1991) and described further by Porter (1999).

Finally, to three aspects of language employed in this book. First is the use of what is called 'people first' language, in which, rather than referring to children who have disabilities as 'disabled children', the contributors refer to them as people who also have some atypical requirements. Second, we use the term additional needs to signal the inclusion of gifted children as well as children with developmental difficulties. Historically, children with disabilities have been referred to as having special needs. Finally, we use the term 'educators' to refer both to early childhood teachers and to professional caregivers in child care settings, in the belief that it is not possible to care for children without giving them an education, and equally impossible to educate children in the early years without caring for them.

EFFECTS OF EARLY CARE AND EDUCATION

High-quality centre-based care has been found to benefit children's cognitive and language development and their confidence and positiveness in interacting with peers, while producing no deterioration in attachment to their parents (Burchinal et al. 1996; Field 1991; Field et al. 1988; Ochiltree 1994; Phillips & Howes 1987; Rubenstein et al. 1981). As well as such immediate benefits, Andersson (1989, 1992) demonstrated that these gains were still present at the ages of 8 and 13 years in children who had attended child care as infants.

As for children with disabilities, such clear findings about the benefits of early intervention are difficult to obtain. This is because programs differ in their content and method of delivery; it can be difficult to determine whether developmental gains were due to maturation or resulted from the program; success could be manifested as the prevention of developmental regression or the avoidance of secondary disabilities—both of which are difficult to measure; and gains could be attained in skills that were not specifically targeted or measured, such as social or emotional qualities or parents' confidence (Bailey & Wolery 1992; Casto & Mastropieri 1986; Guralnick 1991; Kemp & Carter 1993; Simeonsson et al. 1982). Moreover, the findings on the efficacy of intervention programs with one type of disabling condition might not necessarily hold for other disabilities (Bailey & Wolery 1992).

Timing of intervention is also a factor in outcomes: it has been assumed that children benefit most from early intervention when it is begun as soon as a developmental anomaly is detected. This, however, seems to be true only for educationally disadvantaged children, those with milder disabilities and children with autism; for those with other severe disabilities, earlier is not necessarily better (Casto & Mastropieri 1986; Guralnick 1991)—perhaps because very young children with significant developmental delays might not yet be ready to take advantage of formal instruction.

The general conclusion, despite the research difficulties and issues of timing, is that early intervention is both beneficial and a natural right of children and families (Kemp & Carter 1993). Although research cannot yet identify the specific program components that are most essential, the philosophical foundation of early childhood education has generated some core values and these, in turn, have spawned some recommended practices.

CORE VALUES OF EARLY YEARS EDUCATION

Early childhood education and special education both endorse the premise that early learning is important and cannot be left to chance: young children's programs must be tailored to meet their individual needs, however these are manifested. Underpinning this process are the following core values.

Ethical service delivery

The first fundamental tenet of early years education is that professionals must treat children and their families in an ethical fashion—that is, must do what is right, just and good, rather than what is merely expedient, convenient or practical (Katz 1995). Given children's lack of power to advocate on their own behalf, practitioners must use their influence over children in the children's best interests (Australian Early Childhood Association 1991). This generic principle gives rise to some specific ethical guidelines.

The first of these is **promoting the good** of others. When catering for children with atypical development, this principle implies that you must promote their independent functioning and support the parents' ability to remain in command of their family. Thus, early years education is aimed at promoting the abilities of children and families to exercise choice—both through teaching children decision-making skills and offering them and their parents or other caregivers a range of options for them to choose between (Brotherson et al. 1995).

The second principle is that you must **do no harm**. This means that you will not 'participate in practices that are disrespectful, degrading . . . intimidating, psychologically damaging, or physically harmful to children' (NAEYC 1989: 26). As well as ensuring that provided services will actually benefit the children and their families, the injunction to do no harm requires that you do not fail to deliver a necessary service. Furthermore, any service must be delivered competently by staff with adequate training, experience and supervision.

The third principle is that recipients of services deserve **justice**—which means giving all those with whom you work equal and fair treatment, both in the sense of not discriminating against individuals because of their culture, gender, religion and so on, and in the sense of balancing the rights and interests of one group with those of another group. For example, although your main concern might be a child who has additional needs, you must balance that child's requirements with those of surrounding adults, non-disabled children and other members of the child's family. It is unjust if one child's rights are allowed to eclipse those of surrounding individuals.

The fourth principle is that parents must have enough information to be able to give **informed consent** about the program being provided for their child. Voluntary consent requires that they not be threatened with a withdrawal of services for their child if they select a service option that professionals do not endorse, and neither can they be promised extravagant benefits if they do participate (Alberto

& Troutman 1999). Furthermore, professionals cannot use emotional blackmail to coerce parents' consent (Norris & Closs 1999). Your professional status could mean that parents are subtly pressured into consenting to your plan of action, so the onus is on you to ensure that what they are agreeing to represents best practice (Rekers 1984) and that a range of viable service options have been fully considered and explored with them (Martin & Pear 1999).

Finally, children and families have a right to choose who has personal information about them, especially when that information could be used to discriminate against them (Coady 1994). Exceptions to this **confidentiality** principle occur when team members must share relevant information so that they each have sufficient knowledge of a child's or family's circumstances to provide relevant services, and when there is a threat of harm to children—such as when you suspect child abuse.

An ecological perspective of childhood and development

Across time, early childhood education has adopted various views of childhood, each with corresponding models of education. At any one time no single model has achieved unanimous support, although each has been dominant at various points in history.

An early view was that infants start out as **empty vessels** or 'adults-in-waiting' who are impoverished of adult knowledge, skills, values and culture, and who passively await the transmission of these to prepare them for later life (Dahlberg et al. 1999; David 1999). This deficit-based view focuses on achieving pre-determined outcomes, including the imperative to get young children 'ready' for school. Just as in a factory, the children are seen to be the raw material which is acted upon or manipulated to arrive at a finished product (Moss 1999). Achievement of this necessarily relies on adult-directed teaching, and perhaps the use of behaviourist methods in which educators determine what children should know then model desired skills and reinforce (reward) children for producing these.

A second early view is of Rousseau's **innocent child** who will achieve virtue if uncorrupted by the adult world and permitted free and playful self-expression (Dahlberg et al. 1999). This view of children as potential victims leads to efforts to shield them from 'negative' outside influences while offering enriching environments. Other than planning the environment, however, this perspective implies little adult mediation of children's learning for fear of 'interfering' with the natural unfolding of children's process of self-discovery.

A third view springs from **developmental** psychology whereby children of any given age are seen to share universal characteristics (Dahlberg et al. 1999). This view sees children as separate from their social context—as psychological rather than social beings. It leads to a maturational or linear perspective of development which upholds that children's skills unfold sequentially according to a biologically-determined sequence (Richarz 1993; Sandall 1993). Under this model, the educator's role is to fashion an environment that will support the emergence of new skills while recognising that, even so, children's developmental sequence cannot be altered substantially.

A fourth, postmodern or **ecological**, view refutes the concept shared by the previous three perspectives that, compared to adults, children are weak, helpless, passive, incapable, deficient, dependent and isolated, but are instead integral parts of their various social environments, actively constructing their own experiences (Dahlberg et al. 1999). They are thus rich, inventive and competent individuals who can communicate with others from birth and, in so doing, can construct their own identities and understandings (Dahlberg et al. 1999; Fraser & Gestwicki 2002). This shifts the educational emphasis away from *telling* children what they should know so that in future they acquire valued skills, towards *listening* and responding to the richness of their present lives.

In contrast with a developmental perspective, an ecological view sees children's development as holistic, dynamic, transactional and singular (Dahlberg et al. 1999; Ludlow & Berkeley 1994). Taking each of these aspects in turn, holism tells us that all domains of development (cognitive, language, physical, social and emotional) are interrelated (Bowman & Stott 1994). This implies that we cannot assess and program for skills in a single developmental domain, without regard for their impact on children's overall functioning and wellbeing.

Second is the appreciation that development is dynamic—which is to say that individuals' needs change throughout their lifetime and so the environmental features that are ideal at one age might not be the same ones that are required at another. This perspective is expressed as the principle of 'goodness of fit' which states that in order to remain facilitating, the environment needs to alter in response to individuals' changing needs (Horowitz 1987).

Third, development is transactional, which means that individuals change their environments just as their environments change them (Sameroff 1990). Rather than biological and environmental factors being additive in some static linear equation, instead the two aspects work hand-in-hand to shape children's lives. The result is that children will acquire various skills and behaviours at different times, as dictated by the experiences offered by their immediate social environment and wider culture (Bowman & Stott 1994). Individual children's skills must therefore be compared not to the milestones achieved within the dominant culture but in light of whether their behaviours are functional in, and valued by, their home setting (Bowman & Stott 1994).

Finally, rather than regarding knowledge or development as universal, the postmodern view sees it as singular, which is to say that individuals construct their own unique perspectives. This could be seen as a threat to conformity but is instead valued as recognising complexity, diversity and difference. This, then, leads naturally to explication of the concept of pluralism.

Pluralism

A 'melting pot' perspective includes children with additional needs in early education, but requires the children to conform to the setting; in contrast, pluralism accepts and honours differences and adjusts the setting to fit the children's (and adults') various needs (Lieber et al. 1998). This pluralistic perspective pertains to the full range of cultural, family and developmental differences. It requires that programs are not only developmentally and individually appropriate but also culturally and humanly appropriate (Stonehouse 1994). To achieve this, educators cannot apply a formula or packaged curriculum but must respond to the diversity of children and families in their setting (New & Mallory 1994).

The concept of **normalisation** is inherent in pluralism. It states that all children and their families deserve access to all the usual aspects of community life (Bailey & McWilliam 1990; Guralnick 2000). Over the past 30 years, this concept has led to a push for **mainstreamed** education, whereby children with atypical needs are educated in regular schools, and for **integration**, which refers to a continuum from segregated to inclusive placements, depending on which settings are deemed best to meet individual children's needs (Cook et al. 2000; Gow 1990; Guralnick et al. 1995; Wolery et al. 1994b). Still more recently, the term **inclusion** has gained increasing favour. This concept goes a step further than integration in connoting that children with additional needs are fully part of, rather than being additional to, natural settings (Roffey 1999). Inclusion assumes that most children are best served in regular settings (including schools, homes and community services), as this is where they will need to exercise their daily living skills (Guralnick et al. 1995). It refers to a pluralistic system where there is not a focus on accommodating children with atypical needs within programs but on designing programs that can support all children, whatever their needs (New & Mallory 1994; Salisbury 1991).

The importance of process

At all levels of education, processes of teaching and learning are increasingly being given more signficance than *what* the children are being asked to learn. This is partly in recognition of the rapidly expanding pool of information in society, which means that knowing facts (content) is less important than knowing how to acquire them (process). When educating young children, the process that is considered most crucial is the quality of their relationships with adults. High-quality relationships comprise adults' sensitivity to—that is, awareness of—children's needs, and their willingness to respond to those needs, as appropriate. These two aspects are the key to facilitating children's acquisition and consolidation of skills, to disposing them positively to put in the effort required to learn, and to meeting some of their need for intimacy (which within early childhood settings is also satisfied through facilitation of the children's relationships with each other).

RECOMMENDED EARLY EDUCATION PRACTICES

The difficulty of researching the effectiveness of programs for children with disabilities means that we cannot draw definitive conclusions about essential

program components (Kemp & Carter 1993)—not least because what could si
one child might not be beneficial for another, as reflected in the 'goodness-of-f..
principle. Nevertheless, research and the above core values do suggest some
ideal practices to which I shall now turn and which are summarised in Box 1.1.

Box 1.1 Values and recommended practices in early childhood education

Value	Recommended practices
Pluralism	Inclusion
Ecological perspective	Individually appropriate practice
• Respect for parents	Collaboration with parents
• Interrelatedness of development	Multidisciplinary programming
• Cultural awareness	Consideration of quality of life
Focus on processes	Naturalistic teaching
Ethical service delivery	Support for staff

Inclusion

Simply locating children in regular settings does not on its own ensure that educational practices are normalised (Bailey & McWilliam 1990). Instead, a fully
inclusive program requires three elements (Winter et al. 1994):

- *access*—children's ability physically to enter a setting with safety;
- *engagement*—their ability, once present, to take an active part in the activities on offer and to engage socially with surrounding children and adults;
- *options*—the provision of various activities from which children can select
  those that suit them.

When children with highly atypical needs are educated alongside typically
developing children, practitioners often express doubts about whether those with
additional needs truly fit in. This question has three dimensions: first, the effects
on non-disabled children; second, the developmental effects on children with
atypical development; and third, the social outcomes for children with atypical
needs who are in a group of children dissimilar to themselves.

Taking each question in turn, it is clear that inclusion must not lead to a
diminution of the care and education received by the children without disabilities
(Gow 1990). Evidence on this issue indicates that inclusion helps children with
typical development (and educators) learn about, understand and accept diversity
among individuals (Diamond et al. 1994, 1997; Favazza & Odom 1997; Guralnick 1994; Janney et al. 1995; Peck et al. 1992). However, mere contact alone is
not enough to ensure this: the contact between children with and without disabilities must be positive, and staff must have the expertise to respond appropriately
to the additional needs of children—particularly those with severe intellectual disabilities and behavioural disturbances (Green & Stoneman 1989; Guralnick 1994;
Stoneman 1993). Another documented outcome is that inclusion gives typical

children opportunities to practise altruism through supporting their peers who have additional needs (Hanson et al. 1998)—although this is beneficial only as long as it is not condescending (Stoneman 1993).

As for the developmental outcomes for children with disabilities, model inclusive programs and segregated early intervention settings achieve similar improvements in the children's intellectual and language development and sustained group play (Bruder & Staff 1998; Cole et al. 1991; Cooke et al. 1981; Harris et al. 1990; Mills et al. 1998). Nevertheless, the effect of setting on these developmental skills differs for varying degrees of disability (Cole et al. 1991; Hundert et al. 1998; Mills et al. 1998).

In terms of the social effects, inclusion does significantly increase the rate of social interaction and level of constructive play of children with disabilities, although it does not affect their social problem solving (Guralnick 1981; Guralnick & Groom 1987, 1988; Guralnick et al. 1995; Hauser-Cram et al. 1993). Again, findings differ across degrees of disability, with children with mild developmental delays deriving more social benefit from inclusive settings than those with more severe disabilities (Holahan & Costenbader 2000).

Importantly, probably as a result of their lesser social competence, children with disabilities in inclusive settings are less popular than their typically developing peers (Diamond et al. 1997; Guralnick et al. 1995; Maris & Brown 2000) and are less likely to develop true reciprocal friendships both within the program and after hours (Buysse & Bailey 1993; Guralnick 1999; Stoneman 1993). As well as producing loneliness, this could result in their having fewer opportunities to profit from the example provided by typical children. Social isolation is not necessarily an inevitable outcome, however, and could be improved by a specific focus on social interaction (see chapter 11); although friendship formation is less amenable to change (Guralnick 1999).

It must be borne in mind that in most instances these results were obtained in model settings where, moreover, at least one-quarter of the children had disabilities; it is not certain that the same findings would be attained in regular settings in which only one child with a disability was enrolled, as is common practice. Nevertheless, the interim conclusion can be drawn that the quality of the setting and its appropriateness for individual children is more crucial to program success than its segregated or inclusive nature (Fewell & Oelwein 1990; Odom 2000). In turn, the capacity of a setting to respond appropriately to individual children's unique needs depends on the following aspects.

- The physical environment (indoor architecture and outdoor play areas) must be adjusted to assure the children's safe access to the curriculum.
- Educators must actively facilitate interaction between the children with and without disabilities.
- The numbers of children per educator must be low enough to give children the specialised teaching that they require (Fewell & Oelwein 1990) without having so much adult support that the children do not relate to peers or learn to master challenges independently.

- Staff require adequate training and support, including planning time (Bennett et al. 1997; Buysse et al. 1998).
- Educators require consistent support from specialist personnel such as speech pathologists, occupational therapists or physiotherapists (McDonnell et al. 1997; Wolery et al. 1994a).
- Services must be well coordinated (Buysse et al. 1998).
- The children's parents must endorse the inclusive program, which they are likely to do when it is consistent with their own priorities (Bailey et al. 1998).
- Management of the children's behaviour must minimise disruptions to surrounding children and adults (Harris et al. 1990).

If these conditions cannot be met, it is unacceptable that children with disabilities be harmed simply to serve a civil rights agenda that demands inclusive placements for everyone (Cole et al. 1991; Gow 1990). Although the ideal of inclusion is laudable, 'one size does not fit all' and so a continuum of service options—to respond to a spectrum of needs—must be available to children and their families (Holahan & Costenbader 2000; Mills et al. 1998).

Individually appropriate practices

The principles of developmentally appropriate practice (Bredekamp & Copple 1997) state that programs for young children need to be appropriate for the children's ages (the assumption being that this will usually equate with their level of development)—but also individually appropriate, to take account of children's unique pattern and timing of development, personality, learning style and family and cultural background (NAEYC 1986). In terms of curricular content, this means that the activities on offer must be similar to those available to same-aged peers but also modified, where necessary, to enable all children to access them (Bredekamp 1993).

An emphasis on developmental appropriateness also has implications for teaching methods. Early childhood education upholds that young children learn by relating to and acting on their physical and social environment. This implies that early education cannot simply employ formal instructional methods in a downward extension of schooling, as these are not always relevant or benign when applied to younger children (Elkind 1986).

Some of the negative effects of formal teacher-directed instruction of young children are that, although it can advance children's learning in the short term, the skills can be lost again through a lack of consolidation and so result in less skill generalisation (less learning) than a child-oriented approach (Mahoney et al. 1992). Meanwhile, the children's ability to learn in less structured teaching environments—and thus their successful inclusion in regular settings—can be compromised (Copland 1995).

Highly directed programs have additional disadvantages in that children can become passive in their learning style rather than self-driven, so that their exploratory play is inhibited and self-initiation is reduced. In turn, this creates greater reliance on adults and reduced contact with peers (Hauser-Cram et al. 1993). Another disadvantage arises when children receive remedial training in many developmental domains at once (e.g. speech therapy and physiotherapy), putting them under pressure to progress in both simultaneously rather than sequentially as is the normal developmental pattern. Furthermore, such programs can confront children repeatedly with their weaknesses, whereas it can be important to balance remedial work with opportunities for children to engage in activities in their stronger skill areas and which they enjoy. Finally, highly directive teaching might increase children's compliance with adult instruction, which can render them vulnerable to overt abuse as they are taught not to resist adult commands.

Therefore, teaching methods must embrace naturalistic learning. This, however, does not prohibit using direct instruction to help children acquire skills that they are not able to learn independently (Bredekamp 1993). This option takes account of Vygotsky's notion of the zone of proximal development and notions of scaffolding or mediating children's learning which state that with suitable support from adults children can achieve more than they can independently. In this way, teaching processes do not simply follow children's independent achievements but also anticipate and impel children towards higher functioning (Fleer 1995).

Emphasis on play

These disadvantages of high levels of adult-directed instruction lead to the conclusion that play is the best vehicle for advancing young children's learning (Hanline & Fox 1993), as knowledge discovered is more meaningful than knowledge that is transmitted.

In the Piagetian perspective, play is understood to reflect children's present level of development. In contrast, others believe that children's play does not *reflect* their development so much as *drive* their attainment of the next developmental skill (Dockett & Fleer 1999)—principally metacognitive skills such as generating their own structure, solving problems, adjusting their perspective to accommodate playmates, and so on. These metacognitive skills are crucial for children's intellectual development (see chapter 10). According to this view, play persists in children's lives as the main vehicle for development until other activities take its place in driving their development (Dockett & Fleer 1999).

This perspective disputes the notions that children play merely because they have nothing better to do or that play is only fun and therefore not a significant activity (Dockett & Fleer 1999). It also counteracts assumptions that play is immature and that we should rush children through the playing phase so that they can get on with the more important business of growing up. Instead, the benefits of play, as listed in Box 1.2, imply that we cannot 'allow' children to play only after they have completed 'work'—that is, activities that adults have structured for them—as they will learn more in play than in other forms of activity.

Box 1.2 Benefits of play

Play serves many purposes: it meets children's need for recreation; advances their skills in all domains and the dispositions that support ongoing learning; meets their social and emotional needs; and provides an apprenticeship or means of acquiring everyday skills needed throughout life.

Recreation
- Play offers immediate **enjoyment**, **entertainment** and **fun**.

Development of skills
- Because it usually involves high levels of physical activity, play advances children's **physical** development.
- Through exploration, experimenting and inventing, play allows children to build knowledge and skills such as abstract thinking, hypothesis testing and problem solving. Play is the process by which children construct their knowledge of the world and so advances their **cognitive** skills.
- Although play precedes the advent of **language**, it is itself a system of symbolic representation that equips children to learn language. At the same time, play propels them into situations where they must employ communication skills. It also allows children to explore the rhythms of speech, as seen in their chanting and invention of nonsense rhymes.

Promotion of dispositions
- Play offers children opportunities to exercise **initiative** and autonomy.
- It advances **metacognitive dispositions** such as planfulness and self-regulation of thinking.
- Play allows children to experience their own potency (**efficacy**) in the process of play—that is, a sense that they can control events in their world. Toys are designed for just this purpose: they are created because the 'real thing' is too difficult or dangerous for children to manipulate.
- Play teaches children **persistence**, as they apply themselves more conscientiously to this than to most other activities.
- It teaches them **self-restraint** because, although during play children are free to follow their own impulses, they are constrained by the context or game that they have chosen to play.
- Children who engage in most fantasy play tend to develop high levels of **imagination** and **creativity**.

Social–emotional functions
- By promoting children's skills, play increases their **confidence** in their abilities.
- Play allows children to act out and thus **resolve emotional issues**.
- When engaged with peers, play gives children a vehicle for understanding how to **form and maintain relationships** with others. It requires them to coordinate their actions with playmates.

Apprenticeship
- As well as advancing the skills and dispositions that are functional in their lives (as listed above), play **socialises** children as contributing members of their culture by teaching them adult roles, rules and behaviours.

Sources: Athey (1984); Berk (2000); Glover (1999); Sheridan et al. (1999).

Collaboration with parents

The ecological perspective recognises that children both influence and are influenced by their families. This means that the wellbeing of children is promoted by supporting their whole family and having regard for the impact of services on all family members, rather than on the child with additional needs alone. This perspective implies a bidirectional relationship between educators and parents, in which educators learn from parents about their child and their aspirations for him or her while also providing support for the family. Such support must respond to family requests and can comprise a completely child-oriented service if that is what parents want, or can encompass a wider form of support that is focused on family needs. (This theme is expanded in chapter 2.)

Support for staff

Although educators' accepting attitude towards children with atypical needs is essential, that alone is not enough to make inclusion work. Instead, educators must feel empowered to manage inclusive programs. They will feel empowered when they know how to secure relevant services to meet children's needs, can collaborate with other service providers and, when appropriate to their role, can deliver an effective service themselves (Turnbull & Turnbull 1997). To be confident that they can successfully meet children's additional needs, educators require experience with these children, knowledge about typical and atypical development, personal support, time to plan, and extra resources including environmental adjustments and access to specialist personnel and education assistants (Buysse et al. 1998; Dinnebeil et al. 1998; Janney et al. 1995; Malouf & Schiller 1995; Stoiber et al. 1998; Wolery et al. 1993, 1995). Of these, knowledge is within your most immediate control. To that end, the appendices describe some potential causes of developmental disabilities (Appendix I), typical developmental milestones (Appendix II), and signs of advanced development (giftedness) in young children (Appendix III).

Interdisciplinary team work

Because of the interrelatedness of children's development and the complex pattern of atypical development, it is recommended that programs be designed to meet needs across developmental domains, including children's unique social and emotional needs. On occasion this will require that educators have access to specialists from a range of disciplines to guide program planning and implementation. This can occur at any of the following three levels (Bondurant-Utz 1994; McLean et al. 1996):

- **Multidisciplinary** endeavours comprise separate assessment and programming by various professionals.
- **Interdisciplinary** assessment and programming occurs when all professionals share information with parents and each other, and incorporate the

findings of others to yield a unified assessment and program plan but nevertheless deliver these components independently.

- **Transdisciplinary** assessment and programming occurs when team members and parents cross disciplinary boundaries to conduct assessment jointly, perhaps with just one member charged with the tasks of assessment and subsequent program delivery.

The last format sounds less overwhelming for parents and children, respects children's development as integrated, and offers valuable opportunities for individual professionals to learn about other disciplines (Bondurant-Utz 1994), However, in my experience it is difficult to implement unless specialists are co-located, and is highly inefficient as it takes enormous amounts of time for the various professionals to pass on their detailed skill and knowledge to a novice in their specialist field. It is perhaps unrealistic to expect the uninitiated to learn what a specialist has attained in up to five years of training and perhaps the equivalent again in professional experience. The result can be that the primary service provider acquires information but cannot know how to adjust the program if it is not proceeding as planned.

Thus, transdisciplinary work can mean that children and their families receive a less skilled service—which is particularly untenable when the stakes are high, as is the case when children's development is significantly delayed— and that fewer families can receive a service as team members' time is absorbed by lengthy and multiple training sessions. As with other aspects of services, then, the constraints within each setting will dictate which style of program delivery is most effective in individual circumstances.

CONCLUSION

In total, children with recognised disabilities and with advanced development constitute 6–10% of children. A further 15% will have developmental difficulties (see Figure 3.4) that, although mild, if left unassisted could have serious repercussions for the children's continued development. Virtually all of these children will be receiving early care and education in regular settings.

For many reasons, I believe that this is as it should be. Early childhood professionals are inherently child-focused, have a flexible enough structure to allow them to cope with the demands of a mixed-ability group, and are aware of the imperative to focus on children's social, emotional and physical needs as well as their intellectual skills. Finally, young children tend to respond to each other non-judgmentally, in which case social inclusion in the early years is possible— and made more probable with specific adult mediation (see chapter 11).

On the other hand, the small size of most early childhood centres means that staff are sometimes isolated from colleagues, which makes it difficult for them to exchange information about programming for children with atypical development. This means that early childhood professionals must have additional support to cater appropriately for these children.

ADDITIONAL RESOURCES

For a detailed review of early intervention, see:
Shonkoff, J.P. and Meisels, S.J. (eds) 2000 *Handbook of early intervention* 2nd edn, Cambridge University Press, Cambridge, UK

For further information on the ethics of early intervention, see:
Porter, L. & McKenzie, S. 2000 'Resolving ethical dilemmas in family-centred work' in *Professional collaboration with parents of children with disabilities* (pp. 152–78) Whurr, London (also MacLennan & Petty, Sydney)
Stonehouse, A. 1991 *Our code of ethics at work* Australian Early Childhood Association, Watson, ACT

For a United Kingdom perspective on collaborative early intervention, see:
Roffey, S. 1999 *Special needs in the early years: collaboration, communication and coordination* David Fulton, London

For a discussion of the importance of a play-based curriculum:
Dau, E. (ed.) 1999 *Child's play: revisiting play in early childhood settings* MacLennan & Petty, Sydney
Dockett, S. and Fleer, M. 1999 *Play and pedagogy in early childhood: bending the rules* Harcourt Brace, Sydney
Fraser, S. and Gestwicki, C. 2002 *Authentic childhood: exploring Reggio Emilia in the classroom* Delmar, Albany, NY
Macintyre, C. 2001 *Enhancing learning through play: a developmental perspective for early years settings* David Fulton, London

2

COLLABORATING WITH PARENTS

LOUISE PORTER

KEY POINTS

- Parents' support for their child's program is considered a crucial factor in its success.
- In order to meet the needs of all family members—including the child with additional challenges—parents must be able to remain in command of their family life. This means that interventions with a child must not undermine parents.
- Parents might require a range of services during their child's early years, some of which you can supply directly and some of which you can help them to secure from elsewhere.

INTRODUCTION

The involvement of parents or other primary caregivers in their child's program is thought to be the main factor that allows the initial gains of early intervention to be maintained in the longer term (Cook et al. 2000). Having said this, two limitations must be mentioned. First, any evidence on this score is anecdotal: the only study concerning children with disabilities which gathered empirical evidence found no benefits for children's developmental gains, parent stress or parent–child interaction patterns from parent-centred early intervention compared with child-centred programs (Mahoney & Bella 1998). Second, for benefits to accrue, the form of parents' involvement is crucial (White et al. 1992): placing parents in the role of their child's instructor does not improve outcomes for children—and can even be detrimental to them and their family (Ramey & Ramey 1992; White et al. 1992). Instead, the emotional support parents receive from their child's educators is likely to be more beneficial than training them to teach their child formally.

The perspective in this chapter is that children's needs are best met by taking every family member into account, by promoting the whole family's healthy functioning and maintaining the parents' confidence in their ability to care for all their children. In turn, their empowerment will improve outcomes for their son or daughter with additional needs.

RATIONALE FOR COLLABORATION WITH PARENTS

The active inclusion of parents in their child's early care and education is predicated on the dual notions of parents' rights to be involved and of the benefits for children that arise from continuity between their home and care or educational environments (Powell 1994). These benefits are assumed to arise for the following reasons (Dale 1996; Sebastian 1989).

- Parents have the most important and enduring relationship with their children.
- Children learn more from their home environment than from any other setting.
- Parents have a strong commitment to their children and families and to voicing their needs.
- Parents have more detailed knowledge than professionals about their child across time and in a variety of settings; moreover, this knowledge is more personal and in-depth than that of professionals.
- In the case of children with recognised disabilities, many parents will know more about their child's particular disability and about the service system than many professionals.
- Parents know their aspirations for their child and family and what is best for their family.
- Parents' involvement in their child's education contributes to children's positive attitudes to learning and to themselves as learners (Jones & Jones 1998).
- Parental involvement in their child's education promotes mutual respect and understanding between the home and centre or school.
- Accountability is more open when parents are involved in their child's program.
- Some parents need extra support and guidance to understand and cater for their child's atypical needs.

Through participation in their child's program, parents can gain skills and confidence in their ability to meet their child's atypical needs. Meanwhile, educators can work more effectively when they have information from parents about previous interventions and about what works for them at home.

Parents and professionals share a common desire to pursue what is best for the child. By working together, you can fashion a program that maximises the chances of achieving an optimal outcome for the child, family and yourself professionally.

THE EVOLVING PARENT–PROFESSIONAL RELATIONSHIP

Although working with parents has been an aim of professional services for much of their history, over time our views of disability, of parents, of professionals and of their relationship have changed. Half a century ago, parents tended to see professionals as having high status by virtue of their specialised knowledge, and so deferred to professionals' opinions. Subsequently, as notions of dominance receded, professionals would communicate more routinely with parents but still held the decisive role as experts who 'knew what was best' for children. Next, parents became involved in their child's education, but mainly in peripheral ways (e.g. organising an excursion or helping to raise funds). In this way, parents and professionals worked in parallel with each other.

The next major trend was towards coordination between parents and professionals, which comprised some joint planning and sharing of information. Still the focus was mainly on teaching parents skills so that they could work with their children under the direction of the professionals. However, some parents perceived this educational approach as patronising; much parent training was redundant, as parents already had excellent skills and did extensive informal teaching of their children (Foster et al. 1981); while some found that a formal teaching role violated the uniquely personal aspect of their relationship with their children (Seligman & Darling 1997).

Finally, the most recent emphasis has been on collaboration, with parents and professionals determining priorities and planning strategies jointly (Daka-Mulwanda et al. 1995; Turnbull & Turnbull 1997). Although many parents want to take an active part in decision making, some are content to leave the decisions to professionals. For some parents, the process of formulating an individualised education plan is disempowering rather than empowering, as they find themselves facing a barrage of professionals and advice in the expectation that they will make a prudent decision based on incomplete understanding of the information they are being given. Also, the formality of the meeting and the need to cover so much at once can leave parents feeling discouraged.

Underpinning a collaborative approach was professionals' recognition of parents' strengths and skills for meeting their child's needs. This was an advance on the earlier focus on assessing what resources and skills they lacked (Powell et al. 1997), but still placed professionals in charge of determining service priorities, which is inconsistent with a collaborative philosophy (Sokoly & Dokecki 1995).

A more recent view is that parents' equal status does not necessarily mean day-to-day participation in their child's program (Arthur et al. 1996)—as many parents have other commitments both within and outside the family. It is also acknowledged that, like parents of typically developing children, parents whose child has additional needs have a right *not* to participate in their child's education.

This trend towards shared power is dynamic and ongoing, and in my view has one further step to achieve, as a collaborative stance gives too much power to the professionals (Porter & McKenzie 2000). Parents consult us for our knowledge and experience of young children and employ us to support them in advancing their child's educational or other needs. Thus, more than being mere consumers or even equal participants in a partnership with you, parents are actually your employers. They pay considerable taxes for public services and high fees for private services; thus, as with all employers, you are directly accountable to them for your practices.

Under this 'parents-as-employers' model, parents are in charge of steering the services that their child requires. In arguing against such a demand-based model, it could be asserted that some parents do not know what they need (Dale 1996). Nevertheless, they *do* know what they wish their children to achieve, and in response to this message we can apprise them of the services we can offer. Our main role, then, is listening, rather than talking or telling (Dunst et al. 1988, 1994; Sokoly & Dokecki 1995). At the same time we must recognise that the most educated and well-resourced parents (in terms of available time, income and personal support networks) are likely to be those who are most able to articulate their goals and thus to receive a wide range of services (Mahoney & Filer 1996). Less-well-resourced parents might be aware of a difficulty but do not ask for help, as they cannot foresee being able to use it because of the constraints imposed on them by their circumstances (Dunst et al. 1988). These families will require additional information about the menu of services available plus support to overcome any barriers to their access to these (Dunst et al. 1988).

Box 2.1 Summary of trends in parent–professional relationships

Nature of relationship	Parents' roles
Professional dominance	Compliance
Routine communication	Passive acceptance of decisions
Parallel cooperation	Involvement in peripheral activities
Coordination	To learn skills deemed by professionals to be necessary
	To act as formal teachers of their children
Collaboration	To share power but choose their own role and level of involvement
Employer–employee	To direct programs so that these meet their child's and family's needs

A FAMILY-CENTRED STYLE OF SERVICE DELIVERY

A family-centred style of service delivery upholds that the interests of a child who has additional needs are best met by taking every family member's needs into account, by promoting the whole family's healthy functioning and maintaining the parents' confidence in their ability to care for all their children, rather than by focusing solely on the child with additional needs. It is underpinned by recognition that there are many family types and structures that can raise healthy children but that this outcome is more likely when families receive a range of informal and formal social supports.

The family-centred model comprises three key ingredients, the first of which is building rapport with parents. This is achieved by working on their desired outcomes for their children, which requires you to have knowledge and skills about children, typical and atypical development, and the particular needs of each individual child in your care. When services for their child meet parents' expressed needs, child-focused intervention is compatible with a family-centred approach (McWilliam et al. 1995, 1998). The second aspect of family-centredness—and the ingredient that most empowers parents and gives them confidence—is parents' participation in decision making (Dunst 2000). These first two aspects relate to *what* services families receive; the third aspect refers to *how* you relate to families. Crucial relational skills comprise positiveness, sensitivity, responsiveness and friendliness (McWilliam et al. 1998).

Positiveness

Positiveness involves thinking the best about children's and families' strengths, your own skills and the possibility for advancement of children's development. This must be balanced with realism, however: it is no kindness to parents to withhold information about their child's atypical development out of a misguided wish to shield them or to protect yourself from confronting them with unpleasant information. (I give a suggestion for balancing positiveness with realism in the section on presenting child-focused information.)

Sensitivity

When working with families, it is important to be **sensitive to their circumstances**, as these will affect what they are able to contribute to their child's education. If the parents are in the process of separating or of establishing a step-family, or if one adult is parenting alone, there may be little surplus energy left to devote to a child's remedial program, even though in other circumstances the parents would be willing to participate.

Such demands can fluctuate from time to time, whereas families who are living in poverty must often endure its many disadvantages in the long term. When, added to this, the parents themselves have a disability, come from a non-majority culture or otherwise lack support from the wider community, their participation can be severely compromised as they focus instead on personal and family survival.

Meanwhile, all families must fulfil many functions in addition to caring for and overseeing the education of their children. These include: ensuring the family's financial viability, engaging in recreation, socialising outside of the family, and maintaining close relationships among family members (Turnbull & Turnbull 1997). Sometimes the demands of a special program violate these other needs: for instance, placing parents in a formal teaching role can interfere with the amount of time they have available for recreation, and can limit the exchange of affection between parent and child as the parent becomes task-focused rather than nurturing.

A second aspect of sensitivity involves listening to **parents' reactions to their child's disability**. Children's early years are often the time when parents first encounter their child's additional needs. This means that at this time they may be experiencing an array of conflicting emotions. Some parents may grieve about the loss of their fantasised perfect baby; some grieve for the loss of control over their own circumstances because they now have to defer to the decisions of service providers; some grieve about the changes in their own personal circumstances—such as when a mother who was planning to return to paid employment now finds that she cannot do so (Porter & McKenzie 2000); and, most poignant of all, many grieve for the limitations that the disability imposes on their child him- or herself. Having said this, we know more about the reactions of white, middle-class parents than about other parent groups—even then, exceptions are common and each person reacts in an individual way.

Whatever their initial emotions, over time most adjust to their unanticipated circumstances, particularly when they have support from within and outside their family; and many come to appreciate the positive contributions that their child makes to their lives (Grant et al. 1998; Sandler & Mistretta 1998; Stainton & Besser 1998). But in these early days they may still be experiencing uncertainty, anger, depression or isolation arising from the sense that no-one else understands what they are going through. They might lack confidence in their ability to meet their child's additional needs, and experience sheer exhaustion from going the rounds of many professionals in an attempt to achieve a diagnosis and design a suitable intervention.

Meanwhile, parents whose children are intellectually advanced experience many of the same reactions to their child's atypical needs as do parents whose children have disabilities. Specifically, parents of gifted children may (Porter 1999):

- be confused about giftedness in general or its particular manifestations in their child (Hickson 1992);
- feel sad on their child's behalf when he or she does not fit in;
- lack confidence in their own ability to supply what their child requires in the various developmental, social and emotional domains (Colangelo & Dettman 1983);
- grieve at the loss of a 'normal' child whom they could plug into the school system at the age of 5 or 6 and extract at the other end with only the usual challenges and transitions along the way;
- experience frustration at the unsuitability of regular curricula for their child;
- have difficulty advocating for their child's additional needs;
- feel embarrassed at appearing to be 'pushy' when they request a developmentally appropriate program for their child (Silverman 1997);

- feel the need to support siblings who might have average learning abilities, so that all family members can accept differences without allowing these to define any one member as deficient or more special than others (Cornell & Grossberg 1986).

Unlike parents whose children have a disability, however, parents whose children are advanced often experience little support and sometimes outright hostility from educators and other parents (McBride 1992), which means that they lack the personal support and educational adjustments which they and their child require.

A third aspect of sensitivity is **listening to parents' aspirations** for their son or daughter. Professionals must listen to parents' priorities rather than imposing their own goals on parents, as this will facilitate parents' support for the resulting program (Ketelaar et al. 1998).

On the other hand, although sensitivity and empathy towards families are clearly beneficial, you must avoid feeling sympathy for their predicament and allowing demands on you to escalate unreasonably. Pity does not give families confidence in their own ability to overcome adversity, and can overwhelm professionals with 'compassion fatigue' and result in burnout.

Responsiveness

Responsiveness involves providing, arranging for, or recommending services that the family asks for. However, if requested services contradict your professional judgment about best practice, you may not feel it possible to supply these (Powell 1994). Explaining the rationale of programs to parents is one option, but in so doing we cannot attempt to change parents' values (Powell 1994). Persistent disagreement is not easily resolved because a fundamental principle of a pluralistic service is to respect parents' views. On the other hand, professional knowledge must also be respected, and so educators cannot be expected to sacrifice their beliefs in the interests of working collaboratively. Perhaps parents can select another service that more closely reflects their values, but in reality few options can be available when children have additional needs.

Responsiveness can also mean not imposing services that parents do not want. Although services could potentially benefit a child, this gain can be outweighed by the additional stresses placed on the family (Winton 1993). Thus, some parents might choose not to participate in services, in which case their wishes must be accepted.

Although responding to families' requests is important, as with the other aspects of family-centred services this too can be overdone. Too much helpfulness can unwittingly undermine parents, creating dependence on outsiders and reducing their confidence in their ability to solve their own problems.

Friendliness

In order to receive emotional support, parents mainly want an emotionally rich relationship with their professional advisers, rather than formal and distant interactions (Summers et al. 1990). However, for a range of reasons, being friendly is not the same as being friends. First, friendship has no agenda, whereas a helping relationship has a particular purpose; second, being paid to deliver a service renders it a non-friendship; third, personal relationships with clients can exploit both parties: clients might feel reluctant to question your recommendations in case doing so jeopardised your relationship, while friendships can increase clients' dependence on you and burden you with escalating work-related demands. Therefore, friendliness must be balanced with limits on your professional relationships.

FAMILIES' SERVICE NEEDS IN THE EARLY YEARS

Parents require a range of services in their efforts to assist their child with additional needs. It will be within your role to deliver some of these, whereas others will be supplied by outside agencies. Even when you do not deliver a particular service yourself, you have an important role in helping parents to locate appropriate services.

Child-focused information

Parents' first need is for information—on a range of topics as listed in Box 2.2, which will change through the years. The information that we impart must be accurate and up to date so that parents can make informed decisions about their options. This information must be of high quality and easily accessible. To that end, you might need to help parents to identify, understand and synthesise various sources of information, including interpreting other professionals' reports. This will involve knowledge of disciplines other than your own and a close working relationship with other members of a multidisciplinary team so that they can teach you some of the terms in their specialty fields.

Imparting information about disability at times involves using labels to describe children's learning difficulties (see chapter 3). In so doing, it is important to be sensitive to parents' understandings of these terms, as in the example in chapter 1, where I inadvertently talked at cross-purposes with a parent about intellectual disability. Although their estimates of their children's abilities and needs generally tally with that of professionals, parents might resist a particular label because they regard their child as a whole person who is more complex than a single label implies (Harry 1992). Their resistance to a particular label, however, need not stand in the way of participation in their child's program.

Once their child's program is under way, parents most often want information about how their child is progressing (Westling 1996). This can be a delicate issue, as you must convey that the child is continuing to learn while not implying that the child's skills are approaching the normal range if they are not. You might find it useful to say something such as, 'James is communicating more clearly now, and uses a number of words. This is a big advance on earlier

Box 2.2 Information sought by parents

Parents tend to want information about:

- their child's additional needs;
- their emotional reactions and those of other family members;
- typical and atypical child development;
- how to recognise and respond to any atypical cues that their child uses to communicate with them (Guralnick 1991);
- their child's learning characteristics and future potential or prognosis;
- how to support their child at home;
- how to play with their child at home;
- the range of available services such as respite care, relevant extracurricular activities, financial assistance to offset additional costs, future schooling options;
- behaviour management strategies;
- parent support groups.

Source: adapted from Westling and Plaute (1999).

in the year, when he was not speaking at all. His skills then were below the 1-year level. Now they are closer to 2 years' (say, when James is aged 4).

Participation in planning

Most parents, particularly those with high levels of education, want to exercise choice about their children's programs (Freeman et al. 1999; Westling 1996; Westling & Plaute 1999). To that end, it will help to prepare them in advance for meetings and listen to them so that their agenda drives the meeting, rather than topics for discussion being determined by the professionals. While conducting the meetings efficiently, you will need to allow enough time—and double the usual period when interpreters are being employed (Lynch & Hanson 1996)—so that there is enough time to discuss your thoughts, listen to the parents and answer their questions (Abbott & Gold 1991). Listening to their responses will help you to choose terms that they use themselves, which will ensure that they understand what you are telling them. Where you can, you will need to avoid jargon and define those terms that you cannot avoid (Turnbull & Turnbull 1997).

One successful strategy to avoid overwhelming parents with new assessment information and service options is to tape the meeting, so that they can review it later or so that an absent parent can still hear the conversation. Alternatively, minutes of the meeting can be forwarded to parents for them to review what was discussed. It will help if you can invite parents to meet you briefly again to discuss issues and questions thus generated.

Identification and assessment

Sometimes you will be the first to observe the signs of atypical development in individual children. Naturally, you cannot diagnose the cause of these irregularities if that is outside your realm of expertise (Chandler 1994). However, you can talk with the children's parents, giving them specific examples of what you have observed that has raised concern in your mind. When conveying such potentially upsetting information, it is crucial that you be honest and do not try to shield the parents from the facts out of some misguided desire to protect them. However, keep in mind that not all parents will react to your concerns with alarm. Sometimes they will be relieved because your feedback confirms their own misgivings and empowers them to seek more information.

If as an outcome of your discussions a specialist assessment is launched, parents need to be involved in all its phases: their participation is essential to provide a history of their child's development and to detail their priorities for his or her immediate and longer-term program, and to ensure that resulting discussion addresses their issues and that programs are designed to meet their needs. Most want such assessment to be comprehensive, without a sole reliance on testing, as it can be difficult for their children to display their optimal skills in a formal setting (McKenzie 1993; Ryndak et al. 1996). When children receive a wider-ranging assessment in which their parents have been active participants, the parents are more likely to understand and endorse both the assessment process and recommendations that arise from it.

Education

Parents usually want educators to be receptive to the information they impart on their child's history and present needs, without becoming defensive (Ryndak et al. 1996). Above all, they want their child's curriculum to be individualised and challenging, with specialist services provided (Hodapp et al. 1998; Ryndak et al. 1996). They want their teachers to know about disability in general, and about their child's specific disabilities and their impact on his or her development (Hodapp et al. 1998).

In terms of placement, some parents of children with disabilities prefer inclusive settings for reasons of convenience, the availability of positive role models in general settings, socialisation benefits and, in the case of less severely disabled children, for the extra educational challenge (Bennett et al. 1997; Freeman et al. 1999; Guralnick et al. 1995; Hodapp et al. 1998; Ryndak et al. 1996). Even so, they tend to realise that co-location alone is insufficient for friendships to develop, and so want teachers to take active steps to facilitate friendships between children (Palmer et al. 1998a; Ryndak et al. 1996).

Other parents feel that their children's educational needs are best met in segregated settings (Palmer et al. 1998a, 1998b; Ryndak et al. 1996). Some prefer these because they are concerned for their child's physical and emotional safety in inclusive settings (Bentley-Williams & Butterfield 1996; Westling 1996); they believe that inclusive settings cannot provide the resources and individualised programming that their child requires (Hanline & Halvorsen 1989; McWilliam et al. 1995); and some want their son or daughter to be educated alongside children who have additional needs on the grounds that these children might be more 'forgiving and accepting' (Hodapp et al. 1998).

Thus, although local preferred practice may be to encourage inclusive placements for children with disabilities, some parents will need to explore both regular and special placement options and make their selection on the basis of their own and their child's particular requirements.

Direct therapy services

Despite evidence that direct therapy—in the form of speech pathology, occupational therapy and physiotherapy—is not superior to the incorporation of therapeutic activities into the natural setting (Washington et al. 1994), and despite the lack of evidence that more therapy is better (McWilliam et al. 1996), during their children's early years parents tend to seek intensive therapy when their children have disabilities.

In the face of insufficient therapists and a preference for naturalistic instruction in early childhood settings, when children are receiving specific remedial services you will need to negotiate with their specialists to incorporate, where relevant, their goals into your program. This will aid skill generalisation, provide the children with more practice than they might receive from infrequent therapy sessions, and is likely to meet the families' expressed needs for direct intervention.

Social support

Parents who have a high level of contact with friends and relatives tend to have higher morale than those with few such supports (Greenberg et al. 1997). However, parents whose children have additional needs tend to be isolated from the other preschool or child care parents unless educators enact specific measures to foster interactions between them (Hanson et al. 1998; Winton 1993). Ongoing contact avoids the parents' social isolation, while the children also benefit from after-hours contact with peers while their parents socialise with each other.

Advocacy

Although parents can normally be their own advocates, this can sometimes antagonise service providers, in which case you might have to deflect any criticism that arises within your own service when parents are active in advocating for their children's needs (Bennett et al. 1997). On other occasions you might have to advocate on their behalf for particular services within or beyond your agency. One commonplace occasion for this role is during meetings between parents and members of a multidisciplinary team, in which it is easy for parents to feel overwhelmed and outnumbered. The measures already discussed for involving parents in planning can be useful here.

Transition planning

The time when parents and their children are most likely to be stressed is when they are moving from one service to another, such as from preschool to primary school (Wolery 1989). Like all parents, those whose child has a disability are excited at the prospect that their child will start school, but it is also a stressful time (Bentley-Williams & Butterfield 1996). They have to leave familiar programs and staff, and accept that at school there is generally less opportunity for their involvement (Bentley-Williams & Butterfield 1996; Fowler et al. 1991; Hadden & Fowler 1997).

Transition times can reaffirm to parents their child's different needs (Hanline 1993). Parents must face the reality that the early intervention program did not and could not have 'cured' their child's disability. If the parents have been actively involved in the delivery of remedial programs, they can feel cheated and disillusioned that they gave up so much to achieve so little of what they had hoped.

The choice of school is a great concern. Like all parents, those whose children have atypical needs have to adjust to the notion that no school is going to provide all that their child requires. However, there is likely to be an even greater than usual disparity between the atypical needs of their child and the schooling options that are available. Furthermore, sometimes even this choice of school is out of parents' control: their child might not be considered eligible for the school of their choice (Fowler et al. 1991). This adds another layer of complexity and stress to the family's planning for transitions.

In order to help plan for their child's next placement, you will need a long-term perspective on the family's concerns, aspirations and involvement to date. Parents will need information well in advance about the transition process and their child's future schooling options (Fowler et al. 1991; Hanline 1993). It is important to listen to what the family wants of the next service which they and their son or daughter are entering, so to that end you could ask the following questions (Hutchins & Renzaglia 1998):

- What do you want your child to achieve in the new setting?
- What experiences has the child already had that could prepare him or her for, or could be useful in, the new setting?
- What does your child most enjoy doing?
- What sort of assistance and support will your child need in the new setting?
- How does he or she communicate with others?
- In what ways do you (the parents) want to become involved in the new setting?
- What sort of feedback do you need (a) in the initial days and (b) subsequently, about how your child is settling in and performing in the new setting?

As you gather parents' answers to such questions, it will be important to be clear with them if a service that they want is not available: it does not benefit them if you promise something that subsequently cannot be provided. Part of your joint planning, then, might be to develop a plan for surmounting gaps in services.

Respite care

Respite care is one of the most requested services for families, especially when their children have behavioural difficulties (Hayes 1998; Rimmerman et al. 1989). The use of respite care increases mothers' feelings of wellbeing, and as a result has positive effects for the functioning of families as a whole (Botuck & Winsberg 1991). Child care can function as a natural source of respite but can be inaccessible to many parents because of its cost, limited hours, distance from home or work, and inability to accommodate children's additional needs (Warfield & Hauser-Cram 1996), in which case parents might need information about alternative respite care options.

Counselling

We must not assume that parents with a child with a disability will need counselling—any more than would other families (Seligman & Darling 1997). They might require different information about their child's atypical needs compared with other parents, but this does not necessarily mean that they will need more emotional support in the form of counselling.

The counsellor who is supporting parents of a child with disabilities may need to adopt a variety of roles with respect to the services already described: helping parents to gather information; assisting their access to services; interpreting assessment reports; acting as a sounding board, ally or advocate; and supporting their decisions. In performing these roles, your task is to help parents to use their present skills to make effective choices in their lives and to act on these (Nelson-Jones 1988). Thus, counselling does not involve convincing others of what they should do, but allowing them to discover for themselves which solutions fit for them (Geldard 1998).

Coordination of services

A crucial aspect of service provision is service coordination (McWilliam et al. 1995). Privatisation, outsourcing and increasingly restrictive eligibility criteria for publicly funded services can make it difficult for parents to locate appropriate services for their children (McWilliam et al. 1995). Faced with such difficulties, many parents find a case manager to be an asset in helping them to negotiate a complex service system, especially when their child has multiple needs (Dinnebeil et al. 1999; Westling 1996; Westling & Plaute 1999). Others want to assume this role for themselves to retain control of their own circumstances

(Dunst et al. 1988). The implication, clearly, is that professionals need to ask parents about their preferences.

Referral to other services

A final service that parents might require from time to time is referral to an agency that can supply a service you are not equipped to offer—such as specialist practitioners or community-based leisure activities. To perform a referral function, you will need to know about a range of services, including their location, eligibility criteria, waiting time, costs and contact phone numbers. For leisure activities for children with disabilities, it can be particularly beneficial to locate a program attended by one of the non-disabled children in your centre, as the children's contact in two locations can help them to socialise in both (Beckman et al. 1998). Your group of parents can supplement your own knowledge by nominating services they have personally found useful, which you can then collate into a resource list.

COMMUNICATION ISSUES

Communication between parents and service providers and within an interdisciplinary team has been identified as crucial to collaboration (Dinnebeil et al. 1996, 1999). Trust and mutual respect underpin the three clusters of communication skills—namely, listening, being assertive, and solving problems collaboratively. Each of these is best employed according to who is feeling concern at the time. Three scenarios are possible.

First, when parents have an issue to discuss with you, your main task is to listen to these. Listening entails giving speakers your attention, avoiding judgment and resisting imposing your solutions on them. It requires that you accept their feelings—even when you do not understand why they feel as they do.

Second, when you are disturbed by someone else's actions, you need to be assertive by stating the effect of the behaviour on you, without being aggressive. This requires using the word 'I' rather than 'you', as this distinguishes assertiveness from aggression. I have found that the most useful assertive method is an empathic assertive statement (Jakubowki & Lange 1978). This comprises a three-part statement whereby you reflect the other person's concern, state your alternative perspective, and then ask how the two can be reconciled.

Third, when you both are being inconvenienced by an issue, you will each need to be assertive, listen to each other, and then solve the problem jointly. This entails defining the problem, listing potential solutions, selecting one of these, implementing it, and then checking that the solution is achieving the desired outcome.

These three skills will need to be variously employed during challenging communications with parents.

Problem solving with parents

When a child is experiencing a difficulty at your centre, you will need to collaborate with the parents to find a solution. In so doing, it pays not to give parents advice about what should be done, as dispensing solutions is an exercise of power and, as Bailey (1987) observes, is something done *for* families rather than *with* them.

Instead, Heath (1994) suggests that, before selecting which course of action you will follow, you and the parents could:

- restate your priorities for the child;
- identify the types of solutions that are possible in the circumstances, based on parents' information about what works for them at home and on your knowledge of what has already been tried in your setting;
- identify the relevant characteristics of the child—temperament, age, size, abilities, interests, responses to earlier interventions, and so on;
- identify the needs of the surrounding adults and children;

so that you can select a solution that is compatible with your broader goals for the child and which satisfies the needs of all those involved.

If during your discussion parents are expressing their concern in a way that you find intimidating, you nevertheless need to respond with courtesy. Generally the parents feel that they have a valid reason for their behaviour, and their frustration is seldom directed at you personally but at their own powerlessness. When they express their complaints offensively, however, you could redirect the discussion to what they want to accomplish (Jones & Jones 1998). For example: 'I accept that you are angry that Simon's clothes went missing. Perhaps now we can plan for it not to happen again.' It might be useful to impose a time limit or schedule a subsequent appointment to give parents time to calm down and yourself time to gather additional information.

Communicating with parents from non-majority cultures

Just as you plan for the diversity of needs of the children in your care, so too do you need to plan to work collaboratively with parents whose cultural backgrounds vary. In a culturally diverse society it is not possible or even desirable to work with every parent in the same way (a'Beckett 1988).

Culture can affect many aspects of parent–professional interactions. First, it can disenfranchise migrant parents, as they are more likely to be living in poverty and have the least access to support from social services (Salend & Taylor 1993). Their experience of discrimination and the fact that they do not know the local education system (as they received their education in their home country) can mean that they are reluctant to engage with professionals or join parent groups, thus leaving them particularly isolated (Marion 1980).

Second, their competence and confidence in speaking English can deter some parents from being involved (Lynch & Stein 1987). In turn, this disengagement and their lack of facility with language denies you information about their child that would assist you in programming for him or her. Obviously, it also affects how much information they can receive from you as, even when they can use everyday language, they might have difficulty comprehending technical terms and jargon (Rosin 1996; Salend & Taylor 1993).

For parents who speak but are not confident about reading English, informal contacts will be more important than written exchanges. Rather than waiting for difficulties to occur and meetings to become formal, it will help if you can locate a culturally sensitive translator or invite a community volunteer to accompany non-English-speaking parents on a regular basis at drop-off or collection times so that you can pass on day-to-day information about their child's experiences. It is wise to avoid using their son or daughter as a translator, as that burdens a child with inappropriate responsibility, while translators who are children or family friends can be exposed to information that parents regard as personal and so can make parents feel uncomfortable both at the time and in their subsequent relationship with their interpreter (Lynch & Hanson 1996; Salend & Taylor 1993).

Third, culture affects the esteem in which professionals are held. Some parents will regard professionals as experts whose opinions cannot be questioned and with whom they must relate formally, while others who value interdependence between individuals will seek a collaborative style of interaction with you (Lynch & Hanson 1996; Salend & Taylor 1993).

Fourth, their cultural beliefs can dictate how parents understand the cause of their child's disability: some are reluctant to expose their child and themselves to outside scrutiny, as they believe that the disability reflects negatively on them (Salend & Taylor 1993), or they might passively accept it as 'God's will' or as a justified punishment for their own former misdemeanours—and so resist intervention measures (Lynch & Hanson 1996).

Fifth, parents' cultural background can cause parents to emphasise priorities for their children in domains other than academic achievement, which is the traditional focus in Western cultures (Lopez 1996). Many value social cooperation above competition and social and emotional development over academic success. Therefore, you will need to clarify parents' priorities for their child's education.

Sixth, their culture affects family membership. In some families, grandparents or other extended family members have a crucial role either as an elder or as a major care provider for a child. It will be important, therefore, to negotiate which family members should be included in any meetings (Salend & Taylor 1993).

Finally, culture affects communication styles—differences in personal space, use of eye contact, wait time, voice intonation, which words are permissible, facial expressions, emotional expression, and the use of touch (Rosin 1996; Salend & Taylor 1993). There is no guaranteed way to avoid the miscommunication that can arise when others misinterpret your body language, but problems can be minimised when you are aware of the potential for crossed wires.

Cultural competence can be attained by becoming aware of the assumptions and values implicit in your own culture, being sensitive to the fact that these will not be universally shared, and attaining and applying information about other cultures through reading and personal and professional contacts with individuals who bridge cultures (Lynch & Hanson 1996). When you are ignorant of parents' cultures, it can be a simple matter just to ask them about the practices in their country. Generally, they do not expect others to know the practices of every country in the world and are glad to explain some of the values they hold dear. Asking them about their beliefs also avoids assumptions that they will conform to cultural stereotypes.

Communicating with parents of typically developing children

Parents of the typically developing children in your care have a right to reassurance that a child with a disability will not require a disproportionate amount of staff time, resulting in reduced care of their own child. However, you will need to decide on a case-by-case basis how much information you should tell the other parents about the attendance of a child with a disability, as disclosure could create unnecessary anxiety or be construed as a tacit invitation for protest (Chandler 1994); conversely, if you do not discuss the issue with your parent group, some might feel that you are not receptive to their legitimate concerns. Your decision will need to be made in consultation with the parents whose child has additional needs.

CONCLUSION

Whether working with parents whose children have previously recognised disabilities or gifts, those whose disabilities or gifts emerge during their participation in your program, or those parents whose children have typical needs, you must be sensitive to their requirements and respond, where appropriate, to their expressed needs.

In so doing, you must take care not to add to the demands that parents are already experiencing, particularly at the time of discovery of their child's additional needs or during transitions from one service to another. It will be important to listen to their concerns and aspirations and endeavour to adapt services to their individual circumstances, rather than asking parents to conform to program demands.

ADDITIONAL RESOURCES

For more detail on collaborating with parents of children with disabilities and an extensive reading list for further reference, see Porter, L. and McKenzie, S. 2000 *Professional collaboration with parents of children with disabilities* Whurr, London (also MacLennan & Petty, Sydney)

3

IDENTIFICATION AND
ASSESSMENT

LOUISE PORTER

KEY POINTS

- Assessment is a systematic process of data gathering, aimed at establishing children's strengths and educational needs.
- Testing is but one part of the assessment process which can allow educators to prioritise children's needs.
- Labels can lower expectations for children's achievements but at the same time can help describe, explain or predict their developmental pattern, which can help parents and educators to anticipate children's needs.

INTRODUCTION

Early childhood educators have an ethical obligation to collect information that helps design an appropriate service for children and their families (McConnell 2000). For those children whose additional needs have already been recognised, much assessment information will already have been gathered, perhaps by a range of specialists. In that case, your job will be to interpret their assessment reports so that you can adjust your program to meet the children's additional needs. However, the language of these reports can seem impenetrable at times, and so this chapter explains some of the information you might encounter in them.

A second group of children—who constitute a far greater number—will have atypical developmental patterns that formerly have not been recognised. For these children, assessment comprises talking with the parents about their son or daughter's developmental history and observing the children in a variety of contexts. In order to make sense of the information you have received in these ways, it will be useful to refer to checklists that tell you when children usually achieve the various skills in each developmental domain (see Appendix II). Having recognised the ways in which particular children's development is departing from the usual, you can make necessary adjustments to your program and, when the departure from the norms seems extreme, can advocate that parents seek more detailed specialist assessment.

DEFINITIONS

Educational **assessment** refers to the gathering of information about children's learning levels, style and skills in order to make instructional decisions about meeting their needs (McLoughlin & Lewis 2001). **Testing** is but one element of educational assessment and involves eliciting children's responses to questions under structured conditions (McLoughlin & Lewis 2001). These two definitions tell us that there is far more to educational assessment than purely testing—that is, assessment requires gathering information in a range of ways from a range of sources, in a range of situations and over time. This process will need to be *systematic* and *collaborative* and follow a logical sequence from data collection to design of an educational program (McLoughlin & Lewis 2001).

Two remaining terms include **diagnosis**, which refers to the effort to establish the cause of a condition and to outline appropriate treatment implied by that condition; and **evaluation**, which examines the effectiveness of a program, as distinct from focusing on individual children (Cook et al. 2000).

PURPOSES OF ASSESSMENT

For children who are suspected of having delayed or advanced development, assessment can serve many purposes (Taylor 2000). *Why* we are assessing individual children will have implications for *how* we proceed with that assessment (McCormick & Schiefelbusch 1984):

- **Screening** occurs before concern has been raised about individual children's developmental pattern. It takes a broad, naturalistic look at children's development, aiming to identify individuals who might need additional assessment.
- **Description of current skills** determines *whether* children's development is atypical and reveals the *nature* of children's developmental patterns (McLoughlin & Lewis 2001), which will involve identification of their strengths and relatively weak skill areas.
- **Curriculum planning.** Having established the nature of children's additional needs, assessment must be able to guide decisions about what supplementary services individual children require and how to deliver these.

- **Decisions about placement.** Placement decisions will involve making a choice about which settings will most benefit children with atypical development and which age group of peers will best support their learning and social and emotional growth.
- **Classification.** This is a common reason for the assessment of children who are suspected of having developmental delays or advances. Classification is a controversial function of assessment, although by definition giftedness and disability are relative to normal development and so issues of classification are inevitable. This is not necessarily negative, as classification can perform a social justice function of highlighting those individuals who need tailored educational provisions.
- **Monitoring children's progress.** A final purpose of assessment is to monitor how children are responding to an educational program. Monitoring serves three purposes (Wolery 1996b): to check that the conclusions and priorities generated by earlier assessments are still relevant; to build a record of children's progress over time so that educators' accountability is promoted and to celebrate children's achievements; and to determine whether and how programs should be modified in response to children's accomplishment or non-attainment of earlier goals. For reasons discussed later in this chapter, normed tests are not ideal for this purpose, so more naturalistic measures will be preferable.

PRINCIPLES OF ASSESSMENT

A key principle of assessment is that it must be multidimensional—that is, it must employ multiple measures, from multiple sources, over multiple developmental domains and fulfil multiple purposes (as just listed) (Neisworth & Bagnato 1988). A second fundamental principle is that assessment must examine not only the qualities and needs of individual children but also the environmental factors that contribute to their present developmental status (Neisworth & Bagnato 1988). Third, assessment must recognise that, although skills in the various developmental domains can be assessed separately, the domains are in fact interdependent (Meisels & Atkins-Burnett 2000). This implies that specialist assessors must share information so that they can develop a multidimensional picture of the whole child, not just isolated skills.

The following additional principles should guide the assessment process for children who are suspected of having additional educational needs.

Advocacy
The principle of advocacy contends that assessment should uphold the interests of all children and aim to improve services for individuals (NAEYC 1988). Methods should be selected on the basis of whether they meet children's needs, rather than being administratively convenient, for instance. They must also avoid

the negative effects on children that arise through misuse of the findings or from labelling children.

Programming relevance (utility)

Assessment must measure skills that are relevant either to an intended program or in the child's life (Hansen & Linden 1990). That is, the information gained must be educationally useful. Assessment methods must be able to answer the educational questions being asked so that children's strengths and needs can be assessed and thus built into the educational program. To achieve this, tests that yield only a single global score will be less useful than those which provide scores for varying domains of development, for example.

Defensibility

This criterion refers to *how* we assess individual children (Miller 1978, in McCormick & Schiefelbusch 1984). Methods used should be based on the best available research and knowledge. Any tests that are part of the assessment process must be used only for the purpose for which they were designed and must be valid and reliable—that is, technically sound in their construction and suitable for the ages and ability levels of the children being tested (Hooper & Edmondson 1998; NAEYC 1988). Second, not only must the tests have acknowledged strengths, they must also have few limitations, particularly for the purpose for which they are being used (Hansen & Linden 1990).

Equity

Although based on knowledge of the typical sequence of development, assessment must also take into account those cultural experiences which will alter children's developmental milestones (Meisels & Atkins-Burnett 2000). Assessment methods must be culturally fair—which is to say that they should not disadvantage any groups within the community (Hooper & Edmondson 1998). This is a particular issue for children whose primary language is not English or who are bilingual, and for those whose mode of communication is not spoken language. It is imperative that children's lack of facility with English is not mistaken for a developmental delay or disability (Gonzalez 1974; Marion 1980). To minimise error with these children, examiners could provide the test in the children's first language (McLoughlin & Lewis 2001). However, this is not a complete solution, as items have differing levels of difficulty across languages, and so the norms might not apply when a test is delivered in a language other than the one intended (Figueroa 1989). Also, children from various cultures will interpret the demands of the testing session differently and, given that examiners are not allowed to clarify what is being asked of the children, this can penalise those whose experience to date has not prepared them for the formality of such an endeavour (Lynch & Hanson 1996; Miller-Jones 1989).

A second element of equity is that examiners must satisfy themselves that the child being assessed has been exposed to opportunities to learn the skills being measured. For example, young blind children have not yet had the time to compensate for their lack of vision and learn concepts that can come more naturally to sighted children (Brambring & Tröster 1994).

Mainstream tests are often accused of bias for producing differential results across cultures. However, the same groups that routinely perform less well on the tests also perform less well in educational settings (Pyryt 1996). That is to say, the test results are accurate in that they equate to real-life performances. The issue instead is that society is biased in disadvantaging particular groups within it.

Comprehensiveness

Assessment procedures must minimise what is termed false negatives—that is, when children with additional needs are overlooked. To avoid false negatives, assessment must sample a wide range of behaviours across various developmental domains, in a range of settings, gathering information from many sources (Hansen & Linden 1990). Particularly when children have additional needs in many domains, it is important that many professionals are involved in assessment and can collaborate to build a comprehensive picture of the children's skills and needs. This comprehensiveness is particularly important when classification or placement decisions rest on the findings (NAEYC 1988).

Skilled administration

Personnel who are skilled at and familiar with assessing young children should be the ones to administer tests to this age group (NAEYC 1988). On the other hand, assessment should not rely on tests that can be administered only by specialists if (as is usually the case) there are too few of these to administer the tests. Such scarce resources can be saved by identifying most children by other means and reserving tests for the remaining minority of children whose skill levels are difficult to assess in more naturalistic ways (see Figure 3.1).

Second, testers must know how to communicate their findings appropriately to both lay and professional readers of their assessment reports (Hansen & Linden 1990). To aid communication, it is useful if parents and others working with individual children are told something about the content of the test, what information it can provide and its limitations.

Pragmatism

Assessment should be efficient in terms of the administration time and cost and should not unduly burden children with prolonged testing (Fallen 1985). On the other hand, comprehensiveness requires that when children's developmental difficulties are already suspected, for instance, screening devices not be used as they sample too few skills and may result in false negatives.

ASSESSMENT METHODS

When assessing to identify individuals' atypical needs, the stakes are high (Hart 1994, in Taylor 2000). The conclusions drawn will affect which services the

Box 3.1 Early screening for neonates

The Apgar scale is an early screening test for newborns that reflects the degree of oxygen deprivation occurring during birth (Heward 2000). Measures on the five dimensions listed below are taken one minute, and again five minutes, after birth. A low total score at the first minute is not alarming but signals the need for some resuscitation; the five-minute measure assesses how successful that action has been (Heward 2000). If there has been little improvement between evaluations, this signals that the baby is 'at risk' and thus requires paediatric follow-up.

		Points given
Heart rate	Absent	0
	Less than 100 beats per minute	1
	Over 100 beats	2
Breathing	Absent	0
	Slow or irregular	1
	Regular	2
Skin colour	Pale, blue	0
	Body pink, extremities blue	1
	Pink all over	2
Muscle tone	Limp	0
	Some movements	1
	Active movements	2
Reflex response	Absent	0
	Grimace only	1
	Crying	2

children are eligible to receive, the type of program designed for them, and perhaps their placement. Therefore, the instruments used for assessment must be more than impressionistic and must have the power accurately to identify additional educational needs. Thus, performance-based assessments such as portfolios are not described here, as their purpose is generally to document children's products for purposes other than monitoring children's development (see Helm et al. 1998). Nevertheless, the measures described in this section represent a combination of subjective and objective measures, whose aim is to give a comprehensive picture of individual children's particular needs.

Parental reports

Assessment must begin with establishing effective communication with the people who know children best—which is usually their parents or other primary caregivers (Meisels & Atkins-Burnett 2000). You can gain parents' knowledge of their child's development by asking them about his or her milestones, needs and interests—both at enrolment and subsequently throughout their child's participation in your program.

Despite often being dismissed as inaccurate, parents have detailed knowledge of their children's development, motivation and personalities which allows them to be accurate reporters of their children's abilities. For children with typical and mildly delayed development, parents' assessments generally coincide with teachers'; although for children at the extremes of development (severe disabilities or giftedness) parents tend to underestimate their children's skills (Chitwood 1986; Hundert et al. 1997). Even so, parents' identification of giftedness is still more accurate than teachers', as evidenced in studies reporting teachers' accurate recognition rates of between 4.3% and 22%, compared with parents' accuracy of between 61% and 100% (Ciha et al. 1974; Jacobs 1971; Silverman et al. 1986).

Thus, the additional information you receive from parents will be invaluable in program planning, to inform your intervention with immediate difficulties, and for opening the communication channels that will permit longer-term problem solving. (More is said about parental communication in chapter 2.)

Observation

Given that you are in many cases the first education professional with whom children will have contact, your role in recognising children's additional needs is a crucial one. Observation involves describing in specific terms what individual children do, either in spontaneous situations or in activities you have contrived in order to observe specific skills. Structured observation can enhance the picture of children's skills and can help identify those whose abilities are mixed—who, perhaps, have adequate knowledge but are unable to demonstrate it because of how they approach tasks.

A successful approach to observing children's development is to nominate a small group of children to observe for a week, rotating your focus children week by week until you have detailed observations of all the children in your group. In this way you can collect dynamic data about all the children, allowing you not only to assess their needs but also to gauge the adequacy of your program in meeting those needs.

As well as focusing on individual children, you can observe the educational program in order to assess its appeal and effectiveness in general, for particular children, or for fostering particular behaviours such as cooperative play (Taylor 2000). You might park yourself near to, say, the puzzle table for some minutes on consecutive days and observe whether the supplied activities are actually proving too difficult for the majority of children to access, are too easy for the children, or are unattractive in some way. Recognising this will allow you to substitute more suitable activities.

Compared with more formal assessment means, observation has the advantage that tasks can be varied to suit individual children, giving them the best opportunity to display their skills (Fallen 1985). However, without reference to checklists that detail the usual timing of developmental milestones, simply observing children's activities would be like 'solving riddles without clues' (Tannenbaum 1983: 60). Unguided observations are likely to underidentify the needs of many children.

Developmental checklists

Without consuming considerable amounts of staff time, at enrolment you can record on a checklist individual children's current development and update the record each time they achieve what is for them the next developmental milestone. This process can sensitise parents and educators to atypical development and avoid some local bias. Some centres, for instance, serve advantaged families that support advanced development in their children, whose sophisticated development might be overlooked because staff come to see it as 'normal'. Similarly, when children from educationally disadvantaging backgrounds cluster in the one location, all might seem to possess average skills when instead a significant number could have learning difficulties.

On the other hand, checklists can have their problems. The main one of these is that they can detail *when* children attain particular skills but are less useful guides to *how* the children should be approaching tasks. This can be overcome partly by what Neisworth and Bagnato (1988) describe as **judgment-based** assessment, in which children's attention skills, comprehension, memory and concept development can be observed and an intuitive judgment formed about their present skills and needs. Second, checklists can indicate that children's skills are delayed or advanced, but not by how much. Without understanding the extent, some children will be burdened unnecessarily with special programs, while others will wallow without receiving needed assistance. This introduces the need for normed tests.

Normed tests

Ultimate confirmation of children's developmental status can be achieved only by comparing their attainments to typical or 'normal' development. Tests that can do this are termed 'norm-referenced' or normed tests. They can cover a range of developmental domains, such as the psychologist's IQ test; or one single domain, such as an assessment by a speech pathologist or occupational therapist. Resulting scores are usually expressed in terms of 'mental age', 'reading age', 'developmental levels', 'intelligence quotients' (IQs) or other comparative measures.

The purpose of comparing children's results with each other's is to determine whether individual children are progressing at the expected or normal developmental rate. This type of comparative information can be useful when previous assessment measures have not been able to clarify the nature of children's needs or when educators need to compare how efficiently children can perform certain tasks compared with typically developing children, perhaps to assess the likely success of a transition to a regular setting.

While this endeavour of comparing children's performances with typical development attracts little dissent in the domains of language or motor skills, there has been a long-standing chorus of criticism of normed 'intelligence' or broad developmental tests (also known as IQ tests), so it is on these that this discussion will concentrate.

The first criticism arises from what is usually taken to be a strength of these tests—namely, that reputable tests are reliable. This means that individual children attain similar results on a number of administrations of the test, and that different testers will score the same child similarly. However, this degree of reliability has been achieved only by highly prescriptive administration procedures, which might not excite children's best performances and so do not represent adequately their everyday behaviours.

Second, detractors claim that, although the test results for young children tend accurately to describe their performances *at the time*, scores are less consistent over months and years and so predictions are not possible. This comes about because very young children's ability profiles can change dramatically during the developmental years; their environments can alter; and because test tasks at the younger ages bear very little resemblance to mature intelligence, in which case scores on tests for young children are less likely to tally with those for older individuals (Anastasi & Urbina 1997; Gallagher & Moss 1963; Neisworth & Bagnato 1992). Nevertheless, individuals with extreme scores are more likely than those in the average range to attain similar results in future testings (Sattler 1992): their actual scores might change by perhaps five to nine points over one to six years (Cahan & Gejman 1993; Spangler & Sabatino 1995), but their rankings within a group will alter very little (Tannenbaum 1992). These predictions are based on groups, however, and so for individuals—and young children in particular—we cannot be confident of their future developmental trajectories. This, perhaps, is unnecessary, however, as program planning requires only that we understand their needs as they are manifested *now*, not as they might be in the future.

Third, normed tests can include only those items on which scoring disagreement is minimal. This restricted sample of items leads to the accusation that the tests—especially IQ tests—are not valid (e.g. see Sternberg 1982). Validity refers to whether the tests measure anything worthwhile. Critics say that because the sample of items in normed tests is so limited, the resulting score is itself of limited use. This complaint is true, to some extent. However, other, more valid or relevant skills could be included in the tests but could not be scored accurately, which would be akin to measuring length using a piece of elastic. Measuring length is, in certain circumstances, a valid thing to do, but if your instrument is unreliable there is no point in using it at all. The result would be even less meaningful than a reliable but restricted measurement.

A related criticism is that, as test items are selected simply because they distinguish among children of varying developmental levels, they can have little functional relevance in children's lives. Colour naming, for instance, does tend to distinguish between 2- versus 3-year developmental levels, yet is a skill that has minimal functional application. This makes it difficult to design teaching activities based on test content: all the tests can do is indicate a general area in which additional instruction might be useful (Bondurant-Utz & Luciano 1994; Neisworth & Bagnato 1992). Conversely, when the tests *are* used to guide program content, educators might set about teaching skills (such as colour naming) that have little educational value, when instruction time could instead be used for teaching more ecologically useful skills. Perhaps, however, we are expecting too much for one instrument to be a tool both for assessment and for determining specific program content.

A further shortcoming of the tests is their assumption that all children enjoy roughly similar opportunities to acquire typical skills and knowledge, which clearly is not so for children from educationally disadvantaging backgrounds or those with particular disabilities. In instances when this assumption is not accurate, testing can result in mislabelling as delayed or disabled children from disadvantaging backgrounds and the underidentification of these same children as gifted.

Advocates of testing recognise this flaw but pose two rebuttals to this criticism. The first is that testing can result in the delivery of services to those social groups who generally achieve least well on the tests; in this way, social justice is advanced for those who are disadvantaged. Second, advocates claim that bias would not be eliminated by abolishing testing and would still leave us with many decisions to make, with less defensible bases on which to make them: subjective impressions of children by advantaged members of the dominant culture would disadvantage certain children even more than testing currently does (Pendarvis & Howley 1996; Worthen & Spandel 1991). Thus, although imperfect, the tests are still the most technically sound instruments presently available and should not be displaced by even less sound assessment measures (Kaufman & Harrison 1986).

A final criticism arises from the fact that test results are used by agencies to determine priorities for service allocation. If children are deemed eligible for services, normed testing is of direct benefit to them and their families. However, limited services mean that some needy children miss out. This, though, is due to the restricted amount of funds society allocates to service provision. The fault does not lie with the tests.

The potential for overreliance on normed testing requires that assessment involve many phases (as depicted in Figure 3.1). Furthermore, assessment must look more widely than test scores alone, as is only sound practice. This is confirmed by the originator of one of the most common batteries of IQ tests, David Wechsler (1958: 7), in his definition of intelligence as:

> The aggregate or global capacity of the individual to act purposefully, to think rationally, *and to deal effectively with his [or her] environment* (emphasis mine).

This definition implies that assessors must not only establish children's inherent skills but also assess children's functional adaptation to their particular environment. By supplementing test findings with other assessment procedures and information across developmental domains, most of the above disadvantages of IQ tests can be overcome.

ISSUES WHEN TESTING CHILDREN WITH ATYPICAL DEVELOPMENT

Normed tests have limitations that apply variously to individuals across all ages and ability levels. However, young children and especially those with disabilities pose some unique assessment challenges, particularly related to the principles of defensibility, equity and skilled administration described earlier in this chapter. These challenges relate to the unique characteristics of the child being tested, the impact of these on the relationship between the child and tester, and the soundness of the test itself when applied to young children with atypical developmental patterns (Taylor 2000). A further issue for this population is the

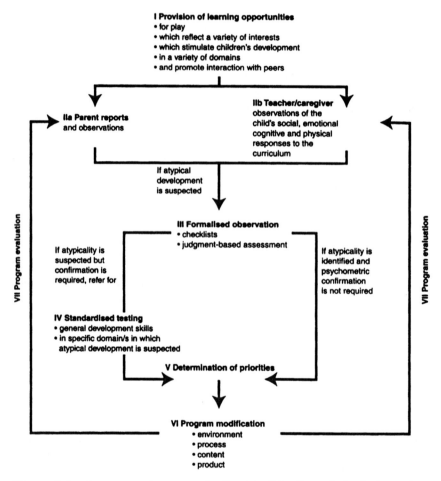

Figure 3.1   A proposed process for the identification of atypical needs in young children

overreliance on developmental tests as the only tool of assessment and overuse of these tests for individuals.

Characteristics of the child

As with testing children of any age, a wide range of variables can influence test results (McCormick & Schiefelbusch 1984). These factors can comprise immediate influences such as medication side-effects, illness, lack of sleep, anxiety, lack of motivation and numerous other temporary variables that can interfere with children's performance on the day. The younger the children and the more compromised their arousal system (see chapter 7), the more significant these issues become in assessment.

A deeper problem relates not to children's immediate wellbeing during the testing session but to the opportunities that they have had for learning. When children's disabilities have imposed frequent or extended hospitalisation or otherwise resulted in restricted exploration of their environment, they will have had fewer opportunities to learn the usual skills that typical children can acquire naturally. Yet test norms compare children with disabilities with others whose life experience is dissimilar to theirs. Thus, when individual children have not been exposed to typical experiences, either a normed test should not be carried out, or testers should interpret the findings as a reflection of both the children's capacities *and* their restricted experience, with the relative impact of each being indeterminable.

A second issue affecting children with disabilities in particular is that when they have difficulties in one developmental domain, these can contaminate their performance in another—for example, inattention can impair their demonstration of their intellectual skills; language comprehension difficulties can restrict their ability to self-instruct—to guide themselves—through each step of non-verbal problem-solving tasks; behavioural difficulties and their management can limit children's engagement with testing; and their sensory or physical disabilities will impair their performance of gross or fine motor tasks. Sometimes the testing is aimed at establishing the nature of such difficulties, but if it actually aims to measure children's intellectual functioning, the test content and assessment process must circumvent these other disabilities (McLoughlin & Lewis 2001).

Relationship between the child and tester

The very formal manner of normed testing is at odds with the needs of very young children (Kaufman 1990), and that formality can impede building rapport with them and encouraging them to perform at their best. Other personal characteristics—such as racial differences between the tester and child—can also impede the building of rapport (Taylor 2000). Furthermore, children with developmental delays appear to be particularly penalised when being assessed by adults whom they do not know (Fuchs & Fuchs 1986; Fuchs et al. 1985). This is probably because when being asked by an unfamiliar adult to complete items that they find difficult, their anxiety interferes with their performance; whereas anxiety is less likely to be provoked in children who find the items easier. This implies that prior acquaintance between the tester and children is likely to improve the accuracy of results.

A further issue affecting the relationship between children and testers is where the testing is carried out. Although there are advantages in testing children at home where they and their parents are less anxious and more comfortable (Lynch & Hanson 1996), natural domestic interruptions can disrupt the testing session. Of even more significance is that the children are seldom accustomed to such a formal situation at home and might refuse to participate, whereas in another familiar location—such as a preschool or care centre—the children are more apt to follow adults' directives. Thus, decisions about location need to be made in consultation with parents informed by knowledge of the children's temperament and emotional needs.

All of these issues affect children across the ages and ability ranges but are of more significance to those with disabilities as, in many cases, so much rests on the findings—including the children's placement, diagnosis and eligibility for services. Because the stakes are so high, then, errors in testing are of increased importance for this group of children.

Qualities of the test

Tests need to be suitable for use with the target population—in our case, for use with young children or those with atypical development. Although few gifted children are untestable on broad developmental measures, almost one-half of very young children with disabilities cannot be tested on currently available tests (Neisworth & Bagnato 1992). This signals that, particularly for this population of children, other measures must either replace or supplement the information gleaned from formal testing.

- **Reliability and validity.** One reason for children's untestability is that, as already mentioned, normed tests have been carefully constructed to produce reliable results. This is essential, but imposes inflexible administration procedures on testers and children. This particularly penalises young children and those with atypical development, as testers cannot take the children's unique individual needs into account and alter the testing conditions to allow them to display optimal performance.
- **Test design and format.** A second reason for children's untestability is the high floor of most tests: for instance, when test items begin at a developmental level of 2 years, 4-year-old children with considerable developmental delays might pass few or no items, thus giving no information about where their individual strengths and needs lie. To overcome this, testers might deliver a smorgasbord of items from a range of tests. This destroys norming, but can at least give some descriptive information on which to base educational planning.

Another issue to do with test format is the duration of testing sessions. Children with certain disabilities will be slow at performing the test tasks; while those with advanced development might complete most items in every subtest. In either case, the testing session is prolonged, requiring of these children a superlative concentration span. If they cannot sustain this, their results could reflect fatigue rather than their actual abilities.

Repeated administration of tests

Children with additional needs are more prone than most populations of children to be overtested, which wastes their time and uses up valuable resources, often unnecessarily. Although ongoing assessment is essential for monitoring children's progress and to evaluate their programs, it is a dubious practice to use normed tests for this purpose because the tests are not sensitive to small increments in development (Bondurant-Utz & Luciana 1994) and because children's learning occurs in growth spurts followed by periods of skill consolidation. Figure 3.2 shows that if our first testing (at T1) happened to fall after a spurt, and our second (at T2) was unwittingly timed before the next spurt, the child would seem to have made no progress in the interim.

On the other hand, our two assessments could take in two growth spurts, and happen to miss one period of consolidation, making it seem as if the child's progress is double what it is in fact, creating unrealistic expectations for the child's future developmental progress. This is depicted in Figure 3.3.

Another issue with repeating normed tests is that the children sometimes remember the items. Practice effects can mean that you cannot rely on the results

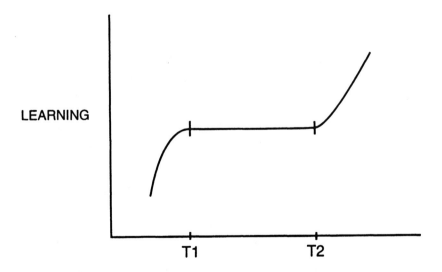

Figure 3.2   Timing of two testings coinciding with a learning plateau

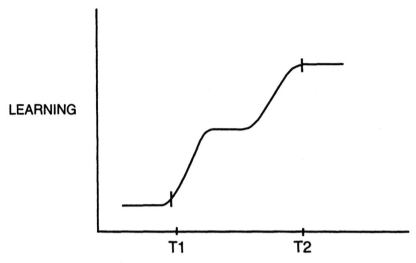

Figure 3.3 Timing of two testings measuring two growth spurts but only one plateau

of the likes of IQ tests, which attempt to assess children's ability to perform novel tasks (because, if the tasks were familiar, all you would be measuring is children's access to an enriching environment, in which case parental income would be an equally good measure).

PARENTAL INVOLVEMENT IN ASSESSMENT

Many of the shortcomings of tests can be overcome by involving parents in all phases of assessment. Having parents attend testing sessions is often advised against on the grounds that they might later teach the test items to their children. However, I caution them that this would contaminate the results of future assessments, on which they might need to rely for educational planning.

I find that parents' attendance during testing improves the accuracy of the results: the children do not have to accompany a stranger, with consequent reductions in their performance, and parents can explain an answer which seems unusual or which I do not understand because the child's speech is unfamiliar to me. When the parents and I subsequently talk about what I observed, they can tell me whether their child's performance on the day was typical or whether it surprised them in any way; and they can supplement and clarify the findings with their own intimate knowledge of their son or daughter. Finally, their participation demystifies the testing process, allowing us to discuss the tests' limitations and what these mean for the confidence we can place in the results.

These discussions can enable parents to clarify the meanings of terms that will appear in the assessment report and to understand its conclusions. Finally, their participation thus far empowers them to contribute to recommendations, which cannot be framed without information from parents and any other professionals who have ongoing contact with the child.

EQUATING CONTRADICTORY RESULTS

A skilled and experienced tester is able to choose a test that can provide the information being sought, as long as those who know the child give information about the questions they need answered. If the subsequent information gained from a test does not tally with the referring person's knowledge of the child, it is possible that the test results are flawed, given the many aspects that can contaminate test findings.

If you encounter an apparent contradiction, you can ask the tester for an explanation of discrepancies. It may be that the child was ill or otherwise uncomfortable during the assessment; that a test of, say, memory might tap only short-term recall, whereas in natural settings you tend to see the products of long-term memory and so the test is measuring skills that are slightly different from those suggested by its title; or there may be a more suitable instrument for obtaining the information being sought.

Sometimes an assessment is flawed simply because it is not comprehensive enough (Wolery 1996a); in other cases, the data are adequate but there is a difference in judgment about their implication for programs. A second opinion or further assessment procedures could assist with such differences in judgment. This must be balanced, however, with requirements that assessment be efficient and the realisation that sometimes, even if we assessed children in great depth, we might arrive at a diagnosis but be no closer to knowing how to respond to the child's day-to-day behaviour and needs.

SOME INTERPRETIVE STATISTICS

When children have been referred for testing, specialists' reports will contain some numbers which are important to understand so that the information conveyed is meaningful and can be used to help plan individual programs for children. This section describes some key statistics used in specialist assessments, which are also summarised in Figure 3.4.

The first statistic to know is the *average* score on the particular test used in an individual child's case. Many normed tests have borrowed the formula originally devised for IQ tests of reporting the average (or *mean*) score as 100 points; if not, practitioners might add a note explaining what the average score is on a particular test.

Comparing individual children's scores to the average is a good place to begin interpreting their results. However, you will also need to know whether an individual child's score is different enough from the average to warrant special programs. For this purpose we need another statistic, which is called a *standard deviation*. This figure tells you whether a particular child's score falls near to or a long way from (that is, deviates from) the average. If the score falls near the average, a child is likely to be well provided for by a regular program; if the score deviates a long way from the mean, the child is likely to need some special educational provisions.

When a child's score is converted into a standard deviation, an average score obviously has a standard deviation value of zero, because the score does not depart at all from the average. Thus, a standard deviation score of zero is 'normal'. However, because individuals do not achieve each developmental milestone at exactly the same age as all others, scores with values near to zero are also regarded as normal. In terms of standard deviation values, this normal range falls between −1 and +1 standard deviations. Children achieving scores within this range are developing typically. This comprises just over 68% of children.

As to scores falling outside this range, taking the lower end of the continuum first, traditionally we have defined children whose scores fall between −1 and −2 standard deviations as being 'at risk' or potentially developmentally compromised. Just over 13% of children fall within this category. When children's reported scores fall within this range you might offer some extra stimulation activities, perhaps in a naturalistic way, with the aim of advancing their skills nearer to the norm. You would monitor their progress and institute more formal programs if their scores subsequently encroached into the disabled range.

Standard deviation scores of −2 and below signify the disabled range. Over 2.5% of children achieve such scores. These are the children for whom it is important to supply modified educational experiences.

This pattern of scores is mirrored at the upper end of the ability continuum. That is, children whose scores fall between +1 and +2 standard deviations are said to have abilities in the 'high average' or 'bright–normal' range. Just over 13% of children achieve at this level. Meanwhile, standard deviation scores of +2 and above are taken to indicate significantly advanced development, or 'giftedness'. As is the case in the disabled range, over 2.5% of children are considered to be gifted. And, similar to children with disabilities, this group of children may well require program adjustments.

A final statistic that you might encounter is the percentile rank (PR). This number tells us that this child 'did as well as, or better than, x% of the cohort'. For instance, if the child's percentile ranking was 23, this means that she achieved as well as or higher than 23% of children of her age. However, this score quickly becomes extreme: for instance, within the normal range of −1 to +1 standard deviations, percentile ranks span from 16 to 84! This points to two disadvantages of percentile rankings: first, they incorrectly give the impression that tests are capable of making very fine discriminations between children;

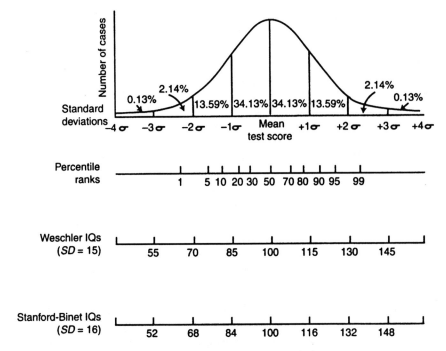

Figure 3.4   Distribution of abilities within a population

Source: adapted from Sattler (1992:17). Reproduced with the permission of Jerome M. Sattler Publishing Co.

second, they imply that these differences are clinically significant, when in many cases they are not—all the children between PRs of 16 and 84 are within normal limits, and yet their numbers seem very disparate.

SETTING PRIORITIES

The above statistics allow us to prioritise goals for children's programs by permitting us to compare their scores across tests. If, for instance, a child is achieving on a developmental test at 84 and a language comprehension test at 34, how can we compare these two numbers? The answer is to convert both raw scores to standard deviations (which testers do by using tables supplied in the test manual). As an example, let's say that we found that the child's achievement on the developmental test was at −1 standard deviations (that is, at the lower end of normal limits), but on the language comprehension test her score fell at −2.5. This tells us that she has a specific language difficulty—within the disabled range, and considerably below her other intellectual skills. Accordingly, we can now design a language program for her.

A second criterion by which we can set priorities for children's programs is to consider the impact of instruction on individuals' quality of life. For instance, when children have delays in two domains—say, forming grammatical sentences and not having toileting control—the latter might be deemed a higher priority because a lack of independent toileting control can significantly increase parents' workload and jeopardise children's social inclusion and so has a greater impact on the quality of life of children and their families.

A WORD ABOUT LABELLING

In the assessment process there is a trend away from diagnosing children's deficits because of the stigma that labels can attract. The focus has shifted to analysis of children's specific instructional needs and determination of the services they require as a result (Cook et al. 2000). However, notwithstanding the sometimes negative effects of labels on the individuals who receive them, diagnostic labels that arise from assessment can be useful to families, by describing, explaining and, at times, predicting the developmental progress of their child.

- **Description.** A label can cluster together an otherwise confusing array of symptoms into a single known entity. Attention deficit hyperactivity disorder (ADHD), for instance, groups together a cluster of inattentive, impulsive and overactive behaviours which otherwise might seem incomprehensible. The danger, however, with descriptive labels such as ADHD is that they can be misinterpreted as explanations.
- **Explanation.** A label can explain why a child has particular impairments. For instance, it is known that children with Down syndrome often have some cardiac problems, in which case a diagnosis of that syndrome will alert medical practitioners to screen for heart problems as well as developmental effects. The danger with explanatory labels, however, is that they are some-times used to excuse underachievement, in the belief that one impairment causes or 'explains' others, when the two might not inevitably coexist. For instance, sometimes gifted children's emotional outbursts are blamed on their giftedness, or behavioural difficulties are attributed to children's intel-lectual disabilities, when the two could be unrelated.
- **Prognosis.** A label can give parents some idea of the expected progress of a child's condition throughout life. The obvious danger here is that most prog-nostic information is based on groups of children rather than individuals which, given our incomplete theoretical knowledge and brief acquaintance with young children, means that we must be cautious in predicting their developmental trajectories.

Thus, when labelling any children—particularly those who are young and so have a short developmental history on which to base conclusions—we must keep in mind the explanatory limits of a particular diagnosis. Also we must be aware that children who share a diagnosis nevertheless can manifest it in differing ways. This implies that educational interventions must focus more on the individual than on the label.

CONCLUSION

Rowe (1990: 544) asserts that some professionals rely on tests 'like a drunk might depend on a lamp-post—for support rather than illumination'. Instead, our best assessment instrument is human (Borland & Wright 1994), and requires us to know individual children well (Shaklee 1992). Tests do not allow us to see everything, so comprehensive assessment requires that educators use a range of informative measures to gain the fullest possible understanding of children's abilities and educational needs.

Naturally, assessment is not an end in itself but a means to achieving an end—namely, translating the information gained into a relevant program for individual children (Wolery 1996a). Thus, selected assessment measures must be viewed as tools only, which in themselves accomplish little: what counts is how these tools are used (Rowe 1990). Properly used, great benefits can accrue from identifying the needs of individual children and devising programs to meet those. This leads into the subject of program planning, which is the topic of Chapter 4.

ADDITIONAL RESOURCES

Anastasi, A. and Urbina. S. 1997 *Psychological testing* 7th edn, Prentice Hall, Upper Saddle River, NJ

Beaty, J.J. 2002 *Observing development of the young child* 5th edn, Merrill Prentice Hall, Upper Saddle River, NJ

McLean, M., Bailey, D.B. Jr and Wolery, M. eds 1996 *Assessing infants and preschoolers with special needs* 2nd edn, Merrill, Englewood Cliffs, NJ

McLoughlin, J.A. and Lewis, R.B. 2001 *Assessing students with special needs* 4th edn, Merrill, Upper Saddle River, NJ

Taylor, R.L. 2000 *Assessment of exceptional students: educational and psychological procedures* 5th edn, Allyn & Bacon, Boston, MA

4

PRINCIPLES OF PROGRAM INDIVIDUALISATION

LOUISE PORTER

KEY POINTS

- Children with additional learning needs require an educational program which is guided by the same principles as any early childhood curricula.
- Such children require an individualised program that is integrated, inter-disciplinary and differentiated.
- Modifications to the learning environment, teaching processes, program content and learning products will be necessary for children who are not learning typically within the regular early childhood program.

INTRODUCTION

Just as a range of views of children (see chapter 1) give rise to various approaches to teaching, so too various views of the purposes of early childhood education underpin the design of curricula (Dahlberg et al. 1999; Moss 1999). Early childhood education has been seen to fulfil a range of functions: from off-setting the disadvantages perceived to be posed by some children's homes, in which case the educator is a protector; to providing substitute parental care; to supporting parents' participation in the labour force, in which case educators become 'service providers' promoting 'consumer' satisfaction (Dahlberg et al. 1999). A fourth model conceptualises child care and preschool centres as places *for* children whose dual role is to provide educational experiences that comple-ment the learning children gain elsewhere and to strengthen social networks within the community (Dahlberg et al. 1999; Moss 1999).

Because centres are located within particular local contexts, their specific workings will be individual to them, arrived at in negotiation with their com-munity. Thus, it is neither possible nor desirable to describe appropriate programs for every setting as practices must be tailored to suit individual children and their contexts. This chapter therefore confines itself to the description of some principles for guiding your decisions about curricula planning and about which adjustments might be appropriate in your environment and for individual children with additional needs.

PROGRAM PLANNING

There are two broad approaches to curriculum programming. The first is a *top-down* approach in which adults determine which skills and information are of value to children and then set about teaching these. The top-down approach is largely adult-driven, with educators framing programs:

- in accord with their philosophy of education;
- guided by their understanding of childhood;
- on the basis of their theory of learning;
- drawing on their own training and experience;
- in light of guidelines and policy directions provided by their governing authorities;
- according to parental values and preferences;
- in response to awareness of each child's interests, experience and abilities in a range of domains; of how each child learns; and knowledge of with whom each child plays (Theilheimer 1993);
- taking into account their resources and constraints.

This top-down process of generating a program is not necessarily unresponsive to children's needs, but is nevertheless largely originated by the educator. It is also at the heart of the push to impose on young children a more academic curriculum (see Rodger 1999), which is often advocated in the interests of developing an increasingly skilled future work force.

In contrast with imposing a curriculum on children, a *bottom-up* approach sees children as already enriched and vibrant human beings (Dahlberg et al. 1999) whose need to generate identities and understandings of the world are the starting point for, rather than an afterthought in, curriculum planning. Advocates of this model say that the fact that many young children *can* learn an academic curriculum does not mean that they *should* (Katz 1988). They argue that children's dispositions and indepth understanding can be harmed by confronting them too early with tasks whose content and processes are too demanding, that when children are deprived of physical play in favour of academic work, neural pathways in the brain that are essential for academic success cannot be strengthened, and that young children's eyesight (being long-sighted and not yet able to track) can be compromised by prolonged close work.

Rather than attempting to instil a predetermined curriculum, the bottom-up approach respects and responds reflectively to the skills and interests of children and their parents. However it does not simply indulge these or rely on improvisation or chance: it utilises educators' expertise and active teaching while also engaging children's (and parents') competence (Fraser & Gestwicki 2002). It is 'child originated and teacher framed' (Forman & Fyfe 1998, in Fraser & Gestwicki 2002: 168).

This, then, generates a reciprocal process of planning, in which educators pay attention to children's thinking and analyse the topics that are engaging them, while also taking into consideration which topics will be of long-term value to the children (Fraser & Gestwicki 2002). This information will generate the basis of the program, to which the children and parents, in turn, will respond, upon which further adjustments will be made, and so on.

AIMS OF EARLY CHILDHOOD PROGRAMS

The broad aim of education is for children to acquire knowledge and skills in a variety of areas and to develop the dispositions and ability to use their information and skills to solve problems and generate understandings of themselves and their world (Dahlberg et al. 1999; Johnson & Johnson 1992). Beyond this general goal, the following specific aims of early childhood programs have been nominated by various authors (Bailey & Wolery 1992; Katz & Chard 1989; NAEYC & NAECS/SDE 1991; Smidt 1998; Wright & Coulianos 1991).

Facilitate competence

This involves skill acquisition, fluency of use, skill maintenance (the ability to use skills after instruction has ceased) (Wolery & Fleming 1993), and the ability to detect when to employ a particular skill so that competence can be transferred (generalised) across situations (Perkins et al. 1993). It also encompasses being able independently to use functional skills in natural settings (this aim tending to be highlighted mainly for children with disabilities).

Naturally, the aim to foster competence spans all developmental domains, including:

- using language to communicate and to facilitate thinking and learning;
- understanding the relationships among objects, people and events;
- developing conceptual knowledge of the world;
- practising higher-order thinking and problem-solving skills;
- becoming literate;
- developing numeracy skills;
- becoming competent in management of one's body;
- acquiring basic physical skills and maintaining a desirable level of health and fitness.

Positive dispositions towards learning

A second aim is to encourage in children positive attitudes to learning and to themselves as learners so that they remain willing to put in the effort required to achieve. These dispositions include, for example: engagement, playfulness, motivation, persistence, independence, cooperativeness, curiosity, enthusiasm for learning, confidence, patience, exploration, planfulness, adventurousness, intellectual rigour, creativity, open-mindedness, self-awareness and self-control (Lambert & Clyde 2000; Perkins et al. 1993).

Emotional support for children

Early years education also aims to safeguard children's emotional development by:

- establishing a safe and caring physical and emotional environment that supports and protects all children's right to learn and grow personally;
- helping children establish satisfying and successful social relationships;
- developing in each child a healthy self-esteem.

A supportive community

The aim to support social networks encompasses the following aspects:

- collaboration with the children's parents (or other primary caregivers) in achieving their goals for their child;
- connecting with the cultures of the families participating in early childhood programs and the broader community;
- imparting understanding of and respect for social and cultural diversity;
- supporting educators, both personally and professionally.

Clearly, these aims are not value-neutral. This is inevitable, as a key function of education is to socialise children; it becomes problematic only if we forget to question the legitimacy of our aims for children in general, for our particular context, or for individual children.

PROGRAM DIFFERENTIATION

Curricula are an organised framework, detailing (Richarz 1993):

- the **environment** in which learning and teaching will occur;
- the teaching and learning **processes** to be employed—that is, what educators will do to help children grow in understanding of themselves and their physical and social world;
- the **content** that children are to learn, which encompasses the planned or spontaneous opportunities that will be provided;
- the **products** that will record what individual children have achieved.

Curriculum or program differentiation refers to adjustment of all these elements as required, so that activities are relevant to children with differing learning needs and preferences (Kulik & Kulik 1997). Individualisation or differentiation of programs or curricula must allow for differences in both the pace (quantity) and depth (quality) of children's learning (Piirto 1999). At the same time, it should build on what the children already *can* do, rather than on what they *cannot* do (Smidt 1998).

Individualisation of the curriculum necessitates greater flexibility in your role, organisation of the setting and structure of the program. While keeping in mind long-term goals, your moment-to-moment decision making needs to remain fluid and opportunistic, taking advantage of spontaneous opportunities to capitalise on the children's ideas and interests (Kostelnick 1992).

It might go without saying, but adjustments to programs for children with additional needs should be based on need. This has two implications: first, that it is important to identify those needs accurately; second, that just as need is the criterion for adjusting programs for children with disabilities, so too must it be the criterion when children's development is advanced. Program adjustments for gifted children are instead often provided on the basis of whether the children are 'deserving'—that is, displaying exemplary behaviour (Borland 1989). However, the fact that these children are able to function within expectations indicates that the present program is already meeting their needs; the children who actually require adjustments to their program are those whose behaviour attests to some difficulties.

When planning for the individual needs of children with disabilities or gifts, local policy might dictate that an individualised curriculum plan be negotiated. Around the world, these go by many titles, including negotiated curriculum plan (NCP), individualised education plan (IEP) or an Individualised Family Service Plan (IFSP) (Cook et al. 2000). Whatever its title, the plan will contain a summary of the assessment information, a statement about the family's aspirations for their son or daughter and resulting program priorities, and a description of the services to be provided and their setting (Cook et al. 2000). Less formal plans are likely to be used for children with lesser developmental difficulties and those with advanced development, although all efforts at individualisation will encompass adjustments to the learning *environment*, teaching *processes*, program *content*, and the *products* through which children demonstrate their learning (see Table 4.1).

Differentiation of the environment

The environment refers to the physical structure of a setting, its organisation and its social climate. Within an ecological perspective, the environment is seen as the 'third teacher'—with the first being the children themselves and the second being their social relationships with adults and other children (Fraser & Gestwicki 2002).

As Fraser and Gestwicki (2002: 100) observe, 'Space does indeed speak': appropriately arranged settings can further many program aims. First, the space communicates a welcome to children, families, educators and visitors and signals their ownership of the space by reflecting their personal interests and requirements (Fraser & Gestwicki 2002). Second, the level of stimulation, attractiveness and fun influences the participation of the children. Third, the structure

Table 4.1 Common and differentiated features of programs for young children

Environmental organisation	Process	Content	Product
Common elements • structured yet flexible organisation • supportive climate • encouragement of exploration • high but realistic expectations • high-quality teaching	• facilitative relationships between educators and children	• programs based on children's interests • an integrated curriculum	• demonstration of key knowledge and skills • a range of mediums

Differentiation methods
• adult-child ratios
• group size
• flexible time allotment
• adaptation of buildings and play areas
• placement
• grouping
	• naturalistic instruction
	• adult-directed teaching
	• mediation of social interaction
	• facilitation of transitions
	• technological adaptations
		• tailored activities:
		  – simple vs complex
		  – concrete vs abstract
		  – small vs large steps
		  – knowledge acquisition vs concept mastery
		  – uni- vs multi-faceted
		  – structured vs open-ended
		  – breadth vs depth
		• tiered activities
		• selected toys and activities
		• access to specialists
			• tiered products
			• teach expressive skills

Source: adapted from Porter (1999:174).

should help children to feel safe, allow them to exercise choice, invite investigation, permit them to use ideas and materials creatively, and give them independent access to materials and play, thus giving them confidence that they can have control of themselves during their play (Fraser & Gestwicki 2002; Robson 1996; Smidt 1998). Fourth, the physical layout allows the program to flow smoothly, for example by keeping traffic areas free of congestion.

Various elements of the physical and social environment can be adapted to enable children with atypical development to engage in purposeful and meaningful activity (Kostelnick 1992). Environmental adjustment will not only promote children's development but has the advantage of being naturalistic and relatively unobtrusive (Sandall 1993).

Maintain appropriate adult–child ratios
Although an accepted canon of early years education is that there should be high numbers of adults to children to foster optimal development, particularly when the children have additional needs, the presence of a greater number of adults makes it less likely that children with disabilities will interact socially with peers and increases their dependence on adults during mastery tasks (Hauser-Cram et al. 1993). Thus, when extra adults are available to assist children with additional needs it is important for adults not to shadow those children constantly and thus create dependency or act as a barrier between the children and peers.

Restrict group size
The size of a group will either enable or hinder personal interactions between group members. Groups could have one adult to five children (with a total group size of six people) or three adults to 15 children, which maintains the same adult–child ratio but yields a group size of 18 members. The dynamics in these two groups will differ considerably, with very young children and perhaps older children with developmental delays being less able to cope well in a larger group. These children may require smaller groups, particularly at times when their skills are being extended such as during group story time, or when group size imposes extended waiting time on children with limited concentration.

Allot time flexibly
In many instances children need prolonged and continuous periods of time in which to develop and sustain the themes of their play, consolidate their skills, or complete engrossing projects. Therefore their time must not be fragmented and intruded upon unnecessarily by the imposition of timetabled activities. In other cases, individual children's limited concentration skills or quick mastery of concepts might call for rapidly changing activities.

Adapt buildings and play areas
The judicious placement of displays, toys and equipment can stimulate children's interactions with their environment (Sandall 1993). In addition, children with disabilities can require specific environmental adjustments so that

they can safely access the setting independently. For instance, blind children need their environment to be laid out logically so that it is predictable; there needs to be sufficient room for specialised equipment and the negotiation of obstacles; children with sensory impairments might require adjustments to the acoustics or lighting in the room; those with physical or vision disabilities will require even walking surfaces, ramps for wheelchairs, and toys and equipment that are safe and adapted for successful use. On the other hand, educators must avoid environmental adaptations being so extensive that it becomes difficult for children to adjust to natural settings where few such adaptations exist (Lewis & Taylor 1997).

Place children with true peers

Placement decisions centre on the age and ability levels of surrounding children. In terms of age, to foster modelling, children with developmental delays might be suited to placement within a group of younger children with similar developmental levels to their own. On the other hand, typically developing 3-year-olds are less able than 4-year-olds to adjust their communication style to accommodate older children with delays, in which case they might not be ideal social companions (Guralnick et al. 1998).

Even when placed alongside younger typically developing children, there are likely to be differences not only in *what* the various children can achieve but in *how* they achieve it (McCollum & Bair 1994). Also, if the children with disabilities are physically large, they might look out of place among a group of younger children, rendering such a placement unsuitable.

On the other hand, placement alongside age mates can put children with delayed development in danger if, for instance, they are still mouthing or eating materials such as glue or nails which are part of the regular children's activities, or if the climbing equipment that suits typical children is dangerous to them. If the children with disabilities are unsteady on their feet, they can be scared of being knocked over by very active children and so lose confidence in moving about independently.

Meanwhile, gifted children might have no intellectual peers within a group of same-aged children and so need access to children who are older than themselves. This is a main reason for their early entry to school, as older children are not generally available in preschool settings in the year before school. (See Box 4.2.)

Plan group composition

Grouping refers to the span of ages and developmental levels within a group. Heterogeneous (also known as mixed-age, mixed-ability or vertical) grouping offers children a wide range of potential playmates, giving younger or less able children access to older companions who can extend their learning and allowing children to adopt a variety of roles within their play (Bouchard 1991; Katz et al. 1990; Lloyd 1997; Roberts et al. 1994). This is of less benefit to the older and gifted children, of course, while same-ability grouping can be more beneficial for language-based activities such as story time (Bailey et al. 1993).

Box 4.2 Developmentally appropriate placement for gifted learners

One method of meeting gifted children's advanced learning needs involves what is usually termed 'acceleration'. This entails allowing them to enter school early or, once in school, to skip an entire grade (or more) or go up to a higher grade for certain subjects (which is termed 'partial acceleration'). Some writers argue, however, that the term *acceleration* is a misnomer as it implies an attempt to speed up the children's development itself, when the term really only means providing gifted children with a curriculum that matches their needs and abilities. Therefore, Feldhusen et al. (1996) suggest that we replace the term *acceleration* with the concept of *appropriate developmental placement*.

Appropriate developmental placement aims to enhance children's achievement by providing a closer match between their needs and abilities and the curriculum they receive and to allow them to socialise more successfully as there will be a closer intellectual match between them and their older classmates (Benbow 1991; Rogers & Kimpston 1992). Despite a few documented cases of children being disadvantaged by early entry to higher grades at school, the bulk of research consistently reports that acceleration meets gifted children's academic, social and emotional needs, particularly for carefully screened children. (For a full review, see Porter 1999.) In light of such findings, the following criteria have been found to be crucial to the success of early placement (Bailey 1997; Braggett 1992, 1993).

- The **school** has to be willing to accept the child.
- The **classroom** where the child is entering needs to be flexibly structured.
- The receiving **teacher** must be sympathetic to the idea of early entry and must be willing to fill any gaps in a child's skills that have resulted from missing some educational experiences.
- The **child** must be interested in early entry, although adults must be careful not to give children the impression that it will solve all of their academic or social difficulties.
- The **parents'** wishes are crucial as their support will affect how well the children cope.

As well, it can help (but is not essential) for the children to be socially mature, to be willing to mix with older classmates, and to have the requisite fine motor and reading skills to be able to cope with academic tasks. These skills are not essential because within any class there is a wide range of abilities in such domains, and so lack of maturity in any of them need not on its own preclude an early placement if all other criteria are met.

Any advanced placement must be treated as a trial and its effects monitored closely (Braggett 1992) and other means of meeting gifted learners' needs—such as enrichment—must also be set in place, as simply offering the children the same curriculum earlier is unlikely to meet their needs adequately.

Having a broad span of ages is a challenging teaching arrangement (Mason & Burns 1996) which, on its own, does not generate the above advantages (Mosteller et al. 1996; Veenman 1995, 1996): the benefits of heterogeneous grouping appear to come from the adults' acceptance of diversity and corresponding philosophical commitment to meeting children's individual needs (Bouchard 1991; Lloyd 1997).

Conclusion: environmental adjustments

A conducive environment is necessary but not sufficient to promote children's learning: setting up activities does not amount to providing a program but instead is only the context in which learning can occur (Lambert & Clyde 2000). It is children's experiences within a setting that provoke their learning. Hence, the next section highlights the importance of the teaching and learning processes employed in the setting.

Differentiation of teaching and learning processes

It is self-evident that teaching processes need to be efficient in helping children acquire and practise skills and dispositions that are a priority for them but, at the same time, educators must minimise the extent to which teaching methods intrude on or restrict children's natural learning (Atwater et al. 1994; Bailey & McWilliam 1990; Carta et al. 1991; Johnson & Johnson 1992; Wolery & Bredekamp 1994).

The dominant teaching method employed will differ at various stages of children's development, as shown in Table 4.2, ranging from showing, telling and describing what infants are experiencing, to facilitating exploration and self-discovery, explaining cause-and-effect relationships and assisting children's experimentation (Belgrad 1998). These methods will also differ according to whether the children are acquiring a new skill, consolidating a skill or extending their mastery (Lambert & Clyde 2000).

The following measures can allow you to individualise teaching methods in response to particular children's needs.

Develop a facilitative relationship with children

In keeping with the concept that early years education must be responsive to and designed for children, the pedagogical role of the educator is to facilitate children's understandings of themselves and their world, rather than to impose preconceived concepts on them. This will empower children to drive their own learning (Lambert & Clyde 2000).

A key means for helping children to understand their world is to engage in dialogues with them about what they are discovering. Being the most experienced communication partners, adults are responsible for shaping such conversations with children. To describe this responsibility, Wells (1986 in Smidt 1998) uses the analogy of teaching a child to catch a ball: when teaching a young child to catch, the adult prompts the child how to hold her hands and makes sure to lob the ball gently and directly into the child's outstretched arms—but the

LIVERPOOL JOHN MOORES UNIVERSITY
LEARNING SERVICES

Table 4.2 Young children's modes of learning and corresponding modes of teaching

Developmental level	Modes of play or learning	Modes of teaching
0–18 months	Imitation	Direct instruction • showing • telling • describing
18–30 months	Exploration Inquiry Discovery	Provision of a safe environment Questioning
30–48 months	Prediction testing (trial-and-error learning) Discovery	Mediation Explaining cause-and-effect
4+ years	Construction	Facilitation Provision of opportunities Mediation

Source: adapted from Belgrad (1998:374).

adult is prepared to run wherever necessary to retrieve the ball when it is thrown back to him or her. Thus, conversations with children have to follow their lead, with adults responding to children's ideas and questions and elaborating on their experience so that they can make sense of what they encounter (Smidt 1998).

Having touched on the intellectual aspect of dialogues, it must be emphasised that conversations must also be emotionally engaging: the intellect cannot work without affective involvement (Maxwell 1996), while intimacy with adults will go a long way towards meeting children's emotional needs. Therefore, your interactions with children must be warm and fun and offer opportunities for personal two-way discussions in which you listen to what is engaging them, rather than asking questions whose answers you already know (such as, 'What colour are you using now?'), offering corrections or giving directives (Maxwell 1996; NCAC 1993). Further, your feedback needs to focus on the learning processes and dispositions that the children are exercising—such as the underlying ideas, problem solving efforts, planning, persistence, and so on—rather than commenting only on end products.

Use predominantly naturalistic instruction

Early education rests on two fundamental principles: first, that children learn best when they are actively engaged rather than only passively participating; second, that children need opportunities for autonomous learning (Bredekamp & Copple 1997). Together, these principles highlight that children must be proactive in their own learning (Maxwell 1996), which implies a preference for naturalistic teaching over formalised instruction. Naturalistic instruction encompasses a number of approaches which share the following characteristics (Rule et al. 1998):

- The context comprises routine events—although these are not accidental, as the educator will structure certain events to evoke and sustain children's engagement so that they can acquire and practise those skills that are a priority for them.
- Interactions follow the children's lead or capitalise on their interests.
- Natural consequences prevail, whereby the children's success—rather than a contrived external reward—reinforces their efforts.
- Because instruction occurs in natural contexts, teaching focuses on functional skills.

You can use activity-based instruction to promote children's learning by inspiring exploration through the provision of attractive toys and activities, embedding your intervention into the children's self-initiated activities, and offering specific activities that both interest the children and allow you naturally to incorporate their developmental priorities (Diamond et al. 1994). Responding to child-initiated activities is likely to encourage higher-order skills such as exploration, persistence and problem solving, and thus will promote the generalisation that is possible only with true mastery (Losardo & Bricker 1994; Mahoney & Wheedon 1999).

One common naturalistic teaching strategy is termed mediation. Mediated learning—as distinct from direct learning through the senses—occurs when adults interpret the environment for children, reflecting the children's interests, needs and capabilities (Klein 1992). This is also known as *scaffolding* and takes considerable adult skill: to set the stage, to recognise the children's responses, and to follow through with support in order to advance children's thinking skills (Barclay & Benelli 1994).

In mediated learning, adults initially direct children's thinking processes towards a higher level than they can achieve alone, and then the children progressively acquire the ability to take over this executive control function themselves (Moss 1992). To achieve this transfer, they need many opportunities to participate actively in the joint problem-solving process (Moss 1992).

Once children's engagement is recruited, mediation involves responding to and provoking children's ideas and suggestions, providing cues or prompts, demonstrating approaches to tasks, asking open-ended questions (which usually start with *who, why, what, when* or *how*), asking challenging questions that provoke thoughtful responses, identifying problems, reflecting on the children's inferred emotions, and offering and asking for feedback (Cavallaro et al. 1993). The aim is for the adults and children to co-construct understandings (Fraser & Gestwicki 2002). This reciprocal process will incorporate the following five key strategies (Klein 1992).

- **Focus.** You can select salient aspects of the activity and help children to focus on these through accentuation or exaggeration (Klein 1992; Moss 1992). For example, with young babies, you might 'dance' a toy to within easy reach; with older infants, you could point out important features: 'Hey, look at this! What do you think it's for?'

- **Meaning.** You can convey your intellectual interest in and emotional excitement about an activity. Children will then internalise (learn) to find such activities interesting and develop the commitment that is necessary for sustained effort and success.
- **Expansion.** You can expand children's cognitive awareness beyond their immediate activity by making spontaneous comparisons between the present task and others they have achieved, pointing out strategies for memory storage and recall, and so on.
- **Simplification.** You can remove elements of the task that are too difficult for a child, or complete those aspects yourself so that the child is able to complete the remaining aspects independently. For example, when completing a difficult puzzle, you might remove only a few pieces from the completed puzzle and allow the children to replace just those missing pieces so that they experience success.
- **Feedback.** You can express excitement and satisfaction with children's achievements by, for example, making explicit positive statements about their efforts (e.g. 'You took care balancing that block and now it's staying put!'). This teaches children how to monitor and judge outcomes for themselves and will enhance effort and reflection (Moss 1992).

This mediating process will be reciprocal, wherein you respond to the children's actions as well as requiring them to respond to you (Lambert & Clyde 2000). In this way, the children can control the pace of their learning and, ultimately, are empowered to practise new skills independently.

Provide adult-directed teaching, as required

To be effective in meeting the diverse needs of children, educators must have a range of teaching methods at their disposal (Carta et al. 1991). Thus, although early childhood curricula are based on children's exploration and discovery, when children are acquiring new skills or concepts, having difficulty becoming engaged or sustaining attention, developing high-level cognitive strategies, or requiring remedial instruction, you will need to guide their learning. Once they are engaged, you might need to offer those with learning difficulties extra cues, prompts and encouragement to continue to be involved (McCollum & Bair 1994) and give them additional time in which to respond to your overtures or directives (Wolery et al. 1994).

The balance between naturalistic and adult-directed instruction will depend on the skill to be taught, its functional priority and the context, with more directive methods employed only once children have shown that they are not profiting sufficiently from more naturalistic approaches (Atwater et al. 1994).

Facilitate social play

Adult involvement in children's social play is essential to support the children when their play flags and to guide the extension of their ideas. Children with disabilities—especially intellectual delay—are likely to need particular assistance to interact with typical peers and, once engaged, to maintain their interactions with others (Cavallaro et al. 1993). In supporting the children, you might choose one of the following strategies (Ward 1996).

- **Play in parallel with children** so that they will begin to copy you. This adds to or extends their own play ideas.
- **Become an active co-player.** At the invitation of children, you can become a co-player, joining in their existing play and responding to their comments or actions, thus complementing and extending their ideas.
- **Direct the play.** Sometimes you might take more control of the direction of children's play, either by making suggestions from the side or by participating in the play. This is useful when children do not seem able to engage in more advanced play without adult prompts. As soon as they can assume control of its direction themselves, you can ease out of the play (Ward 1996).

At all of these levels you can pose questions, make suggestions, and expand on the children's thinking and cooperative skills to enable them to elaborate on their ideas and exercise increasingly sophisticated thinking processes.

Facilitate transitions between activities
When children cannot move about the setting independently, you will need to plan alternative means by which they can change activities. This will assist them to remain engaged and to act on their preferences, and will provide them with the challenge necessary to prevent secondary disabling conditions such as when an inability to move limits their exploration and hence their cognitive development (Erwin 1993).

Make technological adaptations
Some children will require vision or hearing aids, electronic toys, voice-activated computers or augmentive communication systems to help them independently negotiate and interact with their environment. Specialists in each developmental domain can advise you about the appropriate use of such equipment within your program.

Differentiation of curriculum content

There has been a passionate debate in early years education and special education about whether developmental theory offers adequate guidance for selecting the content of early years programs. The debate centres on whether the developmental sequence tells us what young children *should* be learning, or merely describes what most typically learn (see Kessler 1991). Advocates of a developmental model claim that teaching skills in the sequence in which they usually unfold means that children are not set up to fail; but critics contend that slavish adherence to a developmental model can mean that educators hold back from teaching functional skills on the grounds that the children are not developmentally 'ready' to learn them. The results are that programs can remain childlike and irrelevant to children and their families, and educators' low expectations can render children unnecessarily incompetent.

Those who favour the alternative, ecological, model of program planning instead recommend that educators teach skills that are useful in children's environments—particularly their present settings but also having regard for the skills that children will need in their next placement, such as school. This model recognises that there are many pathways to achievement other than the purely sequential route through developmental milestones (Sandall 1993). Developmentalists, however, claim that this approach can result in teaching skills that are too sophisticated for the children's abilities (Mirenda & Donnellan 1987), forcing them to learn by rote rather than fully comprehending what they are encountering (Katz 1988). The result can be that the children are less likely to maintain their skills over time or apply their skills in other settings (that is, generalise what they have learned).

A blend of the two models is possible: educators could decide to teach the next skill in the typical developmental sequence in each domain, but prioritise these according to whether the skills are likely to be useful to the children; or, in reverse, they could establish priorities on the basis of which skills will be functional for children but adjust teaching in light of awareness of the children's current developmental status which will imply how difficult the task might be for them to achieve (Mirenda & Donnellan 1987).

However, you might have recognised that this is a 'top-down' debate that fails to question the implied role of adults as originators of children's learning and whose intrapersonal focus does not take sufficient account of children's social and cultural environments. The debate reported earlier concluded that rather than imposing a set curriculum on children, educators need to follow children's lead, responding to their engagement in a way that allows them to construct their individual understandings of themselves and their world (Dahlberg et al. 1999).

This model has two caveats: first, educators cannot simply wait around for children to become involved but must actively initiate ideas and provoke children's questioning by the content of the program. Second, when children are not managing naturally to learn skills or acquire dispositions that will be useful to them in the long term, you must be willing to assist them to do so. This, after all, is the basis of early intervention.

Despite these debates about how to select priorities for individual children's learning, a core principle of the bottom-up approach to programming is that, in order to foster positive dispositions towards learning, program content should be drawn from the children's interests and educational needs rather than from a predetermined sequence of instruction (Dunn & Kontos 1997; NAEYC & NAECS/SDE 1991). Children's interests are significant because they help them resolve inner conflicts, so it is important that adults help children to explore their own topics rather than redirecting them to more traditional tasks (Cohen 1998). Focusing on these interests avoids their erosion and children's consequent underachievement and deflects from a deficit model of education, in which the focus is on what children *cannot* do (Cohen 1998).

While children's interests change over time, the underlying themes of their play are remarkably similar throughout childhood (Cohen 1989, 1998). Some children are interested in being in *control* of themselves and their world; some are fascinated by the *natural world*; some centre their play on exploring social *relationships*; some seek to *express themselves* artistically and emotionally; and others are interested in learning about *symbols* such as words and numbers (Cohen 1998). These interests can be encouraged by helping the children to gather resources, asking them questions and, when the time is right, extending an interest into a new curricular area (Cohen 1998).

A second principle is that all young children share a fundamental need for opportunities to make sense of their world through an integrated program. Integration encompasses a range of aspects: first, it implies that traditional content areas are incorporated naturally into all activities (Barbour 1992; Nidiffer & Moon 1994). Second, it recognises that all learning is interrelated and so the whole child is the focus, rather than dividing children's skills into the various developmental domains (Sandall 1993). Third, integration also implies an integration of the children's worlds—home, the school or preschool, culture and community (Holden 1996).

Because all children have these core requirements in common, many early childhood experiences are equally valuable for all. At other times children with additional needs will require adjustments to the content of their programs in response to their disparate needs. This individualisation of program content can entail the following measures.

Offer tailored activities
The following features of activities can be varied in line with the ability levels of the children and the complexity of the learning task (Tomlinson 1996).

- **Simple versus complex tasks.** When children are acquiring new content or processes, they will need tasks to be simple; when they are consolidating knowledge and skills, they will be more motivated by tasks that are complex.
- **Concrete versus abstract examples.** At entry level, children will need concrete learning experiences; if children are advanced in the task at hand, they will be more able to apply their sophisticated knowledge to abstract problems.
- **Small steps versus larger leaps.** When a task is intellectually demanding, children will need it to be broken into smaller steps; when children already possess the requisite subskills, they can take larger leaps in their learning.
- **Knowledge acquisition versus concept mastery.** Children whose development is advanced will often have more prior knowledge than their age mates so will need less repetition, revision and consolidation time than less able children (Kanevsky 1994). Thus, there can be less need to teach them isolated facts, leaving time for them to focus on broader concepts. The reverse is likely to be the case for children whose development is delayed. They will require more repeated practice of skills before achieving mastery (Wolery 1991).

- **Unidimensional versus multifaceted.** When children are novices within a field of interest, they might need to explore it along a single dimension; when they already grasp the basics, they can explore it in a more multidisciplinary manner, making more connections between ideas and examining issues from various perspectives.
- **Structured versus open-ended.** When children are comfortable with an area, they can cope with open-ended activities; when they are not sure of their grounding in a domain, they are likely to prefer more structured activities.
- **Breadth versus depth.** All children will need to acquire a broad range of skills across domains; when they have attained these, they can be encouraged to achieve deeper understanding (Patton & Kokoski 1996; Van Tassel-Baska 1997).

Provide tiered activities

The provision of tiered activities takes two forms (Montgomery 1996):

- differentiation of **inputs**, whereby you provide *different* activities at different levels of difficulty but which share a common theme. The children can self-select which activities suit them or you could target certain children and support them to attempt more demanding tasks;
- differentiation of **outcomes**, whereby you set a *common* task which children enter at their own level and then respond according to their level of sophistication.

Offering tiered activities requires that you establish appropriate starting points for the children, based on your recognition of their prior knowledge (Eyre 1997).

Select toys and activities that further program goals

Materials do not teach children as such, but they do set the stage for social and physical interactions that promote learning (Wolery & Fleming 1993). Children with developmental delays and disabilities tend to interact with toys and materials less spontaneously and for shorter periods of time, and so may need additional guidance to become engaged and support to remain on task (Kontos et al. 1998; Richarz 1993). Toys that will invite engagement include those that the children prefer, are functional and relevant in their daily lives and appropriate to a wide range of abilities (Bailey & Wolery 1992). Such naturally attractive materials can draw children's interest, while suitable adjustments to toys and materials can make it easier for them to manipulate these and so remain engaged.

Meanwhile, when your goals for individual children are social, you can provide toys that invite social play. These comprise the likes of dress-up clothes, dolls and doll houses, large blocks, housekeeping materials, puppets and vehicles such as wagons, as against toys that tend to lead to isolated or parallel play such as small building blocks, playdough, books, and craft activities (Ivory & McCollum 1999).

Purposeful selection of activities can be guided by observing how the children typically use the materials provided. If they are not engaging with the materials as intended, the tasks can be modified to further their participation and enjoyment.

Arrange access to specialists

Children with disabilities can benefit either from direct instruction from a relevant specialist or from consultation between yourself and specialist educators so that therapeutic activities can be incorporated into the early childhood program.

Conclusion: teaching processes and content

Teaching processes and curricular content, while distinguishable in theory, are inseparable in practice: children cannot learn problem solving unless there is a problem (some content) to solve, and they cannot learn any content unless they have adequate learning processes and the disposition to employ these (NAEYC & NAECS/SDE 1991). One example of a union between content and learning processes is provided by project-based learning in which, with adult guidance, children apply a range of cognitive and metacognitive skills (processes) and dispositions to answering a question or solving a problem (content) that they have selected for themselves (see Katz & Chard 1989).

Product differentiation

Products allow children to demonstrate the knowledge, skills and dispositions that they have exercised during their participation in the program. They make children's learning visible, communicate to the children that their efforts are valued, communicate to parents about their children's learning, and invite the children's reflection on what they have achieved (Fraser & Gestwicki 2002; Helm et al. 1998). They are 'a visible trace of the process that children and teachers engage in during their investigations together' (Fraser & Gestwicki 2002: 129).

Products can reflect individual or cooperative effort and can span samples of the children's writing and art; lists recorded by the educator but generated by the children, as in brainstorming discussions; extracts from children's journals or educators' logs; displays of children's constructions; photographs of impermanent constructions such as sand creations; or audio or video tapes of children's music or language experiences (Helm et al. 1998). These can be assembled in individual children's portfolios, displayed within the centre or sent home.

The National Association for the Education of Young Children (1986) cautions that such outputs should not be inhibited by adult-imposed standards of completion, achievement or failure. Instead, to help parents appraise their children's products, they need an accompanying explanation of what their children have been doing and how it is significant, both in its breadth and depth (Fraser & Gestwicki 2002).

A curriculum that is negotiated between the children and educators will necessarily result in products that are different for different children. Thus, the final aspect of the individualisation of programs—the differentiation of products—will occur naturally. Nevertheless, the following measures could be additional means of ensuring product differentiation.

Solicit tiered products

Some children will be interested in and capable of producing mature expressions of their learning. Meanwhile, children with disabilities might need simplified modes of expression of their learning: for instance, they might not draw until a much later age than other children, and so you might instead photograph a construction they have made so that they have lasting evidence of their achievements. When children are often absent because of a chronic illness or disability, it can be important to take particular care to document what they do produce during their limited attendance so that they too have proof of their achievements (MacNaughton & Williams 1998).

Teach expressive skills

For children with language disabilities, their ability to communicate may limit their ability to record and express what they have learned. In such cases, additional speech or language therapy can both assist them in that domain and give them the means to express their learning. In other domains, children may seek to demonstrate their skills through musical expression and dance or drama, so these will be necessary components of your program.

PLANNING TRANSITIONS

The goals for transitions include (Hanson et al. 2000; Wolery 1989):

- ensuring that services which individual children continue to need are uninterrupted, while implementing new services that respond to the children's changing needs;
- avoiding a duplication of assessment and planning procedures in the former and future settings;
- minimising disruption and stress for the children and their families so that the children are well prepared to function successfully in the new setting and the parents can become independent of personnel in the former program while still receiving adequate support.

Chapter 2 provides a discussion of how to involve parents in planning the transition of their child to the next setting, such as primary school. This is also a curricular issue of preparing children to function successfully in the next setting—teaching both some essential content and necessary learning processes or behaviours, such as being able to wait for teacher attention, observing routines, following directions, working independently, participating in groups and socialising with peers (Hanline 1993; Rule et al. 1990; Salisbury & Vincent 1990). However, these skills must be taught only when the children are developmentally able to succeed at them: for example, requiring 3-year-olds to attend a group story time on the grounds that they will need to know how to do it when they are 5 is developmentally unsound. Furthermore, if schools cannot accommodate children with atypical development, perhaps we need to consider restructuring classrooms rather than demanding developmentally inappropriate splinter skills of young children.

Thus, at the same time as providing activities that will prepare children for their next environment, it is important that you accept where the children are now, not just have an eye on where you want them to be (Stonehouse 1988). It is important not to rush children into learning the next developmental skill as if their present developmental state is deficient in some way, but to give them time to consolidate what they already know so that they will be able to generalise it to new settings (Kostelnick 1992). Katz (1988, in Richarz 1993) calls this 'horizontal' relevance, whereby the experiences that children are offered in early childhood are relevant to their lives at the time, in contrast with 'vertical' relevance in which their curriculum is aimed at preparing them for the next environmental setting.

In terms of the actual transition, it is common practice to integrate children who have been attending a segregated facility into regular schools gradually, sometimes on a part-time basis for one or two terms. My practical observations have been that this can lead to a prolonged period in which the children feel out of place in both settings and are regarded by peers (and teachers) as not truly part of either group. For this reason, all things being equal, when entry to a new setting is occurring, it might be best for preparatory visits to span no more than a few weeks.

PROGRAM EVALUATION

Once modifications have been enacted, programs must be monitored to check that they are catering appropriately for individual children (Wolery 1996). To facilitate program evaluation, the original intervention plan needs to describe who will collect what kinds of monitoring information and how they will do so and in what settings; and it should give responsibility to particular team members to review the updated information and plan any necessary program revisions (Wolery 1996). The decisions involved in this last aspect are illustrated in Figure 4.1.

Monitoring can detect whether goals need modification because they have been attained or are proving unrealistic. It can also detect those times when children are not progressing because, although the original plan is still relevant, it is not being enacted as intended (Wolery 1996). This can come about because unanticipated or changed circumstances have made it impractical to implement the original measures, in which case these need to be redrafted, or because team members have unwittingly lost sight of the goals and need only a reminder to enact the planned measures.

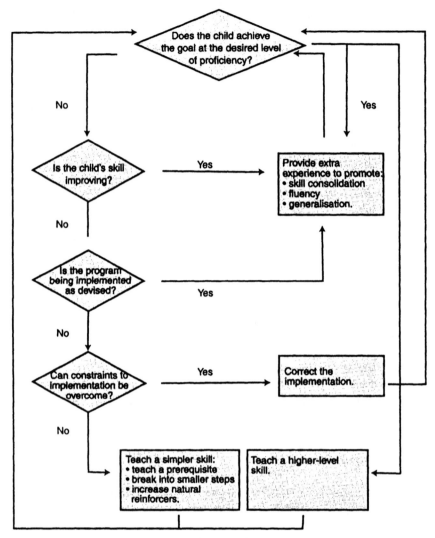

Figure 4.1 Process for program evaluation

CONCLUSION

Modifications to programs need a clear rationale and to be planned systematically so that changes meet the children's unique needs without disrupting the overall program. Thus, program differentiation for children with atypical development comes down to a question of balance: providing for their unique learning needs while also keeping in mind what needs they have in common with all children, and balancing what you can offer one child while still meeting the needs of the group.

For children with disabilities, the most significant challenge is designing instruction so that they are, first, *motivated* and, second, *able* (as a result of true mastery and skill consolidation) to apply their new skills in natural settings. Only then can true learning be said to have occurred. Although this goal is universal, we must recognise that all learning occurs within local and wider social contexts and thus that no one approach will suit every child: it is important to be flexible about meeting individual children's needs and to be responsive to their social context as well as their personal characteristics.

ADDITIONAL RESOURCES

The following text describes teaching techniques for young children, with extensive reference to children with disabilities:
MacNaughton, G. and Williams, G. 1998 *Techniques for teaching young children: choices in theory and practice* Longman, Sydney

For a detailed description of the policy on developmentally appropriate practices that underpins the US system of accreditation of early childhood centres and guides the Australian accreditation system for child care centres, see:
Bredekamp, S. and Copple, C. (eds) 1997 *Developmentally appropriate practice in early childhood programs* revised edn, National Association for the Education of Young Children, Washington, DC
National Association for the Education of Young Children website: http://www.naeyc.org

The following text gives a rich account of child-centred programming:
Fraser, S. & Gestwicki, C. 2002 *Authentic childhood: exploring Reggio Emilia in the classroom* Delmar, Albany, NY

The following texts contain extensive advice on program modifications for young gifted children:
Harrison, C. 1999 *Giftedness in early childhood* Gerric, Sydney
Morelock, M.J. and Morrison, K. 1996 *Gifted children have talents too: multi-dimensional programmes for the gifted in early childhood* Hawker Brownlow Education, Melbourne
Smutny, J.F., Walker, S.Y. and Meckstroth, E.A. 1997 *Teaching young gifted children in the regular classroom: identifying, nurturing, and challenging ages 4–9* Free Spirit Publishing, Minneapolis, MN

PART II

PROGRAMMING FOR ATYPICAL DEVELOPMENTAL NEEDS

Having detailed in Part I the principles that underpin early years education, authors of the chapters in Part II will describe some common instances of atypical development in each of the developmental domains in turn, and will detail how practitioners can adjust early education programs to accommodate young children's additional needs.

It must be borne in mind, however, that although it is necessary to discuss each developmental domain separately, children can have difficulties in more than one skill area, and so the recommendations about fostering development in one domain need to be set alongside and balanced with the recommendations for advancing children's learning in another. For example, although it might be beneficial to give children additional experience in physical skills which they are not acquiring as expected, their current emotional status might instead mean that they would become overwhelmed if put under pressure to learn new skills at this time. Thus, as mentioned in Part I, children's development must be viewed as a whole, such that their needs in one domain must temper decisions about intervening in another.

All the authors in Part II have framed their recommendations with this in mind, and emphasise that activities provided for young children need to be playful and enjoyable for them. Their social needs must also be considered by not singling out individual children for specific intervention—instead offering groups of children modified activities that might specifically benefit a given child but which all can equally enjoy.

5

VISION

James D. Kenefick

KEY POINTS

- Vision teaches infants about the world beyond their immediate grasp. Moreover, it allows them to interpret auditory input and information about the position of their body, and so also assists language development and motor skill learning.
- During the early childhood years many children are naturally long-sighted, but this is resolved if their visual system is functioning normally and they are exposed to rich visual experiences.
- Caregivers and educators can observe for signs of vision impairment in children, but routine specialist assessment is recommended for all children prior to school entry.
- Children with significant vision impairment often have associated disabilities, necessitating a coordinated program based on specialist advice about their individual needs.

INTRODUCTION

Blindness refers to the inability to perceive light; legal blindness is diagnosed when, even with corrective lenses, an individual's field of vision is restricted from the usual 180 degrees to 20 degrees (which is commonly termed 'tunnel vision') or their visual acuity is below 6/60 (which means that they can see at 6 metres what a normally sighted person can see at a distance of 60 metres, the imperial equivalent being 20/200 feet) (Pagliano 1998). Only one child in 3000 is legally blind (Heward 2000).

A further one child in 1000 has a significant vision impairment, which refers to conditions of the visual system that interfere with efficient learning but still permit the children to rely on their vision as their main means of learning (Lowe 1990). Together, children who are blind or have a vision impairment constitute

1% of the population of children with disabilities (Heward 2000; Menacker & Batshaw 1997).

Half of all cases of childhood blindness are genetic and thus present from birth, with a further third of children losing their sight before 1 year of age, usually as a result of infections or other traumas (Howard et al. 2001; Lowe 1990; Menacker & Batshaw 1997). This has such a pervasive effect on all developmental domains that blindness in infancy is considered a 'developmental emergency' (Hyvarinen 1994, in White & Telec 1998).

There are, however, many children with less severe vision difficulties that will affect their learning, particularly when their difficulties are not detected and treated. Perhaps as many as one-third of children have refractive errors (defined below), although the majority of these (all but 2%) respond to corrective lenses or other means (Pagliano 1998).

DEVELOPMENTAL EFFECTS OF IMPAIRED VISION

Like the auditory system, vision provides information from beyond arm's reach. The visual system is used during early development to direct infants' hands to an object that interests them so that it can then be manipulated and inspected to gain understanding and concept knowledge. As children acquire 80% of their information about the world through vision, **concept development** can be fragmented and delayed if their vision is impaired (Pagliano 1998).

Combining visual and auditory information allows children to **interpret spatial distances and positions** (Getman 1993). If their visual system is faulty in some way, children might not be able to integrate anything more than whatever they can reach or place in their mouths. As a result, their development of discrimination skills will take far longer.

Children also use vision to make sense of their own **movement** and changes in posture. The world looks and feels different when infants are lying horizontally from when they are sitting upright. However, when infants' vision is distorted, they can become confused and later have difficulty when moving around in space independently (Lowe 1990; White & Telec 1998). If children have poor vision on one side of their body or have difficulty using their eyes together, their visual image may not match how their bodies feel when they move. In children who have physical disabilities a similar process occurs, where it is difficult for them to integrate their visual and physical feedback. These children can learn to adapt, but more usually they compromise—either by not looking or by avoiding particular movements that confuse them.

Children who have vision difficulties may have associated problems with **hand–eye coordination**. They might not be able to locate a toy with their hand—that is, direct their hand to where they think the object is. When they miss the object with their hand, children with normal vision will look again, redirect their hand, look again, and so on, until they successfully grasp the object. However, children with vision difficulties will tend to look once, feel for the object, and if they continue to miss it will search for it tactually rather than by looking again. This can set up a developmental difficulty, in that the children will not use their visual system as a directing system but only as a rough guide. Later development of difficulties with eye–hand coordination can have this as its basis.

There is also a relationship between vision problems and **hearing difficulties**. One of the advantages of a long-distance receptor such as vision is that it enables individuals to interpret or localise the origin of particular sounds. If there is a clear visual image of the sound source, babies can understand noises and what causes them. When infants cannot generate a visual image to match a sound, they can become frightened or alarmed by noises. This can occur even when their sense of hearing is intact.

As might be expected, **language** and **social skills** are also affected by significantly impaired vision. Eye contact sets the stage for social interaction while eye gaze establishes and maintains topics of conversation, without which children with severe vision impairments can be deprived of the necessary practice at language and with observing the subtleties of social interaction (Howard et al. 2001; Kingsley 1997). Furthermore, infants need vision to imitate mouth movements, so the **speech** of blind children can be delayed.

Finally, while low vision can restrict visual and motoric inspection of the environment, **motivation** to explore can be reduced, as children with severely impaired vision can experience the world as chaotic and unpredictable and so withdraw (White & Telec 1998). Also, fearful of their safety, parents and other caregivers can unintentionally limit these children's investigation of their environment (Hallahan & Kauffman 2000).

COMPONENTS OF VISION

When light enters the eye, it is bent (refracted) at the cornea and focused by adjustments to the shape of the lens—see Figure 5.1. The light then passes on to the retina at the back of the eye, whereupon a message is sent through the optic nerve to the occipital (pronounced ok-sip-it-al) lobe of the brain, which is responsible for interpreting visual input.

The nervous system
Vision impairment can be caused by damage to the optic nerve or occipital lobe of the brain. Early infections, particularly in the first three months of fetal development, traumatic brain injury or seizures are common causes of cortical vision impairment (Howard et al. 2001).

The eye
Impaired vision can result from irregularities in the eye. During the earliest days of life, babies' vision is quite blurred beyond 1 metre (Leat et al. 1999). But as the eye grows during childhood it changes its shape and thus its focus. After babies' initial few weeks, during which time their refractive status is unstable,

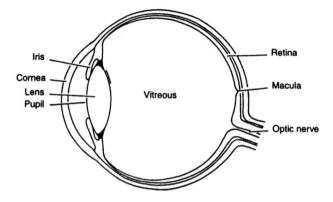

Figure 5.1 Structure of the eye

the eyes gradually settle to become moderately long-sighted (or hyperopic). Over the proceeding months and years until adolescence, the vision system sets up a process of reducing that hyperopia. In adults the ideal outcome is emmetropia (see Figure 5.2a), which is where the vision components are in balance. Distance vision is clear and no effort is required to maintain clarity of vision. The process of achieving emmetropia is termed emmetropisation.

Chronological age gives children time, but might not give them the experience necessary to initiate appropriate emmetropisation. For example, infants with physical or other developmental disabilities might not experience the same rich environment as non-disabled babies. This can delay the development of their visual skills and the emmetropisation process.

Eye use
In some cases the visual system is healthy and the child able to see clearly but the control of the eyes may be immature. From being a purely reflexive system during the earliest days of life, the visual system subsequently develops dramatically. The nerves in the critical area at the back of the eye, which is called the macula, become increasingly sensitive and fine detail can be detected, as long as infants receive appropriate stimulation in the form of light and patterns of light (Kavner 1985), without which there can be a lifelong negative effect on individuals' vision.

The next stage is that babies start to move their eyes, which allows a wider view and the inclusion of more objects. Eye movement fosters the early development of visual skills for discriminating between objects with various colours, movements or sounds associated with them, allowing babies to look selectively at objects to discern their relative value or interest. In order for all this to happen there needs to be integration between the clear vision of the central field and peripheral vision.

To be truly efficient, children's eye movements need to be accurate. Ordinarily, the first eye movement for babies is a very basic horizontal saccadic movement—that is, a movement from left to right. This can be a reflexive response to sound, light or movement and becomes more deliberate when inspecting or satisfying their interest in a stimulus, such as a mobile above the crib.

To increase peripheral vision it may be more efficient to move the head, which in turn requires some motor control. In other circumstances it can be more efficient to move only the eyes. Therefore, it is important that children develop the skill to move their eyes independently of their head, which is dependent on their integration of early reflexes.

ATYPICAL VISION

This section introduces the commonest cases of atypical vision, comprising strabismus (turned eye), amblyopia (lazy eye), nystagmus (oscillating eye movements) and high refractive errors. Defective colour vision is also described.

Strabismus

Strabismus is also termed 'cross-eyed', as it basically describes how the eyes look. The turning in form of strabismus is known as **esotropia** and is by far the commonest variant found in younger children, with between 2% and 4% of the paediatric population affected. Most children with significant esotropia present from birth are identified readily. However, variable esotropia can go unnoticed for some years. This is when the angle of the eye-turn varies during the day, according to the child's wellbeing or health, or depending on the task being performed. Variable esotropia can appear for the first time when children begin to do work at close range for continuous periods. Prior to this, toddlers may only ever have scribbled, and in many cases scribbling can be done without any attention from the vision.

The reason that esotropia is such a significant problem is that the eye which has turned in does not receive adequate information or visual stimulation to develop fully. It is crucial that the eye develop an appropriate connection between the nerves and the part of the brain that interprets visual information. If the eye is turned in, it will not develop its true visual potential. This is one of the leading causes of amblyopia, or 'lazy eye'. When this condition develops children can experience significant problems with binocular vision—that is, using both eyes together. In some cases of alternating strabismus (where one eye will go in and the other remains straight, then the eyes later change to give the opposite effect), neither eye might develop weakness but the eyes learn to work independently rather than together.

A second form of strabismus, **exotropia**, is not simply the opposite of esotropia. From the point of view that the eye turns out rather than in, it may seem the opposite, but its significance for vision development is quite different. Exotropia typically happens at a later age, usually after 3–4 years of age. This means that one eye is unlikely to become weak or 'lazy'. This therefore is a good thing. However, children with exotropia still have the difficulty that they are using one eye, rather than both eyes together. This will affect their eye–hand coordination in the future. Another effect is that when reading their two eyes do not aim together, creating confusion and occasionally even double vision. These children will also have difficulties with catching a ball because they cannot accurately judge the speed of a ball as it approaches them. Throwing balls, however, may not present a problem for them. Therefore, when a significant difference in throwing and catching skills is obvious, an eye problem should be considered as a possible cause.

Obviously, then, it is important to have the eyes as straight as possible as soon as possible, which will require intervention from a vision specialist. In some cases, corrective lenses or glasses will be sufficient; specific training for amblyopia might be useful (i.e. patching or other activities to stimulate the development of vision in the neglected eye), although often a combination of lenses, exercises and surgery is required.

Amblyopia

Amblyopia refers to reduced visual acuity, usually in one rather than both eyes, which cannot be corrected by lenses (Caloroso & Rouse 1993). It affects 2% of the population and arises when the individual's two eyes see with differing acuity, and so the brain ignores the picture from one eye (Menacker & Batshaw 1997). Strabismic amblyopia is due to one eye being turned in; refractive amblyopia is due to an imbalance in the power of the eyes. When treated early, lenses might be all that is required to allow the development of normal vision. However, in some cases additional specific treatment will be necessary.

Nystagmus

Nystagmus is characterised by a rhythmical oscillation of the eyes (Leat et al. 1999). Individuals with nystagmus typically have a relatively normal variation of refractive error—that is, they can be long- or short-sighted. I believe it is as if the eyes, unable to see clearly at the macula, then start performing a searching motion to gain information as best they can. The visual system of individuals with nystagmus is like a camera taking many very quick photos, trying to work out exactly what it is they are looking at.

Near vision is often very difficult for children with nystagmus, and they often require additional help through magnification or enlargement of text. In the short term or as young children, their coordination will develop reasonably well, but they will have underdeveloped eye–hand coordination skills.

High refractive errors

Refraction simply means the bending of light—in this case, so that it focuses in one point on the retina to generate a clear image (Heward 2000). Errors in refraction can result in the rays of light converging in front of the retina, which is termed myopia or short-sightedness (see Figure 5.2b); in the rays being destined to converge behind the retina and so being out of focus at the retina itself, which is termed hyperopia or long-sightedness (see Figure 5.2c); or in distorted convergence due to irregularities in the shape of the cornea, which is termed astigmatism (see Figure 5.2d). All three errors result in blurred vision, with individuals who have myopia having better acuity of vision at close range and those with hyperopia functioning better at distance.

Clinically I have found that only a small percentage of children under 5 years of age have significant refractive errors, although in uncommon cases high levels of hyperopia, myopia and astigmatism can occur. Given that it is most likely that young children will be hyperopic (long-sighted), any suggestion of myopia (short-sightedness) in preschool children should be carefully followed up. It is such an unusual visual condition in this age group that it must be investigated. Furthermore, any sudden change in the child's vision should be considered urgent as refractive changes usually occur gradually, so eye disease must be investigated as a possible cause of the sudden change.

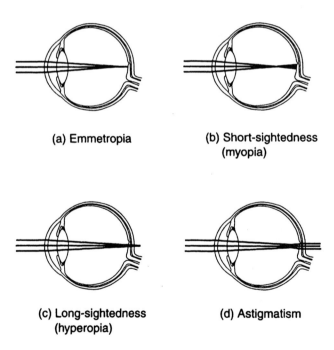

(a) Emmetropia

(b) Short-sightedness (myopia)

(c) Long-sightedness (hyperopia)

(d) Astigmatism

Figure 5.2 Refractive errors

Defective colour vision

The retina comprises millions of cells, those on the periphery being known as rods (which are responsible for black/white detection and night vision) and the central cones for colour vision (Pagliano 1998). The latter are of two types: red/green and blue/yellow colour receptors. Colour blindness is very rare in that it involves the complete failure of colour detection by the cones, with resulting absence of colour perception. More commonly in Europeans (at a rate of around 8% in males and 1% in females), the red/green receptors are slightly defective, resulting in colour confusion (Menacker & Batshaw 1997). Only Polynesians have been recorded to have genetic defects in blue/yellow receptors and even then at a much lower rate than for the corresponding condition in Europeans.

The defective gene occurs on the X-chromosome and so in the absence of damage to the retina is likely to appear in boys when their maternal relatives have colour vision deficiencies and in girls when, in addition, their father has a colour vision defect. The defect is evident when individuals are viewing small patches of colour rather than large-sized items, when locating a colour within an array of multiple hues, or when lighting is inadequate. In these circumstances, affected children will confuse green with brown and navy with purple, for instance, the discrimination between each colour pair relying on the amount of red that is present in the blended colour.

Colour vision deficiencies have no practical disabling effects, although in adulthood some occupational fields such as cosmetic consultancy, interior design and various branches of medicine might not be ideal vocations for those with impaired colour perception.

IDENTIFICATION OF VISION DIFFICULTIES

Ideally, vision screening should be conducted by vision professionals—but only in Kentucky in the USA is this required by law (Shaw 2001). Until such time as compulsory screening becomes a more widespread phenomenon or parents voluntarily take young children more routinely for vision checks, non-vision practitioners need to be alert to signs of potential vision difficulties so that a higher percentage of children with vision difficulties can be identified and subsequently assisted.

Observation

Screening kits and checklists are available to aid identification, but there are also specific behaviours that practitioners can look out for to identify children who are experiencing vision difficulties that require specialist assessment. These signs are listed in Box 5.1.

Box 5.1 Indicators of vision difficulties in young children

Eye use

Children with vision difficulties might:

- Avoid looking at objects.
- Be surprised at expectations that they should see things in the near distance.
- Frown or squint in an attempt to focus due to refractive errors or problems with binocular vision.
- Experience recurrent frontal headaches, but if these are constant might not report them as they do not realise that headaches are abnormal.
- Display excessive head tilt, cover or close one eye, or place books dramatically to one side (particularly on vertical surfaces such as easels) while doing close tasks. These strategies allow one eye to receive the majority of visual information and so indicate that the children's eyes are not working together.
- Have to get extremely close to the page. This could be due to a refractive error or to problems with binocular vision or eye coordination.
- Have difficulty using their two eyes together. This can show up by the early school years as difficulties in visual inspection and with scanning lines of printed words. While reading, these children skip words or lines and often lose their place on pages. They might complain that the print blurs after a short time. To compensate for their vision difficulties, they might whisper to themselves while reading or use a hand or finger to keep their place on the page, both of these persisting past the typical age.
- Have unusually large pupils (which can indicate myopia) or very small pupils (suggesting possible hyperopia).
- Experience increased photophobia (glare sensitivity). Glare sensitivity in dark-eyed children may be particularly significant, as ordinarily they are less likely to be sensitive to glare than children with light-coloured irises.
- Experience frequent reddened or watering eyes and rubbing of eyes after short bursts of close work. This can be caused by mild eye strain or uncomfortable or tired eyes, which the children do not report as they assume it to be normal.

Gross motor skills

Children with low vision can display:

- Late or hesitant walking not due to other causes.
- Asymmetrical posture.
- Difficulties with coordinated movement such as throwing, catching, running, hopping, skipping, kicking, jumping, climbing stairs and self-swinging.
- Physical clumsiness, particularly when their two eyes themselves are poorly coordinated. This can result in behaviours as obvious as bumping into, stumbling or tripping over objects, which is especially worth noting if individual children constantly bump into objects on one particular side.
- Misjudgment of depth and contours: some children seem often to stop short of obstacles, as if they have poor depth perception. This can occur particularly if one eye is out of focus compared with the other.

- Dramatic reactions—even fear—to a change in contours, such as where there is a change of floor covering from carpet to tiles. This is an extreme problem with depth perception. It is as if these children perceive the change but do not appreciate whether it is significant or not.
- Frequent placement of objects just on the edge of the table rather than nearer the centre, as if they cannot judge where the edge is. This is an indication that the visual system and motor skills are not well integrated.

Eye–hand coordination
Vision difficulties can lead to the following effects on eye–hand coordination.
- Children are very slow at developing their hand preference, which can cause them to be reluctant or less skilled at eye–hand tasks. As the development of eye preference closely mirrors both in direction and in time the development of hand preference, delays in establishing hand dominance can imply delays in establishing eye dominance.
- They might continually swap hands during tasks (past the usual age).
- Delayed eye–hand coordination can be due to incoordination of the two eyes and can be seen in difficulties with: cutting out, pasting and other paper tasks; using a knife and fork together; completing puzzles; assembling small construction toys (e.g. Lego); drawing; and dressing themselves.

Behavioural signs
Children with vision impairments can display:
- Impulsive reactions to visual input. This can come about when children have difficulty visually attending to objects. They might inspect these extremely briefly and then act quickly to approach or escape, without giving themselves time to judge the objects' interest or danger value.
- Caution in moving about in strange places.
- Avoidance of close work.
- Distractability. Children with vision impairments can be peripherally driven and thus be distracted by what is going on around them rather than what is in front of them in their central field of vision.
- Signs of exhaustion such as tiring readily, becoming disengaged, or constantly fidgeting or shifting in their seat during prolonged close work. The effort to achieve optimal vision can result in these behaviours.

Sources: Getman (1993); Lowe (1990); Pagliano (1998).

Professional assessment

Children who have been identified to have potential problems with their vision should be assessed by an appropriate clinician. The relevant vision professionals include the following:

- **Optometrists** are practitioners who have a university degree and who look at how the eyes work. A doctor's referral is not necessary for an appointment. Optometrists are able to recognise diseases of the eye, but will refer individuals to an ophthalmologist for any medical treatment. Behavioural optometrists have special postgraduate training in developmental and functional vision.

- **Ophthalmologists** are medically trained doctors who specialise in diseases of the eye. A referral is necessary for an appointment with an ophthalmologist.
- **Orthoptists** are trained in the area of, and deal specifically with, problems with the muscles of the eyes. In some instances, a referral from an ophthalmologist to an orthoptist is necessary.

For young children, the best option is to have them assessed by a paediatric specialist in ophthalmology or optometry. If serious problems are suspected, the children might then be referred to a low-vision clinic (Pagliano 1998).

Because of the developmental nature of vision skill acquisition and because it is rare for a vision problem to exist in isolation, the clinician will want background information on the children's gross motor, language and social development as well as performing a vision assessment. The aim of a vision assessment is to observe the children performing a series of visual tasks, as well as actually measuring the eyes. In almost all cases, the initial consultation will be able to achieve the following:

- assessment of children's visual acuity—that is, the clearness of sight;
- objective measurement of their refractive status—that is, the presence of myopia, hyperopia or astigmatism;
- assessment of basic binocularity—the use of the two eyes together;
- examination of eye movement, looking for a full range of unrestricted movement that indicates the degree of children's control of their eyes;
- basic saccadic (horizontal) eye movements and the ability to separate head and eye movements;
- pupil assessment;
- eye health.

During an assessment by a behavioural optometrist, eye–hand development, hand preference, sighting eye preference (eye dominance) and basic pencil grasp and release will also be observed. Ideally, children should be observed drawing or playing with blocks at some time during the assessment, perhaps while they are in the waiting area.

CHILDREN WITH ATYPICAL DEVELOPMENT

All children and particularly those with recognised disabilities require careful observation of their ability to use their eyes efficiently.

Children who are blind

Blindness can be an isolated disability, although most of its causes—such as prenatal infections—simultaneously cause other disabilities as well. The outcome is that around 70% of congenitally blind children also have other disabilities: 25% have an intellectual disability, 10% also have hearing losses, 8% have epilepsy, 6% have cerebral palsy, and 6% have congenital heart defects (Lowe 1990). These children need an individualised program devised in consultation with a range of specialists to assist them in domains where they experience an impairment and to capitalise on their residual sensory perception and developmental strengths.

Children with cerebral palsy

Virtually all children with cerebral palsy experience focusing and eye movement problems, with the majority having strabismus (a squint) and between 50% and 60% having refractive difficulties, the most common of which is hyperopia—that is, long-sightedness (Duckman 1987; Pellegrino 1997; Wesson & Maino 1995). Those whose CP is due to prematurity can have retinopathy, which is where, without early detection and treatment, vascular damage to the retina causes it to become detached and blindness results (Bernbaum & Batshaw 1997; Pellegrino 1997). Children with ataxia (see Chapter 6) can have nystagmus (the oscillating eye movements described earlier), while children with hemiplegia often have impaired vision of one part of their visual field (Pellegrino 1997).

These children, therefore, commonly need corrective lenses as well as assistance for their dynamic visual skills—that is, how they use their eyes. It is often beneficial to provide them with opportunities to move their eyes in a more coordinated manner through basic eye aiming and tracking activities. Monocular (one eye) and binocular activities should be attempted. These can be designed by the children's vision specialist and, where appropriate, included in their early childhood program.

Children with Down syndrome

Children with Down syndrome have a higher than usual incidence of significant vision problems including hyperopia, myopia, astigmatism, nystagmus, and 10 times the usual incidence of strabismus (Roizen 1997; Wesson & Maino 1995). Difficulties with eye–hand coordination and depth perception are common.

Given these vision problems, both ophthalmologists and optometrists need to be involved in the assessment of these children's eye health and vision (Roizen 1997). Assessment needs to be carried out at an early age with routine check-ups periodically, as some children do not have any outward signs of eye health problems and seldom complain about their vision.

Prescribing lenses is important, and encouraging the children to wear their glasses is also crucial so that they learn to tolerate their lenses. Training sessions need to be brief to take account of the children's reduced concentration span, but it is imperative that they have the opportunity through individualised programs to develop their visual skills so that they will be able to use their vision more efficiently and so that they do not become overly reliant on their other senses, such as touch.

Gifted and talented children

The natural inquisitiveness of gifted children often means that they are interested in reading and other close tasks at an earlier age than usual. As the visual system requires time to develop fully, problems may arise from excessive demands on the focusing or tracking systems of these young children.

The signs of focusing difficulties are the same as already mentioned for all children; tracking difficulties can become evident as the children move to books with more text or more lines of text with fewer picture cues. A sudden loss of interest in reading or avoidance may indicate a developmental mismatch between the children's visual and intellectual abilities.

This mismatch can be dealt with by vision exercises and perhaps lenses in an attempt to let the visual system 'catch up' so that the children can pursue their advanced interests in close work, or by restraining the children's overuse of eyes by restricting the time they spend reading or by making reading and other close tasks less demanding visually. Porter (pers. comm.) advises explaining to the children that, although their brains are growing up more quickly than usual, their eyes can only grow up at 'body speed'. This helps the children to understand their tracking difficulties and encourages them to be patient with their physical limitations until these are resolved naturally with improved maturity of the visual system.

PROGRAMMING FOR CHILDREN WITH VISION DIFFICULTIES

Depending on his or her particular vision difficulties and residual vision, each child will function differently in the environment. The aim for children with significant vision impairment is to give them knowledge of the realities around them and the confidence to cope with these (Lowe 1990).

Environmental adjustments

Children with significant vision impairment need their environment to be **arranged** logically and consistently, with floor surfaces plain and matt to avoid glare, fittings painted in contrasting colours to highlight their location, and changes in floor levels signalled well in advance by texture or colour changes (Lewis & Taylor 1998; Pagliano 1998). Doors should be left open or closed, but not ajar (Pagliano 1998).

These children tend to require double the usual **illumination** levels but with glare-reduced lighting so that shadows do not create visual confusion (Lewis & Taylor 1998). Enhanced illumination is likely to be particularly necessary for children with macular disease or retinitis pigmentosa (which is a degenerative condition of the retina). Their requirement for additional light suggests the need to remove artwork from windows and to provide portable lights (Pagliano 1998).

The children need to be **seated** where they can function best and where there is minimal glare (Lowe 1990). Those who are short-sighted will need to be close to the adult in group activities; those with tunnel vision might need to be at the back of a group, as their viewing area widens with distance; those with photophobia should sit away from windows (Lowe 1990).

Other physical **aides** such as a sloped book rest or desktop easel can help the children avoid fatigue from crouching closely over books or drawing paper (Lowe 1990). Aids such as Braille machines or large-print books will be necessary for those with more severely impaired vision.

Teaching to overcome secondary difficulties

Children with low vision need assistance in all developmental domains:

- awareness of their body in space—that is, orientation training that teaches them to use their other senses to gauge their position;
- mobility training to give them confidence to move independently;
- training in self-help, language and social skills;
- listening training, teaching them to be aware of, discriminate between, identify the source of, and assign meaning to sounds (Arter 1997; Heward 2000; Pagliano 1998);
- specialist teaching of early literacy skills and Braille (if required);
- specific remediation for any associated disabilities.

Some of these topics are covered in this book; for specific guidance relevant to blindness, you will need to consult the children's vision and other specialists.

Vision training exercises

Exercises can improve children's use of their eyes—specifically their ability to use their eyes and hands together, track moving objects, shift their focus efficiently from one object to another (horizontally, vertically and near-to-far), and use both eyes together to develop eye convergence or eye teaming skills. Having identified children's vision difficulties, behavioural optometrists will devise vision therapy activities that encourage these skills. This programming is usually done in a prescriptive way—that is, by identifying individual children's needs and designing relevant remedial activities. Most of these exercises require brief but repeated practice, much of which will take place at the children's homes. Nevertheless, to afford additional practice, under instruction from an optometrist, it might be possible for you to conduct some specific eye skill exercises with individual children during their time in your care.

CONCLUSION

Children's vision skills can be promoted in early childhood environments in order to prevent and minimise vision problems later on and to promote the development of eye–hand coordination skills, the ability to read comfortably and efficiently and to change focus rapidly with changes in visual demands.

Vision difficulties are often subtle yet very significant educationally. When children can be assisted before their vision problems become entrenched and before they have experienced repeated failure, we can avoid detrimental effects to their self-esteem, their attitude to themselves and to learning (Howell & Peachey 1990).

ADDITIONAL RESOURCES

Within Australia, to obtain the names of local behavioural optometrists, you can refer to the website of the Australasian College of Behavioural Optometrists (ACBO) (www.acbo.org.au) or contact the ACBO National Secretariat on (+61 3) 9729-5822.

Currently available screening tests by health professionals have generally focused on detecting vision anomalies rather than vision skills. Therefore there is a need for a new 'family' of screening tests. These are slowly becoming available in the marketplace. You can contact info@visionandlearninginstitute.com.au for preschool and primary school vision screening kits. The observations checklist is available from OEP USA (at www.oep.org). This looks at the development of vision from 6 months and earlier and gives general guidelines for what is to be expected.

For texts on children with severe vision impairments, I recommend:
Arter, C., Mason, H.L., McCall, S., McLinden, M. and Stone, J. 1999 *Children with visual impairments in mainstream settings* David Fulton, London
Mason, H., McCall, S. Arter, C., McLinden, M. and Stone, J. (eds) 1997 *Visual impairment: access to education for children and young people* David Fulton, London
Strickling, C. 1998 *Impact of vision loss on motor development: information for occupational and physical therapists working with students with visual impairments* Texas School for the Blind and Visually Impaired, Austin, TX

6

MOTOR SKILLS

MARGARET SULLIVAN

KEY POINTS

- The aim of programming for young children with movement difficulties is to help them become active solvers of movement challenges and enjoy moving safely and confidently about their environment.
- Children's motor learning depends on the growth and maturation of many biological systems and on their having extensive experience with goal-directed, active movement.
- Children need a range of playground skills in their early years: climbing, balancing, running, jumping and ball skills. Aside from the enjoyment these activities bring, all have an important role for fitness and in the musculoskeletal and skill development of young children.

INTRODUCTION

Generally speaking, young children with an obvious physical disability and a clear diagnosis will already be receiving services from relevant therapists whom you could consult about inclusive curricular practices. On the other hand, you might be the first to notice that certain children in your care have delays in learning to sit or walk, experience many subtle difficulties on playground equipment, fall often, or move in an unusual way. This large group of children warrant our special attention. Often they do not meet the criteria for specialist services, yet they struggle to keep up with their peers because of their sensorimotor problems.

Programming for young children with movement difficulties aims to help them become active solvers of movement challenges and enjoy moving safely and confidently so that they may benefit from the social, recreational and fitness opportunities of physical activity throughout life. Depending on the children's particular difficulties, additional specific aims can comprise promoting the best use of their sensorimotor ability, preventing deformity, correcting muscle imbalance and improving muscle strength.

The methods used to assist children will vary according to the type and degree of their motor difficulties, the presence of associated problems such as sensory or health concerns, and the wishes and expectations of the children and their parents or carers. Interventions will need to focus on the children's most urgent sensory or motor needs at the time, updating interventions as these needs change. Physiotherapists can advise you on functional movement training and on how to overcome problems of physical access as appropriate for each child and setting and, with other specialists, can assist with programming advice and differential diagnosis between the various conditions where motor difficulties can be seen.

A multi- or interdisciplinary approach is needed because often more than one developmental domain is affected, such as when children with cerebral palsy also have vision or hearing impairments. There may also be medical issues, such as the use of medication to influence muscle tone or to control epileptic seizures or respiratory infections, the use of orthotics or orthopaedic surgery to prevent or correct deformities of the trunk or limbs, or orofacial or abdominal surgery to manage severe and prolonged difficulties with eating and drinking.

FACTORS INFLUENCING MOTOR LEARNING AND PERFORMANCE

When we are assisting young children to move about the nursery or playground, we are attempting to promote their motor learning. Children's motor learning depends on the growth and maturation of their anatomy and physiology, in particular the nervous and musculoskeletal systems, plus extensive practice of goal-directed, active movement—and a dynamic interaction between all these elements (Shumway-Cook & Woollacott 2001). An example of this interplay is that toddlers have better head control than babies. This comes about because toddlers' nervous system is more mature, their ratio of head to trunk size is smaller than for infants (see Figure 6.1) and so their neck muscles do not have to work so hard to hold their head steady (a musculoskeletal factor), and because toddlers have had more practice at a variety of movements requiring different types of head control (i.e. task-specific practice).

Motor learning also depends on children's knowledge of the results of movements that they have attempted—that is, sensory feedback (Gentile 1987). This feedback allows children to fine-tune motor control as the movement continues or is repeated; sensory feedforward mechanisms then help children to anticipate or prepare for future movement (Shumway-Cook & Woollacott 2001). Motor learning and performance are also subject to individual differences and prevailing environmental conditions. For example, although all human beings learn to walk using roughly similar patterns of movement, the gait pattern they choose to use at any given time will be shaped by their biomechanical characteristics (height, weight, leg length and bony alignment; see Figure 6.2);

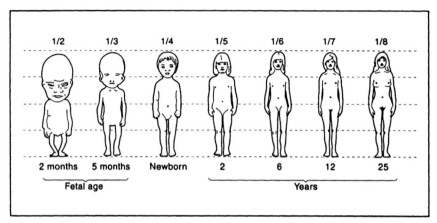

Figure 6.1 Changes in proportion of the human body during growth

Source: Papalia and Olds (1992:94).

current level of alertness, motivation and perhaps aerobic fitness; prior experience and habit; cultural and gender-specific conditioning; and other environmental features such as their footwear, the type of surface, and whether and how they are carrying a load.

CONDITIONS ASSOCIATED WITH ATYPICAL PHYSICAL SKILLS

Some children consistently appear 'clumsy' or awkward in their gross and fine motor play. Others avoid physical activity. These difficulties can be due to a range of conditions such as vision impairments (see Chapter 5) and physical or other disabilities, some of which I shall now discuss.

Cerebral palsy

One group of children with coordination difficulties are those who have cerebral palsy. Cerebral palsy refers to persistent disorders of movement, postural control and muscle tone resulting from non-progressive damage to the developing brain (Stanley 1994) (see Appendix I). Brain injury occurring later in childhood is called traumatic or acquired. Although with cerebral palsy the damage to the central nervous system is not itself progressive, when young infants with cerebral palsy begin to move their ability to control their movement may appear to worsen. For example, children may have normal muscle tone when they are lying and resting, but when they pull to standing at furniture their calf muscles may become very tight, preventing heel contact with the floor. (For further information on these children, see Additional resources.)

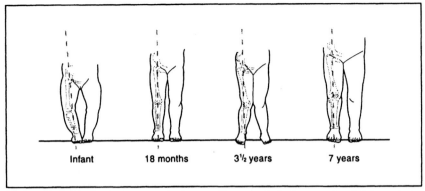

Figure 6.2 Typical changes in bony alignment during early childhood relative to the appearance of 'bow legs' and 'knock knees'

Source: Tachdjian (1997:119).

Children with mild cerebral palsy can be slow to achieve independent sitting; have difficulty moving from lying to standing; have immature balance, resulting in frequent falls; have difficulty climbing, especially descending; become stiffer in their affected limbs when making strong efforts with other body parts; and have difficulty modulating the speed and strength of their movements. There may also be slight problems in the apparently 'unaffected' body parts. For instance, children with diplegia (see Box 6.1) may have minor problems with hand skills (Shumway-Cook & Woollacott 2001).

There are many types and degrees of severity of cerebral palsy (one system of classification of which is given in Box 6.1), so no two children have exactly the same abilities or potential disability. Functional problems can range from barely noticeable to 'profound', with the mildest forms not always evident early in infancy.

The commonest types of cerebral palsy in children who are walking independently are spastic hemiplegia and spastic diplegia. When their difficulties are mild, these children's condition is the most likely to go undetected. Therefore, it is important to look out for indications of these two forms of cerebral palsy. Children with mild spastic hemiplegia:

- commonly use one hand much more than the other;
- avoid weight-bearing on their affected side, so may creep or crawl leaning mostly on their sound side;
- may bottom-shuffle in sitting instead of crawling;
- walk and run with a slight limp;
- appear to stand on their toes on one foot;
- dislike touch on their affected limbs such as when dressing or bathing;
- tend to ignore their affected arm and leg and any toys placed on that side of their body;

Box 6.1 Classification of cerebral palsy

Type of muscle tone
- Hypotonic: tone is too low—child looks 'floppy'.
- Hypertonic: tone is too high—movement is jerky and restricted.
- Fluctuating: extremely variable tone.

Body parts affected
- Hemiplegia: mainly one side of body affected.
- Diplegia: mainly lower trunk and both lower limbs affected.
- Quadriplegia: all four limbs, neck and trunk affected.

The terms hemiparesis and quadriparesis are sometimes substituted for hemiplegia and quadriplegia to signify a mild degree of movement disorder.

Type of movement disorder experienced
Many children with cerebral palsy have problems with eating, drinking and speech because of their abnormal muscle tone, neonatal reflexes being either weak or persisting beyond infancy, and reduced control of posture and movement. Some also have poorly coordinated eye movements. Most have muscle weakness.

- **Spastic:** restricted, jerky movement, stiff postures, muscle imbalance around joints (with potential for joint contracture), low tone at rest but high tone on effort.
- **Rigid:** consistently high muscle tone, very restricted movement and postural reactions.
- **Athetoid:** involuntary writhing or jerky movements accompanying excitement or efforts to move; extreme variations of muscle tone (with children with tension athetosis having high muscle tone).
- **Ataxic:** low muscle tone, incoordination; poor postural stability; some have upper limb tremor accompanying volitional movement.
- **Hypotonic:** very low muscle tone consistently; extreme difficulty moving or holding postures against gravity; weak survival reactions (e.g. gag reflex).
- **Mixed:** a combination of more than one of these types.

In North America, the term 'dyskinesis' is sometimes applied to the various forms of the athetoid type (Wilson-Howle 1999).

- compensate very well with their sound side and resist your efforts to have them use the affected limbs.

The second group of children whose mild cerebral palsy sometimes goes unrecognised are those with mild spastic diplegia. These children:

- do most of the effort of creeping and crawling with their upper body—for example, by drawing their knees together and using short strides of the knee or bunny-hopping (leaning on their hands and dragging their knees behind);
- commonly sit between their heels;
- persistently pull to stand at furniture with their knees drawn together, overusing their arms and upper trunk, then standing up on their toes;

- have a lot of difficulty lowering from standing at furniture;
- walk with short strides, often on toes, and with movements that look stiff and jerky, bracing one knee against the other;
- may be slightly clumsy with fine motor skills.

Spina bifida

Another group of children with difficulties in movement control are those who have spina bifida (described in Appendix I). Children with its most severe form, myelomeningocoele (pronounced mi-lo-men-in-jo-seal), will have partial or complete paralysis of the muscles supplied by nerves below the level of their spinal lesion. They usually also have reduced sensation and bladder or bowel control. Reduced tactile awareness of their lower limbs can result in the children not noticing friction burns caused by creeping and dragging their bare legs and feet across rough carpet. Therefore, you will need to be vigilant of their skin condition and teach the children to use their vision to check their limb placement. They may also have osteoporotic or fragile leg bones resulting from reduced weight-bearing and walking. You may need to take special care that classmates do not trip over their legs when preschoolers are asked to sit together on a mat.

Many children with spina bifida will use standing frames, various assistive walking devices and wheelchairs (often beginning with castor carts low to the floor) from early in their preschool years. They will usually be in the care of a physiotherapist and other medical and allied health professionals who can advise you on their mobility training, manual handling, continence care and related needs. Detailed information can also be found in such texts as Burns and Mac-Donald (1996).

Developmental coordination disorder (DCD)

Some children's coordination difficulties cannot be explained by recognised physical or intellectual disabilities or rapid growth spurts. Historically, a variety of descriptive labels have been applied to this group of children, although an international symposium in Canada recently decided to adopt the term 'developmental coordination disorder' (Fox & Polatajko 1994), as defined by the American Psychiatric Association (1994).

Simply put, children with DCD usually have normal intelligence with no overt disability but minor difficulties in many sensory domains, which combine to interfere significantly with fine and gross motor skills, social development and their ability to function in daily life (see Box 6.2). These difficulties may manifest differently at different ages, with specific learning difficulties and low self-esteem often becoming evident in the school years (Gillberg & Gillberg 1989; Losse et al. 1991). However, appropriate intervention programs can do much to help these children (Watter 1996).

Interdisciplinary assessment is essential to distinguish DCD from other conditions such as specific language impairment, the attention deficit disorders,

Box 6.2 Characteristics of young children with developmental coordination disorder (DCD)

The following features are common in preschoolers with DCD (and are sometimes present in part in other conditions), although not all are present in any one child.

- **Muscle tone** is often unusual, commonly too low; sometimes too high.
- **Range of joint movement** may not be age-appropriate, commonly being excessive; sometimes limited.
- **Habitual toe-walking** may persist beyond the toddler years.
- **Reduced proprioception** (reduced joint position sense) can show up in poor limb placement during climbing; fidgeting; leaning on the back of the hand instead of the palm when sitting or pushing objects; and poor pre-writing skills (see chapter 7).
- **Weak motor planning (dyspraxia).** Children with DCD can have motor planning problems because of various sensorimotor difficulties, including poor proprioception and visuospatial perception. Motor planning difficulties show up as difficulties using appropriate muscle groups in the correct order and timing (Lundy-Ekman et al. 1991); difficulties starting a movement; being slow to learn a movement sequence and so needing much repetition and verbal or physical cueing; having trouble with action songs or copying gestures; having difficulty transferring a new motor skill to another context.
- **Balance difficulties.** Children with DCD often cannot right themselves quickly if pushed off balance; fall over often without being tripped; like to keep on the move or act the clown by falling (to avoid having to balance); avoid activities that challenge their balance; have poor single-leg stance; and sit, walk and run with their feet widely spaced.
- **Reduced functional strength and endurance**, such that they fatigue easily.
- **Coordination difficulties** of upper and lower body, left and right sides, and eye–hand skills. The children's movement lacks rhythm and smoothness and may look heavy; strong effort is accompanied by unwanted background movement; they exert too much or too little force (Lundy-Ekman et al. 1991); cannot perform rapid, alternating movements (e.g. drumming); and have difficulty crossing their body midline (e.g. in ball-catch or drawing).
- **Difficulty with visual judgments about space** leads to frequent collisions with other children or equipment; weak ball skills; climbing difficulties such as bumping their head and misjudging heights; and weakness at copying another's gestures.
- **Unusual responses to touch** (see chapter 7).
- **Weak memory for visual or auditory patterns**, as shown when the children have trouble remembering rhythms or a short sequence of verbal instructions, or the rules in games or dances (Watter 1996).
- **Reduced attention span or impulsivity.**
- **Behavioural difficulties.** As a result of frustration at their awareness of their failures or because of the effort of compensating for their sensorimotor difficulties, children with DCD may exhibit difficult behaviours, especially when tired. These may include irritability, low frustration tolerance, aggression, low self-esteem and withdrawal or, conversely, clowning rather than making a serious attempt at a task.

global developmental delay, autism spectrum disorder or mild cerebral palsy, all of which share some of the sensorimotor and behavioural features of DCD.

Your programming adjustments will depend on children's specific combination of sensorimotor difficulties, but are likely to span sensory preparation activities (see chapter 7) and activities to promote well-timed and coordinated movement, motor planning, balanced muscle length, functional strength, fitness and confidence.

Intellectual disabilities

As is the case in all other developmental domains, children with intellectual disability acquire motor skills more slowly than average and take longer to generalise motor skills learned in one context to another slightly different situation. When intellectual disability is the sole cause of their motor developmental delay, the children commonly have low muscle tone and poorly developed postural adjustments and balance reactions. This leads to difficulty with control of movement against gravity, distrust of situations that challenge their balance, and assumption of a wide-based stance. Low tone in facial muscles can lead to eating, drinking and speech difficulties.

Children with intellectual disability often have trouble initiating functional movement, but can complete a familiar movement sequence if it is begun for them. Motor planning, especially in novel situations, is weak. Arousal levels (see chapter 7) and motivation strongly affect their rate of learning. Behavioural techniques can assist (see chapter 12).

One category of children with an intellectual disability are those who have Down syndrome (see Appendix I). In terms of the effect of this syndrome on motor learning, these children's low muscle tone, lax ligaments and sensory difficulties affect their control of posture and movement. Infants with Down syndrome are often tactile-sensitive on the soles of their feet and dislike weight-bearing in standing. (See chapter 7 for sensory preparation techniques.)

Of those individuals with Down syndrome, 14–20% have atlantoaxial instability. This is excessive movement between the top two vertebrae of the neck, associated with lax ligaments. This may cause no symptoms and go undetected, but children with identified instability should avoid contact sports, diving, or any activity likely to put strain on the neck such as somersaults or strenuous trampolining. In extreme cases surgery can be necessary to relieve pressure on the spinal cord. If in doubt, refer the children's parents to their paediatrician or local Down Syndrome Society.

Toe-walking

When typically developing infants first learn to walk or when toddlers are carrying an object, they can walk on their toes for a time (Van Sant & Goldberg 1999). When it is the only unusual feature in a child's movement, it can resolve itself in time. However, all persistent toe-walking warrants careful assessment, as it can lead to shortening of the Achilles tendons and weakness of calf muscles.

In children with sensory processing problems (e.g. in DCD, mild cerebral palsy or the autism spectrum disorders), toe-walking may occur in association with other 'soft neurological signs', including unwanted background movement such as upper limb flexion or mouth-opening accompanying strong effort or emotion. In that case, tendon and muscle stretches and sometimes orthotics or therapeutic taping may be useful.

Toe-walking can also occur in a more sinister condition affecting boys, called Duchenne muscular dystrophy (DMD) (see Appendix I). Three-year-olds with DMD typically will walk with a waddling, high-stepping gait, up on their toes, with a pronounced 'sway back'. They may appear to have excessive bulk in some muscle groups around the hips, thighs and calves (pseudohypertrophy). If the children are still walking they may show a positive Gower's sign: that is, when asked to stand up from sitting or kneeling on the floor without using props to lean on, they tend to 'walk their hands' up their thighs to assist their hips to straighten. Some resort to Gower's manoeuvre only when tired, so observe them after strenuous play. A firm diagnosis of Duchenne's muscular dystrophy requires a full medical work-up including history, muscle biopsy and blood tests. Discussion with a physiotherapist can help you determine whether to suggest that parents seek such an assessment. Subsequent management of the toe-walking will occur as part of programming for the children's overall neuro-muscular difficulties.

Limps

Although children will limp briefly when they have hurt their leg or foot, per-sistent limps can be caused by a variety of factors, including muscular imbalance or coordination problems, as in cerebral palsy or developmental coordination disorder; leg length discrepancies; disease or malalignment of any lower limb joint; trauma; hairline fractures; soft tissue damage; low back injury; and even bone cancer (although this is rare). Any painful limp that persists for more than two days and cannot be explained by a minor local injury should be investigated, initially by the family's general practitioner.

Giftedness

Children with advanced learning capabilities often acquire motor skills early—particularly skills that require cognitive control such as balance, compared with skills that rely only on strength or endurance (Roedell et al. 1980). They can generally learn new physical movements with ease (Moltzen 1996), can locate themselves readily in the environment, and have superior coordination, environ-mental perception and planning skills (Porter 1999).

On the other hand, some gifted children take little interest in physical activity. Instead some prefer literacy-based activities; some consider the unsophisticated active play of their age mates trivial or dislike its boisterous or competitive element; some shun physical activity because, compared with their extremely advanced intellectual skills, they feel relatively incapable in the physical arena (Porter, pers. comm.). These children can be at risk of reduced physical fitness, while a lack of practice of motor skills can lead to declining proficiency over time. In my clinical experience, a very small subgroup of gifted children can also have developmental coordination disorder. Even as preschoolers these children are acutely aware of their lack of physical prowess and are adroit at avoiding physical activity.

To overcome these children's avoidance of physical activity, you can encourage them into activities that have a high intellectual component, such as active dramatic play where they can develop their own rules. (This is less likely to be successful, however, if they have no playmates at their own intellectual level with whom to share such play.) Parents can also be alerted to extracurricular activities such as gymnastics, while in the school years sports such as orienteering, archery and horse riding can appeal to these children's intellect at the same time as offering physical exercise. Teaching children responsibility for their own health and fitness, perhaps using children's health websites to set up their own fitness program, can empower and motivate these children to be more physically active.

TRENDS IN THE DEVELOPMENT OF MOVEMENT CONTROL

Within a population of able-bodied children with optimal development, large variations exist in the rate and order at which they learn new motor skills (Shepherd 1995). Even individual children do not learn these skills at the same steady pace throughout childhood: at times they may consolidate rather than acquire new skills or even regress temporarily while they are acquiring new abilities in other domains (Alexander et al. 1993). Nevertheless, the following are recognised trends in children's development of movement control (see also Appendix II). Children with atypical development may acquire some of these key components of movement control but imperfectly, or in a different developmental sequence. This has implications for programming, as listed in Box 6.3.

Stability and mobility, and antigravity control
Efficient movement control requires body orientation (involving a dynamic interplay between stabilising a body part and moving it), and manipulation of objects (Gentile 1987). This ever-changing interplay involves a constant controlled response to gravity—either bracing a body part against its effect, or moving against gravity.

Three-dimensional control, weight shift and rotational elements
Infants and young children must learn to control movement in three dimensions relative to their long body axis. This includes learning to control weight shift in

Box 6.3 Principles of programming for motor learning

- Young children with low levels of motivation or arousal associated with prolonged illness, significant intellectual disability or sensory deficit will be at risk of delayed development of motor skills. Providing these children with an environment conducive to optimal arousal levels (see chapter 7) and opportunities to explore and practise pleasurable, active, goal-oriented movement (Bower et al. 1996) will help motivate motor learning.
- In order to achieve their potential for motor learning, children with sensory deficits will need programming that includes sensory enhancement or assists them to compensate with their stronger senses (Freeman 1993).
- Because motor learning is task- and context-specific (Shepherd 1995), infants and young children need many opportunities to practise similar-but-slightly-different motor tasks, to assist them to generalise skills to other contexts. For example, a new walker could be encouraged to walk on level floors at first, then on floors with different surface texture, then on rugs, in the sandpit, on grass, pavement and on gentle slopes.

all directions, and to twist one body segment on another, as in crawling or running.

Reduction of unwanted background movement

Young infants' actions are characterised by mass, poorly scaled movement. As control develops throughout early childhood, only the body part directly involved with the action moves, and other joints are held stable (Wolff et al. 1983). Refined, precise movement gradually becomes possible.

Sequencing and scaling of muscle activity

As superfluous background movement is progressively reduced, infants and young children become more adept at ordering the sequence in which teams of muscles will act (often across several joints at once), and the force and duration of that muscle activity. With practice these muscle synergies become increasingly automatic.

Muscle length

Because of restricted space for movement in the last two months prior to birth, full-term infants are born with shorter flexor muscles (those mainly in the front of the neck, trunk and limbs which bend the body part forwards) and longer extensors (muscles mainly on the back of the body which straighten the trunk or limb). One of the byproducts of early motor learning is to balance muscle length around joints to permit efficient control of movement.

Postural control or balance

These terms refer to individuals' ability to make rapid and subtle postural adjustments in order to maintain or realign their body's centre of mass over their base of support (Horak 1987). For balance, we need sensory input signalling a threat to our equilibrium, and motor output to respond to that threat. Sensory input for balance (some operating in both feedback and feedforward modes) comprises:

- vision—both structural aspects of the visual system and efficiency of eye movements. This sense is the most dominant, especially in infants and preschoolers;
- proprioception (or somatosensation in US terms), which contributes information about joint position and muscle tension and becomes useful from around 3 years of age (Foudriat et al. 1993);
- the vestibular sense in the inner ear, which matures later and, from around 7 years of age, can assist individuals to resolve situations of sensory confusion about balance (Shumway-Cook & Woollacott 1985).

Motor output for balance involves activating teams of muscles in the right order and at the right force to adjust our posture effectively. Children with difficulties sequencing and scaling muscle activity will lack precision in the postural adjustments required for balance (Shumway-Cook & Woollacott 2001). There is a large learning component to this process, beginning in infancy, superimposed on developmental and maturational changes to the nervous and musculoskeletal systems.

As well as maturation and experience of locomotion and physical activity, for efficient postural control we need reasonably normal muscle tone and strength and adequate range of joint movement. Children with stiff ankles (e.g. as caused by juvenile chronic arthritis or mild cerebral palsy) may maintain standing balance by making compensatory movements around hip level. If that fails, they may take a step to reposition their base of support, rather than relying on their limited ankle movement. Considering all these sensory input and motor output factors, it becomes evident that there are many potential ways to assist the balance difficulties of preschoolers.

PROMOTING MOTOR LEARNING

To assist children's motor learning, the aim is to enable them to perform goal-directed movement (e.g. when infants reach for and grasp a toy or when toddlers climb onto their parent's lap for a hug). If children are not achieving this or if their movement is inefficient, practitioners will analyse the component skills (sensory and motor) that are weak or missing in the children's performance and train these aspects specifically in programming. In so doing, it is crucial that the activities given to assist children's motor learning are purposeful and appealing. Sensory preparation may sometimes have to begin a movement lesson.

Once children have partial mastery of the component skills and the goal-directed movement, the next step is to help them generalise skills to similar-but-slightly-different contexts, with less and less direct assistance from adults. In this way, children can develop an expanding repertoire of sensorimotor skills, which they can adapt and modify to solve new movement challenges. By this process they learn confidence and enjoyment of physical activity.

Suggestions for promoting motor development in infants or toddlers who are not yet walking are readily available elsewhere but it is important to highlight five issues here. First, children need to experience the world from different heights and angles so those with physical disabilities will need opportunities to play at floor level as well as from their wheelchair or standing frame, so that they can see the world from different perspectives (Nixon & Gould 1999). There are also musculo-skeletal, physiological and social reasons for these children to experience a variety of play positions, including assisted standing, each day. A second issue is that when young children require you to help them move about in their castor cart or wheelchair, it must be borne in mind that infants and toddlers typically pause to inspect what they discover in transit. Therefore, your speed of pushing will sometimes need to mirror this slow pace so that children with physical disabilities have similar opportunities for exploration. Third, children who cannot move about independently will need systematic assistance to move from one activity to another so that they are not stranded at an activity that they have completed. Fourth, children who cannot move independently will need active assistance to become involved in physical play. Finally, in all instances when you are lifting or moving children, you will need to avoid injury to yourself and them by practising safe handling techniques. For detailed guidance about these issues for individual infants and children, you will need to consult with their visiting allied health professional. (See also Additional resources.)

The remainder of this chapter concentrates on strategies to promote fitness and gross motor skill development for preschoolers who are walking independently but experiencing some difficulties of motor learning or performance. As no two children have the same mix of abilities and disabilities, the following programming suggestions cannot be applied in a recipe-like fashion but call for improvisation and adjustment, according to how the children respond.

If you have any worries about children's safety while engaging in physical activity—such as when children have asthma or other cardiorespiratory problems, or the neck instability sometimes associated with Down syndrome—you should consult their parents and, with permission, their medical practitioner or allied health professional for advice. (See also Additional resources.)

Weight shift and weight-bearing

Weight-bearing is a powerful sensory stimulation, and improved weight shift is necessary for improved gait and running and to enable children to change positions. For infants with hemiplegia, many techniques of handling, lifting and carrying have been devised to promote weight-bearing through the affected side (see Additional resources). Toddlers and preschoolers can be motivated to practise weight shift on and off the affected leg by moving or marching to music and action songs. Walking up and down stairs and climbing also teach children to weight-bear through both sides alternately.

To improve upper body weight shift and weight-bearing in children with hemiplegia, DCD, intellectual disabilities or sensory processing difficulties, any functional activity involving pushing through two hands or leaning through an affected hand achieves weight-bearing through the palm. Examples include rolling a big barrel, propping on an affected or neglected hand while side-sitting on the floor for story time, or leaning on both hands while climbing over a bolster.

Reduction of unwanted background movement

Unwanted background movement sometimes results when children with cerebral palsy or DCD attempt a task that proves too difficult. They might draw their legs together, stand on their toes, have unusual arm posturing or jaw opening or, like any children, simply become irritable with tiredness. If this happens, try simplifying the task: giving the children a rest, or alternating between sitting and standing activities. You could also modify their position in relation to equipment: for example, children with hemiplegia will have less unusual arm posturing if you move their toys or work from the side to midline, or encourage them to grasp the edge of their book or table with the affected hand. For older preschoolers, gentle verbal or physical prompts (e.g. to close their mouths or swing their arms) can teach them to self-regulate unwanted background movement. If these strategies do not work, seek a physiotherapist's advice.

Sequencing and scaling of muscle activity

Poor coordination can lead to children's using muscle groups in the wrong order or at incorrect force. This can cause jumping that looks and sounds heavy, with poor shock absorption, endurance and rhythm. Climbing, balance and ball skills can also lack finesse and children may be impulsive and unsafe. Sequencing and scaling of muscle activity is one skill component that is fostered by the playground games mentioned later in this chapter.

Moving one body part independently of another

Children with diplegia have trouble moving one lower limb independently of the other and have poor control of rotation around their long body axis. For these and other children, games to assist their development of movement control include:

- climbing;
- stomping;
- using giant strides;
- kicking;
- 'twister' game or similar, involving working out how to place hands, feet, elbows or knees on different-coloured circles on a floor mat;
- reaching around behind in sitting or standing, as in two-handed batting with

a baton at a suspended ball, or reaching around to pass a ball to the child behind in a file;
- 'animal walks' on their knees;
- action songs involving asymmetrical movements of limbs and body rotation;
- marching and stepping through a horizontal ladder (either flat on the ground or raised to thigh height);
- bike riding.

Balancing muscle length and strength

Premature infants are born with less of the physiological flexion of full-term infants, and often need extra help to learn control of their flexor muscles. Positioning them in 'nests' or hammocks and special techniques of handling, carrying and dressing them can also promote the balanced use of flexors and extensors for head and trunk control and reaching (Creger 1995).

In children with cerebral palsy, DCD or intellectual disability, certain muscle groups can become short because of postural habit and persistent imbalance of muscle strength. Weight-bearing through the palm, crawling through tunnels, and rolling out playdough with the palms are all useful muscle-stretching activities for the upper limbs. Climbing and squatting to play can help active lengthening of tight hip, calf and foot muscles. Meanwhile, children with diplegia can also take part in 'twist-and-turn' games to elongate tight trunk muscles.

For toddlers with persistent toe-walking, parents or carers can perform manual calf stretches and encourage the children to squat to play, while older preschoolers can be taught a simple form of the jogger's wall stretch (see Figure 6.3). In more severe cases, serial casting is required. This can produce gains lasting five months or longer (Cusick 1990), and can be repeated at intervals throughout the children's growth years. Other management options include orthotics, drug therapy (muscle relaxants), therapeutic taping to re-educate children via sensory feedback about the new position of their ankle to achieve heelstrike, and orthopaedic surgery later in childhood to lengthen the Achilles tendon or calf muscles.

PLAYGROUND GAMES THAT FOSTER MOTOR LEARNING

The playground is a natural setting in which to help children achieve goal-directed movement, as in this environment children naturally want to participate in games that involve climbing, balancing, jumping, hopping, running or using balls, and so are inherently motivated to learn the motor skills that will assist their lifelong participation in physical activity. As well as enabling expertise in the preschool playground, these motor skills are necessary for sport and dance. When teaching component skills, it can help to work with children in small groups, so that no one child feels singled out. Also, it makes sense to modify how you use your present equipment, so that activities are novel without requiring a huge financial outlay for customised materials.

The instruction during a stretching activity such as the one illustrated here could be: 'Keep your feet pointing forward. Lean forward and keep your heels on the ground. Can you feel that "comfy stretch" and count to twenty? No bouncing!'

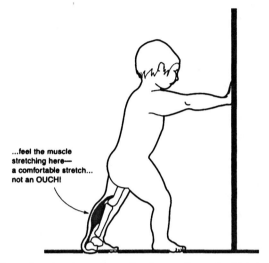

...feel the muscle
stretching here—
a comfortable stretch...
not an OUCH!

Figure 6.3 Preschoolers' version of a jogger's wall stretch

Source: Rang (1993:15).

Climbing games

Climbing gives children improved access to their environment and has an important role in their musculoskeletal development: it can improve their strength, motor planning, aerobic fitness, and control of movement involving rotation of one body segment on another. As well, it teaches them to shift their weight in various directions without falling and enables them to learn visuospatial relationships—that is, how much space their body requires to negotiate obstacles.

Thus, teaching horizontal or vertical climbing can be particularly beneficial for children with weak muscles (e.g. those with cerebral palsy) and for those with shortened muscle groups or immature lower limb bony alignment (e.g. children who are 'pigeon-toed' beyond the age of 4 years). Whenever climbing raises one knee past waist level, it causes rotation outwards of the raised leg. The muscles that cause this outward rotation exert a cranking-out effect on the lower limb bones and so with repetition may help to realign the limbs (Cusick 1990). This is possible in young children as their bones are softer than those of adults.

While playing games such as follow-the-leader, animal walks or completing an obstacle course, you can encourage horizontal climbing by having the children crawl over floor cushions, through tunnels or portholes, under or over rungs of a climbing frame or in and out of supermarket cartons (turning hands and body for descent; see next section). If necessary, offer extra help in the form of

LIVERPOOL JOHN MOORES UNIVERSITY
LEARNING SERVICES

manual or verbal prompts to duck their head, shift their weight, lean on their palms not the backs of hands, and so on.

Vertical climbing can be up and down stairs or the ladder to a play fort or a toddler's slide, or on and off a rocking horse. From 4 years of age, you can help children to descend a platform above waist height (e.g. trampoline, play fort) using the following sequence: sit on edge, turn onto stomach, push back with arms, feel with feet for rungs or the ground.

From 4 years of age, children can climb over a climbing trestle, turning to face the equipment to descend. For children with motor planning or proprioceptive problems, it helps to teach each stage of the trestle sequence separately. For example, a simple rhythm of 'hand, hand, foot, foot' with verbal and manual prompts can assist practice of limb placement for the ascent, reversing this order for descent. Once this is established, show children how to swing one leg over the top bar and turn to descend. Children with poor coordination or safety sense may need to 'sit on the bar, stop and think'. They should then 'turn and swap' their hands, thus initiating upper body rotation towards the trestle, then 'keep holding on, and stand up'. Help them to swing the trailing leg over the top bar, then use that foot to 'find the bar' below to begin the descent.

For a strong handgrip, encourage preschoolers to wrap their thumbs around each rung, to meet their fingertips 'like a bird on a perch'. For children who are afraid of heights, let them practise the 'turn to descend' while one foot remains on the ground, perhaps climbing into a large supermarket carton, or over a low fence.

Balance games

As discussed earlier, balance or postural adjustments accompany and underpin all movement. Young children can have poor balance or postural control for one or a combination of reasons, and you may need to consult a paediatric physiotherapist to work out where individual children's main problem lies. Nevertheless, there are many preschool games that you can use to help develop postural control on a broad front, particularly the ability to shift weight for single-leg stance activities, and the ability to make rapid postural adjustments 'on the run'. Because balance accompanies all movement, children need to practise their balance skills in a wide variety of task settings and under various sensory conditions—for example with shoes on and off, indoors and outdoors, and on the various types of terrain they are likely to meet in their everyday life.

To promote weight shift and single-leg stance, the following activities can be useful:

- Kicking a ball softly.
- Marching to music, emphasising lifting knees.
- Simon says: 'Stand on one leg and count to three.'
- Taking giant steps from island to island (hoops or paper circles).
- Stepping over shin-high bars without hand support in an obstacle course.

- 'Stomping' toys and games (e.g. a foot catapult which throws beanbags for the children to catch, or stomping on bubble wrap).
- Swaying activities in sitting, quadruped or standing on a trampoline (one child at a time). You can stimulate the sway by gently applying pressure to the trampoline mat, in various directions. The children can then sway themselves from foot to foot, being an elephant swinging its trunk.
- Side-stepping along a line, or between the rungs of a ladder laid flat on the ground.
- Using low cup-type stilts.

To promote rapid postural adjustments 'on the run', you could encourage the following activities either in the playground or during indoor music and movement times:

- Walking, running or completing rapid turns on slopes and uneven terrain.
- Playing a 'traffic game', in which the children are cars that have to stop and start rapidly on your traffic officer's signal. Begin on level ground, then progress to a gentle slope. A variation is 'freeze' on a verbal or musical signal.
- Retrieving and returning a rolling ball without falling.
- Walking along a line, beam, or the brick edge of a garden bed. From 4 years of age, try heel-to-toe walking (Burns 1992).
- Ball catching and throwing (seated or standing).
- Moving to music, later simple folk dance.

Jumping, hopping and running games

Jumping requires, and in turn promotes, children's motor planning, visuospatial perception and proprioceptive awareness. It also assists their ability to coordinate in space and time their upper and lower body and left and right sides; and turning muscles from hip to foot on and off quickly and repeatedly, in the correct order and strength. It requires functional joint range and improves children's propulsive strength and endurance, which in turn may assist running—and vice versa.

Soon after they learn to stand with support, infants enjoy bouncing (softening then straightening their knees) as a repetitive activity. Toddlers love to squat to play. These activities are important for learning about switching from controlled lowering (shock absorption, preparation) to controlled push-off (propulsion), as preparation for jumping. Children with poor coordination may have missed these stages. Thus, to encourage bouncing, you can use a mini-trampoline or mattress, have the children complete five bounces and stop, showing them how to bend their knees to stop ('like riding a motor-bike'). You can gradually progress from bouncing to assisted jumping. (An adult's foot may add rebound on a mini-trampoline.)

From the age of 3 years, children can practise controlled lowering and push-off with activities such as squatting then jumping like a frog, or kangaroo jumps forward with feet taking off and landing simultaneously. They can jump off a low step (at ankle then knee height), with help from you if necessary by drawing their hands forward. Walking on tiptoes and running improve the propulsive strength needed to jump. Preschoolers benefit from opportunities to run free on open ground with safe boundaries. From 3 or 4 years, children can attempt hopping, although many 4-year-olds cannot hop (Shumway-Cook & Woollacott 2001). Pushing down with their hands on a waist-high bench while hopping may assist.

From 5 years of age, children can be challenged to jump zig-zag along a line, sideways, or backwards. Many children of this age can be taught to use the balls of their feet to help them in landing, although for some, this may require specific training from a paediatric physiotherapist.

A useful strategy is to involve the children in jumping, hopping or tiptoe relays (preferably not a race) in which three children move as a team together. This avoids spotlighting individual children with difficulties.

Ball games

Basic proficiency with kicking, throwing and catching a ball is a great advantage to children beginning school, as much of the socialisation that occurs in school playgrounds involves ball games. Ball games advance children's:

- eye–hand coordination;
- visual attention and pursuit;
- coordinated use of both sides of their bodies;
- ability to cross their body midline;
- strength, endurance and cardiovascular fitness;
- ability to stop and start quickly;
- rapid postural adjustments while manipulating or chasing the ball;
- rhythm and timing;
- group interaction.

This list implies that there are many possible reasons why young children might be weak at ball skills. If children over 4 years of age have persistent problems with ball-catch despite interest in and experience with the game, arrange for their vision to be checked and look at these other potential sources of their difficulties, including some of the physical disabilities already discussed.

Great variation exists in the sequence of ball skill development. For instance, preschoolers with coordination difficulties may be at a 4-year level with kick, but at a 2-year level with catch. Start at the children's current functional level and move them on in the general sequence that follows.

Catching
- **Roll and stop.** Start with a 20–24 cm ball. From the age of 2 years, sit on the ground with your legs in a 'V', facing the child, and roll the ball back and forwards between you. From 3 years, emphasise pushing through open palms, with wrists cocked up. (This relates to pre-writing skills.)

- **Two-handed catch.** For 3-year-olds or reluctant older children, toss a beach ball, in midline, from 1–2 metres away. Progress to a firmer 20–24 cm ball. Initially, the children will scoop the ball to their chest, with unreliable eye-follow, and from 4 years can trap the ball in their forearms or hands (Burns 1992).
- **Clap-catch.** From 4 years, teach children to 'catch like a clap' to encourage eyes and hands to ball.
- **Hanging ball in a net.** From 3 years of age, suspend a 20 cm ball in a net at their waist height, asking them to catch it as it swings. This is useful for reluctant children or those with poor eye-follow. Older preschoolers could bat the ball with a baton held two-handed, with wrists cocked up.
- **Catching away from or above midline.** From 5–6 years, children can learn to catch a 20 cm ball tossed in line with their shoulder. The next stage is to step to the side to catch, learning weight shift first, then adding catching. Using a mitt to catch, and catching above their heads, are generally left until school age.

Kicking
Infants enjoy crawling or running after a rolling ball and running into it in an attempt to kick. Use a soft beach ball initially or have them chase balloons. Teach youngsters who have poor balance or are impulsive to 'kick softly'. If 4-year-olds display excessive 'pigeon-toeing', show them how to contact the ball with the inside edge of their foot, as in a 'soccer pass'. From 4 years, teach leg backswing.

Propulsion (toss, throw, bounce)
Begin with teaching an underarm toss two-handed, as this improves aim. Children at this stage can also learn to bounce a large ball between themselves and an adult then catch two-handed, and later bounce the ball in front of their own feet at hip level and catch.

For 4-year-olds or those seeking more challenge, proceed to a chest pass or two-handed overhand throw. Show the children how to position their elbows 'like chicken wings', with fingers cupped loosely around the ball. Have them throw at a wall initially. Balloon volleyball can be played with a net improvised from rope and paper streamers. Teach the children to throw the balloon straight upwards, then reach up and bat it forwards to the child across the net, using both hands initially. Another useful activity involves tossing small beanbags underarm into hoops. Demonstrate a palm-forward position of the tossing arm, and hand-opening for release. You can also try various-textured balls.

CONCLUSION

In this chapter, the focus has been on the more subtle problems in movement control or avoidance of physical activity seen in preschoolers who are walking. Because some sensory and movement difficulties are common across a range of childhood conditions, many inclusive programming ideas can be modified to suit various children. Nevertheless, the complexity of sensorimotor development means that it is important to consult specialist allied health professionals if additional programming ideas are needed.

ADDITIONAL RESOURCES

Box, J. and Lancaster, A. 1997 *From cuddles to coordination* Royal Blind Society, Sydney

Finnie, N. 1997 *Handling the young cerebral palsied child at home* 3rd edn, Butterworth-Heinemann, Oxford, UK

Klein, M.D. and Morris, S.E. 2000 *Pre-feeding skills* 2nd edn, Therapy Skill Builders, Tucson, AZ

For information on other neurological or orthopaedic conditions, and orthotics and mobility aids for children using wheelchairs, see:

Burns, Y. and MacDonald, J. (eds) 1996 *Physiotherapy and the growing child* Saunders, London

Eckersley, P.M. (ed.) 1993 *Elements of paediatric physiotherapy* Churchill Livingstone, Edinburgh

7

DAILY LIVING SKILLS

Zara Soden

KEY POINTS

- To perform everyday tasks, young children need to be able to organise the information that they receive through their senses, use their hands effectively, and perform basic self-care functions.
- Efficient hand use requires object grasp and release, grasp strength, manipulation skills, tool (pencil and scissor) grip, use of two hands together and established hand dominance.
- Self-care activities that are relevant for young children include dressing, toilet learning, basic grooming and hygiene measures, and self-feeding.
- We can enhance children's success in these areas through carefully selected and directed activities and through influencing the environment.
- To assist children who are experiencing difficulties in basic play, pencil and scissor work and self-help skills, it is essential to understand the role of sensory processing in enabling them to attend, perform and self-correct in order to achieve.

INTRODUCTION

To perform the tasks that are typical of their age, young children need to be able to organise the information that they are receiving through their senses, use their hands to carry out activities, and begin to take care of their physical needs. These three areas are the typical domain of an occupational therapist and are the subject of this chapter. Naturally, success in each of these areas rests on the successful functioning of numerous other systems such as the visual and auditory senses and motor skills (see chapters 5, 6 and 8). Furthermore, each is complex and can be described only in overview in a text such as this; consultation with an occupational therapist might be useful if a child in your care is experiencing difficulties beyond those covered here.

117

SENSORY SKILLS

Young children learn about themselves through their senses. We are all familiar with the five basic senses of touch, taste, smell, vision and hearing. Of these, problems with seeing and hearing are the best recognised and understood (see chapters 5 and 8). Less well understood is how children process and interpret information from the other senses—known as 'near-body' senses because they give us direct information about our bodies and what is happening to them.

These lesser-known senses comprise the three systems of touch, the vestibular (or movement) sense, and the proprioceptive or body position sense. These last two are sometimes referred to as the combined vestibular-proprioceptive sense because they work so closely together.

- **Tactile (touch) receptors** are located in the skin. The touch system is the first part of the nervous system to begin functioning in utero and is the most mature of the sensory systems at birth. Of any organ of the body, the skin sends the most sensory information to the brain. It comprises two subsystems: the protective system that warns of danger (the 'flight' or 'fight' response); and the discriminative system that gives information about the properties of objects so that children can recognise objects by feel. The discriminative system develops more slowly and can override the protective system.
- **Vestibular (or movement) receptors** are located in our inner ear. From these we receive information about how we are moving, the effect of gravity on our bodies, and the position of our head in relation to the horizon. Vestibular information helps us to regulate muscle tone so that we can maintain posture, and coordinates with our visual system to allow us to control eye and head movement.
- **Proprioceptive receptors** are located in our muscles and joints. These receptors allow children to know where their body is in space and to perform tasks automatically without looking. This takes some years to develop: most under-4-year-olds, for instance, find it difficult to maintain standing balance with their eyes closed, indicating that they are still relying on vision to regulate their body position.

SENSORY PROCESSING

For infants and children to function effectively, information from the three near-body senses must be integrated well together and with visual and auditory input. Information from all these sources must be registered, sorted, combined and related to past experiences. Doing so keeps children alert, safe and responding correctly to their environment (Steer 1999). With successful sensory integration, infants can develop eye movement (tracking), posture, balance, muscle tone, gravitational security (so that they are comfortable with movement), sucking, eating, and a sense of tactile comfort which can promote parent–child bonding and attachment (Ayres 1981). These are all necessary foundation skills to promote learning.

As illustrated in Figure 7.1, to achieve successful integration of sensory input, children need to be able to moderate two processes: their level of arousal or alertness, and their information processing. Although in reality these two aspects occur almost simultaneously, to assist with conceptualising them they are illustrated separately in Figure 7.1 and discussed individually here.

Alertness

Most children in a group can be calm when required, such as when listening to a story or settling to their afternoon nap. Others seem to function in 'overdrive' and have great difficulty settling. These children are often in constant motion, yet their activity levels seem to lack purpose, they might jiggle or rock constantly during quiet activities such as group story time, flit from activity to activity so often that it interferes with their play (Dunn & Westman 1997), need extensive help to get to sleep, or seem to become anxious or stressed with little reason. These problems can be exacerbated in summer, when the children are sleeping under light covers, thus depriving them of the deep pressure of heavier bedding that can help to settle them as they sleep.

Conversely, some children seem too calm or appear tired or disengaged even when they have sufficient sleep. These youngsters might spend long periods in sedentary activities, appear not to be tuned in to what is going on around them, or are distracted by extraneous sights or sounds even during activities that you would expect to hold their interest.

Children's level of alertness is dynamic and so *will* vary throughout the day; difficulties arise only when their alertness levels are not suitable for the activity at hand. When these overactive or underactive behaviours occur often, they will interfere with the children's ability to engage in developmentally appropriate activities. Although it can appear that these children are being disruptive, disengaged or have behavioural difficulties, these patterns may be due to poor regulation of their state of alertness. This means that the children themselves are not able to organise automatically the sensory information that they are receiving. Because of this, they require adults to structure their sensory experiences for them so that it is easier to organise their bodies and achieve a state of calm alertness.

Those who are underaroused can require alerting activities that offer a high level of stimulation, while those who are overwhelmed or overaroused can benefit from activities that help them to calm. Both measures can help children achieve optimal attention and alertness, thus assisting them to learn (Levine 1998)—see Box 7.1.

An important sensory integration principle is that activities work best if they are directed by the children themselves. When children enjoy the experiences and are active in directing these, there is more potential to improve their brain organisation and so to make them more successful in their interactions with their world. A second key principle is that trial and careful observation are required to ensure

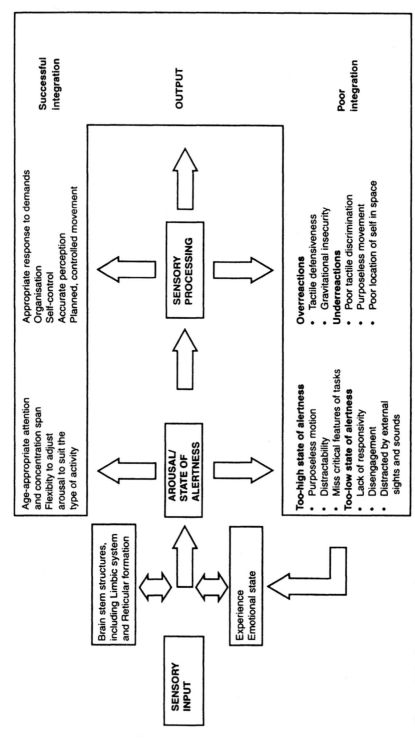

Figure 7.1 Sequence of sensory processing

that the activities are enjoyable and of benefit to the children. The amount of extra stimulation needed, its frequency, intensity and duration, will vary from child to child and for the same child over time. As the children's level of alertness improves and they are better able to participate in activities, their intrinsic motivation for the task will help reduce their need for additional sensory stimulation.

Sensory integration

Normally we receive so much sensory information all at once that we are unable to pay attention to it all effectively. Consequently, we are forced to select out some of it and focus only on what is important for us to function well. This selection process is called sensory modulation (Spitzer et al. 1996). When children's sensory systems appear not to be able to recognise and effectively screen incoming sensory input, it can lead to what might simply be viewed as under- or overreactions to sensory input (the latter being termed 'sensory defensiveness') (Wilbarger & Wilbarger 1991).

These over- and underreactions can occur in any sensory modality and are manifested by various unusual behaviours (see Figure 7.1) which, we can assume, are an attempt by the children to organise and control the currently confusing sensory input they are receiving. Although the resulting behaviours can seem unusual, these have a physical basis and an adaptive function that reflect the children's efforts to meet their atypical sensory needs, or are simply an emotional outburst in reaction to the distress caused by their unreliable nervous system.

Dysfunctional reactions to touch
You might observe that children who overreact to touch avoid hugs except on their own terms; become disturbed by the feel of new clothing or rough textures; are upset when touched unexpectedly, particularly by other children; avoid messy activities such as playdough, sand, paint or glue; take extraordinary care not to spill food on their face while eating; restrict themselves to particular food textures; avoid having bare feet (or, conversely, are irritated by the feel of shoes and socks); seem to require a larger than usual personal space; and are hesitant around splashing water. These children are sometimes referred to as being 'tactile defensive', suggestions for assisting whom are given in Box 7.2. Subsequently, their avoidance of touch is likely to have led to impoverished experience of exploratory play with their hands, so they can also require additional practice at hand skills (see later in this chapter).

Meanwhile, some children underreact to touch. They might continually touch objects, certain surfaces, textures or other people to the point of irritating others; mouth objects beyond the usual age; show decreased awareness of pain or temperature; and be less aware of their clothing, perhaps leaving their clothes twisted on their body when other children would notice that these needed adjusting. Activities to assist these children aim to enhance the touch input that they receive so that they notice it more. If this can be done within a natural activity, it will prove most meaningful to the children. Some strategies are included in Box 7.2.

Box 7.1 Activities to help children modulate their alertness

At various times, individual children might need a mixture of both alerting and calming activities. Some of these require direct, hands-on assistance; others comprise indirect ways of influencing the sensory environment.

Alerting activities

- Prior to commencing a task requiring more concentration, provide linear movement with faster tempo, including stops and starts (e.g. giving children a swing, jumping together on a trampoline, or rocking in a rocking chair).
- Give the children a small 'feely' fidget item (e.g. putty or a 'stress' ball) to hold during group time to aid sitting in the one spot.
- Give ice cubes or ice chips to crunch or snacks of crunchy and/or spicy food (e.g. celery sticks, soya crisps).
- Use a focused light source such as a torchlight on an object on which you wish the child to focus.

Calming activities

Clues about suitable calming experiences come from noting what sensory activities help to calm young babies and adjusting these to make them appropriate to individual children's ages. Another clue to what might calm children is to look at what input they seem to be seeking. For example, some children like to squeeze into small gaps behind a sofa or a cupboard (suggesting that they are seeking deep pressure), to rock when stressed (indicating a need for rhythmic movement), or hum with their hands over their ears (which can mean that they need quiet, blocking noise). The soothing activities include:

- using rhythmic movement through rocking the child in your arms, a pusher, hammock, or rocking chair; or jumping on a trampoline—at first quickly and then more slowly to prepare for a quiet activity;
- giving firm proprioceptive input through swaddling, patting, massage and use of a dummy (pacifier);
- providing deep pressure input through massage or a firm hug, by having the children lie between heavy cushions, or roll up in a blanket pretending to be a hot dog. You can then add 'sauce' and 'mustard' by stroking firmly down their back;
- 'chair push-ups': having the children raise their bottom off the chair by pushing their hands against the sides of the chair and straightening their arms, keeping their feet off the floor. This is useful partway through a table task when they are becoming restless;
- giving chewy food such as bread with thick crusts or thickened drinks to provide deep pressure to the mouth. Keep flavours mild;
- place a weighted fabric bag filled with dried beans (or similar) on the child's lap when sitting (such as during meals or group time).

Box 7.2 Activities to help children integrate their sense of touch

Activities for children who overreact to touch

- Start by giving deep pressure touch, as firm touch tends to override tactile irritation. If the children do not tolerate direct touch, give firm pressure through another surface such as via a cushion squash, crashing off a swing into soft cushions, wearing a vest weighted with beanbags, or additional firm towelling after swimming.
- Have children perform 'heavy work activities' such as pushing or pulling a trolley or wheelbarrow filled by them with blocks or sand; cutting through playdough with a plastic or wooden knife; pulling velcro pieces apart; riding a bike; swimming; or jumping on a trampoline.
- Gradually introduce more tactile play experiences to develop the hands' ability to discriminate between different textures, shapes and sizes. Keep these activities brief initially and have a face cloth handy during messy activities for the children to wipe their hands clean if they desire.
- Allow children to sit on the edge of groups or be last or first in lines to avoid unnecessary jostling.
- Ensure that there are quiet corners in play areas for them to withdraw to when they are overwhelmed.

Activities to help children who underreact to touch

- Provide tactile activities as part of daily play, such as having a large box of dried peas with scooping and pouring utensils available, and providing manipulative play with textured objects.
- Have a collection of different and special textures in a feely bag for the children to feel.
- Use massage.
- Employ messy play.
- For children who mouth objects past the usual age, provide mouth stimulation via using straws or blowing on whistles or other musical instruments.

Dysfunctional reactions to movement

Some children overreact to movement. This is termed *gravitational insecurity* and is seen when children become anxious or distressed when their feet leave the ground or when they are held upside down; when they avoid climbing or jumping; avoid uneven ground; seek sedentary play; and avoid playground equipment or moving toys. You might notice these children holding their heads upright, even when bending over or leaning, or turning their whole body to look at you. These behaviours are aimed at avoiding movement because the children misinterpret vestibular feedback and so movement scares them. Some suggestions to help are given in Box 7.3.

Key principles of working with these children are to respect their fear of movement as it is real to them, to prepare them for what they are being asked to do by explaining the activity, and to give them control over their movements by beginning with safe movements and introducing others only as the children become more confident. To help children feel in control give them choices, be predictable, and use equipment they can control. Keep close to the children to give them security.

Rather than overreacting to movement, some children underreact. They might seek out all sorts of movement to the point that their movement levels interfere with daily routines; rock or spin constantly; spin objects; walk on their toes; or take movement or climbing risks that compromise their safety (Dunn & Westman 1997). Some ways to help these children integrate their sensory reactions to movement are given in Box 7.3.

Box 7.3 Activities to help children's reactions to movements

Activities for children who overreact to movement
- Start with linear movement, such as jumping backwards and forwards or swinging. This is more focusing and calming than rotational movement.
- Start with low demands and work close to the ground, such as riding on a scooterboard or walking along a plank on the ground.
- A fun and reassuring way to broaden movement experiences is to sit on a trampoline together, bouncing gently. The children could initially sit on your lap.
- Time in a warm swimming pool with a capable, understanding adult can dramatically increase the children's ability to cope with movement experiences. In water they might tolerate more movement than on land.

Activities for children who underreact to movement
Aim to help the children become calm and alert by providing large doses of the movement they are seeking. This is particularly effective when combined with heavy muscle work (proprioceptive input).

- Provide a range of movement experiences during the children's day, remembering that linear movement (forwards and backwards and up and down) is the most organising. These children can probably cope with strong, fast movement and then the tempo can gradually be reduced to a calm pace.
- Supply activities that require hanging by the arm, such as swinging from a trapeze swing.
- Offer trampolining.
- During table activities, have the children sit on a large ball or a cushion filled with air, to give background movement as they work.
- Encourage hobbies such as swimming or walking.

Dysfunctional proprioceptive reactions

Children cannot have too much body position awareness (or proprioceptive feedback); the only group of children mentioned clinically are those who underreact to information from their muscles and joints about the position of their body. This group of children will deliberately fall over or jump off heights without regard to their personal safety; can seem to have weak muscles, including a weak handgrasp; fidget excessively as they have trouble maintaining a steady position, such as maintaining cross-legged sitting; lock their elbow or knee joints to achieve stability; tire easily; or might use other people, furniture or objects as a physical prop for support (Dunn & Westman 1997). Box 7.4 lists some suggestions for assisting these children.

Box 7.4 Activities to help children who underreact to proprioceptive feedback

- Use some calming strategies (as listed in Box 7.1).
- Provide extra opportunities for proprioceptive input throughout the child's day via heavy work activities.
- Many household chores offer strong proprioceptive input. These include vacuuming, mopping, putting the wheely-bin out, using a tin opener, mixing cake mixture and kneading bread dough.
- Use heavy quilts, layers of blankets or pillows over the children's body at nap times. (Make sure that the children do not overheat, however.)
- Provide 'hidey holes' in play areas with plenty of cushions for children to pile on top of themselves.

Dysfunctional reactions of other sensory systems

Just as is the case with the near-sensory systems, children can experience atypical under- or overreactions to taste, smell, visual or auditory sensations. Some of the sensitivities in these domains (especially auditory sensitivity) can be assisted by the activities recommended above, as calming one sensory modality can help calm others as well. However, when individual children continue to show extreme reactions that interfere with daily living (as commonly observed in children who have moderate or severe disabilities), you will need to consult specialists to advise you about designing individual programs for them.

HAND FUNCTION

Hand function is vital for many daily living skills throughout life. In terms of adults' focus on children's development, with the understandable emphasis on walking and talking in toddlers, hand function often takes a back seat until later activities such as writing and using scissors are introduced. Yet for skilled 'tool' use such as using a writing implement, a toothbrush, scissors or a knife and fork, much behind-the-scenes work needs to occur to ready the hand. Much preparation for manipulation occurs in babies' early years as part of their gross motor development—for example, while weight bearing on their hands during crawling. These large motor skills and ongoing refinement of grasps set the scene for controlled hand use. Thereafter, to develop precision, toddlers and preschoolers need to practise manipulative activities during quiet indoor time rather than replacing these entirely with watching television or using a computer.

When looking at hand function and suspected difficulties, it is important to look at not only *what* children can do but also *how* they perform an activity (Exner 1997). While some children might be able to 'get there in the end' to achieve a particular hand task, it can require considerably more effort and time than would normally be expected. This can come about because of difficulties in any of the following systems affecting hand function:

- **Alertness.** This affects persistence at, and thus practice with, tasks that require the use of the hands.
- **Sensory integration** permits the use of two hands as a team, planning of movement and accurate positioning of hands, all of which are essential to children's fine motor skills (Exner 1989).
- **Gross motor development**, particularly children's ability to maintain stable trunk, shoulder and neck control, affects their proficiency with fine motor activities (see chapter 6).
- **Vision.** Vision is crucial for directing hand movements (see chapter 5). Visual perception is the ability of the brain to interpret and use what is seen (Levine 1998). It guides movement, particularly for developing pre-writing, puzzle and scissor skills.
- **Motor planning.** This is our ability to plan and execute a sequence of steps to complete a task successfully. As we become more proficient in a skill, our movements can become less conscious and more automatic, leaving thinking capacity available for higher-order problem solving.
- **Intellectual development** affects children's interest in persisting with complex tasks (Exner 1989).
- **Social, cultural and emotional factors** influence children's exposure to and interest in fine motor activities.
- **Physical abnormalities** such as an absent thumb, severe dermatitis or juvenile arthritis, for instance, will affect children's ability to use their hands proficiently.

Grasp development

Hand skill development follows reasonably predictable trends, driven by nervous system maturation and influenced by children's experiences. Sequences for the development of grasp and hand skills are outlined in Appendix II, with mature grips illustrated in Figure 7.2. Behaviour that you might observe that suggests difficulties with grasp development includes the following.

- You will observe grasp patterns that are immature for age, such as when 2-year-olds hold beads using the whole hand rather than fingertips when attempting to put beads on a stick. A fisted grasp like this means that the children cannot see the bead to line the hole up with the stick, which will lead to failure at the task.
- You might also observe that individual children can use a mature grasp when their hand is still, but not once they start to move their hand to manipulate

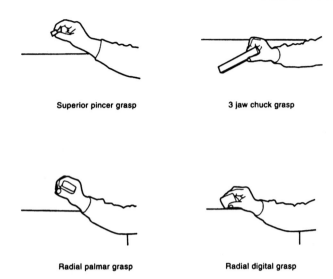

Figure 7.2 Mature grasp patterns

an object. This indicates that the mature grasp is not a well-established, stable position.

- Some children could also be limited in the variety of grasps they are able to use. This is a problem because everyday tasks require a wide range of grasp positions (including those in Figure 7.2). Sometimes the awkward grasp is a result of a problem 'further up' the arm such as poor control of the forearm. Examples of this are when children hold their wrist in a bent-in (or flexed) position when grasping, or hold their palm face down (pronated) instead of the thumb pointing upwards (midpronation). Both these positions prevent the children from being able to see the object and do not allow for a precise placement.
- Other children might not be achieving age-expected functional independence because of their weak grasp, such as when they cannot pull their trousers up.

Activities to encourage grasp and hand-use development are included in Box 7.5. If individual children continue to experience difficulties, referral to an occupational therapist is recommended.

Bilateral hand skills

The ability to use two hands as a team is important for many daily living tasks. Activities which require children to use their two hands together can assist those who are having difficulty with this aspect of hand use. It can help to present toys on a slippery surface so that one hand has to stabilise the item, or to use toys or objects that have a handle to encourage one hand to hold while the other

Box 7.5 Activities to encourage grasping and hand-use skills

To help children control their postural muscles, start them in a supportive position, giving them a chair of correct height with armrests or sitting on the floor with their back to the wall. Tables need to be at or slightly above elbow height. This helps position the upper arm so that the thumb and the index and middle fingers (the 'skill fingers') are more accessible. Different positions can also be used to add variety: not all hand skill tasks need to happen at a table—some can be done sitting on the floor, standing, side-lying and, for activities that require a small range of movement only, lying on the stomach. It is essential to give activities that engage the children, afford pleasure in their accomplishment and fuel a drive to try more of the same activity.

As the wrist is a key control point for the hand, assist wrist stability with weight-bearing activities such as animal walks, 'wheelbarrows', climbing and handing from a trapeze swing.

Wrist supination (the 'keep your thumb up position') is necessary to facilitate fingertip grasps. To foster this, present objects to be grasped (e.g. pegs, pencils or crayons) in a vertical orientation and to the side rather than in the midline of the child's body, with the object offered to the thumb side of their hand (see Figure 7.3). Ask them also to carry the object in this position. An example is grasping large birthday candles and inserting them into a playdough cake, with the wrist maintained in the thumb-up position.

- Start with large objects and gradually reduce size.
- Start with square objects then other shapes such as a cylindrical pegboard peg (for three jaw chuck grasp), handbag handle (for hook grasp), holding pieces of paper (to develop intrinsic muscles of the hand), perhaps posting papers in a 'letter box' (with help if required).
- To improve stability, put objects to be grasped on a very firm surface such as a table or hard floor.
- Hand objects to the thumb side of the children's hands to encourage them to use their thumbs in opposition to fingers.
- Expect a palmar grasp for objects that are unstable (e.g. are squishy, round or lightweight).
- Initially place objects in the children's hand rather than have them reach for objects.
- For tools which require a power grasp, such as a toothbrush, hairbrush and hammers, the handle size may need to be enlarged, or handles with finger indentations might be useful. Practise this grip in activities that do not require much power, such as hammering objects into playdough.

For release
Voluntary release can be a problem when children have involuntary movement or tremors, abnormal tone or immature grasp patterns. To encourage release, ensure that the children's wrist is straight or slightly bent back (in extension).

- Have the children release objects into a container placed lower than their seat. This position with the elbow straight makes it is easier to extend the wrist and thus facilitates a good release pattern. Bring the container gradually higher and closer to the children.

- To release into a small space a good-quality grip is needed, in which case you may need to position the children's fingers on the object to be released.
- To help maintain the forearm in position and keep the object visible, remind and/or manually guide children to keep their 'thumb up'.
- Gradually reduce the size, weight and solidity of the object. For example, go from a rubber to a paper ball.
- To increase interest, have the children use tweezers, or release balls or marbles into a tin to enhance the noise effect; drop magnets into a tin, upturn it and see if they hold; drop sultanas or currants into cake mixture.

manipulates—for instance, having children decorate with stickers a cup that has a handle. Once children are comfortable using one hand to hold and the other to manipulate, move on to activities that require both hands to manipulate, such as easy threading tasks.

Grasp strength

Weakness in the hands, for whatever reason, interferes with children's ability to sustain good-quality grasp and to perform self-care tasks and engage in age-appropriate play. Children with weak hands will have difficulty pulling up their pants, fastenings snaps or pulling on their shoes (Case-Smith 1996); carrying heavy objects; hanging from monkey bars or the 'flying fox'; and opening lids. Any activity that involves pushing and pulling with the arms and hands will strengthen muscles. Examples include playdough, snaplock beads, and pulling a partly loaded trolley or pushing a wheelbarrow.

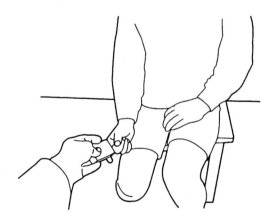

Figure 7.3 Handing an object to be grasped to encourage forearm supination and thumb opposition

Manipulation skills

Very young children use simple open-and-close patterns with their fingers. However, as they get older, they need to be able to manipulate objects between and within their hands. The latter is known as in-hand manipulation and comprises:

- **translation** of multiple or individual small objects from the fingertips to the palm and retrieval of the objects back to the fingertips. When some objects are retained within the hand during this manoeuvre, that is termed translation with stabilisation;
- **simple rotation** which involves rolling a small object between the pads of the thumb and fingers;
- **complex rotation**, which involves using the thumb and fingers to turn an object end over end (as when children pick up a pencil upside down and have to rotate it so that the tip points down);
- **shift**, which comprises moving linearly on an object, as when children creep their fingers down a pencil to be nearer its tip.

These skills are necessary for many daily tasks such as opening jars, replacing lids on textas (felt pens), doing up buttons, and adjusting the position of a pencil in the hand to permit comfortable use.

Checklists of fine motor development often overlook manipulation within the hand (Case-Smith 1996; Pehoski et al. 1997). As a result of a lack of norms, some children with significant manipulation difficulties are overlooked. These children might avoid challenging hand skills or might drop objects while turning, storing or positioning them in their hands.

To help develop in-hand manipulation skills (remembering to practise using only one hand at a time), try handing children individual shiny stones or toy coins with their fingertips to 'store' in their palm. They then can retrieve these using the thumb of the same hand and insert the coin into a 'treasure chest'. Start with one coin at a time and gradually build up the number. (More than one is not common prior to 3 years of age.)

Another idea to encourage object rotation: when replacing texta (felt pen) lids have the children practise orienting the lid in their fingertips, again without the assistance of the other hand. Place pencils or crayons in their hand so that their fingers are well away from the tip; they then have to crawl their fingers down to the tip. You will know that these activities have helped if the children's manipulative movements in daily activities become faster and more efficient.

Pencil grip

There are many reasons why children might use an awkward or inefficient pencil grip. Before much time is spent with paper and pencils, it is important that the muscles of the hand be ready. This is because prevention of awkward grips is better than cure: it is hard to change a dysfunctional grip that is 'locked in'. If the hand is well prepared, many later difficulties experienced by learner writers—such as poor grip and fatigue—could be prevented. When the muscles are overstressed, children compensate for the discomfort and lack of stability by developing what is in the long term an inefficient pencil grip.

Signs that children's grip development is not progressing well include:

- deviation from the normal developmental progression of grips (see Figure 7.4 and Appendix II);
- an overly tight grasp, which often indicates the need for additional position sense feedback (Schneck & Henderson 1990) but leads to fatigue and additional strain on joints;
- poor position during pre-writing and drawing activities;
- excessive arm tension;

Primitive grasps: typical of a 3-year developmental level

Radial cross palmar   Palmar supinate   Digital pronate grasp (only index finger extended)

Transitional grasps: typical of a 4½-year developmental level

Brush grasp   Grasp with extended fingers

Cross thumb grasp   Static tripod grasp   Four finger grasp

Mature grasps: typical of a 6-year developmental level

Lateral tripod grasp   Dynamic tripod grasp

Figure 7.4 Developmental progression of pencil grip

Source: adapted from Schneck & Henderson (1990). Reproduced with the permission of the American Occupational Therapy Association.

- use of whole-arm movements rather than fine finger movements when directing a pencil;
- no establishment of hand preference.

As to the last of these, children are less likely to have a mature grasp if their hand preference is not well established by 4 years of age (Chapparo 1998; Schneck & Henderson 1990), in which case it will be more useful to focus intervention on establishing hand preference than on correcting their grip.

A skilled fine motor activity such as threading provides a good opportunity to assess whether children's hands have sufficient muscle control to begin writing. While observing such an activity, you will need to note whether the children are able to hold their hands in a cupped position (palmer arches are developing); whether they can hold their wrist up; are able to use their thumb, index and middle fingers separately from their other fingers (they have developed a 'skill side'); the 'skill fingers' can move together at the end joints; and the children have an open circular-shaped web space between their thumb and index finger (Myers 1992). Children who lack these skills need to be given opportunities to perform activities requiring manipulation. Such activities include threading, lacing, using tweezers, tearing paper strips for use in art projects and cutting with scissors. At the same time, use of vertical surfaces can have a dramatic effect on preparing the hand. Vertical surface activities include drawing or playing with magnets on a whiteboard, playing with felt pieces on a vertically positioned felt board or painting at an easel. Pen grips can provide comfort and anecdotally seem to help children's grip, but they are treating the symptom not the cause of the inefficient grip, whereas vertical surfaces and manipulative activities address the cause and in my experience are more effective.

When observing the progress of grip development in young children, consider that grip is influenced by:

- the children's age: most 4–6-year-olds use a dynamic tripod or a lateral tripod grasp (see Figure 7.4);
- the children's gender: girls tend to use more mature grasps earlier than boys and more often use a lateral tripod grasp for colouring;
- type of task: the bigger the drawing, the less fine movement is required; when colouring the middle of an object, a less mature grasp is used than when colouring the edges; tracing elicits a more skilled grip than free drawing;
- time at the task: when a pencil grip is being used which is not yet firmly established, children may revert to a less mature grasp because of fatigue (Burton & Dancisak 2000; Schneck & Henderson 1990).

Once children are physically ready to practise pre-writing, it is important to vary activities. Examples are duo drawing, which involves taking turns to add to a drawing such as parts on a face; using stencils; writing with shaving or sorbolene cream on a table or mirror; using chilled paints or warmed sorbolene cream; adding essential oil to paints (peppermint to alert, lavender to calm); or copying simple drawn designs such as a circle or cross using pipe cleaners, laces or even bodies. (Other resources with more detail on prewriting activities are listed at the end of this chapter.)

Children with advanced intellectual development can lack motivation for or experience frustration with their fine hand skills, as these tend to be less advanced than their intellectual abilities (Tannenbaum 1983). Their hands cannot move as quickly as their ideas and so they experience frustration, particularly with tasks involving writing. By school age, they might not be as interested as others in getting the mechanics of hand writing and spelling correct, taking greater interest instead in their ideas and concepts. If the discrepancy between their fine motor and intellectual development bothers them, these children need to know that this is just because their hands grow up at 'body speed' whereas their brains are growing up faster (Porter, pers. comm.). Similarly, teachers need to attend to the quality of these children's ideas, rather than insisting on perfect writing output.

Use of scissors

As well as offering an enjoyable constructive activity, scissor activities exercise the same small muscles of the hand as are needed to manipulate pencils, and are therefore useful for building muscle strength and control. The developmental progression for the attainment of scissors skills is given in Appendix II. Children who are experiencing difficulties with scissor control may ask for adults to hold and direct the paper during cutting, might complain of fatigue, and be unable to stabilise and control their wrist during cutting because of muscle weakness.

Activities to prepare for scissor use include water pistols, squeeze toys, use of a hole punch and play with tongs and tweezers. When introducing scissors, ensure that you offer good-quality, clean-cutting scissors that fit the children's hand, with the lower loop being larger than the upper. Adapted scissors such as

---

Box 7.6 Correct scissor grip

There is divided opinion about the best scissor grip. One version is when the thumb occupies the top loop of the scissors and the third (middle) finger is inserted into the bottom loop, with the index finger being used beneath it to stabilise the grip. A second version employs two fingers in the bottom loop (where the scissors permit) with, once again, the thumb in the upper loop. Both grips are correct; it is safe to encourage whatever finger arrangement is most comfortable and functional for a particular child. Meanwhile, it is important that the hand holding the scissors is not bent forwards (flexed) at the wrist but is in line with the forearm (except when cutting around curves), and that the assisting hand can hold and guide the paper (or other object to be cut) with accuracy.

squeeze or spring scissors can be used to build confidence initially. To encourage snipping, cut playdough sausages or soft sweets for variety. When cutting paper, start with heavier paper to give greater stability. Next have the children combine two snips by using wide strips. Then they can cut along lines of reducing widths and finally cut around shapes. Remember to show them what to do with their stabilising hand to support the cutting hand.

Hand preference

Hand preference is a complex area. Handedness is biologically determined, and means that the arms and hands are asymmetrical in use and function so that individuals reliably favour one hand or the other for a range of tasks (Murray 1995). Handedness refers not only to which hand is preferred but to the degree of preference shown. Some research has indicated that hand preference is observed from as early as 2–3 months of age, as displayed in infants' favoured head orientation. By the age of two-and-a-half to 3 years, handedness is well established for the majority of children and remains consistent thereafter (Murray 1995). Subsequently, the degree of handedness and proportion of activities performed with the preferred hand increases over time.

    If children are aged 3 years or older and have not yet established firm hand preference, you might see that they use the hand closest to their activity; both hands might look awkward during skilled activities such as writing, cutting or drawing; or the children might swap hands during writing or drawing, often accompanied by frustration or avoidance of skilled hand activities.

    If children aged four years and over do not have a clearcut left-handed preference, it is probably better to guide them gently towards right-handedness (Chapparo 1998; Murray 1992). Alternatively, if the left hand is clearly the more accurate during particular tasks such as drawing, then support the dominance of that side. Keep in mind that some left-handers being taught activities by adult right-handers can feel confused as they attempt to imitate the adults. If individual children use the left hand for drawing and other pre-writing activities but choose the right hand for cutting, do not interfere unless their accuracy is clearly better with the left (Levine 1998). It is beneficial if the same hand is consistently used for the same tasks, but using different hands for different tasks is acceptable (Chapparo 1998).

    Activities that develop hand dominance include finger painting or reaching tasks where the children are encouraged to cross the midline of their body, and activities that encourage the hands to work together so that the children get into the habit of using the same hand to manipulate and perform the most skilled movements with the other hand holding and stabilising.

    Left-handers make up 10% of the population, although this proportion is slightly higher among people with learning or motor disabilities. This is thought to be because of some interference with brain development on the left side (remembering that the left side of the brain controls the right side of the body). This causes a naturally right-handed child who has some brain impairment to favour the left, in a pattern which has been termed 'pathological left-handedness' (Murray 1995). These children have to contend with living in a right-handers' world as well as with their learning or motor difficulties.

Some left-handers develop an awkward grip to allow them to view their work (Levine 1998). A common example is the hook grasp, where the wrist is bent around and above the writing. To prevent maladaptive patterns becoming established, ensure that children's tables are not too high so that they can rest their forearms on the table, position their hand to the left or below the writing line, encourage tripod grasp of the pencil but with the thumb slightly further away from the tip than is the case for right-handed children, and position paper to the left of the children's midline with the paper slanted left-side high at 45 degrees.

Because right-handed scissors, when used in the left, do not allow a view of the line being cut, provide left-handed or either hand scissors.

SELF-CARE ACTIVITIES

Their ability to perform self-care tasks independently gives children some control over their environment. Lack of ability in self-care skills compared with others can be isolating and lead to frustration.

Children's attainment of self-care skills will reflect cultural, class and family expectations as well as their intrinsic abilities (Henderson 1995), and closely reflects their acquisition of hand skills. With increased exposure at younger ages in playgroups and child care to children of the same age, observation of others performing independence tasks appears to motivate young children to learn the same skill.

Self-care skills have varying degrees of manipulative, perceptual and cognitive components (Henderson 1995). Encouraging development in self-care needs to focus on functional outcomes that will make a difference for the children and their families. Training is best achieved by direct practice of the desired skill, rather than concentrating on components of the task (Case-Smith 1996).

It is beyond the scope of this text to detail the many self-care tasks with which young children might have some difficulties. However, some general guidelines follow.

Dressing

When teaching dressing, begin with undressing, as this precedes dressing as a developmental skill. Meanwhile, remember that children learn one-handed skills before two-handed and so teach such tasks as doing up buttons at a later age. Another suggestion is to use the children's favourite clothes, those with an obvious front and back (e.g. those with designs or pictures on the front), and clothing and footwear large enough for easy donning. Hand garments to the children in such a way that they are already oriented to them, and allow children with poor balance to sit down when pulling on pants.

Toileting

This is another important independence skill. Children with sensory processing difficulties are unable to perceive correctly information from their touch and pressure receptors, and so have reduced awareness of their need to empty their bladder or bowel. Similarly, children with language difficulties often have difficulty gaining independence in toileting as some do not talk to themselves about the sensations that signal the need to use the toilet.

For children with mild developmental difficulties, the general guidelines suggested by and available from your local community health organisation for introducing toileting are likely to be useful. These will comprise advice such as ensuring that the children have ready access to a toilet and can remove their own clothing quickly and easily; that their feet are able to reach the floor while sitting on the toilet to maximise the use of muscles that assist with elimination; ensuring that they can reach and use taps; and helping position their hand for wiping their bottom. If children have suspected constipation, they will need to be assessed by a paediatrician or a general practitioner interested in family health. If failure to learn toileting has no physical or other developmental cause, psychologists or occupational therapists can assist with toilet learning, such as with the 'sneaky poo' program (White 1984).

Grooming and hygiene

Most preschoolers require assistance with the third area of self-care tasks—namely, grooming and hygiene tasks such as bathing and cleaning their teeth, hair and nails. When children have additional developmental needs, it often seems easier for carers to perform these tasks for them, but the children's ability to perform even aspects of these tasks can build feelings of mastery and promote later independence. Therefore it is useful to encourage the children's active involvement as soon as they show some interest. You can help by ensuring that they can reach the sink, taps and mirror; that they can sit if balance, postural control or stamina are problems for them; and that brushes have large handles that are easy to hold.

Self-feeding

Self-feeding is a crucial self-care or independence skill. It requires the motor skills of trunk stability, head and mouth control as well as eye–hand–mouth co-ordination. Sensory information needs to be interpreted accurately to facilitate an efficient eating process. Children with significant eating difficulties are likely to be managed by a paediatrician aided by a 'feeding team'—that is, a multi-disciplinary team with expertise in feeding issues.

When children have feeding difficulties (see Box 7.7) you might observe the following signs, with those with mild difficulties in this area exhibiting more subtle expressions.

Box 7.7 General suggestions to assist children with feeding difficulties

For detailed guidance, with parental permission refer children to your local relevant health professional—such as a speech pathologist for mouth control and swallowing difficulties, an occupational therapist for issues with sensory awareness and utensils, a physiotherapist for positioning and problems of muscle tone, and a dietitian for dietary requirements.

- Position children to maximise their function. To assist with postural security, use a chair with arms and ensure that the children's feet can be flat on the floor. The table should be at elbow height when the children's upper arms are at the sides of their body.
- Use utensils with large handles and which are attractive and comfortable for the children to hold. Some come with grip positions indicated by bumps on the handle. To help guide movement, support the children at the upper arm or elbow or, if required, have the children rest their elbows on the table to give additional support. For part of the meal, give some finger food to ease frustration.
- Remind children to close their mouth during eating. A visual cue could be used to minimise embarrassment in front of peers.
- Have a damp face cloth handy for children to wipe their face clean as part of their routine at the conclusion of mealtime.
- For children with hypersensitivity to textures, mouth preparation needs to occur prior to the meal. You can do this by giving firm pressure around the mouth by gently massaging the upper and lower lips using warm, clean or gloved fingers. Older preschoolers might be able to do this for themselves. Alternatively, to reduce sensitivity in the mouth, you can give deep pressure through the use of thickened fluids requiring firm sucking, such as custard through a thick straw. Crushed ice given prior to food can also reduce sensitivity. Once desensitising has been achieved, a new texture could be introduced to the child. Start with a small amount mixed with an already accepted texture.
- For children who lack mouth awareness, try activities to get their mouth ready such as imitation games with tongue, lips and cheeks, or have them 'brush' their teeth and lips with their finger covered by a face cloth.
- When low muscle tone is a difficulty, provide chewy food to develop mouth muscles such as sugar-free bubblegum, dried fruit straps or bread with thick crusts.
- Involve children in food preparation to assist their acceptance of food.
- New tastes take on average 10 presentations before they are accepted (Birch et al. 1995)—so keep trying. Avoid mixing too many tastes at once, and use the peer group to help encourage acceptance of new tastes.

- The children might drool excessively, and this is not better explained by teething or a blocked nose. This can indicate poor sensory awareness around the mouth so that the children are unaware that they do not have adequate lip seal. Another explanation would be that the children have low muscle tone in the facial muscles and so have trouble lifting their jaw against gravity.
- They might be very messy when eating, with food left around outside the mouth. This can indicate poor sensory awareness of the face, poor handling of utensils, poor hand-to-mouth control or a combination of all three.
- They could have excessive tongue movements, again suggesting poor sensory feedback and awareness of the tongue, and poor planning and control of tongue movement.
- Some children are hypersensitive to textures of food within their mouth and manifest this by eating only a limited range of foods, being reluctant to try new textures and gagging on food. Hypersensitivity to food textures is often associated with hypersensitivity to taste and even temperature of food and, predictably, to mealtime anxiety.

CONCLUSION

This chapter has explored children's sensory needs and their development of hand function and self-help skills and how these areas affect children's daily lives. The aim of programming for children in these domains is to assist them to gain independence and thereby contribute to their sense of mastery and self-worth. The suggestions offered provide starting points for helping children meet their own needs and develop their skills and can all be integrated into ongoing programming for routine activities in early childhood settings. By necessity, the information offered is simplified: some children will present with more complex difficulties about which it will be necessary to consult an occupational therapist or other relevant health professional.

Occupational therapy is a profession that has a significant contribution to make to children with atypical development. Nevertheless, not all gains must be made in direct therapy sessions: many can be attained through collaboration between therapists, educators and parents, whereby beneficial activities can be incorporated naturally into children's everyday activities in natural settings (Washington et al. 1994). Ongoing links between therapy settings and the children's homes and education venues will enhance the benefits of each to the children and their carers.

ADDITIONAL RESOURCES

Henderson, A. and Pehoski, C. (eds) 1995 *Hand function in the child: foundations for remediation* Mosby Year-Book, St Louis, MO

Klein, M.D. 1983 *Pre-dressing skills* rev. edn, Therapy Skill Builders, Tucson, AZ

——1990 *Pre-writing skills* rev. edn, Therapy Skill Builders, Tucson, AZ

——1999 *Pre-scissor skills* 3rd edn, Therapy Skill Builders, Tucson, AZ

Klein, M.D. and Morris, S.E. 2000 *Pre-feeding skills* 2nd edn, Therapy Skill Builders, Tucson, AZ

Shellenger S. and Williams, M.S. 1995 *The Alert program with songs for self regulation* Therapy Works, Albuquerque, NM

The following internet site has a good home page with information about paediatric occupational therapy: OTnetwork.com.au

8

HEARING

LINDSAY BURNIP

KEY POINTS

- Although hearing might seem to fall along a continuum from normal hearing to total deafness, there is a point along this continuum when vision replaces hearing as the main communication channel, in which case quantitative differences in hearing produce qualitative differences in learning style.
- Time is not a benign factor in childhood hearing impairment. The longer an impairment remains undetected, the more affected will be children's language acquisition and the more likely it is that this will result in secondary difficulties such as behavioural or social problems as well.
- Early childhood practitioners can assist children whose hearing is impaired by looking out for signs of impairment and recommending a hearing test, creating a helpful communication environment, developing an effective communication style, supporting the children and their parents emotionally, and helping the children to manage their hearing aids.

INTRODUCTION

Hearing loss in childhood takes many forms, from the slight reduction in hearing sensitivity that can occur during a heavy head cold through to the total inability to hear spoken language experienced by a small number of children. On the surface, it seems reasonable to assume that hearing ability forms a continuum, with normal hearing at one end and total deafness at the other. However, this continuum view can be misleading when we consider the effects of hearing loss on developing children. As McAnally and colleagues (1987:198) state:

> somewhere along the . . . continuum . . . hearing ceases to be the major communication channel and is replaced by vision; the child becomes linked to the world of communication by eye rather than by ear. This is the point at which a child can be

140

considered to be deaf rather than hard of hearing. The impairment shifts from being a difference in degree to being a difference in kind.

The management of severe and profound hearing loss in childhood is too broad to deal with in any real depth here. Instead, this chapter considers some of the common elements of childhood hearing loss and focuses on the more usual forms of hearing loss that occur in the early years, particularly those that arise from middle ear problems.

THE IMPORTANCE OF HEARING

Those of us with normal hearing can hear for some time before we are born, and come into the world already familiar with the sounds of daily life and with the sound of voices, particularly that of our own mother. These familiar sounds remain the background music to our lives. Our ears are our connection to our world and, unlike the sense of vision, our hearing sense is switched on at all times: when we go to sleep, we close our eyes but not our ears. The unfamiliar creak of a floor board or the all-too-familiar cry of a child can bring us instantly awake. Even in deep sleep, some level of our consciousness is listening to the world.

As children, we hear the speech of those around us and, long before we can understand the meanings of words, we learn to identify and draw meaning from the patterns of speech. The many adaptations that adults make to their speech when addressing babies and young children are well recorded and readily observable. A major figure in the area of language development, Roger Brown (1973), coined the rather delightful term 'Baby talk' to describe these adaptations which include exaggerated pitch changes, frequent repetitions, short utterances, and conversational role-play in which the adults provide both their own and the children's conversational turns. Babies and infants are very attracted to these speech styles, which most caregivers use instinctively and unselfconsciously. Researchers believe that these early baby talk interactions provide the 'scaffolding' or support structures within which young children learn how to produce the language of their community and how to use that language in conversation. Almost all of this learning—social, communicative and linguistic—occurs through hearing.

It is easy to appreciate the difficulties that a significant hearing loss might cause when learning a spoken language, but some other effects on communicative interactions are less straightforward. For example, when parents interact with their normally hearing children they observe the child's actions, predict the likely object of their attention and offer appropriate commentary on that object, while the child is engaged with it. That is, parents guess what their child is thinking, then talk about it. This match between child attention and parental language is referred to as 'contingency' (Bamford & Saunders 1991).

In contrast, for children with limited hearing it may not be possible for parent and child to establish 'mutual gaze' and talk at the same time as they look. In such cases the adult must attract the child's attention, then communicate. When the child's attention must be gained before communicating, the conversation is no longer contingent on—that is, related to—the child's engagement: the probability will be higher that the child is no longer thinking about the object or event when it is being commented on. The linguistic interaction between parent and child becomes sequential rather than occurring in parallel. Thus, children's awareness of contingency—of the connection between language and action—is believed to be reduced by significant childhood hearing impairment (Wood et al. 1986).

The early communicative experiences of children with impaired hearing are likely to be quantitatively and qualitatively different from those of normally hearing children and, in general, less useful in helping them to develop social and linguistic skills in a normal manner. It is possible to use visual rather than spoken communication styles (e.g. a sign language) but this requires first that the child's hearing loss is identified very early, which it usually is not, and second that the parents quickly learn a new set of unfamiliar skills, which is a very difficult task.

Hearing impairment does not in itself affect children's acquisition of social skills. However, where the development of communication skills is delayed, regardless of whether speech or sign is used, interactions with parents and other adults can become more difficult (Jamieson 1994), and the acquisition of some social skills may be delayed (Sass-Lehrer 1999). Children with hearing impairments with delayed language skills can also have difficulties in their interactions with other children, and have been found to show a strong preference for playmates who also have impaired hearing, suggesting that even at 4 years of age they have already established a sense of social-self which is distinctively different from that of their normally hearing peers (Brown & Remine 1996).

THE NATURE OF HEARING LOSS

The mechanisms of the hearing apparatus are illustrated in Figure 8.1. In order to hear a speaker or other sound source, the sound must:

- pass down the ear canal of the listener;
- vibrate the ear drum;
- pass through the middle ear;
- create a pressure wave inside the cochlea, causing a group of hair cells to 'fire'.

The nerve impulse created by the hair cell firing must pass out of the cochlea and through the various processing stages en route to the brain.

This can be thought of as the 'hearing chain', and hearing impairment occurs when the transmission of sound is reduced or blocked at any point in this chain. Three important parameters of hearing loss are its degree, type and age at onset.

Degree of hearing loss
The degree of loss is usually described as being mild, moderate, severe or profound, and is plotted on a form called an audiogram. This plots intensity against frequency, which is roughly the same as loudness against pitch. Interpreting an

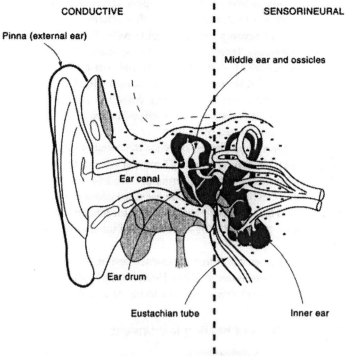

Figure 8.1 The ear in cross-section showing regions of conductive and sensorineural hearing loss

audiogram is not straightforward, as these graphs are intended to convey information from one audiologist (hearing scientist) to another, not to indicate to lay persons what a particular child can and cannot hear. To obtain this information you should seek the assistance of an expert in the area, such as the child's audiologist or a specialist teacher of the deaf. However, it must be understood that the degree of a hearing loss will not be, in itself, a reliable indicator of the impact of that hearing loss on a child's development. Numerous other factors must be considered.

Age of onset of hearing loss

Because childhood hearing impairment of any degree can affect language development, the age at onset of the loss is most important. All else being equal, a hearing impairment acquired after the development of normal language skills will have a much less disabling effect than a loss present at birth or soon after. The management of a prelingually deafened child (as the condition is known) is significantly different from that of a later-deafened child.

Type of hearing loss

There are two types of hearing impairment: sensorineural and conductive. Sensorineural impairments are caused in the inner ear or beyond; conductive loss occurs when the transmission of sound is impeded by a blockage in the outer or middle ear (see Figure 8.1). A problem in both is referred to as *mixed*.

The two forms of hearing loss are qualitatively different from each other. With conductive hearing losses, sounds can be inaudible but, if made loud enough, are understandable; whereas sensorineural hearing losses can cause both inaudibility and sound distortion. Using a radio analogy, conductive hearing impairment has an effect similar to turning down the radio's volume, while a sensorineural hearing impairment has an effect analogous to a radio with the volume turned down and tuned off station.

Conductive hearing impairment is by far the commonest form of childhood hearing impairment, generating around 24 million visits to the doctor in the USA alone (Mitka 1999). Many different terms are used to describe this condition, including ear infections, glue ear, middle ear disease/disorder and, more technically, otitis media. This last term is simply Latin for middle ear inflammation, so they all mean much the same thing—problems in the middle ear that are likely to affect hearing.

It is believed that most children experience one or two bouts of otitis media in their early years (Bluestone & Klein 1988). Despite this high prevalence, in general otitis media is seldom serious in terms of its impact on development,

---

Box 8.1 The effects of hearing impairment

Degree	Likely effects
Mild	Without a hearing aid, children with a mild hearing impairment will probably hear quite normally when close to a speaker and in quiet conditions. At a distance or in noisy settings, that same child is likely to be able to detect speech but might have some difficulty in understanding it fully. (For further information, see Bess et al. 1998; Tharpe & Bess 1999.)
Moderate	A moderate hearing impairment will cause even greater difficulties in hearing speech, and children with this degree of impairment will be at a great disadvantage without a hearing aid.
Severe/profound	Attainment levels in language and academic skills are typically low (Diefendorf 1996).

Unilateral hearing impairment

The erroneous view persists that unilateral hearing impairment—normal hearing in one ear but a loss in the other—is relatively unimportant in young children. (After all, they have two ears and can turn their head if necessary!) But research tells us that this condition can cause difficulties in acquiring language skills and, consequently, in language-based learning tasks (Diefendorf 1996; English & Church 1999). Later difficulties with reading and writing are not uncommon, even though affected children usually develop age-appropriate spoken language skills.

partly because it is usually transient in nature. However, some children have more frequent and more severe bouts, and the hearing impairment that results tends to be greater in degree and more long-lasting.

This more severe form causes a slight to mild hearing impairment which fluctuates over time. The terms 'slight' and 'mild' can be misleading, however, as the long-term effects of recurrent otitis media can be anything but slight (e.g. see Clark & Jaindl 1996; also Roberts et al. 1997), with research linking this condition to reduced language attainment and increased behavioural difficulties (Wilks et al. 1999). Children who are otherwise in good health and with no other impediment to learning may be able to compensate for the relatively small degree of hearing difficulty that comes and goes from day to day, and may suffer no longer-term ill-effects. Other children will be much less able to cope with their fluctuating hearing if, for example, the language of their preschool is not the language of home. This appears to be the case with Aboriginal children with a history of otitis media who experience greater than usual difficulty in listening in noisy environments, particularly when listening to English (Yonowitz et al. 1995).

CAUSES OF HEARING IMPAIRMENT

The hearing mechanisms contain the smallest bones in the body and some of the most fragile structures. Permanent sensorineural hearing loss can result when these vulnerable mechanisms fail to form correctly as a result of genetic or developmental mishaps or are damaged by viral or bacterial infections (e.g. rubella, CMV, syphilis, measles, mumps and meningitis), by ototoxic drugs (e.g. some members of the group of antibiotics whose names end in 'mycin'), and by trauma (e.g. arising from car accidents). A strong risk factor for hearing impairment in children is low birth weight (van Naarden & Decouflé 1999), and admission to a neonatal intensive care unit for 48 hours or longer (Kennedy 2000). This latter risk factor has increased greatly in recent years (Bamiou et al. 1999), presumably as a result of improved medical technologies and procedures helping very low weight and/or premature babies survive in greater numbers.

Very occasionally, children are born with one or both ear canals absent, often with a malformed or absent outer ear. This is called congenital atresia, and gives rise to a conductive hearing impairment that will remain until an artificial ear canal is created surgically.

The commonest form of hearing loss—otitis media, which is of the conductive type of loss—is related in part to lifestyle; as such, its prevalence and severity are considerably higher among some groups than among others. In Australia, Aboriginal children are especially at risk (McPherson 1990), as are similar indigenous groups elsewhere (e.g. McShane & Mitchell 1979). Children who attend child care centres also appear to have higher rates of otitis media (Amarjit & Scott 1999), and there is a suggestion that this might also be the case among children who use pacifiers (CNN 2000) and those who are subjected to passive smoking (Clark & Jaindl 1996). Nevertheless, although some of the risk factors

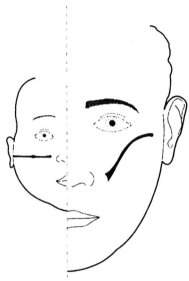

Figure 8.2 Comparison of the angle of the eustachian tube in children and adults

for otitis media appear to be related to lifestyle, the condition is not wholly preventable (Medley et al. 1995).

This is partly explained by considering the structure of the middle ear. It consists of an eardrum over a cavity which contains a string of tiny bones (the ossicles) joining the rear of the eardrum to the inner ear (see Figure 8.1). To function properly, the air pressure inside the middle ear cavity must be the same as the pressure outside. If it is not, the ear drum will not be free to move as it should in response to incoming sound waves, thus reducing the ability to hear.

The tasks of equalising air pressure on each side of the eardrum and of draining any middle ear secretions are performed by the eustachian tube. This joins the middle ear to the back of the nose and throat and is normally closed, but opens when we swallow or yawn, allowing air to flow in or out. In young children the tube lies at a much flatter angle than in adults and as a result functions much less efficiently (see Figure 8.2). Children typically acquire a more adult-like angle of the eustachian tube at around the age of 7, but prior to that are very susceptible to blockage of the tube and thus to a build-up of pressure and fluid in the middle ear. This may remain for a long time and become infected or glue-like, resulting in various forms of otitis media with consequent effects on hearing.

INTERVENING WITH HEARING IMPAIRMENT

Early childhood practitioners can help children with hearing impairment in the following ways:

- Assist in the identification of children with impaired hearing.
- Create a helpful communication environment.
- Develop an effective communication style.
- Provide support to children and their families.
- Support children's mode of communication.
- Assist in the management of hearing aids.

Identify children with impaired hearing

Given the impact that hearing impairment can have on the development of early language, it is important to identify as early as possible children who have a significant hearing loss (Downs & Yoshinaga-Itano 1999; Roizen 1998). The prevalence of serious, permanent hearing impairment in young children is not high: estimates vary depending on the criteria used but are typically around 1 or 2 per 1000 live births (Department of Human Services 1998; Steel 2000), so large-scale screening is called for rather than the more expensive diagnostic testing. Early childhood hearing screening procedures have been available for a long time and, with recent advances in technology, have become cheaper, easier and more accurate.

Expert opinion has it that screening should be performed around 3 months of age and, where necessary, intervention begun before 6 months (Finitzo 2000). However, in most countries we are far from achieving these targets. In 1996 in Victoria in Australia, a state with a relatively good hearing screening system, the median age of diagnosis was 10.43 months (Department of Human Services 1998), but in Australia more generally some areas are poorly served by hearing screening programs, and the majority of children are not tested until after 2 years of age (Winton et al. 1998). In the UK, the average age at detection has been reported to be 26 months, with intervention not begun until 32 months (Abbasi 1997).

Because hearing screening programs are at present so incomplete, many children with hearing impairment remain undetected through their early years. This fact makes it essential for early childhood professionals to be vigilant in their observations. Time is not a benign factor in childhood hearing impairment: the longer the impairment remains undetected, the more developmental opportunities children miss out on and the greater will be their resulting disability.

Thus, until effective universal hearing screening programs become available, we should assume that a proportion of young children in early childhood settings will have an undetected hearing impairment. Even when wide-scale screening is in place, we will still have the continuing problem of recurrent otitis media. Box 8.2 lists some observable behaviours that can be indicative of a hearing difficulty. Of course, some of these indicators are consistent with normal childhood behaviour and thus a checklist such as this should not be used in a prescriptive manner, but if a child exhibits several of these indicators a referral for a hearing test is in order.

If you find yourself or other adults saying of individual children, 'They can hear when they want to', you should consider seriously the possibility of hearing

Box 8.2 Some indicators of possible hearing impairment

Children with hearing losses might:

* have frequent upper respiratory tract infections, coughs, colds or throat infections;
* currently have an ear infection;
* turn their head towards a sound source;
* appear 'blocked-up', snore and breathe through their mouth;
* have some craniofacial abnormalities, including cleft palate;
* report or have a history of ear trouble;
* report earache, 'popping ears', or fullness in the ear;
* have periods of irritability or atypical aggression;
* appear to daydream, and be more 'with it' when close to a speaker;
* want to sit near to the TV, or have volume louder than usual;
* watch a speaker's face intently;
* cup their ear with a hand;
* not turn when called;
* search for rather than locating a sound source quickly;
* ask for repetition of instructions or watch others;
* misunderstand or be slow in responding;
* give inappropriate answers;
* be inattentive and restless;
* show inconsistent listening behaviour, 'switching off' in noise;
* withdraw and not mix well;
* have poor concentration and become tired easily;
* have speech that is unusually soft or loud or indistinct;
* evidence a fluctuating pace of learning.

Source: adapted from Webster (1986).

difficulties. This is a classic comment made about children with fluctuating, conductive hearing impairment. In reality, these children can hear on some occasions and under some conditions but not others.

When a child appears to require a hearing test, staff can assist by encouraging parents to make a referral and by helping them determine the best place to go. In recommending to parents that their child have a hearing assessment, the following information might be useful:

* In Australia, children are not charged for hearing tests.
* These tests are non-invasive and children usually find them fun.
* Parents may wish to involve their child's general practitioner but a medical referral is *not* required for a hearing test.
* Do not try to test a child's hearing yourself: it is too easy to get it wrong.
* It is not appropriate for young children to have hearing tests at the commercial vision and hearing agencies commonly found in shopping centres, as the staff in these facilities will rarely have received specialised paediatric training.

- State health authorities are responsible for hearing testing of children and should be approached first. The contact number for the relevant state health agency will be in your local telephone directory, probably under 'Health' or in the state government section.

Create a helpful communication environment

Children with impaired hearing often use vision to compensate for reduced hearing. To make this easier, ensure that the room is adequately lit but without harsh lighting and reflective glare.

Distance, noise and reverberation are all major hindrances to effective communication for children with impaired hearing. Taking each of these impediments in turn, with distance sounds lose their intensity, and speech delivered across a large room might be quite unintelligible through a hearing aid, especially if contaminated by noise and reverberation.

Noise creates particular difficulties for those with hearing impairment, particularly young children. Normal conversation contains a great deal of redundancy—that is, the same information is present in various forms. So, if one piece is obscured by noise an alternative is often available, if one knows how to interpret it. Young children with hearing impairments can have insufficient knowledge of the structure of language and the rules governing conversation to take advantage of this redundancy. In noise, they are at double jeopardy: the noise hides some of the speech, and their limited linguistic skill reduces the benefit they can derive from what is left.

Reverberation is a little more complex than echo but can be understood in those terms. This occurs in most rooms—especially those with hard, shiny surfaces—and can seriously reduce speech intelligibility for children with hearing impairment, again at levels that might cause no discernible difficulty for people with normal hearing. Reverberation often combines with noise and distance to create a poor communication environment for children with impaired hearing. Reducing noise and reverberation in rooms, although highly desirable, may be beyond the resources and skills of most people. Choosing a less noisy and/or reverberant room may be an option, but one can often compensate for even a poor communication environment by getting close to a child with impaired hearing and using the effective communication strategies suggested below.

Develop an effective communication style

The way we communicate—our voice level, rate of speech, complexity of language—and the strategies we employ can greatly affect how well we are understood by children (and adults) who have impaired hearing. Becoming aware of what we do when we communicate and changing these behaviours is not easy, but becoming an effective and supportive communication partner might be the greatest assistance we can provide to children in our care who have hearing impairment. Some suggestions for effective communication strategies include the following.

- Before conversing, direct the child's attention on you and your face.
- Have the lighting on your face, not in the child's eyes. Avoid having a brightly lit window behind you.
- Identify the topic of conversation early. Use props and gestures as necessary.
- Face children when talking with them: in front and not too high and not too low—and avoid unnecessary movement.
- Don't exaggerate your speech or lip patterns: exaggerations make you look silly and make understanding harder, not easier.
- Don't obscure your mouth with pencils, hands, moustaches etc.
- Use visual aids to support your conversation.
- Speak at a strong normal voice level—that is, at the upper range of your normal level. This should not cause vocal strain.
- Increase the intonation patterns in your voice—that is, the rise and fall in pitch—in much the same manner as one does instinctively with very young children.
- If your voice pitch is naturally very high, try to lower your pitch a little but not so much that you suffer vocal strain.
- Emphasise the key words in your sentences a little.
- Provide non-verbal cues (e.g. meaningful facial expressions and natural gestures).

Support children and their families

For many parents, the initial phases following the diagnosis of a disability in their child are traumatic (see chapter 2). The great majority of children who have impaired hearing are born to hearing parents, and those hearing parents typically have as little knowledge of hearing impairment and its effects as the average lay person. The years following diagnosis can be very stressful as parents acquire new knowledge and attempt to understand and come to terms with the atypical needs of their child. Effective counselling for this group requires skilled personnel who are also knowledgeable about the impact of childhood hearing impairment, although early childhood staff can help by providing an empathic and supportive ear.

Understand that communicating in a hearing-speaking world when one does neither well can be a tiring and frustrating experience. Young children with hearing impairment may expend energy faster and tire more readily than their hearing peers. Where the hearing impairment has resulted in delayed language and perhaps reduced speech intelligibility, children may have greater than normal difficulty in interactions with adults and other children. Such difficulty may result in displays of anger and aggression. These children can be assisted with social skills interventions (see chapter 11).

Support children's mode of communication (speech or sign)

The great majority of children with hearing impairment develop spoken language skills, although these may be delayed and voice quality ('naturalness') may be affected if the hearing impairment is moderate or greater. A small number of children need a visual mode of communication to supplement what they can hear and lip-read. This is a complex field, and determining which children require a visual mode of communication and which do not is difficult and often controversial. To complicate matters further, there is a range of sign languages and sign systems from which to select. There is an extensive literature on this: a good starting point for further study would be Paul and Quigley (1990).

Assist in the management of hearing aids

If a child in your care has been fitted with hearing aids, find out as much about the devices as you can. Information can usually be obtained from the child's parents or, with parental permission, from the audiologist who fitted the aids. Modern hearing aids are sophisticated and expensive devices, but their effective use with young children requires some knowledge and skill on the part of the adults who care for and communicate with them. This is particularly important, as hearing aid technology is advancing rapidly, quickly rendering textbook descriptions obsolete. Nevertheless, the following key features are worth noting.

The primary task of a hearing aid is to pick up wanted sounds, make these louder, and deliver them to the wearer's ear. Secondary but important considerations are that the aids be as uncomplicated and unobtrusive as possible. These two features can be in opposition to each other, in that aids that fit right inside the ear canal (in contrast to those conventional aids that sit behind the ear) usually suffer a reduction in amplifying power and increased difficulty of management for little fingers, making these very small and unobtrusive hearing aids often unsuitable for young children.

Ear moulds and hearing aids are fitted to each ear individually, so care must be taken to ensure that these are replaced correctly. The left-ear hearing aid is unlikely to work well if placed in the right ear, and the ear mould most certainly will not! Also, hearing aids do not work well with ear moulds blocked with cerumen (wax) or tubing that is partly filled with water. Moisture in the tubing can result from perspiration or condensation. It filters out some of the higher frequencies and can even flow into the hearing aid and cause corrosion.

Moisture should be removed using a puffer similar to that used to remove dust from a camera lens. A caution: putting the end of the tubing into the mouth and blowing may visibly remove the moisture in the tubing, but when the wet and warm air from the lungs cools, moisture will be added.

Wax can be removed by washing the mould with warm, soapy water (avoiding strong detergents), but sometimes the wax is rather hard and difficult to dissolve. In such cases, it must be picked out without damaging the ear mould. Scratching with a sharp object such as a piece of wire can create raised edges on the ear mould which, in turn, can irritate the wearer's ear. A device with a closed loop of wire is preferable.

Flat batteries are a major cause of hearing aid malfunction and one that is readily avoidable. Batteries should be checked regularly using a reliable battery tester. To check that you know how to operate the tester correctly, test a battery when it is new to ascertain exactly what the reading should be.

Hearing aids are sophisticated devices but can malfunction, especially if subjected to rough handling. A regular listening test is highly recommended, which is best done using a stethoclip, available from medical supply stores, hearing aid dealers or through the child's audiologist, who can also show you how to carry out a listening test effectively and safely.

Conventional hearing aids amplify all sounds that reach the microphone and work best when a speaker is nearby. However, real-world communication often involves listening to speakers and other sound sources that are not close by. Sounds drop in intensity as they travel through the air and may also get 'mixed up' with other, unwanted sounds. This can be a major difficulty for children who have hearing impairments and has led to the development of various types of FM hearing aid systems. These typically use a microphone and transmitter worn by an adult and a receiver unit linked to the child's hearing aids. FM systems are highly recommended as an addition to conventional hearing aids for young children (ASHA 1991), and as stand-alone systems (i.e. without a conventional hearing aid) for some children with mild hearing impairment (Edwards 1996).

The cochlear implant—sometimes called a bionic ear—is now used with most children in the developed world who are born with a profound hearing impairment or acquire such a loss during childhood. This device consists of a thin wire implanted inside the cochlea (inner ear) and a speech processor worn by the child. When used in conjunction with a high-quality and ongoing intervention program, the cochlear implant can enable children to use auditory means to learn and communicate, rather than relying on their vision as they would if profoundly deaf. This is a rather technical and controversial field, but Tye-Murray (1992) provides a good starting point to understand some of the issues.

CONCLUSION

Hearing impairment in childhood can have a major impact on the development of speech and language, often also affecting later academic and vocational attainment. Time is not a benign factor for young children with impaired hearing and, although early detection and intervention are widely agreed to be essential, they are not as yet a reality for most children. Early childhood practitioners can play an important role in detecting hearing impairment, in modifying the environment to maximise the children's hearing, and in making themselves more understanding and skilled communication partners.

ADDITIONAL RESOURCES

Anonymous (no date) 'Where do we go from hear?: support to parents of deaf, hard of hearing children, infant, baby, and newborns'. Retrieved 8 February 2001 from the World Wide Web: http://www.gohear.org/

ASHA (no date) 'Questions and answers about otitis media, hearing and language development'. Retrieved 18 August 1999 from the World Wide Web: http://www.kidsource.com/ASHA/otitis.html

Deslandes, S. and Burnip, L.G. 1995 'Choosing an early intervention program for hearing impaired children' *Australasian Journal of Special Education* vol. 19, no. 2, pp. 54–61

Flexer, C. (ed.) 1994 *Facilitating hearing and listening in young children* Singular Press, San Diego, CA

Health Pages 1998 'Easing your child's ear infection'. Retrieved 20 February 2001 from the World Wide Web: http://my.webmd.com/content/dmk/dmk_article_6462929

Lane, S., Bell, L. and Parson-Tylka, T. 1997 *My turn to learn: a communication guide for parents of deaf or hard of hearing children* The Elks Family Hearing Resource Center, Burnaby, BC, Canada

NIDCD 1997 'Otitis media fact sheet' The National Institute on Deafness and Other Communication Disorders. Retrieved 20 February 2001 from the World Wide Web: http://my.webmd.com/content/dmk/dmk_article_4461625

Ross, M. 1991 'Hearing aids and systems' in *When your child is deaf: a guide for parents* D.M. Luterman & M. Ross (eds) (pp. 105–36) York, Parkton, MD

9

COMMUNICATION SKILLS

BERNICE BURNIP

KEY POINTS

- Communication refers to the act of exchanging information, ideas, needs and desires. While speech and language are only part of the larger process of communication, they do provide the most important and efficient means for communication by human beings.
- In order to develop typical language skills, infants require a language-rich environment, with caregivers who communicate often with them and respond to their initiations of conversation.
- Difficulties with the acquisition of language affect children academically, socially and personally.
- Intervention for children's language learning difficulties must be based on a sound knowledge of normal language development and a detailed assessment of their language difficulties, with interventions ranging from naturalistic methods to structured teaching of specific language skills.

INTRODUCTION

Communication plays a central role in human development and behaviour throughout life. It allows us to express our needs and desires, to exchange information and ideas, to learn about the world, and to become social beings. As most children seem to learn to talk so quickly and effortlessly, the complexity of this task tends to be taken for granted—that is, until difficulties emerge.

Communication disorders represent one of the most prevalent disabilities in early childhood and are the single most common reason for special education referral (Casby 1989, in Warren 2000). An estimated 7% of preschool children and 2–3% of school-aged children have a specific language impairment that is not related to another disability, while as many as 15% of school-aged children

154

have communication disorders with and without other disabilities (Heward 2000; Shames et al. 1998; Vaughn et al. 2000).

Typically developing children have established a strong foundation in language skills by the time they start school. Thus, the critical period for language acquisition is considered to be before the age of 5 (Chomsky 1957); therefore, if problems with the development of communication skills exist, it is vitally important to identify and intervene with these during the preschool years.

Children who have difficulty making themselves understood or who cannot understand what others say to them are likely to be disadvantaged academically, socially and personally. Academically, language and/or communication disorders are strongly linked to learning difficulties, particularly in the area of reading and writing (Aram & Nation 1980). When children have a problem in the development of language, school readiness will be delayed. Socially, children with delayed language development have been found to be delayed in their pretend play (Rescorla & Goossens 1992). Personally, their inability to communicate effectively may result in their developing alternative and disruptive behaviours—such as pushing, hitting or yelling—to try to get their meaning across. In fact, 50% of preschool children with language difficulties have been observed to have behavioural difficulties (Cantwell & Baker 1987). Alternatively, children with impaired language might seem shy and passive and make little attempt to initiate conversation. Early identification and intervention are crucial to preventing these associated difficulties.

THE COMPONENTS OF COMMUNICATION

Communication refers to the act of exchanging information, ideas, needs and desires (Owens 2001). It involves the organisation and representation of a thought in a mutually agreed form so that it can be shared with another being. Communicative competence indicates an ability to convey a message effectively and appropriately as well as determining how well the message was conveyed (Dore 1986). Communication comprises many aspects, as depicted in Figure 9.1. The two broadest categories are non-linguistic (non-verbal) and linguistic (verbal) communication.

Non-verbal communication

Non-linguistic aspects that contribute to the effect of the spoken message include facial expression, eye contact, gestures, body posture, head and body movement, distance from the listener, manual sign, writing, drawing, or representational symbols (Banbury & Hebert 1992). In face-to-face communication, it is estimated that up to 60% of the information may be relayed in these non-linguistic ways (Owens 2001). Given that there are cultural differences in the use of non-linguistic features, when a signal from one culture is used within another language and culture the intended meaning of a message may be altered (Cartwright et al. 1995).

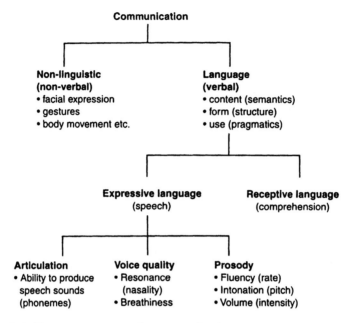

Figure 9.1 The components of communication

Language

The second broad category of communication is **verbal** or language skills (see Figure 9.1). Although these skills are only part of the larger process of communication, they are the most important and efficient means for communication by human beings.

Language has been defined as 'a code whereby ideas about the world are represented through a conventional system of arbitrary signals for communication' (Bloom & Lahey 1978). In order to understand atypical communication skills, it will be useful to explain the complex rule systems of language in terms of its components: content (meaning or semantics), form (syntax, morphology and phonology), and use (pragmatics) (Bloom & Lahey 1978).

Content

The content of language is its meaning—what an utterance is referring to or is about. This is called *semantics*. Words do not refer directly to an event, object or relationship, but to a concept which is built up as individuals' experiences and perceptions are categorised, organised and related to one another. These concepts are then stored in semantic memory, which contains word and symbol definitions and is primarily verbal.

Language form

This refers to the order and form of words. It comprises syntax, morphology and phonological structure. Taking each of these aspects in turn, *syntax* is the system of rules that guides the way sentences are produced and understood. It specifies the way words are organised or combined within different sentence types, which will provide more information than the individual symbols themselves. For example, the words 'Dog the brown is' make little sense compared with 'The dog is brown', and their meaning is different again from 'Is the dog brown?'. The rules for the combination of words give language an order and allow creative use. An infinite number of sentences can be created from the limited number of symbols and rules for combining those symbols (Owens 2001): every day we create sentences that have never before been produced in exactly the same way by anyone else.

Morphology is concerned with the internal organisation of words. A morpheme is the smallest unit of meaning in language; it cannot be divided any further and still remain a meaningful unit. Some morphemes are the content words of a language (nouns, verbs, adjectives and adverbs) and some serve grammatical functions in linking the content words (e.g. articles, prepositions and conjunctions). Some morphemes are grammatical markers, such as 'ed' or 'ing', and cannot stand alone as words. As children learn morphological and syntactical rules they often make errors in applying these, as in saying 'I eated my tea'. The fact that children make such errors suggests that they do not learn the rules merely by imitating what they hear.

Phonology is the sound system of spoken language. Unlike morphemes, phonemes do not carry meaning by themselves but are combined in specific ways to form words. The English language has approximately 45 phonemes, which are reduced to 26 written letters. For instance, the letter 'a' sounds different in the words 'car', 'cat' and 'caught'. As children acquire the individual sounds (or phonemes), they must also learn the phonological rules that govern the sequencing and distribution of phonemes within their language. In terms of sequencing, they must be able to say 'animal' rather than 'aminal', for example. In terms of distribution, English words do not start with /sd/ whereas /st/ is common. These rules vary between languages, and it is only through experience with a first language that a child learns which sounds may go with others.

Use (or pragmatics)

This third aspect of language refers to its purpose or function. It is concerned with how language is used to communicate intent and to gain what is wanted from the environment. In order to communicate effectively, as well as knowing about form and content children need to know about social appropriateness, so that they can use language appropriately in different contexts, depending on the specific topic of conversation, the situation, the relation of speaker and listener, and so on.

Pragmatic rules relate to both verbal and non-verbal behaviours and include turn-taking, establishing and maintaining a topic, implementing repair strategies when the communication is not successful, and terminating a conversation. The acquisition of these skills begins well before children produce their first words, as seen in the prelinguistic acts of pointing combined with vocalisation and eye gaze in attempts to communicate with adults. Children such as those with Asperger syndrome (see Appendix I) who have not developed these pragmatic skills may seem very different from other children in their preschool group (Rinaldi 2000).

In summary, these three aspects can be illustrated in a child's request: 'Can we go to the park?'. The *content* of this utterance refers to a specific place for recreational activity which, in this case, is likely to have children's play equipment; its *form* is a six-word interrogative sentence; and the *use* or purpose of the utterance is to go to the park.

Linguistic competence refers to individuals' underlying knowledge about this complex system of rules. This knowledge is often intuitive in that users and listeners might not be able to state the rules but can use them effectively. In normal conversation this inability is not a problem, as the purpose of language is to share the information. However, when the speaker is a child who consistently produces utterances that do not fit the agreed rules, it becomes necessary for adult listeners to identify the problem, which requires more than an intuitive knowledge of the rules of language.

Comprehension (receptive language)

Children understand some of the language around them well before they produce their first words. The repetitiveness of daily routines and their accompanying verbal and non-verbal exchanges with caregivers allows children to develop an understanding of some of the words that are used in those contexts. Before producing their first word at around 10 months, infants typically understand approximately 10 words heard in context and may understand 50 words by 13 months of age, even though they do not produce their first 50 words until about 18 months (Benedict 1977). Throughout life, receptive language skills continue to exceed expressive language skills: even adults understand many more words and language structures than we typically use in our spoken language.

Speech (expressive language)

Speech involves the use of an auditory-articulatory code to represent spoken language. It is the actual mechanical act of producing phonemes (that is, sounds) within a language. Unless the speaker and listener share the code, speech is a series of meaningless sounds. The speakers of any language have agreed on the symbols that will be used and the rules that will be followed when combining those symbols. Languages are continually changing, with new words being added and others falling into disuse.

Speech comprises three key aspects:

- **Articulation.** The production of the specific sounds (phonemes) and sound combinations of a language is one of the more complex and difficult human endeavours, requiring precise neuromuscular coordination. The unique structure of the human vocal tract allows the production of a variety and complexity of sounds that cannot be matched by any other species (Owens 2001). Box 9.1 details the typical sequence of the production of consonants.

- **Voice quality** (comprising resonance and breathiness).
- **Prosody** (comprising rate, intonation and volume).

The last two aspects are the 'paralinguistic' aspects of communication, and enhance the meaning of a message by signalling the speaker's attitude. For example, a fast rate of production often indicates excitement, whereas slow, hesitating speech may accompany a difficult or upsetting topic of conversation.

FACILITATORS OF LANGUAGE ACQUISITION

Children have a need to communicate long before they have the ability to use language. They begin to communicate so that they can achieve something. This may be to meet a need, such as to assuage hunger, reduce discomfort or gain attention. Most importantly, language provides children with a means of controlling their environment.

Although parents usually consider the appearance of their child's first word as the beginning of language, there has actually been much meaningful communication between parent and child prior to that event. Children's understanding or receptive language skills thus exceed their production or expressive language skills.

For infants to develop typical language skills, they require a reasonably stimulating environment, with reasonably verbal caregivers who provide a reasonably warm and caring atmosphere and who communicate reasonably often with the infants. This will result in an internalised language system which will provide the foundation of the children's receptive and expressive language in early childhood as well as the base for subsequent literacy skills and academic achievement (Quigley & Kretschmer 1982). Note that the word 'reasonably' is used to emphasise that, for typically developing children, some disruptions in the process can take place without resulting in serious language delay.

In many cultures, including English-speaking ones, there is an expectation that babies will communicate from the earliest age. In fact, many parents talk to the fetus in-utero, as if their baby can understand. But such passive exposure to communication is not sufficient for the development of language: meaningful communicative interaction with a mature language user is essential.

Initially, the prosodic elements of language are more important than the words as in the early stages words do not have meaning for infants. Rather it is the aspects of speech such as pitch, intonation patterns and variation in intensity that engage infants in a meaningful way.

Adult input is extremely important to children's understanding of the meaning of words—that is, their semantic development. An understanding of words gradually develops as infants become able to attach meaning to often-repeated phrases that occur in routine happenings. They learn the meanings of

Box 9.1 Typical sequence of the production of consonants in Australian English

Consonants	Typical age of accurate production	Comments
p, b, m, n	By 2½ years	Infants' suckling (moving their tongue in and out of their mouth while drinking milk) and later sucking (moving the tongue within the mouth during spoon feeding) facilitate lip control. Thus sounds made with the lips are the earliest to be produced, followed by those that rely on tongue control. Munching and chewing of solid foods teach jaw control and stablisation, paving the way for the production of the remaining speech sounds.
h, w, t, d	By 3 years	By this age, children's speech should be easy to understand around 80–90% of the time.
g, k, y	By 3½ years	This group of sounds tend to develop at a slightly earlier age in girls compared with boys.
f, sh, ch, /dg/ (as in treasure), bl, fl, sl, sn, st, kr, gr, sm, str	By 4 years +	The consonant blends and clusters may begin to appear as early as 4 years of age but the full range of clusters are not acquired until the ages of 7 or 8 years.
l, z, v, s	By 5 years +	These fricatives and the liquid l develop gradually. Although z and y tend to be acquired a little later, some children may produce these sounds as early as 3 years of age.
th (voiced as in 'thumb' and unvoiced as in 'father'), r	By 7 years	Until this age, children typically continue to use w instead of r (e.g. 'wabbit' instead of 'rabbit').

Source: adapted from Kilminster and Laird (1978).

nouns by looking at or touching an object being named, while to learn the meaning of verbs, activities must be described as these are happening. Having thus acquired new words, children need subsequent opportunities to experiment with their use (Cook et al. 2000).

The first 50 spoken words develop fairly slowly. When children often interact with adults, these early words will usually comprise nouns (e.g. the names of toys, clothes or food) with which the children can interact in some way, in contrast with objects such as a tree or a house which they cannot manipulate (see Box 9.2). When they interact often with other children, social words ('hi' or 'bye') can predominate (Nelson 1973). Nonetheless, children's initial vocabularies are very similar despite differences in environment and upbringing (Gleason 1985; Slobin 1966).

Once children can produce 50 words the expansion of their expressive vocabulary progresses at a much faster rate, with between two and four words being added to their lexicon each day. By the age of 5 years, children will be able to use at least 2000 words.

Similarly, once children have an expressive vocabulary of about 50 words, the length of their utterances grows. The emergence of two-word utterances marks the beginning of the interaction between semantics and syntax. By the age of 5, typically developing children will have acquired a complex syntactic system similar to that of an adult, combined with an extensive vocabulary that will be further expanded and refined throughout life (see also Appendix II).

Communications between young children and their caregivers that focus on the development of turn-taking, topicalisation and sustained reciprocal

---

Box 9.2 Children's first 50 words

Nouns, or naming words, comprise at least 60% of the first 50 words, with action words, or verbs, comprising perhaps 20%. Modifiers and personal-social words make up the other 20%. As can be seen in the list below, the same word can fit into different categories depending on the child's purpose.

Naming words (nouns)	Action words (verbs)
Mummy	do
Daddy	more
Nana	up
Car	all gone
Milk	hi
Doggie	no

Modifiers	Personal-social
no	please
yukkie	bye-bye
hot	yes
all gone	no
nite-nite	
want	

conversational exchanges enable children to learn the underlying organisation of conversation as used by adults for social purposes (Bruner 1975; Kretschmer & Kretschmer 1999; McLean & Snyder-McLean 1999). Box 9.3 outlines the interaction styles that adults typically use to teach infants language. These early social communicative interactions provide the foundations for the development of socially appropriate discourse and language patterns: they help very young children learn how to communicate.

Box 9.3 Communication styles that foster language acquisition

From birth, infants vocalise and move reflexively. Although these behaviours are not under conscious control of babies, adults nevertheless interpret them as meaningful communication and **respond as if the infants were communicating**. They leave pauses between their utterances, giving children an opportunity to take their turn in the conversation.

Adults will then **behave as if infants had taken their turn** and respond accordingly. For instance, in response to an infant's agitated movements and hungry cry, the mother says 'Oh! Are you hungry?' (pause) 'Okay, here's your bottle'.

Later, parents will **focus more on their infants' vocalisations** so that by the time infants are about 10 months old caregivers and infants engage in what are termed 'proto-conversations'. These occur when infants produce a vocalisation to which the caregiver responds and which prompts interactions that can last for many minutes. These exchanges are related to a topic—that is, a task or object of interest to both infants and their caregiver. Although initially the topics are drawn from the immediate environment, these gradually extend to events or objects that are less immediate. Even then, it is infants who draw attention to the potential topic, as when attending to the other parent's voice in a nearby room. The caregiver will then talk about the 'voice' and perhaps take the child to its source.

'Motherese' (also known as 'parentese' or 'infant elicited behaviour') is a form of language which adults reserve for talking with young children. In this pattern, adults' speech is usually:

- enunciated clearly and slowly;
- with emphasis placed on important words;
- with varied pitch and intonation;
- with clear pauses between utterances.

Conversation with young children is usually about the **'here and now'** and involves objects that the children can see, so that they are able to interpret what the words are referring to. **A limited number of words** is used and adults will **repeat the important words** over and over again in subsequent utterances, thus encouraging children to attach meaning to the words. For example, an adult might draw an infant's attention to a brightly coloured ball, saying, 'Oooh! I see the ball' (pause) . . . 'Can you see the ball?' (pause) . . . 'Roll the ball . . . Uh oh! Where's the ball gone?' (pause) . . . 'Here it is! The ball went under the chair.'

Finally, children need feedback about the effectiveness of their language use. As infants begin to use gesture or voice in an intentional way, appropriate adult response is vital. Children use language for a purpose, and therefore adults must respond positively to children's early attempts at communication so that they continue to use and develop language.

CAUSES OF ATYPICAL LANGUAGE DEVELOPMENT

Children can be at risk of communication disorders as a result of environmental events such as neglect, abuse or poor-quality interactions with caregivers, and from biological causes such as genetically transmitted disabilities, trauma, toxins, infections, poor nutrition, drug exposure, anoxia or asphyxia at birth, and low birth weight (Lerner et al. 1998; McCormick 1994; Wetherby 1998) (see Appendix I). Such events may result in disability in the areas of hearing, vision or cognition, all of which are associated with communication difficulties. These disabilities are explained in other chapters of this text, and so will be discussed only briefly here.

Hearing impairment

Hearing is of greatest importance to the development of spoken language, and therefore any degree of hearing loss in the early years can be detrimental to language development (see chapter 8). In turn, as language development is so intricately linked to academic achievement, critical thinking, and social and emotional development, hearing impairment can detrimentally affect all these other aspects of life (Greenberg & Kusche 1993).

Vision impairment

Although vision is not as important to language development as hearing, significant vision impairment in early childhood can affect four key aspects of language development. First, infants who cannot see cannot follow others' gaze, and do not appreciate that their parents can see, and so do not use gestures to draw adults' attention to, and subsequently converse about, an object that interests either partner. This lack of 'joint referencing' by parents and infants delays the children's ability to build vocabulary and to categorise and organise their concepts.

Second, children may repeat words or phrases in an 'echolalic' way because they do not understand their meaning or because they are using language to maintain a degree of social contact that, for normally sighted children, is achieved by non-verbal means. Similarly, children with vision impairment can make much use of questioning in an attempt to understand their environment as well as to maintain social contact. However, their questions are not always relevant to what is actually taking place (Palmer 1998; White & Telec 1998).

Third, vision impairment can restrict infants' ability to imitate mouth movements, resulting in some delays in their speech. Finally, vision impairment can affect the development of pragmatic skills because the children cannot see the non-verbal aspects of language use. Inappropriate use or lack of gesture by children can make their communicative attempts harder to understand, which in turn will affect the quality of their interactions with others. (For more detail on vision impairment, see chapter 5.)

Intellectual skills

Children with intellectual delays usually develop language at a slower rate and with less complexity than their peers. Impaired intellectual development is likely to be associated with impaired memory, which in turn has a significant role in language acquisition. Children with mild and moderate intellectual delays require language stimulation based on their developmental level rather than their chronological age so that they can develop language in the normal way, albeit at a slower rate. Children with severe cognitive delays may require augmentative communication systems, such as manual sign or visual symbols, to enable them to develop functional language. Nevertheless, the decision to use signed communication must be made on an individual basis as, for some children, having to learn verbal communication *and* a signing system results in their learning neither one; for others, having access to some signs takes the pressure off their production of speech, allowing language to develop.

In contrast, intellectually gifted children may begin to say their first words at an earlier age than usual. They are likely to develop a larger and more complex vocabulary and use more complex sentence structures than their peers (Lewis & Louis 1991; Perleth et al. 1993). Gifted children's precocious comprehension of language allows them to follow more complex instructions, modify their language use to suit the listener, and use language to exchange and manipulate ideas and information at a younger age than is typical (Porter 1999). They are able to use language in a more abstract way, rather than being restricted to the 'here and now'. These advanced communication skills allow them to express their needs, ask questions and understand adult explanations from an earlier age than usual.

Oral-motor skills

Children with feeding difficulties—perhaps associated with cerebral palsy, Prader-Willi syndrome or other disabilities affecting their swallowing reflex or tone and control of their oral muscles—can later have particular difficulties with articulation skills, rendering their speech unclear to listeners. (This issue is discussed in chapter 7.)

COMMUNICATION DISORDERS

Although there appears to be uniformity in the pattern of language development for children learning the same language, there is actually much individual variation in both the pattern and rate of development. Children do not always conform to developmental norms, with some being advanced, some delayed, and some developing language in an unusual sequence (Heward 2000). However, when the deviation from the norm is too extreme, children will experience difficulty understanding language, making themselves understood, or both, with resulting social and educational problems.

A difference in communication is considered to be a communication disorder when the ability to receive, send or process information is impaired and/or when the ability to comprehend concepts or verbal, non-verbal or graphic systems is impaired (American Speech-Language-Hearing Association 1982). Communication disorder is categorised further into **speech disorders** and **language disorders**.

Speech is considered to be disordered when it is so unusual that it draws attention to itself, interferes with communication, or causes discomfort for the listener. Speech disorders can occur in articulation, voice quality and prosody (fluency, intonation and volume) (see Figure 9.1), with articulation problems being the most prevalent type in preschool children (Heward 2000). The common articulation errors include:

- substitution of one sound for another (e.g. 'dat' for 'that');
- distortion of certain speech sounds (e.g 'shame' for 'same', or a lisp);
- omission of certain sounds (e.g. 'kool' for 'school');
- addition of sounds (e.g. 'hamber' for 'hammer').

It is quite normal for preschool children to exhibit these types of speech errors, and in most cases they disappear as the children get older. However, if articulation problems do not improve or are causing difficulties in interactions with others, the children should be referred to a speech-language pathologist.

Voice disorders may take the form of a breathy, hoarse, husky or strained voice. There may also be a problem with resonance, where sounds either come out through the nose (hypernasality) or not enough sound comes through the nose, as if the speaker has a cold (hyponasality). Voice disorders are much more common in adults than children, although they can result in children from organic conditions—such as hearing impairment, cleft palate or swollen nasal tissues.

Fluency disorders occur when the normal rhythm and timing of speech are disrupted. Stuttering is an example of a fluency problem and occurs when sounds are repeated over and over again, usually at the beginning of words. In the course of developing normal speech patterns, most young children stutter at some stage and in certain situations. When adults accept these dysfluencies (repetitions and interruptions) in a patient manner and focus on the content of the children's message rather than the delivery, the children are unlikely to develop a fluency problem. However, as with any speech disorder, if their ability to communicate with others is impaired, early referral to a speech-language pathologist is crucial.

Language is considered to be disordered when children have difficulty in comprehending and/or using spoken, written and/or other symbol systems. The disorder can involve the content, form or use of language (ASHA 1982). Where children have difficulty understanding an aspect of language—such as being unable follow a sequence of commands—they have a **receptive** language disorder. Children with **expressive** language disorders may have difficulty with, among other things, the sequencing of sounds in words (e.g. 'aminal' for 'animal', 'psgetti' for 'spaghetti'); may have a limited vocabulary for their age; or they may have difficulty in applying the morphological rules correctly (e.g. 'I wented out').

The terms *specific language impairment* (SLI) or *specific developmental language disorder* (SDLD) are used when there are no other apparent causes for children's language difficulties, such as sensory or intellectual disability (Leonard 1990).

LANGUAGE DELAY

Whereas a language disorder is characterised by a problem in one or more aspect of language (i.e. content, form or use), children with language delays show delay in the acquisition of all aspects of language. They seem to be following the normal progression but at a slower rate, and the expectation may be that they will eventually 'catch up' without specialist intervention. However, as children get older this distinction between language disorder and language delay becomes less relevant, because any children using language that is appropriate for much younger ages will need specialist intervention if they are to catch up to their peers (Rinaldi 2000).

When children aged under 3 acquire two languages simultaneously, their rate and manner of development is similar to those who are learning only one language (Owens 2001). Commonly, however, many bilingual children develop their first language in the home and their second language after the age of 3 in early childhood settings. If they are exposed to their second language before they have developed some maturity in their first language, temporary delays in both may occur, which will be overcome naturally through the provision of rich opportunities to learn language during sensory activities and in meaningful contexts.

However, when children with certain intellectual or language disabilities are required to learn more than one language simultaneously, they might have great difficulty becoming proficient in any. In these exceptional cases, it may be necessary to limit them to one language at a time. This can involve negotiating with the family to use the language of the educational setting at home when communicating with the child. Although initially at least this can limit the child's use of the family's native language, it can help the child to access education. Subsequently, if the child is able to become reasonably proficient in the language of the educational setting, he or she can then learn the language of home in the same way as other children who are bilingual.

ASSESSMENT

All development progresses in uneven steps, which is one of the reasons that assessment of language problems in the preschool years is so challenging.

Another reason is that it is difficult to distinguish whether communication is children's only affected domain, or whether their language difficulties are just one feature of another condition such as autism or intellectual disability.

The indicators of speech or language impairments given in Box 9.4 can alert you to the need to discuss with parents their child's language skills; if there is still concern, recommend an assessment by a speech-language pathologist.

Speech-language pathology assessments

Intervention should be based on a comprehensive assessment of children's language and other skills, based on a sound understanding of the typical developmental sequences in content, form and use of language. An interdisciplinary assessment is required to discriminate whether children's language difficulties stand alone or are part of more generalised developmental difficulties such as the autism spectrum disorders or developmental delay or disability. With this in mind, children are often referred to a psychologist for a generalised test of development, while those whose language difficulties are associated with sensory or other disabilities will be referred to specialists in these domains. A comprehensive evaluation will normally include tests of hearing, auditory discrimination, articulation and vocabulary development, as well as samples of the children's communication behaviour in various settings.

INTERVENTION

When an assessment of children's language abilities indicates delays in some areas, some form of language intervention must be implemented. The assessment information should indicate the children's strengths, emerging language skills and areas of difficulty. Following from this, as mentioned in chapter 4, priorities for intervention will be selected in light of the normal developmental sequence, tempered with ecological information about which skills will be most functional for the children in their present and future environments and which will make the most difference to the quality of life for them and their families.

All adults involved with children's language programs should be aware of the current priorities and strategies to be used to elicit the language, and be able to use everyday occurrences to encourage the use of the language skills that the children need to acquire. To that end, it is extremely important that adults who are assisting children with language difficulties have a good understanding of the normal sequence of development (see Appendix II), the components of language, and a shared 'language to talk about language difficulties' (Martin 2000:28). Effective intervention should be implemented early and carefully monitored so that strategies can be adjusted according to the children's progress.

Box 9.4 Indicators of speech or language impairments

- The most obvious signs of language acquisition problems are delays in the number and type of words in children's vocabulary. At an age when you would expect more sophisticated vocabulary, children with language impairments might use only a few nouns and social greetings, with few other word forms. (This is an impairment of **content**.)
- Children's speech might be echolalic—that is, they repeat part or all of what has just been said to them. Although when communicating together children and adults commonly repeat what they have heard to signal their understanding, children's echolalia can occur because they have learned that it satisfies their communication partner and so will end an uncomfortable communication, or as an attempt to disguise the fact that they have not understood. (This indicates a problem with **pragmatics**.)
- Children might repeat questions over and over again, not appreciating that these have been answered. (This signals a problem with **pragmatics** and **semantics**.)
- Some children fixate on one particular topic of conversation, introducing it even when others are already conversing about another. Others change topic within a conversation, perhaps using a key word uttered by an adult to spark a flight into an unrelated topic. For instance, an adult might comment that one of the building blocks is light and the child might use this as a trigger to introduce his or her favourite topic of Superman, saying 'Superman is light. He can fly'. (This suggests a problem with **pragmatics**.)
- Some children cannot detect that communication has broken down and so do not use language to repair it or to solve social problems. (This is characteristic of difficulties with **pragmatics**.)
- Children might say the same thing in the same circumstance, such as asking 'Where we going?' when in a car, without understanding the meaning of what they are saying. The relevance of the utterance to that particular context can deceive adults into thinking that the children understand, when instead the children simply know that this is the thing to say in these circumstances. (This indicates a problem with **semantics**—or meaning—of language.)
- Children might often make physical contact with other children because they do not have ready access to their words to greet others, make requests or negotiate. This can result in antisocial touching, snatching at items over which they are competing, and aggression. (This suggests a problem with **semantics** and **pragmatics**.)
- Children can be inattentive during language-based sessions such as song or story time, particularly when the content is relatively advanced for their language age. (This suggests a problem with language **form** and **semantics**.)
- They might attempt to participate in song sessions, but have to watch the other children's gestures to know what they are supposed to be doing, and might sing very few of the words. (This suggests a problem with **phonology, syntax** and **semantics**.)
- Some children might have difficulty following instructions that contain many parts. For example, when asked to put their car on the bookshelf and come back with a book and sit down, they might move over to the bookshelf and

apparently forget what they were there for. This can appear to be a lack of cooperation and so is seen to be a behavioural issue, but results instead from their inability to remember the instructions. (This indicates a problem with **syntax** and **semantics**.)

- Some children have difficulty finding the words to express their ideas when age mates are doing so more automatically. (This relates to difficulties with **semantics**.)
- In comparison to their age mates, some children might have difficulty forming grammatical sentences, such as being unable to form questions or use pronouns accurately, as when continuing the use of 'Me do it' past toddlerhood. (This indicates a problem with **syntax**.)
- Some children can use language to communicate about the 'here and now' but cannot use it for a variety of purposes—such as to tell about an event, to gain attention or to make a request. (This relates to difficulties of both **semantics** and **pragmatics**.)
- Some children continue to use immature word endings; as in, 'He wented out' or 'I breaked it'. (This indicates a problem with **morphology**.)
- Some children have difficulty producing speech sounds well beyond the age at which they are normally produced. This can result in 'babyish'-sounding speech, for example 'I fought we were doing out' instead of 'I thought we were going out'. (This indicates a problem with **phonology**.)
- Some children have difficulties acquiring independence skills, such as toileting, because they do not have the language to talk to themselves about the need to go to the toilet; they can have difficulty putting away toys as they cannot categorise them and plan where they belong; they can be impulsive, as their lack of self-talk means that they do not guide (think about) their actions in advance. All of these can surface as behavioural difficulties but can have a general expressive language problem as their basis.

Provide a language-rich environment

An environment that is rich in language experiences will give children repeated exposure to a range of language forms in multiple natural settings and ensure that children's communication is purposeful (McCormick & Schiefelbusch 1990). Early childhood settings can provide children with many natural reasons to communicate, thus allowing them to associate language with the context to which it relates.

Incorporate play into language learning

Keep in mind that children learn to communicate because they have a need to and because they want to, not because someone makes them. This means that play must be an integral feature of children's language programs. Peer interaction through play allows children to use the various types of language according to the roles assumed during play. Adults can assist children to engage in and elaborate on play in the ways suggested in chapter 4, keeping in mind that high levels of adult directiveness can reduce the complexity of children's pretend play (Fiese 1990).

Be a responsive communication partner

Language learning normally occurs in the pleasant, caring interactions between caregivers and children. Thus, any attempt to teach language is likely to fail unless the children enjoy the interaction in which the teaching is embedded. Communication will be enhanced when adults accept and respond to children's communication attempts, including paying attention to their initiations of conversation and verbally and non-verbally expressing acceptance of their attempts. Through this acceptance children learn that communication is reciprocal. Adults can also initiate and elaborate conversations with children using the following means.

- Talk with children about objects and events to which you are both attending.
- Model, imitate and expand children's intended or actual communicative attempts.
- Repeat and clarify any aspect of the language that individual children do not seem to understand.
- Use higher pitch and stress—typical of 'parentese'—to highlight important sentence elements for listening children (McCormick 1994).

However, although frequent interaction with responsive communication partners is a necessary condition for language development, it does not ensure development in all cases. This fact necessitates some more deliberate interventions.

Adjust the complexity of language

When children's comprehension of language is delayed, the language content of stories and song sessions may need to be simplified so that children are able to participate at their level. If the language is too advanced for their comprehension, they will become bored and frustrated and will not benefit from the language activities.

In contrast, when children have advanced language skills, they will seek sophisticated language experiences. Verbally gifted children may come to rely on adults as their communication partners if their age mates are not able to converse with them about sophisticated concepts. Placing these children with older playmates for at least some of their day can allow them to converse and play with intellectually matched peers, so that they do not become reliant on adults and can learn to accept peers as potentially rewarding companions.

Use naturalistic interventions

The least intrusive form of naturalistic intervention is to respond to children's spontaneous language use. Giving their communication your attention and following it with a response or action that reflects their communicative intent is vital (McCormick 1994). Nevertheless, it is not sufficient just to wait for naturally occurring opportunities; thus, at the next level of naturalistic intervention, educators can structure situations so that specific language is elicited and practised.

At the last, most formal level of naturalistic teaching, educators can focus on children's specific language difficulties. For instance, if individual children's morphological development is found to be delayed with 'ed' or 's' endings being omitted, educators could ensure that many examples of these morphemes are provided in a salient way throughout their program, as well as prompting and modelling their use.

Nevertheless, as children with language difficulties have not developed typical skills under normal language learning conditions, many will also require some specific, targeted intervention as well as this more general naturalistic approach.

Provide structured teaching as necessary

While intervention strategies are best placed in children's natural settings, the importance of one-on-one direct instruction in a setting conducive to learning cannot be overlooked. The provision of specific, targeted interventions is justified on the grounds that children have already experienced a normal language environment during their early years but nevertheless have not managed to acquire language as expected. In that case, providing more of the same experience is unlikely to be sufficient to develop their skills.

Thus, in order to progress, some young children—and particularly those who have sensory or intellectual disabilities accompanying their language difficulties—may need specific language elicitation techniques (Yoder et al. 1998). These may include the use of prompts and feedback, quick repetition of target skills, ongoing diagnostic assessment of learning, and daily one-on-one sessions so that they receive intervention of sufficient intensity to ensure optimal progress (Warren 2000).

Chapter 10 mentions that, when teaching children new thinking processes, it helps to apply these to content with which the children are already familiar. The same applies to teaching new language skills: children need to develop new information in the context of known information. For instance, a new sentence structure should be introduced using known vocabulary and experiences so that the children are able to understand and classify this new piece of knowledge. Similarly, new words are best introduced in relation to known words so that these can also be categorised on the basis of known information. Other general strategies are listed in Box 9.5.

Provide early literacy experiences

The ability to identify and manipulate the sounds (phonemes) in words is called phonological awareness. When activities that emphasise the sounds of language are integrated into the preschool program, there is a greater likelihood of children becoming successful readers in their second year of schooling (Bryant & Bradley 1990). Furthermore, children who are good readers become even better readers,

Box 9.5 Strategies for teaching language skills

- Give priority to skills that are relevant to children's everyday communicative needs.
- Give children with language difficulties extra opportunities to practise newly acquired skills across meaningful settings, including home, care or education settings, and the community.
- Before giving an instruction, ensure that the children are attending.
- Check that they have understood by requiring a verbal or behavioural response.
- Allow extra time for the children to respond as it may take them longer to process information.
- Keep directives short and simple.
- When children have not understood, repeat a directive but modify it by simplifying its vocabulary, sentence structure or number of parts or elements.
- Be alert to naturally occurring events that provide opportunities to introduce a new concept or to consolidate a skill being acquired.
- Accept and acknowledge children's attempts at initiations or responding. Model, expand or extend these as appropriate.
- Aim for productivity rather than perfect mastery. It is enough that children can produce the target skill on 60% of occasions, as they will continue to improve in natural interactions without the need for continued direct intervention.

whereas those who are poor readers are likely to fall even further behind (Stanovich 1986).

A language-rich environment promotes children's phonological awareness and thus their reading skills through, among other things, their participation in nursery rhymes, finger plays and stories that are read aloud, developing picture charts and books that describe children's first-hand experiences, and encouraging story telling. Such activities can include identifying rhyme patterns and alliteration (as in 'There's a mouse in my house' or 'Peter Piper picked a peck of pickled peppers'), recognising isolated sounds (as in the 'ssss' for a snake sound), and counting or clapping syllables (e.g. Pe - ter) or sounds in words (e.g. d-o-g). (See the Additional resources section.)

This naturalistic teaching might seem insufficiently formalised, but literacy learning can be likened to an iceberg: most of the learning occurs in hidden or natural ways, with formalised learning, although more observable, being responsible for the smallest proportion of children's literacy skills (Miller 2000). Even those verbally gifted children who are interested early in literacy—and only a minority of these children are (Perleth et al. 1993)—require early reading and writing to be introduced in naturalistic rather than formalised ways so that their disposition to keep learning is not impaired by finding literacy activities meaningless, too abstract, or too challenging.

CONCLUSION

Language does not develop in a linear way: children progress unevenly within and across developmental domains—and at times seem to plateau. Intervention must take this variability into account and be sensitive to children's individuality. At the same time, we cannot fail to provide support when children clearly are not acquiring the language skills that they need to function in everyday life. Caregivers must be aware of the vital role that they have in facilitating the language development of all young children and referring these children for specialist help if naturalistic methods are not progressing their skills as expected.

ADDITIONAL RESOURCES

Owens, R.E. 1999 *Language disorders: a functional approach to assessment and intervention* 3rd edn, Allyn & Bacon, Boston, MA

——2001 *Language development: an introduction* Allyn & Bacon, Needham Heights, MA

The following internet sites might also prove useful:
How Now Brown Cow: Phoneme Awareness Activities for Collaborative Classrooms
    http://www.ldonline.org/ld_indepth/teaching_techniques/cld_hownow.html
    www.asha.org/speech/development/Parent-Stim-Activities.cfm
www.asha.org/speech/development/Pragmatic-Language-Tips.cfm
www.ldonline.org/bulletin_boards/index.html
    members.tripod.com/Caroline_Bowen/acquisition.html
    members.tripod.com/Caroline_Bowen/encourage.html
    members.tripod.com/Caroline_Bowen/wordretrieval.html
www.angelfire.com/nj/speechlanguage/Articles.html
www.speechteach.co.uk

LIVERPOOL JOHN MOORES UNIVERSITY
LEARNING SERVICES

10

COGNITIVE SKILLS

LOUISE PORTER

KEY POINTS

- As well as acquiring information as they develop, children need to acquire skills for managing how they learn.
- As children near school entry age, their main intellectual task is the acquisition of learning skills. It is principally their facility with these that distinguishes advanced, average and delayed learners from each other.
- These skills comprise the *knowledge acquisition skills* of attending and recalling information; *metacognitive knowledge* to plan, check and solve problems; the *metacognitive controlling* skills of self-monitoring, self-instructing and self-evaluation; and aspects of *learning style* or dispositions such as motivation and self-efficacy.

INTRODUCTION

Cognitive development entails acquiring understanding about the world in which we live (Lutz & Sternberg 1999). The processes involved in achieving such understanding comprise mental activities such as conceiving, reasoning, storing and retrieving information from memory, and attending to stimuli (Wolery & Wolery 1992). These abilities are known as knowledge acquisition and meta-cognitive abilities, the latter having to do with managing thinking.

In this chapter I review what information processing theory can tell us about young children's learning processes. This focus is selected because it has specific implications for intervention. The measures described for promoting intellectual development of children with additional needs is built on the concept that, for this group in particular, learning cannot be left to chance (Umansky 1998). Although early childhood programs can supply the materials that provide curricular content, children with disabilities are best served by structured teaching of the *processes* involved in learning that content.

EARLY COGNITIVE ATTAINMENTS

Acquiring the following cognitive skills is important during the first five years (Chen & Siegler 2000; Cook et al. 2000). Achievement of these relies on accurate perception—that is, the ability to assign meaning to sensations—plus intact sensory and motor systems and language skills (Umansky 1998).

Intentionality

Around the age of 8–10 months, infants are able to do things intentionally rather than by chance. Infants learn that they can act voluntarily, and that their actions will have an effect. This is a prerequisite for almost every other skill (Cook et al. 2000). Babies who have an intention—for example, to reach for an object—but cannot achieve this will find it difficult to learn intentionality. This could explain the passive learning style of some children born with physical disabilities. These children might learn that there is little point being curious when they cannot move themselves to explore the item that has engaged their interest.

This potential for acquiring a passive learning style makes it doubly important to facilitate children's development of intentionality. Some means of doing so are suggested by Cook et al. (2000):

- Increase motivation by making objects and activities interesting to the children.
- Create a need to act: by placing an object within sight but where the infant must reach for it; by stopping an enjoyable activity and waiting for the child to indicate a wish for it to start again; by interpreting even accidental movements as signals of intent; and by ensuring that children can activate favourite toys.
- Allow ample time for children to act and let them do things for themselves when they are able.

Systematic exploration

Young infants' exploration is based on trial and error, but once they are able to manipulate objects and their own actions systematically they become capable of self-directed learning and of discovering new ideas for themselves (Cook et al. 2000). To assist in this process, you can guide them to explore solutions and persist at activities until they are successful.

Cause–effect understanding

The ability to explain why an event has happened or will happen is crucial to the subsequent development of problem-solving skills and intentionality. To learn this, children must be allowed to experiment safely so that their explorations teach them the effect of their actions. As well as offering opportunities for them to discover information for themselves, some ways to enhance this learning are to copy their actions in the typical mimicking game which involves your turn, my turn, and by responding to their social cues. This may be difficult when their cues are atypical, such as a blind child's not looking in your direction to gain social contact.

Object permanence

Learning about object permanence is crucial to the development of memory and to being able to predict not only the presence of objects and people but also their behaviour (Wolery & Wolery 1992). This in turn promotes exploration. Games that demonstrate that an object is present even if unseen can teach this concept.

Deferred imitation

While young children may be able to imitate an activity simultaneously or immediately after it has been carried out, their later ability to defer imitation is necessary for pretend play and language development.

Means–end analysis

Means–end analysis involves being able to assess the present situation, envisage a goal, and plan an appropriate strategy to move from the first to the second (Chen & Siegler 2000). This ability is present by the end of the first year of life and is crucial to the subsequent development of more sophisticated problem-solving skills.

Symbolic representation

Symbolic play reflects children's understanding of the world and (as discussed in chapter 1) is important for social and emotional development. The first stage of symbolic play is where the children are the actors in very familiar activities, such as shopping or going to bed. Children with disabilities may need to be assisted to engage in these activities, although this will help their development of symbolic play only if the chosen activities are very familiar to them.

The above represent the earliest intellectual attainments of infants. Subsequently, children develop logical thought, which entails the abilities to use previous experience to make decisions and solve problems, and to transfer solutions from one problem to another (Chen & Siegler 2000; Umansky 1998). To achieve this, children need sophisticated skills for *acquiring* and retaining new knowledge and to *control their thinking* processes (termed metacognitive skills), and a set of *dispositions* or style of learning that will enable them to learn. The remainder of this chapter describes these three processes, which dictate *how* children learn.

KNOWLEDGE ACQUISITION SKILLS

Knowledge acquisition is an active process. Children who have intellectual disabilities tend to be more passive than typically developing children in learning situations, and are more dependent on others for guidance (Whitman et al. 1991). In comparison, children who are developmentally advanced play an active role in eliciting stimulation from their physical and social environments (Damiani 1997; Morelock & Morrison 1996). They can deal with abstract and complex material earlier and gain knowledge in greater depth and breadth than is usual for their age (Morelock & Morrison 1996).

Young children's ability to move around and converse with others shape the opportunities that they have to acquire new information; therefore, their skills in these other domains have a significant impact on their intellectual development. Two cognitive skills that also affect their acquisition of skills and information are their abilities to attend to and remember their experiences.

Attention skills

One of the necessary skills for acquiring knowledge is the ability to pay attention to relevant input. Attention follows a developmental trend (see Appendix II), and comprises five quite separate processes (Zentall 1989).

1. Maintaining a level of **arousal** necessary to attend. As described by Soden (chapter 7), some children with disabilities have difficulty moderating their levels of alertness to suit the task at hand, while gifted children are commonly highly alert and demand constantly changing stimulation (Morelock & Morrison 1996).
2. **Focus** is the second aspect of attention. It requires, first, awareness or detection of an event (Umansky 1998) and, second, ability and interest in attending to it.
3. Maintaining attention over time is termed the attention span, sustained attention, or **concentration**. Having been made aware of a stimulus, the individual must compare it with others that have been experienced previously (Umansky 1998). Children with intellectual disabilities show impairment of both awareness and comparison; gifted children are alert and make ready comparisons with prior experience, and so can quickly lose interest in (habituate to) repeated stimuli (Perleth et al. 2000). For opposite reasons, then, both groups can experience difficulties sustaining their attention.
4. Scanning the field of possible stimuli allows children to select those aspects relevant to the task at hand and ignore those that are not relevant. It requires focus and inhibition of distracting or incidental stimuli. It also involves being able to shift attention rapidly to deal with changes in stimuli or in response to directives from an adult. This form of attention is called **selective attention**, and is impaired in children with intellectual disabilities in that they are less able to screen out distractions in their environment, resulting, for example, in

less sophisticated play in group versus individual settings (Malone & Stoneman 1990).

5. **Divided attention** allows us to manage more than one task at a time, prudently shifting our focus as the tasks require (Sternberg 1999). Children with intellectual disabilities appear to have difficulty attending to many environmental features at once, and if not distracted and disorganised by competing events instead fixedly focus on one activity, screening out all competing information in the wider environment, with the result that their play can become inflexible and repetitive (Krakow & Kopp 1983).

When planning attention training, you will need to distinguish between distractability, whereby children cannot focus on any activity, versus those occasions when they are simply attending to something other than the adults intend (McWilliam & Bailey 1992). If the former, attention training can be useful; if the latter, engagement could be an issue (see below).

Box 10.1 lists some general guidelines relevant to all forms of cognitive and metacognitive training. In addition to using those measures, there are some specific recommendations for helping children learn attention skills:

- Respond to the object or event that has attracted children's interest, rather than directing children to attend to features that you have selected (Jones & Warren 1991).
- In the initial stages of an intervention program, cut down on extraneous stimuli so that it is *easier* for children to attend to relevant information. However, to aid generalisation, these distractions will need to be reintroduced gradually, requiring the children to exercise selective attention skills and thus to be able to function in natural environments.
- To make children more *willing* to attend, use attractive, moderately novel materials of varying complexity.
- Control the pace. Rather than speeding up when the children's attention appears to be waning, slow down to reduce the amount of input to which they have to attend.
- Ensure that children are seated in a position that facilitates their interaction with materials. Many children with physical disabilities need specific seating in order to be able to control their arms and hands (see chapter 7); all children need table and chair height to match, and for toys to be below eye level.

One everyday activity that can enhance attention skills is cooking, as this encourages children to look and listen to instructions (Cook et al. 2000).

Memory function

A second knowledge acquisition skill is use of memory. It can be distinguished by three features: first is the *amount* of stored knowledge; second is how is it *organised*; and third is how *accessible* the information is (Rabinowitz & Glaser 1985).

Box 10.1 General guidelines for teaching cognitive and metacognitive skills

There are two tasks in facilitating children's skill acquisition: first, to help them to be *willing* to put in the effort to learn; second, to structure tasks to be *easier* to learn.

Make tasks relevant
Children will be willing to put in the effort to learn thinking skills when there is a reason to do so—that is, when tasks reflect their interests (Wolery & Wolery 1992). They must be able to see that the task is helping them in obvious ways to make a success of their lives. Although the rationale for a task might seem apparent to you, it might not be as obvious to young children, so it can help to explain it to them.

Give children control of their learning
Where educationally viable, give children choices about what they want to learn; if you deem an activity to be necessary for educational reasons (and there is thus no choice *whether* to attempt it), you can still give children the choice of *how* to do it.

Provide sufficient challenge
The degree of challenge must not be so high that the children do not feel confident that they can meet demands, while not being so low that success on the task is meaningless: work that is too easy will not raise children's opinion of their abilities (Bandura 1986).

Use the children's favoured learning mode
Offer a range of auditory, visual or kinaesthetic, or multisensory experiences that allow children to access information via their favourite mode. At young ages, physical activity is likely to be children's favourite mode of learning.

Teach knowledge acquisition and metacognitive strategies
These comprise the *knowledge acquisition skills* of selective attention, rehearsing and recalling; the *metacognitive knowledge* of how to plan, check and solve problems; and the *metacognitive controlling* skills of self-monitoring, self-instructing and self-evaluation.

Simplify the content
When asking children to use processes that are difficult for them, you will need to simplify the content so that the children are applying the new skill to something they already know and understand well. Gardner (1983) argues that individuals have differing abilities at problem solving across various content areas (e.g. mathematics versus language). It could be useful, then, to begin teaching problem solving in each child's strongest content domain and only afterwards attempt to transfer the skills to other domains.

Give informative feedback
Children who are discouraged about their skills are in most need of feedback, although in giving feedback you do not have to *judge* or evaluate what the children achieve but instead give them *information* about what they are doing.

This must be specific and precise, but also genuine, so that children learn to discriminate success from failure.

Furthermore, rather than commenting on the content of the activities or what the children produce, informative feedback should focus on the *processes* that the children are using to achieve success—such as paying attention, planning what to do, checking whether it is working, and applying what they have learned elsewhere to this present task.

Encourage risk taking

To encourage children to learn new skills, you must avoid implying that they should not make mistakes. Mistakes merely signal that it is time to try another approach. You can guide the children to turn failure into success by changing their strategy, or you can adapt the processes or materials to enable success.

Give repeated practice

One study showed that children with intellectual disabilities required 40 training sessions to teach problem-solving skills (Ross & Ross 1978, in Whitman et al. 1991). It is clear, therefore, that children will need extensive opportunities to practise new skills.

Taking each aspect in turn, there is some evidence that children with an intellectual disability have limited knowledge, presumably because they have difficulties both storing information in and subsequently retrieving information from memory (Umansky 1998). Meanwhile, gifted children acquire more knowledge because they are faster (more efficient) at storing information in their memory and subsequently at retrieving it (Borkowski & Peck 1986; Haensly & Reynolds 1989; Rabinowitz & Glaser 1985). This probably arises because their brain cells transmit information with few errors (Eysenck 1986), allowing them to master a new skill with unusual speed and accumulate deeper knowledge than other children of the same age.

To explain *organisation* in the memory store, it might help to think of memory as being like an office filing cabinet. If over time you toss documents into a filing cabinet until they fill the drawer, you are going to have difficulty locating the document you want when you need it. If, instead, you put each document in a hanging file devoted to that topic, retrieving it is simply a matter of locating the topic and finding the document that relates to it. So it is with memory: when we rehearse information or elaborate on it, we are ensuring that we 'park' that memory near other related information, which makes it easier to locate when we need to retrieve it later.

The third feature of memory is *accessibility*. Here, the analogy of dropping a stone into a pond might be useful. When a stone is thrown with force into the water, it disturbs or sends out ripples to nearby parts of the pond in ever-increasing circles; when the stone lands gently in the water, the ripples are smaller and they spread less far. In the same way, one memory can trigger or activate another, related concept. A person with a superior memory will have strong links between concepts and will activate a large number of related ideas (the 'ripples' will go out strongly from the original idea to a wide range of related memories). If the associative links in memory are weak, then the activation (ripples) does not spread far enough or with enough strength to call up related ideas. In short, related memories are not activated automatically. Thus, individuals with learning difficulties can retrieve information that has been stored in their memory, but only with effort; in contrast, the ability of advanced learners to access a wide range of relevant information easily and quickly permits complex problem solving (Rabinowitz & Glaser 1985; Perleth et al. 2000).

In summary, as individuals become more competent in a given domain, their *knowledge* of that domain grows, they *organise* their knowledge in memory in more sophisticated ways, and much of it can be accessed *automatically* (Perleth et al. 2000; Rabinowitz & Glaser 1985; Shore & Kanevsky 1993). This leaves processing capacity available for carrying out higher-order tasks (Perleth et al. 2000).

Children with intellectual disabilities appear to have both memory storage and memory retrieval difficulties compared with children both of the same age and younger children with the same developmental level (McDade & Adler 1980). This is likely to be due to their language difficulties, which limit their ability to rehearse information (Ellis 1970) and to store information according to its category membership. Both these aspects will mean that information is stored randomly rather than near related concepts, making it more difficult to retrieve. In turn, memory deficiencies limit problem-solving capacity as the children cannot recall information that is relevant to solving the problem (Ellis 1970).

To enhance children's recall, the most crucial dual strategies are to engage them actively in learning (rather than passively receiving information) and to ensure that the information is meaningful and relevant to them. For instance, children may be least motivated to learn by rote the names of colours or to learn letters of the alphabet if they have not yet developed an interest in the written word. General teaching strategies are listed in Box 10.1; some other specific strategies for memory enhancement include:

- asking conversational questions about topics of interest to the children, such as 'What is your new baby sister's name?', 'Where does your puppy sleep?' and, in a story, 'What was Spot looking for?';
- playing games at group time in which the children are asked to recall each other's names;
- having the children report what objects have been removed from an array of three toys;
- asking children where an item they are seeking is stored;
- checking that the children have understood an instruction that has just been given, for example, 'Put your plate on the side table . . . Where do you have to put your plate?' (Allen & Schwartz 2001).

Not carrying out directives can have many causes, one of which is children's inability to remember what they were asked to do. If individuals frequently carry out only part of a task, it can help to simplify what you say and to reduce instructions to fewer parts—perhaps instructing just one step at a time (Allen & Schwartz 2001).

METACOGNITIVE SKILLS

The second cluster of intellectual skills which children need for learning are the metacognitive abilities. **Metacognition** refers to our knowledge about our cognitive processes. It involves monitoring and regulation of our thinking processes and has three aspects (Schraw & Graham 1997):

- **Self-awareness.** This comprises individuals' knowledge about how their mind works, which is crucial for selecting suitable strategies to assist their learning (Borkowski & Peck 1986).
- **Metacognitive knowledge** is information about how to use learning strategies, and when and why to use them.
- **Metacognitive control** comprises planning, monitoring and evaluation to regulate our thinking.

The main task of the year immediately prior to school entry is the acquisition of metacognitive thinking. As can be expected, children with intellectual disabilities are typically less proficient at all three aspects: first, they are less aware of how their mind works; second, they have less knowledge about learning strategies; third, although they can be taught strategies, they are less able efficiently and independently to initiate, regulate and monitor (i.e. control) their use of these (Cole & Chan 1990; Whitman et al. 1991).

In contrast, gifted children demonstrate more knowledge about how their mind works (Borkowski & Peck 1986; Carr et al. 1996) and how to use strategies, and they show early use of metacognitive control (Horowitz 1992; Schwanenflugel et al. 1997). In turn, their early acquisition of these skills might be due to the structure of their brains which permits, among other skills, advanced language abilities and early understanding of cause-and-effect relationships (Borkowski & Peck 1986; Moss 1990, 1992).

Self-regulation (-control) skills

To be effective and independent managers of their own learning, children need to be able to monitor what they are doing, have the verbal skills to give themselves useful instructions, and set appropriate standards or criteria by which to judge their performance.

Self-monitoring

To be successful, individuals have to keep track of or monitor what they are doing so that, if necessary, they can adjust their approach to tasks (Bandura 1986; Lutz & Sternberg 1999). However, few young children are aware of the strategies they can use to acquire new information (e.g. rehearsal to promote recall) and, if aware, do not always employ these when needed (Lutz & Sternberg 1999). This means that all children—even those with advanced development—will need feedback about how they are approaching tasks (see Box 10.1) and, ultimately, instruction in how to monitor their task approach independently.

Self-instruction

This is the use of 'personal verbal prompts' (Zirpoli & Melloy 1997: 187) to guide our actions. When a task is new or challenging to us, we talk about it out loud to ourselves; then our self-talk becomes covert; finally, we no longer need to self-instruct as the task has become automatic for us. When teaching children to self-instruct, you can use the following steps:

- As you complete an activity, talk out loud about what you are doing and how successful you are being.
- Next, have target children perform the same activity alongside you, while you comment on your own and their performances as you go.
- Next, if necessary, children can complete the task while giving themselves out loud the same instructions that you were using, until eventually they can self-instruct quietly in their heads (Meichenbaum 1977).

Throughout, you will need to teach strategies for dealing with failures and ensure that once the children have become competent at a task, they have enough time to practise and consolidate their new skills.

Self-evaluation (self-assessment)

In this phase of self-regulation, children need to assess whether their performance has been successful or not. Only when they can recognise their accomplishments will this information add to their pool of knowledge that can be drawn on during future tasks (Whitman et al. 1991). Setting appropriate performance standards may be the most crucial phase of the self-management process (Whitman et al. 1991). Some children might set themselves very lenient standards, while others are too demanding of themselves (Alberto & Troutman 1999; Kaplan & Carter 1995). To assist them in judging their own efforts, you will need to give clear and specific feedback (see Box 10.1).

Problem solving

Problem solving is a key metacognitive skill. It requires developing a plan to bring about a desired result (Ashman & Conway 1993). In order to achieve this, children need to realise that a problem exists, examine what has to be done, scan a range of options, and select one that they think will be most successful (Ashman & Conway 1989; Kaplan & Carter 1995; Zirpoli & Melloy 1997). This decision will be based on their judgment about whether the chosen strategy is feasible and will meet their goal without generating new problems for them. Next, they need to devise a plan for implementing their chosen solution. This step requires *consequential* thinking, which is the ability to consider the potential outcomes or consequences of a proposed behaviour, and *means–end thinking*. This refers to the ability to plan the steps needed to achieve a goal.

Problem-solving training involves teaching children how to deal with the structure of problems and provides practice in the skills involved. Once again, general teaching strategies are listed in Box 10.1, with additional strategies for teaching problem solving being the following.

Present clearly structured problems

Children with few learning difficulties make the transition readily from well- to poorly structured (novel) problems, generalising the skills across content areas (Ashman & Conway 1989). In contrast, children with learning difficulties cannot apply structure as readily to ill-structured problems. Thus, they will need you to structure tasks well. This requires you to:

- present the task clearly;
- give all the information that is necessary for successful completion;
- teach strategies for solving the problem;
- provide extensive practice.

Teach the problem-solving steps

The formal steps of problem solving comprise the following:

1. Pause.
2. Ask: 'What is the problem?'
3. Ask: 'What do I want?'
4. Ask: 'Is what I'm doing working?'
5. If not, plan solutions: 'What else could I do?'
6. Choose what to do and do it.
7. Evaluate the results. (Go back to step 4).
8. Self-reinforce.

Older children or those with advanced development ultimately can learn and direct the steps independently, but very young children or those with learning difficulties are likely to need you to prompt them at each stage. To be successful, children need to be capable of paying attention, pacing themselves, persisting, and noting feedback, some or all of which might need specific training as well.

Give multiple and varied prompts

To teach them to solve problems, children with mild intellectual disabilities will require repeated instruction and prompts. It may not be enough simply to repeat the original instruction; instead you will need to augment that with active demonstrations and perhaps manual guidance to ensure that they understand how to go about solving a problem (Rynders et al. 1979).

Generalisation skills

As has already been mentioned, children with intellectual disabilities can be taught learning strategies, but have difficulty applying these in new situations and with knowing when and how to change strategies (Whitman et al. 1991). The ability to transfer skills from one task or setting to similar ones is termed generalisation. It requires the ability to scan memory efficiently, knowledge of strategies and, above all, metacognitive control (Borkowski & Peck 1986; Carr et al. 1996; Risemberg & Zimmerman 1992).

The single most effective way to promote maintenance and generalisation of new skills is to teach children self-management skills, rather than having programs under adult direction (Martin et al. 1988, in Whitman et al. 1991). Skill transfer can be programmed for using the same general teaching strategies as the other cognitive skills and which are outlined in Box 10.1. In addition, you can encourage generalisation by specifically teaching for it. This can involve the following measures:

- Make sure that tasks are not too difficult and that they are similar to real-life activities—both to make them more meaningful and to reduce the discrepancy between the skill as it is taught and as it is enacted in real life.
- Highlight similarities between tasks by asking 'How is this similar to what you've done before?' and then teach children to analyse what they already know about solving the problem at hand (Whitman et al. 1991).
- Where their verbal skills permit, teach children strategies such as rehearsal, repetition, labelling, classification, association and imagery. Also teach how the strategy can be used so that ultimately the children can work independently. This is the essence of generalisation.
- Give children numerous opportunities to practise using the strategies in the one context before requiring them to transfer these to other situations (Zirpoli & Melloy 1997).
- Offer a series of similar (not exactly the same) tasks working up to the generalisation task.

EMOTIONAL LEARNING STYLE

The third aspect of intellectual abilities is children's learning style or dispositions. Children's dispositions involve first, an awareness that a particular skill would be useful and, second, an inclination to employ it (Perkins et al. 1993). Metacognitive skills dictate how children go about achieving success; style refers to how they feel about learning and about themselves as learners. Although discussed last in this chapter, this emotional aspect actually makes the greatest contribution to success, because even if children have the ability to do a task, they will not be successful at it unless they are motivated to use their skills. This may be especially so for young children, as they rely more than older children, on their emotional interpretations of events (Meyers et al. 1989).

Many dispositions or aspects of learning style could be nurtured within early childhood programs—some are listed in chapter 4; the discussion in this section will focus on the key processes of engagement, motivation, fostering an internal locus of control in children and encouraging independent learning.

Engagement

Engagement refers to the amount of time children spend intellectually or emotionally involved with materials, peers or adults in developmentally and contextually appropriate ways (McWilliam 1991). It also relates to how they use their time (i.e. to the quality of their involvement rather than its duration) and can span five levels (McWilliam & Bailey 1992):

- **non-engagement**, where children are not involved in their surroundings;
- **transient** engagement, in which they pay attention for short durations but do not become involved in any particular activity;
- **undifferentiated** engagement, in which they play in one given way with objects or people;
- **elaborative** engagement, when the children use a range of different behaviours in their interactions with materials and other people;
- **sustained** engagement, when they display persistent, goal-directed interactions.

High levels of engagement are necessary—but not sufficient—for learning to take place, and are assumed to result in fewer behavioural disruptions; furthermore, engagement is important simply because children have a right to involvement in an attractive and interesting program (McWilliam 1991).

The level of children's engagement reflects the quality of the environment, the level of educators' support for children to engage and maintain their participation, and children's personal characteristics such as developmental level. Young children with developmental delays (aged 2 years) have been found to be less engaged with toys and in overall learning than their age mates, but this difference disappears by age 4 (McWilliam & Bailey 1995).

In terms of program planning and delivery, the following measures could prove useful for engaging children in learning (McCormick et al. 1998; McGee et al. 1991; McWilliam & Bailey 1992; Whaley & Bennett 1991).

Modify the environment
Ensure that the children have independent access to materials that are developmentally appropriate, which encourage a variety of independent, constructive, social and creative play, and are in good supply. You could systematically rotate some of the available toys to renew children's interest in familiar play materials and demonstrate at group time the potential uses of those toys that seldom engage the children.

Having supplied activities within clearly delineated zones but between which transitions are easy, assign individual staff members a particular zone so that they can observe and alter those activities that are not inviting the children's participation and can assist children to manipulate the activities on offer.

Modify processes
Choice over their activities will engage children, as will using naturalistic instruction that provides activities which closely match the children's understanding and interests, is non-directive and facilitates children's achievements rather than providing direct assistance. Small-group rather than large-group activities promote engagement also (Burstein 1986).

However, there will also be a need on occasion to intervene actively when your observations reveal that individuals are disengaged. To assist them to participate, you will need to mediate these children's learning or social play (see chapters 4 and 11). On the other hand, allow children some passive time in which to recharge their batteries and select their next activity (Linn et al. 2000). This breathing space could be particularly useful for those children with delays who focus exclusively on the activity to hand and so do not use surrounding events as a clue about a next possible activity. Within reason, giving them time to plan will allow them to exercise some initiative rather than being under adult control (Linn et al. 2000).

Another process issue is the management of transitions between activities to minimise waiting time so that children do not become disengaged. Yet another is observing routines, as these signal to children to change their style of engagement; on the other hand, you will need to be responsive so that, where appropriate, routines can follow rather than direct children's engagement.

Modify social interactions
Social engagement with adults will be fostered by ensuring that you relate warmly with children, and use authoritative rather than controlling discipline (see chapter 12) so that the children *want* to be involved with you. The children's engagement will also be affected by the nature of their peers: some will be more engaged with same-ability peers and others with same-aged peers. Furthermore, in my research I observed that in order to engage there needed to be a minimum number of children, maximising the chances that one would generate an idea for an activity in which the others could participate: groups can be *too* small to occasion engagement (Porter 1999).

Motivation

Motivation refers to children's willingness to invest time, effort and skills in the tasks that we set for them (Ben Ari & Rich 1992; Cole & Chan 1994). Glasser (1998) believes that all individuals are motivated to meet their emotional needs (see chapter 11) and their need to survive. Therefore, Glasser contends, when we say that children are not motivated, what we are actually saying is that they are not motivated to do the particular task they are being given. In turn, this will be because it is not meeting their needs. Motivation, or a lack of it, then, is not an inherent part of children's personality: if some children are choosing to invest their energies elsewhere, this will have at least as much to do with the way educational activities are structured as with the children's personal make-up (Ben Ari & Rich 1992).

Thus, motivation has the following aspects (Cole & Chan 1994; DiCintio & Gee 1999; Glasser 1998; Jones & Jones 1998):

- children's *expectation* that they can be successful. They will not be motivated to invest energy in tasks that are not intellectually demanding or in tasks where they do not expect to be successful (Chan 1996; Vallerand et al. 1994);
- their assessment of the benefits that success will bring in terms of the fulfilment of their personal needs. This assessment will cause children to place a *value* on being successful;
- the extent to which the environmental *climate* meets their physical, emotional and social needs. The notion that relationships are crucial to children's social and emotional development is mentioned in chapter 11; in chapter 12 the quality of relationships is discussed with respect to its impact on children's willingness to cooperate with others; in the present context, warm relationships are crucial to motivation as they inspire children to put in the effort to achieve (Hauser-Cram 1996).

Jones and Jones (1998) regard these elements as multiplicative, which implies that all three components are necessary for motivation. Thus, their formula (Jones & Jones 1998: 179) is:

Motivation = Expectation of success × expected benefits of success × emotional climate

The general measures for enhancing children's motivation are given in Box 10.1. These can distil down to a three-pronged approach suggested by the above formula: make realistic demands which the children are confident of meeting, ensure that tasks are relevant for the children, and develop a supportive relationship with the children so that they are emboldened to face challenges.

Locus of control

An important belief that children gain through experience is whether they themselves can control outcomes (which is termed having an internal locus of control, or *self-efficacy*), or whether luck, fate or other people control what happens to them. Individuals are said to have an external locus of control or, in its extreme form, to display 'learned helplessness' (Seligman 1975) when they believe that events outside their control are responsible for what happens to them.

When children believe that they can control the outcomes of their actions—that is, when they locate their control internally—they are more motivated to invest effort in learning, are more likely to learn from their mistakes, are more persistent and are more reflective learners (Knight 1995). In contrast, children with intellectual disabilities can be unmotivated because they are not aware that the way they go about tasks will affect the outcome. Because of a history of failure, these children might not apply themselves to a task because they do not expect to succeed. They are more likely to attribute success or failure to uncontrollable outside events such as luck, help from the teacher, or the difficulty or ease of the task (Cole & Chan 1990).

Meanwhile, the picture of the locus of control of gifted children is mixed. Although they tend to achieve an internal locus of control earlier than usual (Brody & Benbow 1986), some take too much responsibility for their mistakes, which can lead to perfectionism, while attributing their successes to the ease of the task (Bogie & Buckhalt 1987); although this pattern is by no mean universal.

Self-efficacy is vulnerable to repeated failures and to criticism (Bandura 1986). Unfortunately, it is not responsive to positive persuasion. Thus, in addition to the general measures given in Box 10.1, the following strategies will be necessary to teach children that they can be successful:

- Children will need to *experience* success, rather than simply be *told* that they are successful. Therefore, feedback needs to be specific and genuine. That is, you should not tell children that they have been successful when they have not, and should give feedback that is specific enough for them to be able to act on the information and correct their errors.
- Give children experience of both success *and* failure, so that they can form a link between their actions and the outcome (Seligman 1975). If they are always successful, no matter what they do, they will feel just as helpless as if they always fail, no matter what they do. In either case, they will show low tolerance of frustration, poor persistence at tasks, and avoidance of challenge.
- To encourage them to persist in the face of setbacks, you will need to teach children to attribute their achievements to their own effort, rather than to uncontrollable factors such as inability or luck. This is called *attribution training*. You will need to guide them to: define the failure as *temporary* rather than permanent; see failure as *specific* to the event rather than a sign of a general or all-pervasive failing on their part; and explain the failure in terms of their *behaviour*, not personality—they need to take personal responsibility without taking blame (Seligman 1995). Without confronting them with their mistakes, you should not allow them to make excuses or teach them to do so, for example by blaming a 'naughty' step for tripping them over, but instead comment that they forgot to watch out for the step.

Independence

Children who have intellectual disabilities can be reliant on adults to present information to them and to help them to make sense of it. They might not spontaneously generate their own play ideas. In contrast, although they can generate their own play ideas, gifted children might learn to rely on adults to give them the stimulation which they seek, partly because adults' ideas are more sophisticated and fascinating than their own or those of age mates. Others prefer to work independently—perhaps because of the discrepancies between their skill levels and those of their age mates. Still others might fiercely insist on doing things independently (e.g. getting dressed) but, once they have mastered the task intellectually and it holds no further interest for them, might then refuse to do it at all. They can be impatient with repetition of activities that they already understand (Clark 1997; Kitano 1990).

Various cultures place differing values on and expectations of independence in children: some encourage early autonomy while others value interdependence of individuals. Furthermore, it is appropriate that children learn to perform both independently and in cooperation with others. Therefore, although it can be valuable to encourage children to attempt age-appropriate tasks independently, it can also be important to allow them to give and receive help.

Even though you might be seeking to foster independent learning skills in individual children, at times they will need adult guidance to learn, particularly when they are acquiring new skills or extending or challenging themselves. This can involve scaffolding or mediation of their learning, as described in chapter 4.

CONCLUSION

When assisting children to 'learn how to learn', the strategies you teach must match their abilities (Cole & Chan 1990). For example, children who have impaired language skills will find it difficult to use self-instruction to guide their completion of tasks, in which case their receptive and expressive skills would be a more fruitful focus of teaching (Whitman et al. 1991). It is also important that you correctly identify whether they most need knowledge acquisition skills (attention or memory training), metacognitive knowledge and control, or adjustments to their learning style. Otherwise, a mistargeted program could frustrate both you and the children.

Some of the measures for teaching thinking processes will involve a behavioural element as well as cognitive training. I refer you to chapter 12 for a review of behavioural approaches.

ADDITIONAL RESOURCES

Ashman, A. and Conway, R.N.F. 1997 *An introduction to cognitive education: theory and applications* Routledge, London

11

EMOTIONAL AND SOCIAL NEEDS

LOUISE PORTER

KEY POINTS

- After satisfying the need to survive, children require security, self-esteem, autonomy and a sense of belonging.
- Security entails more than physical safety: children need to feel nurtured and confident that they can meet adults' expectations of them.
- A healthy self-esteem is achieved by being competent at worthwhile skills, having a realistic picture of oneself and striving for attainable ideals.
- Satisfaction of the need to be self-determining is central to individuals' emotional wellbeing and to their constructive approach to learning.
- Children cannot thrive in isolation; when for whatever reason they are not socially engaged, their social inclusion cannot be left to chance but requires some specific intervention.

INTRODUCTION

Rather than focusing on children with recognisable emotional difficulties, this chapter examines the everyday emotional and social needs of all young children, with particular attention to those whose atypical development makes them especially vulnerable to difficulties.

After the need for physical survival, children's other emotional needs can be categorised as the needs for:

- security—an assurance of protection and safety;
- self-esteem—the need to value oneself;
- autonomy—the need to be self-determining, to have some freedom;
- belonging—the need to love and be loved and accepted.

Two additional needs have been suggested. The first is the need of all creatures—and the young in particular—to have fun, which Glasser (1998:30)

191

defines as the 'intangible joy' that arises from satisfaction of the above needs. The second was posited by Maslow: namely, the need for self-actualisation, which refers to the drive to develop our abilities fully (Peterson 1996). Both of these are probably outcomes of meeting the above needs, so only that list is focused on here.

THE NEED FOR PROTECTION AND SAFETY

Adults can choose to take part in activities and to associate with people who bolster our self-esteem, but children are at the mercy of the contexts in which we place them (Katz 1995). This means that they rely on you to create an accepting environment in which they can feel emotionally safe and confident about their ability to meet the demands being placed on them.

Require considerate behaviour

To safeguard miscreants, victims and onlookers, it is important to require considerate behaviour of all children and adults. The advantage for perpetrators of learning self-control is that doing so will protect them from being shunned by others and will give them a skill to feel proud about. At the same time, teaching individuals self-control will protect surrounding children from being the recipients of thoughtless behaviour. Nevertheless, the means used must themselves protect all parties (see chapter 12).

Supervision of children is essential to oversee their physical and emotional safety. In addition, some of the following measures could prove useful.

- **Prohibit discriminatory comments and actions.** There are few occasions when an outright ban on particular behaviours is warranted, but discrimination is one of these times. So establish a general rule that children cannot use words that hurt other people or unfairly exclude others from their play (Derman-Sparks 1992).
- **Encourage assertiveness.** You can cue children when to be assertive and perhaps teach them diplomatic strategies for rejecting domineering commands of their peers—for example, by offering a reason for not following a peer's suggestion (Trawick-Smith 1988). Explain that if being assertive does not work, they can ask you for help.
- **Follow up.** If any children report that they cannot resolve a conflict, help them to sort it out: do not tell them to go back and be assertive if they have already done so. You might return with them to the other child and solve the problem collaboratively. If one child has been hurt physically or emotionally, in the hearing of the perpetrator, you can tell the victim you understand that it hurt and that the perpetrator might remember next time to use words to solve problems or to speak more kindly (as the case may be). This validates hurt children's feelings without confronting perpetrators with their mistakes and in

so doing avoids a repetition of an aggressive incident. If particular children are repeatedly aggressive or unkind to their playmates, social skills interventions could be useful (see later in this chapter).

Respond to and prevent child abuse

Child maltreatment takes a number of forms: neglect of children's physical or emotional needs, and physical, emotional and sexual abuse. Of these types, neglect constitutes more reported cases than the other forms combined.

Families who are isolated and lacking in support are more prone to child abuse, while parents' substance abuse is an increasing cause of the neglect of children. Although the use of illicit drugs occurs across all sectors of the community, it is likely to have most impact on those families that are already economically disadvantaged (Hanson & Carta 1995). Meanwhile, additional caretaking demands that arise when children have certain disabilities appear not to lead to the documented higher rate of abuse of these children: instead, the children's dependence is the factor that places them at increased risk.

The effects of child abuse differ depending on its severity, chronicity, the child's age when it occurs, the relationship between the child and the perpetrator, and the fact that in most cases many types of abuse are co-occurring. Abuse produces developmental and social-emotional impairments, with children under the age of 5 years being at more serious risk than older children of injury from physical abuse (Bonner et al. 1992). Despite this, the effects of neglect are thought to be more severely damaging (Bonner et al. 1992). When the parents are the perpetrators, the effects of abuse are compounded by the fact that it is happening within dysfunctioning family relationships that are characterised by neglect, indifference, violence, humiliation and terrorisation of children, isolation, corruption of children (as they are encouraged into antisocial behaviours), and unreliable parenting (Harter 1998).

This context leads to insecure attachments between children and their parents, as the children must continue to rely on their parents for survival but are under threat from those same caregivers (Cole-Detke & Kobak 1998; Harter 1998). In this respect, neglected children might be most disadvantaged, in that they are less likely to learn how to form attachments to others; alternatively, while abused children develop attachments, these are often damaging to them (Steele 1986).

Disturbed attachment to parents can cause these children to withdraw from the friendly overtures of caring adults or peers, and to assault or threaten adults, as they have learned that adults can be dangerous (George & Main 1979). Abused children often have difficulty regulating their anger and aggression, which probably arises from copying their parents' lack of inhibition; while neglected children can be withdrawn as a result of learning to avoid relationships: they have few social problem-solving and coping strategies, limited interaction with peers, and lack empathy for others (Hoffman-Plotkin & Twentyman 1984; Klimes-Dougan & Kistner 1990).

The result of such behaviours is that the children tend to be ignored in care and preschool settings—unless behaving disruptively, when their interactions with caregivers often comprise disciplinary measures (Hoffman-Plotkin & Twentyman 1984). This emotional neglect compounds the problems these children experience at home and leads to worsening social difficulties throughout childhood (Cole-Detke & Kobak 1998; George & Main 1979; Trickett 1998).

Emotionally, depression and anxiety are common outcomes (Trickett 1998). In terms of children's self-esteem, child abuse causes children to see themselves in negative terms and to try to be perfect in an attempt to halt the abuse (Harter 1998). Thus, in the terms discussed below, the children develop a devalued self-concept and unattainably high ideals for themselves. Their development is impaired by not believing themselves capable of solving problems.

The signs that abuse is occurring include the above social and emotional behaviours, plus physical signs such as burns or bruises; sudden changes in the children's behaviour (coinciding with the onset of abuse); refusal to accompany a particular adult; declining development or regression to less mature behaviours; and, for sexually abused children, frequent discussion about secrets or about sexual practices, knowledge of which is in advance of the children's years or developmental level.

The above litany of serious effects of abuse make it essential to report any signs that children might be being abused. You cannot wait until you have gathered all necessary evidence. Instead it will be the welfare agency's job to investigate your suspicions, which they will aim to do without further victimising the child or those wrongly suspected of being perpetrators.

If the welfare agency decides on the basis of your information to investigate the family, you will need its advice on whether you should tell the parents that you have reported your concerns and about how to support the family during the investigation process so that the child is not subjected to further violence or emotional abuse as a result of the disclosure.

Meanwhile, you will need to support the children by respecting their feelings but also requiring them to use prosocial means for dealing with their anger and regaining some power (Gootman 1993). They need empathic responses from educators so that they learn to recognise their own and others' pain; they need attention; and they need to know that they will be safe if they make a mistake (Gootman 1993). Predictable reactions and a safe emotional climate will help children who are hypervigilant to signs of danger to know what is required of them and to realise that they will be safe.

Personal safety programs are often recommended for preventing children from becoming victims of abuse, although there is little research evidence of their effectiveness at empowering children to enact the protective skills imparted in the programs (Bevill & Gast 1998; Ko & Cosden 2001), little advice about necessary modifications to ensure age-appropriateness, and few guidelines to avoid side-effects such as increased fears in children (Bonner et al. 1992; Jordan 1993). Nevertheless, incidental or more formal instruction involving modelling, role-play and feedback can teach children to be assertive and seek help in unsafe situations (Bevill & Gast 1998). Meanwhile, raising the topic of abuse with your parent group can highlight how they can keep their children safe, recognise the signs of abuse, and acquaint them with reporting procedures, while using behaviour management strategies that permit children to exercise self-control and do not demand obedience to adults (see chapter 12) will empower children and thus make them less vulnerable to abuse.

SELF-ESTEEM

The second fundamental emotional need is for a healthy self-esteem. In their first two years or so, when young children are learning to trust their caregivers, their self-esteem relies almost entirely on whether they feel loved and *accepted*. After that age, their self-esteem begins to be fed by how much *control* they can exercise over their lives. Subsequently, adults' reactions to their choices allow them to feel proud of or guilty about wanting to act independently, and they begin to define themselves as *competent* or as failures (Curry & Johnson 1990).

So, from the earliest years of their lives, children gain impressions about the type of people they are and how others want them to be. By comparing themselves to their ideals, they learn to feel pleased or disappointed in themselves. In short, then, self-esteem has the following three parts (Burns 1982; Pope et al. 1988):

1. **The self-concept.** This is our picture or description of ourselves. Young children's self-concept is fairly basic and becomes more comprehensive as they get older and learn more about themselves. At young ages, they tend to describe themselves according to how they look, what they wear, their state of health and their possessions. As they get older, they begin to define themselves on aspects comprising their relationships within and outside the family (which includes ancestors as well as living people), abilities and talents at sport and academic work, temperament, religious ideas, and ability to manage their own lives.
2. **The ideal self.** This is our beliefs about how we *should* be. This set of beliefs comes about from actual or implied critical judgments by significant people in our lives or by a process called social comparison, in which we compare ourselves to other people and set our ideals accordingly (Adler et al. 2001).
3. **Our self-esteem.** This is how much we value our characteristics. It is a judgment about whether our abilities and qualities meet or fall short of the standards we believe are ideal. In other words, self-esteem is a comparison between the self-concept and ideal self (Burns 1982), as shown in Figure 11.1.

No-one's self-concept and self-esteem ever overlap completely: most emotionally healthy individuals believe that they have around three-quarters of the characteristics they would like to have. If the two overlapped entirely, individuals would have no ambitions or goals to strive for.

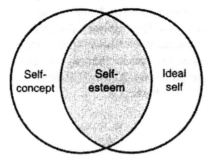

Figure 11.1 Diagram of self-esteem as the overlap between the self-concept and ideal self

Signs of low self-esteem

In contrast with the attributes of a healthy self-esteem as listed in Box 11.1, children who have low self-esteem can display a wide range of less adaptive behaviours. Emotionally, they might seek constant reassurance about your affection for them, might be overly helpful as if they must earn your approval, might be devastated if chastised, and could be highly reliant on parents, as seen with separation difficulties. Socially, they might not be able to have any fun, might be withdrawn, or not be able to enter a group without becoming either too self-conscious ('shy') or too boisterous. Finding and keeping friends can be a problem, and negotiating conflict can be difficult because they do not have enough confidence to assert themselves. They might be bullied on the one hand, or easily led on the other. Their development can be compromised as they avoid trying something new, refuse to take risks or be adventurous, or give up easily. Instead, they might play the same game over and over—such as playing only in the sandpit—because they are afraid to fail at other activities.

Such behaviours can be an effect of low self-esteem but also cause future underachievement. As time goes on, their earlier unsuccessful experiences cause them to approach tasks without confidence and fail at these as a result, thus re-affirming their low opinion of their abilities.

Routes to low self-esteem

Individuals can develop low self-esteem when they actually *are not competent* at skills which they value; when their self-concept is impoverished such that they possess many of their ideal qualities, but *do not realise* it; and when their *standards are just too high*. These pathways suggest three routes for improving their self-esteem.

Promote competence
The first route to a healthier self-esteem is to help children become competent at skills they value, because success breeds confidence. However, success must be personally meaningful. Thus, Curry and Johnson (1990:153) argue that:

Box 11.1 Characteristic behaviours of children with a healthy self-esteem

When children have a healthy self-esteem, they:

- make transitions easily;
- approach new and challenging tasks with confidence;
- set goals independently;
- have a strong sense of self-control;
- assert their own point of view when opposed;
- trust their own ideas;
- initiate activities confidently;
- show pride in their work and accomplishments;
- cope with (occasional) criticism and teasing;
- tolerate frustration caused by mistakes;
- describe themselves positively;
- make friends easily;
- lead others spontaneously;
- accept the opinions of other people;
- cooperate and follow rules, remaining largely in control of their own behaviour;
- make good eye contact (although this can vary across cultures);
- are realistic about their shortcomings but not harshly critical of them.

Sources: Adler et al. (2001); Curry & Johnson (1990); Pope et al. (1988).

Self-esteem is not a trivial pursuit that can be built by pepping children up with empty praise, extra pats, and cheers of support. Such efforts are temporary at best, and deceptive at worst. *Our children need coaches, not cheerleaders* (emphasis mine).

In line with this assertion, coaching children to learn skills that they value could entail the following measures:

- **Break tasks down** into achievable steps and then teach each step until the children can successfully complete the task independently. It might help to keep a record of the children's improvement, using audiotapes, videotapes, photographs or other natural means so that in the course of learning a skill the children can appreciate their progress.
- **Give positive instructions.** We might accidentally set children up to fail by telling them what *not* to do ('Don't run') instead of what they could do: 'Take small steps on the wet floor.'
- **Encourage children to be independent** about performing age-appropriate skills, to give them something to feel proud of.
- **Teach self-instruction skills.** Success at tasks involves not only being able to perform the skill but also being able to organise oneself to do it proficiently. Therefore, teach children how to concentrate, plan each step of a task, check that their approach is working, persist, change approaches if necessary, and so on (see chapter 10).

- **Provide authentic and specific feedback** so that children know precisely what they have to do to be successful.

Embellish children's self-concept

For children to know themselves, they need information or feedback about their attributes:

- **Use acknowledgment.** In my view, the single most powerful way that you can help children develop a healthy self-esteem is to acknowledge and celebrate their successes, without praising these. Children need *information* about their attainments but not *judgmental* feedback in the form of praise or other rewards, as these imply ideal standards and might threaten children's faith in their ability to continue to meet adults' expectations.
- **Focus on processes.** Children's self-esteem will depend on the extent to which they make the most of their potential: if you praise them for inherited characteristics, their self-esteem is not likely to improve, as they had no control over those characteristics. This means that you will need to acknowledge *effort* rather than cleverness, *personality* rather than appearance, learning *style* rather than outcome.
- **Introduce activities that acquaint children with their attributes.** If you would like to supplement your everyday feedback with a formal activity, you could help children make a list of all the many things they can do.
- Do not use—and do not permit surrounding children to use—**put-downs** or nicknames that demean individual children.

Encourage realistic ideals

It is important for children to have realistic standards for themselves; otherwise they can develop a dysfunctional form of perfectionism in which they are dissatisfied with their achievements, no matter how well they perform. A more functional type of perfectionism entails striving for high standards because you know you are capable of meeting your goals. Gifted children in particular can fall into this category. In that case, you do not want to teach them to lower their standards as their perfectionism is the engine that drives them to achieve, but you do need to give them confidence that they can reach their ideals:

- **Accept yourself.** Show children how to talk positively about themselves by occasionally doing so about yourself in their hearing and treat your own mistakes kindly so that children will learn to handle their own errors similarly.
- **Respect children and their feelings,** even when you do not understand why they feel as they do. Respect also requires you to value children's diverse cultural backgrounds. This requires doing more than discussing the exotic customs and dress of other cultures but demonstrating acceptance in your day-to-day interactions with all the children.
- **Encourage risk taking.** If children are told when they are successful that they are 'good' boys and girls, they will assume that making a mistake renders them 'bad', and so will restrict themselves to only the safest of activities. Therefore,

you need to give children permission to be adventurous and risk getting things wrong. If they are not making mistakes, that means they already knew how to do a task—and that is not called learning: it is practising.

- **Teach children to evaluate negative feedback.** When children are disappointed in themselves, your first response must be to listen and accept what they feel. They will think that you do not understand them if you insist on reassuring them that things aren't that bad, or if you tell them to cheer up. Moreover, their disappointment might be a realistic reaction to a failure and might spur them on to becoming more skilled.

  But if they *are* expecting too much of themselves, you might gently question whether they are being realistic, without giving advice or telling them off for feeling what they feel. You could, for example, ask gently, 'You seem disappointed that you didn't finish that. But do you think that 4-year-olds can normally do it all by themselves or do they need help? Perhaps you're expecting too much of yourself to be able to do it alone.'

AUTONOMY

A third emotional need is for self-determination or autonomy. When children feel out of control of what happens to them, they become stressed. Thus, giving children autonomy is fundamental to satisfaction of these other needs.

Give children control

Children need repeated opportunities to exercise choices, initiative and autonomy, so involve them in making decisions that affect them. Asking for their suggestions and listening to their ideas tells them that you value them and believe in their abilities to take responsibility for themselves. This is especially important for children whose disabilities limit their learning of intentionality (see chapter 10) as, without experience of being able to act on their intentions, they can develop a helpless learning style which in turn compromises their development (Seligman 1975).

It is important not to ask for children's participation when there is no choice *whether* to perform a particular activity, but you can still give them a choice of *how* to go about it. For example, at pack-up time you will not ordinarily ask whether children want to help pack away, but could ask if they want to pack away the blocks or the paints.

Provide attribution training

This is described in chapter 10, so it is enough to repeat here only that you must teach children to connect an outcome with their own actions (Seligman 1975), so that they realise they are in command of their decisions and actions.

Minimise stress

Stress is a physical reaction to feeling out of control, particularly of negative events in life. Children whose families are stressed can become overwrought themselves, while children who have emotional or behavioural difficulties can themselves create stress in those around them, which then rebounds on them (Luthar & Zigler 1991).

You can support stressed children, first, by noticing the signs such as behavioural acting out or withdrawal and allowing children to discuss their feelings. Second, you can assist children to solve challenges in a way that enhances their self-confidence, promotes mastery and encourages them to take appropriate responsibility for themselves (Rutter 1985).

To prevent provoking stress in reaction to your program, you must give children activities that they feel able to master. It is important not to overwhelm children who have learning difficulties with remedial programs in many developmental domains at once or to focus only on what they find difficult, but instead allow them also to experience success and pleasure in other skills, even when these are outside the traditional focus of education (Sapon-Shevin 1999).

SOCIAL NEEDS

In order to satisfy children's fourth emotional need—correctedness with others—they need warm relationships with their adult carers and peers.

Educators' relationships with children

In chapter 4, the quality of educators' relationship with children is highlighted as being crucial to the children's willingness to learn; here it must be emphasised that children's attachment to their caregivers will meet many of their fundamental social and emotional needs. To that end, your relationship with children needs to involve the five As of attention, acceptance, appreciation, affirmation and affection (Albert 1989, in Rodd 1996).

With respect to the first of these qualities, it has been found that although educators spend the vast majority of their time interacting with children, nearly one third of the children actually receive no individual attention on a given day (Kontos & Wilcox-Herzog 1997). This signals the need for adults deliberately to make contact with individual children who could otherwise be overlooked. Meanwhile, the other listed qualities do not mean that you should indulge children's emotions or behaviours if these will be detrimental to them in the long run (Katz & McClellan 1997), but simply that you respect children for who they are and respond to them in ways that will make it more rather than less likely that they will continue to cherish relating with you (see also chapter 12).

Children's relationships with each other

Friendship is an ongoing, voluntary bond between individuals who see themselves as roughly equal, have a mutual preference for each other, share emotional warmth and interact reciprocally (Hartup 1989; Howes 1983). It usually requires that the children are at a similar developmental level and behave predictably so that others feel safe in their company.

Peers can make unique contributions to children's development in many domains (see Hartup 1989; Hartup & Moore 1990). This tells us that when children's peer relationships are disrupted, their development as well as their emotional wellbeing can suffer.

Three groups of children are more likely than most to be socially isolated in early childhood centres. First are children with significant intellectual delays: around 30% are actively rejected, which is often related to their behavioural difficulties, while a greater number still are ignored (or neglected) by peers, which is often related to their social reticence (Odom et al. 1999). This social isolation comes about because, even compared with younger children of an equivalent developmental level, those with intellectual disabilities lack the cognitive and metacognitive skills necessary to read social cues and to instigate and maintain peer relationships. As a result, they (Brown et al. 1999; Guralnick & Groom 1987; Hanline 1993; Odom et al. 1999):

- interact less often and so spend proportionately more time either unoccupied or engaged in solitary play;
- initiate fewer interactions with peers (Reynolds & Holdgrafer 1998);
- are less successful in their social initiations—and this can deteriorate over time;
- respond less to approaches from others;
- take the lead less often in social play.

The same is not necessarily true of all disability categories, however. For example, children with physical disabilities appear to be well understood, accepted and included (at least at the level of parallel play) in the play of typically developing children (Okagaki et al. 1998).

A second group of potentially isolated children are those with advanced development. Gifted youngsters are often popular with others but do not experience these relationships as deeply companionable: in short, many are not as attached to peers as their peers are to them. They might develop deep attachments to a best friend at a similar developmental level to themselves or to their parents, but lack a breadth of attachments, making them vulnerable to separation problems and loneliness within groups of age mates. Thus, despite the fact that their advanced problem-solving skills contribute to social finesse, it can seem at times that they lack the ability to form friendships. The main intervention for these children is to give them access to others at their developmental level, as usually their social success improves and they feel less lonely when they have playmates who can share their sophisticated interests.

A third group of children commonly experiencing social isolation are those who often behave aggressively. Although these children initially approach others often, their overtures are commonly rejected because their approaches are boisterous or aggressive, they disrupt others' play and are less cooperative—with the result that over time they initiate less often and become increasingly isolated (Dodge 1983). As a result of their behaviour, these children are disliked by many peers but are liked by and gravitate towards other aggressive children (Arnold et al. 1999; Dodge 1983; Farver 1996; Hartup 1989; Hartup & Moore 1990).

SOCIAL SKILLS INTERVENTIONS

Once isolated, children's social inclusion is unlikely to improve without deliberate intervention: it is not enough simply to place children together and hope they will relate to each other positively (Guralnick et al. 1995). One approach is to conduct formal social skills training programs. However, across a range of learning and behavioural difficulties, such programs have produced improved rates of interaction at the time but little evidence that these gains are maintained. Given that the studies involve intensive and prolonged training—as many as 37 (Antia et al. 1993), 56 (McConnell et al. 1991) and 60 (Odom et al. 1999) daily training sessions, for example—and given that most studies utilise highly trained behaviour specialists and still attain very modest results, it seems that formal social skills training programs are unlikely to be practicable (Odom et al. 1999). More comprehensive, multifaceted approaches focusing on the environment, children's everyday interactions and their developmental skills are more likely to produce lasting results (Strain & Hoyson 2000).

Promote acceptance

When children have a history of being in the same group and have observed adults interacting positively with isolated peers, they are similarly likely to accept and involve these children in their play (Hughes et al. 2001; Okagaki et al. 1998). Your acceptance can also be communicated by talking openly with the children about the many differences and similarities between people (Crary 1992). This can allow you to dispel some of their myths about disabilities, such as that a peer's disability in one domain affects all his or her developmental skills simultaneously, or that it is contagious.

Ensure that the children know each other
Children are more willing to play with someone they know. This requires that, where possible, you maintain a stable group membership and on a daily basis incorporate the likes of name songs in your group story and song sessions so that the children become familiar with each other.

Furthermore, it pays to limit individual children's withdrawal or absences for specialist appointments and the like, so that they have continuity in their contact with potential playmates (Freeman & Kasari 1998). Also, dividing the children regularly into groups composed of the same members for particular activities is likely to highlight their differences, and could make members of the other group seem unsuitable as playmates (Hestenes & Carroll 2000).

Consider placement

Because children choose playmates who are at their own developmental level, it behoves us to provide individual children with potential matches by, where possible, placing children with disabilities with at least one other child with a similar disability (Freeman & Kasari 1998)—and gifted children with older playmates—so that the children have access to peers at similar developmental levels to themselves (see also chapter 4).

Use toys that invite social play

Ensure that the activities on offer invite social play and are more attractive than being alone. Toys that tend to invite isolated or parallel play include small building blocks, playdough, books, sand play, and craft activities; while those that promote social cooperative play include dress-up clothes, dolls and doll houses, large blocks, housekeeping materials and vehicles (Ivory & McCollum 1999). This list is not prescriptive, as most of the latter group can be used in solitary play as well, while the provision of dramatic play equipment will allow children to engage cooperatively with otherwise solitary materials, such as playdough and sand play (Sainato & Carta 1992).

Initiate cooperative activities

You can actively foster cooperative play between children by instigating activities and games that require joint effort and cooperation. Cooperative games aim to involve isolated children and to pair up children who ordinarily do not play with each other. In this way, they expand each child's pool of potential friends; help children form a cohesive group; teach cooperation skills, turn-taking and sharing; decrease aggressiveness; and provide a non-threatening context for modelling and rehearsing social skills (Bay-Hinitz et al. 1994; Hill & Reed 1989; Orlick 1982; Sapon-Shevin 1986; Swetnam et al. 1983).

Examples of cooperative games include non-elimination musical chairs, which involves removing a chair—not a player—whenever the music stops, so that all the children end up having to fit on the one remaining chair. Another example is the frozen beanbag game, which requires children to move around with a small beanbag on their heads, freezing when it falls off, and remaining still until another child helps by replacing the beanbag on their head (Sapon-Shevin 1986).

At the same time you must curb competitive activities, as these increase aggressive behaviours and reduce cooperation (Bay-Hinitz et al. 1994). Competitive games involve taunting or teasing (e.g. 'King of the castle'), grabbing or snatching at scarce toys (e.g. musical chairs), monopolising or excluding other children (e.g. the piggy-in-the-middle game), or the use of physical force (e.g. tag ball) (Orlick 1982; Sapon-Shevin 1986).

Some children are reluctant at first to engage in cooperative games but still benefit from even low participation rates, and can be persuaded to participate by watching the other children enjoying themselves (Bay-Hinitz et al. 1994; Hill & Reed 1989).

Mediate children's use of social skills

When you observe that particular children have no stable friendships, are rejected because of their aggressive behaviour, have disabilities that impair their social skilfulness, or play predominantly alone or in parallel beyond the usual age, you can take active steps to support their social engagement.

Mediate social play

In most instances, it is important to allow children to direct their own play and resolve their non-violent conflicts independently (Harrison & Tegel 1999). However, when children are often isolated, you can be more directive by:

- selecting socially competent children to play alongside the reticent child;
- introducing an activity that will attract that child and others;
- if necessary, prompting their play until the children can direct it themselves (Odom et al. 1999).

Some writers advise educators to structure all elements of play involving children with intellectual disabilities: determining the game, allocating roles and assigning tasks, as negotiating these exceeds the children's cognitive skills and so limits their involvement in dramatic play (DeKlyen & Odom 1989). However, as this denies children without disabilities the metacognitive exercise that negotiation provides, and the imposed structure might not result in generalisation of disabled children's play to less structured settings, this procedure should be used judiciously.

Teach specific behaviours that make up social skilfulness

The first social skill is surveillance: to enter a group, children need to take time to survey the group's activities and members' non-verbal behaviours. This allows hopeful entrants to make their behaviour relevant to the group's, which in turn makes it more likely that their bids to gain entry will be positively received (Asher 1983; Brown et al. 2000). A hopeful entrant can approach the other children and quietly observe their game, wait for a natural break to occur, and then begin to do what the other children are doing (Putallaz & Wasserman 1990). This has been called the wait-and-hover technique and is extremely useful—as long as it is followed by bids to enter; otherwise children remain on the periphery for extended periods (Brown et al. 2000). Moreover, as groupings become more firmly entrenched over time, entry bids have to be increasingly sophisticated, which will disadvantage children with developmental delays (Guralnick & Groom 1987).

This entry process can be facilitated by the use of some social behaviours, as listed in Box 11.2. You can naturalistically prompt and assist isolated children to use any of these behaviours. Once children have located some playmates, they need to know how to maintain the relationship. This too requires a range of skills (see Box 11.2).

Assist children's development

Children need to be competent at talking so that they understand the play themes of others and can sustain and elaborate on their social play (Rose 1983;

Box 11.2 Prosocial behavours

Although social skills differ at various ages and for various ethnic and cultural groups, some skills are universal. These universal skills comprise being positive and agreeable; being able to use relevant contextual and social cues to guide one's own behaviour; and being sensitive and responsive to the interests and behaviour of playmates (Mize 1995).

Entry skills
- **Observe** the group before attempting entry.
- **Initiate** contact by approaching, touching, gaining eye contact, vocalising or using another child's name.
- **Responding positively to others' invitations** is a second way to gain entry to others' play.
- **Avoid disruptive actions,** such as calling attention to oneself, asking questions, criticising the way the other children are playing, or introducing new topics of conversation or new games, being too boisterous and thus out of keeping with the group, acting aggressively or destroying others' play materials (Putallaz & Gottman 1981; Putallaz & Wasserman 1990).

Supportive actions
Supportive behaviours tell others that potential playmates are keen to cooperate and can be trusted. Such actions comprise:

- complimenting;
- smiling at;
- cooperating;
- imitating;
- sharing;
- taking turns;
- assisting others;
- leading diplomatically (i.e. making positive play suggestions) to enlist other children in their play, but without being bossy.

To be supportive, children also need to pay attention to relevant social cues so that they are sensitive to the needs of their playmates. In response to feedback from their peers, they need to:

- moderate their behaviour to suit their friends;
- respond positively when others are trying to make friends.

Finally, children need to be aware of how their behaviour will influence how other people respond to them.

Conflict management skills
To resolve conflict peaceably with playmates, such as when their requests to enter a group are being rebuffed, children need to:

- be persuasive and assertive rather than bossy;
- negotiate play activities;

- obey social rules about sharing and taking turns as leader;
- suggest compromises when someone's actions have been disputed;
- avoid acceding to unreasonable demands from playmates but nevertheless decline tactfully by presenting a rationale for not accepting a playmate's idea or by offering an alternative suggestion (Trawick-Smith 1988).

Rubin 1980; Trawick-Smith 1988). Similarly, they need the requisite motor skills to participate in peers' physical play and to move about the centre, seeking activities and peers to engage them. Therefore, if children speak a language other than English or have delayed skills in any developmental domain, secure them professional assistance to enhance their skills and thus their social inclusion.

Ensure access for children with disabilities
If children are to play together, you will need to ensure that those with disabilities have access to the same activities as their peers. Suggestions given in previous chapters can help here. Nevertheless, being alongside each other is necessary but not sufficient for children to play together and so you will need to enact the following additional measures that allow them to find mutual interests.

Assist peers to engage excluded children
When children are neglected or ignored by their peers, you might deliberately structure an activity that you know will appeal to two children who do not ordinarily play together, or you could await a natural opportunity to point out to a competent child that an isolated child appears interested in what he or she is doing and might want to take part. You could say something like: 'James seems interested in your game. Do you think he could help you with the baby's bed?'

Some social skills programs that train peers to lead the play of less able children (e.g. Odom et al. 1999) generally increase the rate of children's interactions. Even then, educators must continue to structure activities and materials and seek opportunities to facilitate the children's natural social exchanges (Kohler & Strain 1999). Moreover, such programs have disadvantages that suggest caution in their use: first, the children's friendships may not flourish (English et al. 1997), partly because the 'buddy' role must be shared between the able children so that they do not feel burdened by it; second, it is important that time involved in training their less able peers not encroach on opportunities for the able children to extend their own development.

Another instance where you can support individual children is when they are refused entry to other children's play, which is common even when children request entry in socially graceful ways. At times, a rebuff will occur because the children just want to be alone or because they cannot think of a way of involving a new player. In the latter case, you can inquire about their game and ask whether there is room for one more child. You could meet such complaints as 'Matthew wants to be the baby and we already have a baby' with suggestions that this family could have twins, or that Matthew could adopt some other role.

If the children reject these suggestions, you could limit the duration of the exclusion. You could begin by explaining to the excluded child, 'Well, it looks like there isn't room for you in this game just now, Matthew. Children, how long do you think you'll be playing this game before you can let Matthew join in? How long will Matthew have to wait?' This gives a certain end to their exclusion of Matthew and lets him know that his exclusion has to do with the demands of the game, rather than himself.

Assist aggressive children

Troubled and isolated children have troubled and isolated families (Hartup & Moore 1990; Kelly 1996). Furthermore, the behaviour of aggressive children can provoke rejection by their parents, educators and peers, exacerbating their original difficulties. Thus, it is crucial that you do not allow the children's behaviour to provoke the same reaction in you (Kelly 1996). Instead, you will need to:

- build a close relationship with these children, to compensate for their lack of attachments to peers and other adults;
- teach them to manage their emotions so that they can behave prosocially with peers, without using coercive means that invite further rejection (Arnold et al. 1999) (see chapter 12);
- teach the children how to enter a group without disrupting its ongoing activity (Kelly 1996);
- as aggressive children are more likely to interpret their peers' accidental behaviours as intentionally hostile and to respond aggressively, guide them to make more accurate interpretations of others' intent and to overlook occasional mistakes by playmates (Asher 1983; Katsurada & Sugawara 1998);
- teach recipients of aggression how to negotiate with rather than to reject the aggressor, so that rejection does not provoke further instances of aggression (Arnold et al. 1999);
- allow recipients of aggression some time to be assertive independently to establish their own place in the group hierarchy (Farver 1996);
- if safety becomes an issue or resolution is not speedy, step in to protect recipients from intimidation (Arnold et al. 1999);
- give aggressors alternative opportunities to lead and exercise autonomy so that they do not need to exert control in destructive ways;
- consider social skills coaching for all members of an aggressive child's clique, as all group members are likely to display similar levels of aggression, even when individuals have differing popularity (Farver 1996);
- foster cohesion within the peer group in general, as aggression is less common within stable, cooperative groups (Farver 1996);
- where possible, support parents to improve their bond with their children without using controlling disciplinary methods, so that the children experience and acquire an attitude of nurturance and empathy towards others;

- encourage parents to provide additional opportunities for the children to practise prosocial skills in relationships with family acquaintances or other children from the centre (Hartup & Moore 1990).

CONCLUSION

A crucial part of any early childhood program is safeguarding the emotional wellbeing of the children. All children have emotional needs that deserve consideration, while children with atypical development can experience additional emotional and social challenges.

If young children are having difficulty learning social skills naturally, early childhood is an ideal time to intervene: children of this age are motivated to play socially so they are willing to be guided by adults, and there are many natural opportunities every day to be taught social skills. Nevertheless, antisocial behaviour might arise not because children do not know the prosocial alternative but because their aggression works for them. In that case, the issue is behavioural rather than a skill deficit, which leads in to the topic of chapter 12.

ADDITIONAL RESOURCES

Child protection
Briggs, F. and McVeity, M. 2000 *Teaching children to protect themselves* Allen & Unwin, Sydney

Self-esteem
Curry, N.E. and Johnson, C.N. 1990 *Beyond self-esteem: developing a genuine sense of human value* National Association for the Education of Young Children, Washington, DC
Seligman, M.E.P. 1995 *The optimistic child* Random House, Sydney

Social skills
Cartledge, G. and Milburn, J.F. (eds) 1995 *Teaching social skills to children: innovative approaches* 3rd edn, Allyn & Bacon, Boston, MA
Katz, L.G. and McClellan, D.E. 1997 *Fostering children's social competence: the teacher's role* National Association for the Education of Young Children, Washington, DC
Kostelnick, M.J., Stein, L.C., Whiren, A.P. and Soderman, A.K. 1998 *Guiding children's social development* 3rd edn, Delmar, Albany, NY
McGrath, H. 1997 *Dirty tricks: classroom games for teaching social skills* Longman, Melbourne
McGrath, H. and Francey, S. 1991 *Friendly kids; friendly classrooms* Longman Cheshire, Melbourne

Odom, S.L., McConnell, S.R. and McEvoy, M.A. (eds) 1992 *Social competence of young children with disabilities: issues and strategies for intervention* Paul H. Brookes, Baltimore, MD

Sapon-Shevin, M. 1999 *Because we can change the world: a practical guide to building cooperative, inclusive classroom communities* Allyn & Bacon, Boston, MA

12

GUIDING CHILDREN'S BEHAVIOUR

LOUISE PORTER

KEY POINTS

- Behaviour management or disciplinary practices reflect an imbalance of power between adults and children, which is often justified on the grounds of the children's immaturity (Johnson et al. 1994).
- There is a contradiction between teaching children to explore so that they will learn and teaching them to do as they are told so that they obey behavioural limits.
- This tension can be resolved by aiming not for compliance but for thoughtful and considerate behaviour, using means that increase the children's self-control rather than imposing controls on them externally.

INTRODUCTION

Although more common in those who have significant developmental disabilities, clinical behavioural difficulties in very young children are rare—perhaps as low as 2% (Smith et al. 1987). Nevertheless, many practitioners experience significant behavioural difficulties in children who have no recognised behavioural disorder and display otherwise typical development. Such difficulties comprise the following:

- behaviours that are normal but occur excessively—past the usual age or at a higher rate than usual (Herbert 1987);
- behaviours (e.g. head-banging and biting oneself) that are abnormal at any age (Smith et al. 1987);
- a constellation of behavioural difficulties, any one of which on its own would not be a major challenge but when combined pose some management difficulties;

- behaviours that are suitable in one time and place (e.g. moving about) but which disrupt the present context, such as group story time (Apter 1982, in Conway 1998).

These scenarios have been termed primary behaviours (Rogers 1998), and are generally thought to be a problem because they violate the rights of the children performing them or interfere with the rights or needs of surrounding children or adults. Secondary behaviours, however, are probably more common and therefore of greater importance: these are said to occur in reaction to adults' corrective responses to the primary behaviours (Rogers 1998). In my research I found that the disciplinary methods described in this chapter avoided provoking such reactions, thus reducing considerably the number of disruptions (Porter 1999b).

DEBATES ABOUT DISCIPLINE OF YOUNG CHILDREN

The language about behaviour 'management' is problematic, having overtones of controlling others: of doing something *to* them, rather than working *with* them (Kohn 1996). It implies a reward-and-punishment system of behaviour modification: even the alternative term 'discipline', which might seem preferable, has connotations of punishment because our society has such a long tradition of using controlling forms of discipline that the two terms are wrongly thought to mean the same thing.

Locus of control

Some theories—most notably applied behaviour analysis (ABA), which was earlier termed 'behaviour modification'—believe that individuals' behaviour can be manipulated by changing the rewards and punishments that follow it. Guided by this belief, adults give children rewards for 'good' behaviour and punish undesirable actions.

Taking rewards first, these can be social (e.g. praise, hugs or a smile); the opportunity to do a favourite activity (e.g. being allowed to play outside for extra time); a sticker or some other tangible reward that the children value for itself; or food rewards (although these are not recommended; see Birch et al. 1995). Meanwhile, punishment is of two types: withdrawing a positive consequence that children want (e.g. withdrawing access to a privilege, or withdrawing attention through the use of time out), and administering negative consequences such as verbal reprimands and physical aversives such as spanking. In some countries, physical aversives, particularly in professional settings, are illegal; even where this is not the case, experts agree that they should never be used for ethical reasons and because of their ineffectiveness.

A contrasting view of where control is located comes from a group of theorists known as humanists. These writers believe that external events only ever give us information about what might happen to us if we engage in a particular

Box 12.1 Side-effects of rewards

Rewards imply that adults know everything in all domains and so have a right and are able to judge whether children's achievements are adequate. Other disadvantages include the following.

Effects on children's self-esteem

- Children will not feel accepted because they know that they are being judged.
- When ideal behaviours are rewarded, children might expect themselves to be 'good' all the time, lowering their self-esteem when this is impossible.
- Rewards teach children that other people's opinions of them are more important than their own. This can stifle self-reliance.

Rewards can impede learning

- Rewards can cause children to develop external rather than intrinsic motivation.
- Children who strive for rewards might engage in 'adult watching' to assess whether you approve of them. This will distract them from their own learning.
- Rewards cause children's performance to deteriorate: they may do more work but it is of lower quality.
- Rewarded children might strive to please and fear making mistakes, and so avoid being creative and adventurous.

Rewards can provoke disruptive behaviour

- Discouragement about being unable to meet unrealistic expectations can cause some children to behave disruptively.
- Rewards do not teach children to monitor their own successful behaviour and so do not give them the skills to regulate their unsuccessful actions either.
- Rewards might teach children how to manipulate their peers.

Rewards can be ineffective

- Rewards are often delivered to the children who achieve least well (as adults are aware that these children need encouragement) and so, if they work, will reinforce low-quality output.
- Adults and their praise lose credibility if the children's evaluations of their work do not match those of the adults.

Rewards can be unfair

- Adults need a high level of technical expertise to use rewards well.
- While some children can 'pull' praise from adults, others cannot and so receive less praise than they deserve.
- Rewards increase competition between children.
- Their experience that praise is unfair causes some children to reject the adults who administer it.
- Many children come to resent being manipulated by rewards.

behaviour, but that we decide for ourselves whether we will abide by or defy a system of rewards and punishments (Glasser 1998). This decision is based on whether a behaviour we are contemplating is likely to meet our needs (as listed in chapter 11). In short, humanists say that all individuals are controlled internally, not externally.

The debate is difficult to settle through research, but cognitive theory (see chapter 10) highlights the need to promote an internal locus of control for all children and particularly for those who have disabilities—and disciplinary methods are no exception to this edict. Furthermore, even if individuals can be manipulated externally, the humanists contend that it is risky to do so. They cite many disadvantages of rewards and punishments, respectively listed in Boxes 12.1 and 12.2. Many (but not all) of these have been verified by research: for instance, studies have shown that when mothers exercise restrictive control over their children, the children become defiant, uncooperative, withdrawn, anxious, unhappy, hostile when frustrated, and unwilling to persist at tasks (Baumrind 1967, 1971; Crockenberg & Litman 1990).

In contrast, Gordon (1991) believes that adults must achieve authority by virtue of their expertise, rather than through their power to make children uncomfortable for non-compliance. Glasser (1998) describes the first style as leadership and the second as bossing. This authoritative discipline style tends to produce children who are more cooperative, self-controlled, self-confident, independent and social. This is probably because children are more likely to cooperate with adults who have previously cooperated with them (Atwater & Morris 1988; Parpal & Maccoby 1985; Porter 1999b).

In light of such studies with parents and educators, the humanist writers conclude that there are alternative disciplinary measures that are as effective as rewards and punishments, but which do not incur their risks.

View of children

The humanist writers accuse the authoritarian theories of having a sour view of children, namely that they will not behave thoughtfully unless they are manipulated into doing so (Kohn 1996). Humanism believes instead that when adults do not threaten children with punishment or bribe them with incentives for behaviour of which we approve, young people are motivated, will make constructive choices, and are likely to behave thoughtfully (Kohn 1996; Rogers 1951; Rogers & Freiberg 1994).

Goals of discipline

Some theories aim to teach children to comply with adult directives, and indeed use terms such as 'non-compliance' or 'naughty' to describe behavioural difficulties. Most claim that their intent is to use this external control to teach children self-discipline. However, 'self-discipline' means different things to the various authors: in some cases, it simply means getting children to comply

Box 12.2 Summary of disadvantages of punishments

Limited effectiveness
- Children must infringe someone's rights before action is taken.
- Aversive consequences can increase undesirable behaviour.
- Children learn to behave well only to avoid punishment, rather than developing a 'conscience'.
- Adults must be constantly vigilant to detect misbehaviour, and cannot. Failure to identify the full circumstances leads to errors in administering punishment.
- Its effects may not be permanent.
- Punishment may not replace the undesired behaviour with a more desirable one.
- Punishment works only for those who do not need it.

Effects on recipients
- Punishment can produce negative emotional side-effects, including low self-esteem.
- It can teach children to imitate exercising control over others.
- Children might avoid punishing situations either by withdrawing or by becoming submissive.
- Punishment can provoke undesirable behaviours such as resistance, rebellion and retaliation, which in turn attract more punishment.
- Punishment can intimidate onlookers even when they themselves are never punished.
- Punishment can cause onlookers to define a punished child as 'naughty' and, as a result, exclude him or her from their friendship group.

Effects on administrators and society
- Punishment can become addictive and can escalate into abuse.
- It can teach children to ignore adults who threaten but do not deliver punishment.
- Children might push adults who threaten punishment, to see how far they will go or to force them to back down from an empty threat.
- Violence damages relationships.
- Violence in homes, care settings, preschools or schools leads to a violent society.

whether or not they are being supervised. But this might come about simply because the children are not sure when the adult will return and detect any misdeeds. This, then, is simply internalised compliance. Instead, humanism aims to teach thoughtful behaviour, which comprises:

- developing in children a sense of right and wrong so that they act considerately, not because they might be punished for doing otherwise but because it is the right thing to do;
- teaching children to manage their emotions so that their outbursts do not disturb those around them, but more importantly so that they themselves learn to cope with setbacks in life;

- teaching children to cooperate so that all can have their needs met;
- giving children a sense of potency—that is, a sense that they can make a difference to themselves and their world and can act on their values (Porter 2001).

In the vein of Calvin Coolidge's declaration that 'There is no right way to do the wrong thing' (Sapon-Shevin 1996: 196), the humanists reject the authoritarian goal of teaching obedience, as it runs counter to the educational goals of teaching democratic values, problem-solving skills and critical thinking (McCaslin & Good 1992). As McCaslin and Good (1992: 13) observe, 'We cannot expect that [children] will profit from the incongruous messages we send when we manage for obedience and teach for exploration and risk taking.'

Furthermore, training children to be obedient is dangerous in three respects. First, it endangers individual children because they might not resist abuse—and here I'm thinking mainly of sexual abuse—because they have been taught to do what adults say (Briggs & McVeity 2000). Second, it is dangerous for surrounding children, as those who have been trained to follow others might collude with schoolyard bullying when directed to do so by a powerful peer. Finally, whole societies would be safer if people did not follow the commands of a sociopathic leader who told them to harm members of a surrounding community whose race or religion differed from their own.

Definition of disruptiveness

The pluralistic perspective introduced in chapter 1 flows into acceptance of diverse behaviours of children as well as other differences among them. Lieber et al. (1998) observed that teachers who seek conformity accept only a narrow range of behaviours in their young charges. This provokes the recognition that 'misbehaviours' or 'inappropriate behaviours' are mostly defined by adults and are in the eye of the beholder (Kohn 1996). Instead, you need to keep in mind your goals of discipline and define only those behaviours that violate these or interfere with someone's rights as being in need of intervention.

Externally oriented theories such as ABA believe that children's disruptive behaviour is caused when it is inadvertently rewarded or not punished. The humanist view, in contrast, is that disruptions occur:

- as a natural result of children's inability always to anticipate the effects of their actions;
- when children explore their social environment and, not having the skills to predict the outcome in advance, at times do not realise that their actions could negatively affect someone else (Gartrell 1987, 1998);
- when children lose control of themselves because they are temporarily overwhelmed emotionally;
- in reaction to the methods adults commonly use to control children's behaviour (Gordon 1974; Porter 1999b).

All of these reasons, then, are natural childhood events—in which case we should not punish children for such mistakes, because to do so would be to punish them for *being* children. Instead, we should teach them how to act thoughtfully, just as we teach any other functional skills.

SELECTING DISCIPLINARY METHODS

With these debates about the discipline of children as a background, practitioners must choose which approaches they will use when children act thoughtlessly. When selecting these, the issue of justice or ethics is fundamental. As discussed in chapter 1, there are two key ethical guidelines: first, that practitioners must do good and, second, that they must avoid doing harm. The first of these principles implies that when trying to correct disruptive behaviour, any measures used must be *effective*. That is, they must improve the behaviour so that surrounding children or adults are protected from ongoing disruptions. Second, miscreants must likewise be protected: children who are acting inconsiderately must learn self-control so that they can cope with emotional setbacks without becoming overwhelmed and can become proud of their ability to manage themselves, and so that they do not become ostracised by others because of their inconsiderate actions.

The second principle—of *avoiding harm*—implies that while attaining a good outcome in terms of the reduction of thoughtless behaviour, the means of achieving this must not harm miscreants or onlookers in any way: the measures used must not scapegoat, disempower or intimidate any individuals.

Thus, the merit of any proposed disciplinary measures should be assessed on the following dimensions:

- the child returns to considerate behaviour—the disruption ceases;
- the miscreant learns something positive through the process of correction—such as how to solve problems;
- there are no unintended side-effects that could disadvantage the miscreant—such as increased fear of adults, feelings of intimidation, or rejection by peers;
- there are no spillover effects for onlookers—such as intimidation about how they would be treated if they too made a mistake;
- there are no spillover effects for adults—such as a loss of their humanity or violation of their own principles;
- there are no deleterious effects on the adult–child relationship as a result of how a misdemeanour is handled.

Although the theories that use rewards and punishments can cite a considerable body of research demonstrating that these methods often reduce subsequent undesired behaviours and increase desired ones (e.g. see Alberto & Troutman 1999; Kaplan & Carter 1995), such studies typically do not investigate whether there were side-effects on individual and surrounding children. When examining such spillover effects, my research (Porter 1999b) found that the humanist approaches both were more effective at ending disruptions and avoided the negative emotional side-effects of the rewards and punishments used by the authoritarian approaches (as summarised in Boxes 12.1 and 12.2). This suggests that educators should guide—rather than control—children.

SKILLS FOR GUIDING CHILDREN

Based on the research and ethical issues just described, the following methods adhere to a humanist approach to discipline, in which adults guide children and coach considerate behaviour rather than controlling children through the use of rewards and punishments.

Enact preventive measures

Although prevention is by far the most crucial aspect of behaviour management, previous chapters have discussed how to adjust the curriculum for children with atypical needs, so that information will not be expanded on here. In addition, other preventive principles can only be summarised here for reasons of space. These include the following.

- Provide a child-friendly environment in which all children feel emotionally safe and confident that they can meet expectations.
- Give children choices: on compulsory activities you cannot give them a choice whether to participate, but you can give choices about how they carry out the activity.
- Expect considerate behaviour—even from children with conditions that make this difficult, as to expect less of them would be to gain less for them and would disable them doubly with the original disability and rejection by their peers. However, when individual children have more than the usual difficulties learning thoughtful behaviour, balance this with the provision of increased support.
- Use routines where appropriate so that children understand what they have to do and do not need you to supervise their performance.
- Give instructions on what you want the children to do, rather than what you want them to stop doing. For instance, the positive instruction to 'Take small steps' can replace the negative injunction 'Don't run' on wet tiles.
- Be sensitive to what is troubling children and respond suitably so that they can regain emotional balance.

It cannot be emphasised enough that, when individual children are often acting thoughtlessly, you *must* examine the context in which they are currently functioning and make adjustments to the wider curriculum (including group size, teacher–child ratios and developmental demands) to *enable* more considerate behaviour, and you *must* develop caring relationships with troublesome children in order to make them more *willing* to cooperate with you. No intervention—no matter how skilfully employed—can compensate for a program that does not meet children's academic, social and emotional needs.

Establish guidelines, not rules

In collaboration with the children (once they have the verbal skills), you can jointly determine the behavioural guidelines that will help everyone to enjoy their time at the centre. Guidelines define considerate behaviour—that is, what you want children to do (Gartrell 1998). They are reference points that help make your responses predictable across time and different situations, but they leave you free to decide how to respond in each instance, depending on the circumstances.

In contrast, rules tell children what you *do not* want them to do and usually have predetermined penalties: 'If you do that, *this* will happen.' Consequences leave you either having to enforce something that does not make sense in the circumstances, or appearing to be inconsistent, which under the controlling forms of discipline is ineffective.

Acknowledge considerate behaviour

The humanists have generated many criticisms of using rewards (including praise) to encourage children's achievements and thoughtful behaviour, as listed in Box 12.1 (Kohn 1996, 1999; Ryan & Deci 1996). Nevertheless, these writers do recognise that children, especially those who are discouraged about their skills, need feedback about their successes and considerate behaviour, so that they will remain motivated to strive to achieve.

This dilemma is resolved by giving children *information* about what they have achieved (which elsewhere I have termed 'acknowledgment'), rather than praising or *evaluating* them—that is, judging children positively for their achievements. The risk with evaluative feedback is that it can inflate children's ideals, with the result that they become discouraged at their ability to meet expectations (see chapter 11). Acknowledgment instead aims to feed children's self-concept, and so gives them information about what they *can* achieve, not what they *must* achieve to gain adult approval. The humanists contend that children will be equally motivated by informative feedback, with fewer risks to their self-esteem and motivation to act thoughtfully (Brophy 1981).

Acknowledgment differs from praise in the following ways:

1. Acknowledgment teaches children to *evaluate their own efforts*, whereas praise gives your evaluation of these. You can invite children's self-evaluations with feedback such as: 'What do you think of *that*? . . . Was that fun? . . . Are you pleased with yourself? . . .You seem pleased that you did that so well.'
2. Unlike praise, acknowledgment *does not judge* children or their behaviour or achievements. When you acknowledge, you might tell them how what they have done affects you, but this is only an opinion, not an evaluation: 'Thanks

for being quiet while I explained what we all have to do', or 'I appreciate that you all helped pack away: it meant we could all go outside a little earlier.'
3. Acknowledgment is a *private* event that, unlike praise, does not show children up in public or try to manipulate others into copying someone who is behaving to expectations.

We do not reward our adult friends or tell them that they are 'good people' when they help us out: all we do is thank them. So we can do the same for children: it is not up to us to judge or label them, but we *can* say when we appreciate their considerate behaviour. This is a natural outcome (consequence) of their actions, not an attempt to bribe them into repeating the behaviour again.

Nevertheless, on rare occasions I have had to contrive some feedback so that children who find learning very difficult have some physical evidence that they are achieving the many small steps towards success. This is particularly so when using cognitive training approaches (see chapter 10). In these cases I have used stars, placing them inside an outline of a child's favourite cartoon character—not as a reward for listening, attending or whatever, but as a form of *evidence* of that achievement. Placing the sticker on the drawing 'punctuates' the training session, as it were, allowing us to pause and highlight the children's efforts. At the end of the session, when the character is filled with stickers, the children have some physical evidence to remind themselves of their achievements. Meanwhile, the feedback is still informative, not judgmental. It comprises such comments as, 'Congratulations! You did it!' or 'Wow. Did you know you could listen so carefully?' or 'How did you do that?' or 'I think you can be proud of that. Here's another star to remind you that you did it.' This practice might seem similar to delivering rewards but the intent is to help the children recognise their own achievements by giving them visual information when verbal feedback is not meaningful enough to them.

Modify your demands

It is important to 'listen with your eyes' to children's disruptiveness and interpret it as a message that they cannot cope with the present circumstances. Here you have two options: try to help them to regain self-control (see below), or change what you expect (you can change your demands, not the child). For example, when a child is disrupting others' play, you could invite him or her to come with you to help cut up the fruit. To those steeped in the controlling style of discipline, this seems like a 'reward' for poor behaviour, but under a guidance approach it is a recognition that the child is experiencing difficulties and is an attempt to offer support for regaining control.

Let children save face

Because their self-esteem can be tenuous, it is important to give children a way to save face after they have made a mistake. You could comment that sometimes people forget to think before acting, that it was probably an accident, or that now that the children know what can happen when they act in that way they will probably decide not to do it again. Because children cannot always anticipate the effects of what they do, the result can startle them enough to teach them not to do it again, and you will only humiliate them if you preach about something they have already realised.

Similarly, do not force children to apologise when they have hurt another child and do not deliver a lecture about what they have done. They will already know that their actions were hurtful but, in the heat of the moment, could not overcome their emotions and act on this knowledge. Therefore, there is no point explaining this to them again: the issue is not a lack of information but a lack of self-control.

So take the perpetrator and victim aside and soothe the child who has been hurt, responding to his or her feelings, as well as the physical pain. With the perpetrator listening, reflect the *victim's* feelings: 'That hurt you, didn't it? Yes, Shelley forgot to use her words ... She might be feeling frustrated or angry, do you think?' You could add, 'I think that she is sorry that she hurt you. She might be able to say so later.' If you let perpetrators save face in this way, they are likely to choose to say sorry; if they are not ready to, forcing them will not help.

Be assertive about inconsiderate behaviour

The types of behaviour for which intervention is necessary are those which violate someone's rights. Disruptive behaviour can interfere with children's own participation, with meeting the needs of surrounding children or adults, or both. When children's behaviour is violating your needs or those of other children in your care, you will have to be assertive about the effect their behaviour is having on others—without, however, blaming or criticising them, as that would be aggressive. The difference between assertiveness and aggression is that assertiveness tells children about your needs (using the word 'I') whereas aggression tells them about themselves (using the word 'you').

The first principle of assertiveness is to speak up early so that you do not force yourself to be too patient, do not require surrounding children to suffer repeated disruptions, and do not allow the miscreant to develop a habit of acting thoughtlessly.

A second principle is that, if you expect children to listen to your needs, you must first be willing to listen to theirs. This makes the method of 'empathic assertion' particularly valuable (Jakubowski & Lange 1978). In this approach, you deliver a three-part statement which:

• reflects the children's positive motives for the behaviour;
• states what you require;
• asks for a resolution.

For example, when some children are being noisy outside, you could say: 'I know that it's fun to run around and be noisy, but the babies are still asleep inside, so I need you to be a little quieter or move away from the babies' window. What would you like to do?'

Resolve conflict collaboratively

Instead of punishing children for what it regards as natural childhood mistakes, humanism uses collaborative problem solving to resolve disruptive behaviour that is negatively affecting both children and adults. When there is a conflict, leaders look for a solution, not a culprit. Nevertheless, children will need guidance to solve a dispute collaboratively. When disputes have arisen between children, this comprises the following steps:

1. Ask and listen to what each child needs.
2. Explain each child's need to the others involved.
3. Ask the children how they can solve the dispute so that they all get what they need.
4. Guide them to select one of the strategies they have suggested.
5. Gain their agreement to try the chosen solution and thank the children for their cooperation.
6. Once the solution is in place, check that it is working.

Similar steps can be used when you are in a dispute with children over their behaviour, whereby you listen to what they require, are assertive about what you need, and ask how the two of you can resolve the issue.

Teach self-control

Mostly, we assume that when children are not able to behave in a certain way, this is because they do not know the correct form of behaviour. Instead, in my observations, most children know how they should be acting but are temporarily overwhelmed by their feelings and cannot act on that information.

A brief adult example might help to explain this: let's say that at a social gathering you are offered some potato crisps. Despite not feeling hungry, you reach out your hand to take some. At that point, do you need someone to tell you about the nutritional value of potato crisps—or do you already know that and instead need more self-control? The answer is clear: it is not a lack of information that causes us to behave in ways we would prefer not to, but a lack of self-control.

In my experience, children show that they have lost self-control in one of the following four ways (Porter 2001).

1. **Protesting tantrums** occur when children are angry about not getting what they want. This type of tantrum involves crying, screaming, hitting or kicking, and is very active. (This is different from preverbal children's attempt to communicate that they are disappointed. *That* is not a tantrum: it is legitimate communication. A tantrum is where children who can usually say what they need, instead get so worked up that they cannot use words.)

2. **Social tantrums** involve one or more children exchanging verbal abuse, refusing to share or take turns, bullying, name calling, and generally not being friendly.
3. **Whingeing,** sulking or nagging are the passive version of a protesting tantrum and tell us that children feel dissatisfied with something, and cannot get past that feeling to get on with what needs to be done.
4. **Uncooperative** behaviour is the commonest expression of lost self-control, and occurs when children cannot do as they are asked because they do not want to—and cannot overcome their feelings about having to do it.

That young children lack emotional self-control is natural, given that as babies their survival demanded that they communicate every emotion to their care-givers. But this does not mean that we have to wait passively in the hope that somehow they will learn to manage their emotions: we can teach this skill to them by explaining the process of growing up and lending our warm support as they regain command of themselves.

Explain growing up

Growing up is a process of learning how to be boss of our feelings. Adults (mostly) have learned that we cannot act on every impulse. In contrast, infants believe that if they feel something, it is okay to act on it. This is part of normal development. However, as they are approaching school age, they need to be beginning the lifelong process of learning how to be in charge of what they do.

So I tell children that while their body—their outside—is getting taller, bigger, stronger and so on, their insides may have forgotten to grow up. Their feelings boss them around and get them into trouble or get them upset (as the case may be). As they are growing up to be a kindy or school person shortly—or will be *this* old at their next birthday—now is the right time to start *thinking* about growing up on the inside as well.

You cannot talk children into growing up, or they would not want to do it. Also, you cannot give them suggestions of how they can achieve it. But it can help to warn them that it will take them a long time to think about, but you are sure that part of them knows how to do it. After all, they have grown up on the outside so successfully that this shows they know how!

While they are thinking about how to teach their feelings to grow up, you will help them at the times when they get out of control.

Bring children in close

When babies get upset, we bring them in close to us and soothe them. But often our first impulse with older children is to send them away to sort themselves out alone. That, to my mind, is unfair and is too big a task for young children. (It's even too big a task for many adults.)

So instead of sending them away from you, bring upset children in close. Cuddle them, soothe them, let them cry—for as long as it takes for them to feel better. This is meant to be nurturing. The children's behaviour tells you that they are feeling stressed and out of control. There is no point punishing them for feeling like this, but they do need help to learn how to manage their feelings so that, with repeated practice, these do not need to get out of control in future.

Meanwhile, on the grounds that you cannot reason with people while they are being unreasonable, say very little: do not try to hurry them into feeling better or explain yourself or the problem. That can come later, if at all. All you need to repeat is something like, 'I understand that you're upset and I'll sit with you until you feel happier/better.' In this process, children usually go through a range of feelings from anger, sadness, to bargaining, before becoming calm and back in control.

Staying with children in this way tells them that you are willing to help them and teaches them the very skill that you are wanting them to learn—namely, how to get back in control of their emotions. Cuddling them does not do that task for them, but it does give them the support they need to achieve it.

Being with them will work best if you can begin before they get really upset and if you can comfort children often so that they get repeated practice. The early signs that they are losing control could comprise one of the passive tantrums (whingeing or uncooperativeness), which will be easier to manage than the subsequent active versions (protesting or social tantrums).

Sometimes, however, children are too out of control to accept your company or a warm cuddle as they calm down. When there is a risk of injury or the children's distress escalates, you might instead need to use time away.

Use time away

Sometimes you cannot or do not want to accompany children while they calm down, in which case time out might seem an attractive option. This usually involves isolating a child on a chair that is somewhat separate from others and asking him or her to think about a transgression. The child is typically allowed to leave when able to state what he or she did 'wrong' or should have done instead, or when adults judge that the child has calmed down sufficiently; less commonly, a predetermined time limit is imposed. However, time out in this form has many disadvantages:

- It isolates hysterical children.
- It unfairly expects children to regain control by themselves.
- They might damage the area where they have been isolated.
- They can create so much noise that the disruption is unabated.
- They might forget that they are being punished.
- You might forget that a child has been isolated and leave him or her there for too long.
- You cannot teach children more considerate behaviour when you are not together.

Therefore, time out will not work to discourage inconsiderate behaviour. However, when everyone needs a breather you can use time away instead. This involves inviting upset children to go off by themselves to a quiet and pleasant corner, until they feel better. This is not a punishment: they should find their solitude enjoyable and refreshing. If you use it as a punishment, like time out, it will not work.

Reframe your explanation of the behaviour

Your response to children's behaviour will depend on what you think the behaviour *means*. When your approach is not working, maybe that is because your explanation of the behaviour is not helping.

Unhelpful explanations usually incorporate one of two ideas: first, that the children are 'doing it deliberately' (perhaps even 'to get at you'), which will have led to a range of responses that were all designed to make the children stop it; second, that the children cannot help it (because of their personality, disability, events in the past, or their home circumstances). This idea will have led to unassertive discipline methods, where no demands are made on children to act thoughtfully, usually alternated with exasperation—neither of which have much effect.

To find a new solution, you will need to find a new way of looking at the problem. A new view of the problem is called a *reframe*. This will look at what is maintaining the behaviour *now*, rather than what might have triggered it originally. It will identify the *effect* of the children's behaviour rather than seeking a cause. For instance, when children appear to be 'attention-seeking', it might be because they are simply not sure that even when you are busy you will nevertheless insist that they behave considerately.

The new view of the problem will enable you to let go of an ineffective solution so that you can try another instead (Fisch et al. 1982). (Reframing is more complex than this brief overview; see Porter 2000a, 2000b or Durrant 1995 for more detail.)

Interrupt the pattern

Let's say that you cannot figure out a new view or a reframe of a recurring problem. In that case, you could simply use 'pattern interruption' (Durrant 1995). With this approach you allow the behaviour to continue, on the understanding that it is helping the children in some way, even if you do not understand how. In line with the principles of guidance, you cannot frustrate children's legitimate needs; but you can insist that the resulting behaviour is less disruptive to others (Molnar & Lindquist 1989).

There is an old saying that a chain is only as strong as its weakest link. With this in mind, you can break up the chain or sequence of events that occur whenever the children's behaviour is disruptive, producing in its place a new pattern. To disrupt the old, dysfunctioning pattern you could (Durrant 1995):

- change the location of the behaviour;
- change who is involved;
- change the sequence of the steps involved;

- add a new element;
- introduce random starting and stopping;
- increase the frequency of the behaviour.

So when individual children throw themselves down on the floor in a tantrum, you could move them to the sofa so that they are more comfortable (changing the location); you could invite children who often fight over sharing toys to fight now before they enter the sandpit, so that they do not miss out once they start to play (changing the sequence or introducing random starting); you could let children know that it is okay to cry when their parent leaves and that you will stay with them for as long as it takes for them to feel better (increasing the frequency of the crying), and so on.

Even when you do not understand why the children persist with their behaviours, changing the sequence of events will alter the behaviour to a form that is less disruptive.

Try a reversal

If all else has failed, try doing the opposite of what you have been doing so far (Amatea 1989), even if you do not understand in advance how that could help. If you have been:

- ignoring the behaviour, give it your attention;
- sending children away to sort themselves out, bring them in close to you and give them your support to get back in control of themselves;
- trying to talk them out of a behaviour, give them permission to continue with it—perhaps using pattern interruption to ensure that it does not bother anyone;
- thinking that they cannot help themselves, notice the times when the behaviour does not occur, and expect them to do more of what causes those exceptions;
- getting earnest about the problem, have some fun—for example, by pretending to throw a tantrum yourself whenever the child does;
- working on a difficult behaviour, choose an easier one so that you can have some success on which to build.

This suggestion to do something different is based on the advice: 'Always change a losing game' (Fisch et al. 1982:88). Or, put another way: 'If something isn't working, don't do it again' (de Shazer et al. 1986:212).

Provide repeated practice

In order to work at all, rewards and punishments have to be administered consistently. But in the real world things happen that get in the way of consistency, making it unwise or just impossible to apply the same disciplinary methods on every occasion.

Luckily, however, a consistent response to repeated disruptions is unnecessary. An analogy might be useful to explain this: if you give children swimming lessons every day for a fortnight, they might learn to swim in two weeks; if you give them lessons once a month, they might take a year to become competent swimmers. This tells us that the more practice children can get at learning a new skill, the more quickly they will learn it—but either way, they do achieve it. So if you cannot respond in your usual way to a disruption, the children will still be learning how to control their feelings at other times. Consistency is unnecessary, but repeated practice helps.

Support parents

It is inefficient (and inhumane) to undermine the skills and confidence of parents, particularly those whose children often behave inconsiderately. Just as consistency within your setting is unnecessary, so too are common approaches between home and educational settings not a prerequisite to teaching children how to manage their feelings—although it is clearly preferable if children can get practice in both locations. Nevertheless, you would create resistance in parents if you tried to convince them of your approach. Instead, allow your success to be persuasion enough.

CONCLUSION

Discipline will only ever safeguard individual children from abuse and protect society from the behavioural excesses of its members when individuals accept responsibility for themselves and can seek to satisfy their own needs without violating the needs of other people. In the preschool years, the goal of discipline, then, is to give children the confidence to take increasing responsibility for their own actions and for their effect on other people. In this chapter, I have argued that the most effective means to this end is a guidance rather than a controlling approach to discipline.

The guiding skills described here can be very similar to their controlling counterparts. For example, a natural positive consequence can involve virtually the same action as a reward, but the intent is just to acknowledge children, not manipulate them into repeating a desirable behaviour. The difference has to do with flavour or style, with how you communicate your respect for children. In their turn, children can detect the difference and will respond distinctly to the two methods. Nevertheless, because the methods are similar, you do not have to learn a completely new set of skills but can apply the skills you already have, with just a change of purpose and flavour.

ADDITIONAL RESOURCES

If you would like to read more about the ideas introduced in this chapter, I suggest the following titles:

Fields, M.V. and Boesser, C. 2002 *Constructive guidance and discipline: preschool and primary education* 3rd edn, Merrill Prentice Hall, Upper Saddle River, NJ

Gordon, T. 1991 *Teaching children self-discipline at home and at school* Random House, Sydney

Kohn, A. 1996 *Beyond discipline: from compliance to community* Association for Supervision and Curriculum Development, Alexandria, VA

——1999 *Punished by rewards: the trouble with gold stars, incentive plans, A's, praise, and other bribes* 2nd edn, Houghton Mifflin, Boston, MA

Porter, L. 1999 *Young children's behaviour: practical approaches for caregivers and teachers* MacLennan & Petty, Sydney

——2000a *Student behaviour: theory and practice for teachers* 2nd edn, Allen & Unwin, Sydney

——2000b *Behaviour in schools: theory and practice for teachers* Open University Press, Buckingham, UK

——2001 *Children are people too: a parent's guide to young children's behaviour* 3rd edn, Small Poppies SA, Adelaide

Appendix I

COMMON CAUSES OF
ATYPICAL DEVELOPMENT

LOUISE PORTER

Awareness of the primary and secondary characteristics of various disabilities allows you to look out for associated difficulties in children with a known disability. Such knowledge can also alert you to patterns of atypical development that might signal the presence of an as yet unrecognised disability.

Naturally, you cannot diagnose disabilities merely by observing atypical development—nor without a comprehensive assessment can you raise with parents the possibility of a particular diagnosis—but you can encourage parents to seek a relevant assessment and discuss with that specialist your observations of the child (Mazzocco & O'Connor 1993). Once a diagnosis is attained, knowledge of the child's associated needs can allow parents and educators to anticipate and plan for these with more detailed understanding (Hatton et al. 2000; Mazzocco & O'Connor 1993).

Three facts must be borne in mind, however. First, for the majority of children with disabilities, the condition has no recognisable biological cause, in which case detailed observation of their developmental pattern will be more useful than diagnostic categories (Ashman 1998). Second, children who share the same diagnosis can vary considerably in its severity and manifestation. This implies that educational interventions must be planned on the basis of knowledge of individuals rather than their diagnostic label. Third, for all but those with severe disabilities, children's environments are better predictors of developmental outcomes than is the existence of disabling conditions (Sameroff 1990). This means that children can suffer mild impairments (as defined in chapter 1), but in a responsive environment these do not necessarily result in a disability. For example, the link between low birth weight and poor developmental outcome is most pronounced in impoverished families: it is the families' limited resources that cause the risk posed by low birth weight to be realised (Sameroff 1982).

PRENATAL DRUG EXPOSURE

Some of the developmental effects of alcohol and other drugs can be due not only to the damage to the developing brain of the baby but also to the chaotic home circumstances prevailing when a parent is an addict—not least of which is a lack of supervision and stimulation of the baby, poor prenatal and postnatal care and nutrition, impoverished living circumstances, multiple drug use, and diminished social supports for the family.

Alcohol

Fetal alcohol syndrome is now the single biggest cause of intellectual disability in the world, accounting for 10–20% of all instances (Batshaw & Conlon 1997; Howard et al. 2001). Developmentally, delays are mainly in speech, language, cognitive and motor skills, with some behavioural difficulties also being associated with the condition (Batshaw & Conlon 1997). The physical signs of fetal alcohol syndrome are listed in Table AI.1. The degree of intellectual disability and the extent of facial abnormalities are both related to the amount of the mother's alcohol intake during the first trimester of pregnancy in particular, but also subsequently through the pregnancy and during breastfeeding (Batshaw & Conlon 1997). The mean IQ of affected children falls around 70 IQ points, although variation is considerable (Shonkoff & Marshall 2000). Lesser effects on development and physical appearance are experienced at lower doses, when the child's difficulties are usually referred to as 'fetal alcohol effects'.

Other drugs

Exposure to tobacco, marijuana, cocaine and other illicit drugs in utero results in decreased blood and oxygen reaching the fetus, causing stunted growth and increased risk of miscarriage, premature birth, stillbirth and sudden infant death (Batshaw & Conlon 1997; Howard et al. 2001). In the long term, babies whose mothers smoked during pregnancy or subsequently, achieve at below-average levels in cognitive and language skills, and may be more prone to the attention deficit disorders and learning disabilities (Howard et al. 2001).

CHROMOSOMAL ANOMALIES

Most chromosomal anomalies are incompatible with life: the fetus does not survive; a few key anomalies, however, are sustainable while resulting in disabilities in children.

Fragile X syndrome

This condition is now considered to be the leading hereditary cause of intellectual disability, being transmitted from generation to generation in a complex fashion (Batshaw 1997; Howard et al. 2001). It occurs when a long arm of the X-chromosome becomes detached or connected to the rest of the chromosome by only a thin strand.

Boys are more seriously affected by this condition, with 80% of boys and 30% of girls having intellectual disabilities (Howard et al. 2001). Physical signs of the condition (as listed in Table AI.1) are too variable in girls to be of any use in diagnosis; in boys, most signs show up only in adolescence. However, developmental delays are apparent from infancy, showing first as late walking and talking (Batshaw 1997). The main signs of the condition are autistic-like social behaviours, impaired (or disordered) speech and language, hyperactivity, attention deficits and emotional difficulties. The behavioural difficulties appear to relate to sensory processing impairments (Hatton et al. 2000), while the information processing deficits might account for the deterioration in the children's intellectual functioning as they age, which in turn partly accounts for the later identification of this syndrome.

Down syndrome

This is the second-largest genetic (but not inherited) cause of intellectual disability (Howard et al. 2001; Mazzocco & O'Connor 1993). Since the 1970s its incidence has declined from 1.33 per 1000 to 0.92 per 1000, partly as a result of prenatal screening of older mothers, some of whom subsequently choose to abort (Roizen 1997).

It is caused mainly by the existence of a third 21st chromosome (termed trisomy-21) or, in 5–10% of cases, by translocation of extra chromosomal material to another chromosome (Howard et al. 2001). Less obvious is mosaic Down syndrome, in which only 10–12% of the individual's cells have the extra genetic material. Children with this condition will share only some of the characteristics of those with the full syndrome, and as a result might not be recognised unless genetic screening is instigated.

The majority of children with this syndrome have an intellectual disability, ranging in degree from mild to severe (Howard et al. 2001), with the milder degrees of disability usually typical of mosaicism (Fishler & Koch 1991). Low muscle tone leads to delayed motor skills, and significant speech and language delays are the norm. Down syndrome is also associated with many medical difficulties, as listed in Table AI.1. After the first year, the children are commonly overweight and, combined with orthopaedic problems associated with ligament abnormalities, are less likely to exercise. Nevertheless, with adequate exercise and diets and treatment of the associated medical problems, life expectancy can be near the norm (Howard et al. 2001).

As to their temperament, some studies find that children with Down syndrome are more positive in their interaction with peers than children with similar levels of intellectual disability (Hauser-Cram et al. 1993), while others have shown them to have similar personalities to non-disabled children (Roizen 1997). Furthermore, these children experience resistance to rules, ADHD, aggressive or uncooperative behaviour, eating disorders and other psychiatric complaints at slightly elevated rates compared to the general population (Hauser-Cram et al. 1993; Roizen 1997).

Other chromosomal abnormalities

Other chromosomal abnormalities lead to a myriad of syndromes. **Prader-Willi** and **Angelman** syndromes result from a deletion of genetic material from chromosome 15: Prader-Willi occurring when the affected chromosome is supplied by the child's father; Angelman occurring when the mother's chromosome 15 mutates (Shonkoff & Marshall 2000). Children with Prader-Willi syndrome have similarities of appearance to those with Down syndrome, and have small hands and feet. Their low tone at birth leads to feeding difficulties and thus failure to thrive, but subsequently they develop an insatiable appetite that leads to obesity. Children with Angelman syndrome have low muscle tone, seizures, severe intellectual disabilities, a tendency to smile and laugh often and a walk that resembles a marionette (Shonkoff & Marshall 2000).

Rett syndrome occurs only in girls and is characterised by normal early development followed by decelerated developmental progress and head growth (Shonkoff & Marshall 2000). Children with this progressive condition have seizures, develop hyperventilation, lose purposeful hand movement and develop instead wringing of the hands, develop spasticity and often lose the ability to walk independently (Shonkoff & Marshall 2000).

Muscular dystrophy is a term representing many genetic conditions that cause progressive loss of muscle tissue and subsequent muscle weakness, which first shows in the early childhood years following normal motor development during infancy. Progressive physical disability occurs during childhood and, with the commonest form (Duchenne muscular dystrophy), death usually occurs in the late teens as a result of heart or respiratory failure, although other forms of the disease have a longer life expectancy (Howard et al. 2001). Being X-linked, the condition affects mainly boys.

Phenylketonuria (PKU) is an error in metabolism that causes affected individuals to be unable to use the essential amino acid, phenylalanine (which is found in high-protein foods), whose consequent build-up causes brain damage and profound intellectual disability. All babies born in hospitals are screened for the condition, which if detected can be avoided by dietary restrictions.

NEUROLOGICAL CONDITIONS

Many disabilities relate to the integrity of children's nervous system.

Cerebral palsy

Cerebral palsy (CP) is one of the commonest disabilities, and the commonest cause of physical disability in children, with a rate of 1.5–2.7 per 1000 live births in the developed world and higher rates in developing countries (Howard et al. 2001). CP causes disturbances of muscle tone, movement, reflex integration and posture. Prematurity combined with low birth weight (below 2500 grams) is a leading cause, accounting for 36% of cases, as is damage to the brain occurring during gestation (in approximately 30–50% of all cases) or resulting from birth complications (predominantly asphyxia, in 14% of cases) (Howard et al. 2001; Pellegrino 1997). However, many children with these risk factors do not have cerebral palsy and many children without those events do. Therefore, many additional causes are implicated, including infections before or soon after birth and exposure to toxins. Furthermore, the figures just cited may be speculative, and in many instances no cause can be found.

With the hypotonic and ataxic forms of cerebral palsy, babies will have reduced reflexes whereby, for instance, their gag reflex is weak, thus making feeding risky (Sullivan, pers. comm.) Another diagnostic sign is the persistence beyond 12 months of age of babies' early reflexes, whose continued presence affects muscle tone and movement (Pellegrino 1997). One of these reflexes is the asymmetrical tonic neck reflex (ATNR), which is seen when the head is turned to one side. It causes the arm and leg on the chin side to extend, with the other arm and leg becoming more flexed (bent), with related alterations in the trunk muscle tone (Pellegrino 1997). In normally developing children, independent movement of head, trunk and limbs is progressively possible by 3 months of age, but children with CP often cannot achieve this integration.

Another sign is delayed walking, although this is characteristic of many conditions. Treatment involves active movement training and strengthening where possible, positioning to minimise abnormalities in tone and maximise movement, prevention of contractures of muscles through the use of braces and splints, and correction of contractures where necessary through surgery. (For more details, see chapter 6.)

Epilepsy

A second neurological condition which can result from and cause disabilities is recurrent seizures—that is, epilepsy. When epilepsy is combined with neurological damage, intellectual disabilities and young onset, the prognosis is less favourable than when it occurs alone (Howard et al. 2001). Most children with epilepsy have diminished concentration and information processing skills, with a higher than usual rate of behavioural difficulties (Howard et al. 2001). Some of these difficulties can also be the result of medications needed to control the seizures (Tyler & Colson 1994).

Traumatic brain injury

A third neurological cause of disabilities is traumatic brain injury, 90% of which is caused in infants by child abuse, with the remainder being caused by the likes of falls and motor vehicular crashes (Howard et al. 2001). The severity of resulting impairments, of course, depends on the extent and location of the damage to the brain (Howard et al. 2001). As well as intellectual effects and impaired motor functioning, following a traumatic brain injury children can have reduced stamina, seizures and sensory impairments (Tyler & Colson 1994). The prognosis for children who are injured non-accidentally is less positive than for those who experience single traumas, as child abuse can lead to repeated and multiple injuries, and where a parent or parents were the perpetrators of the abuse subsequent treatment must also involve rehabilitating both the injured child and the dysfunctioning family.

NEURAL TUBE DEFECTS

Neural tube defects result from malformation during the third to fifth week of gestation of the neural groove which houses the spinal cord. Spina bifida is the most common of these and only one form of that, *myelomeningocoele*, causes physical disability. It is the second most prevalent cause of motor disabilities in childhood, after cerebral palsy (Shepherd 1995). In this condition, both the spinal cord and its covering, the meninges, push through the defective vertebrae to the skin surface, most commonly in the lumbar region of the spine. This causes flaccid paralysis and reduced sensation below the lesion, whose extent and associated difficulties depend on the location of the lesion along the spine (Liptak 1997).

In the USA the present rate of myelomeningocoele is around 0.3–0.9 live births per 1000 births, with a three to four times higher rate in Wales and Ireland and a much lower rate in Africa (Garber 1991). The prevalence is decreasing in developed countries, partly as a result of prenatal screening (following which 40% of mothers elect to abort), partly because folic acid intake by women prior to and in the first trimester of pregnancy reduces the risk of spina bifida, and partly through a natural decrease in prevalence which might be due to improved nutrition (Liptak 1997).

Three-quarters of children with myelomeningocoele have measured intelligence within the low–normal range, but still experience some learning difficulties as a result of mild impairments of perception, organisation, attention, memory, speed of motor response and hand use; the remaining quarter have an intellectual disability (Liptak 1997).

Of those infants with myelomeningocoele, 80% have associated *hydrocephalus*, which is a build-up inside the head of cerebrospinal fluid caused by obstruction of its drainage system (Shepherd 1995). Untreated, this causes the head to grow in size, placing pressure on the brain and leading to brain damage. When treated soon after birth with the surgical closure of the vertebral defect and insertion of a shunt to drain off excess cerebrospinal fluid, subsequent impairment to intellectual functioning is minimised.

It is crucial to be aware that sometimes the shunt diverting the fluid from the brain becomes blocked, resulting in lethargy, headache, vomiting and irritability as pressure builds up inside the child's skull, while an infected shunt will cause similar signs plus fever and an elevated white blood cell count (Liptak 1997). A blocked or infected shunt can be life-threatening or lead to intellectual disability (Shepherd 1995). It is important to look out for these signs in children with this condition, therefore, so that an early shunt repair can be performed.

As they have reduced sensation of pain, care must be taken that children with spina bifida do not sustain injuries, particularly to their feet and buttocks (e.g. from walking on hot outdoor surfaces).

CONDITIONS OF PREGNANCY

Illnesses of the mother or baby during pregnancy and exposure to toxins can also lead to disabilities in the baby. Still more numerous (accounting for 50% of all disabilities) is extreme prematurity (those babies born at less than 32 weeks' gestation). Nevertheless, birth weight combined with gestational age is more predictive of outcome than degree of prematurity alone, with around 20% of those born at less than 2500 grams being later diagnosed with disabilities, and babies of even lower birth weights being at still higher risk (Bernbaum & Batshaw 1997; Howard et al. 2001).

SYNDROMES WITH UNKNOWN CAUSES

Despite advances in genetic and medical understanding, the exact cause of some syndromes is still unknown, although many run in families and thus appear to have a genetic and biological basis.

Autism spectrum disorders

The autism spectrum disorders are one of a category known as pervasive developmental disorders. In this context, the term 'pervasive' means that the disorders affect all domains of children's functioning and are experienced across various settings. For children to receive the diagnosis of autism, the following three domains must be affected, with irregularities first becoming evident prior to 3 years of age and being present across a range of settings (Mauk et al. 1997; Quill 1995).

- **Impaired communication.** Around half of all children with autism do not develop functional speech; those who do show severely disordered or impaired speech which lacks diversity and is echolalic (i.e. immediate or delayed repetition of something they have heard), and thus their speech is unspontaneous and uncreative. Verbal children also use strange rhythms and intonation patterns in their speech, and use speech to indicate their needs rather than to interact with others.
- **Impaired social understanding** is shown in extreme aloofness and indifference to others and an inability to copy others, including an inability to imitate peers' play. This leads to isolated and stereotypical play with objects (e.g. lining up vehicles or spinning the wheels of a toy vehicle rather than using these toys in pretend road play), with the result that the children lack representational or pretend (dramatic) play.

- **Behavioural abnormalities.** The children have narrow play interests and obsessive adherence to routines, to the point of severe tantrums if routines are disturbed or preoccupations interrupted. The children often display repetitive movements such as hand-flapping or waving, toe-walking, rocking and, particularly in those with severe intellectual disabilities, self-injurious behaviour such as head-banging or biting their arms.

Around 75% of children with autism also have an intellectual disability, with 40% recording IQs below 50, which signifies a profound disability (Howard et al. 2001). These children also have a higher than usual rate of ADHD and perhaps epilepsy (Mauk et al. 1997). Their intellectual disabilities appear to relate to perceptual problems, one of which (termed 'overselectivity') entails perceiving only one aspect of a multifaceted problem, resulting in impaired problem solving and social perception (Quill 1995). These difficulties might arise from problems with coding and categorising information which, in turn, causes information processing difficulties (Quill 1995). Rote memory seems unimpaired (Quill 1995).

Asperger syndrome involves the last two impairments listed above. Children with this condition acquire language at around the usual age, although as a result of the children's impaired social functioning their language use can be unduly formal and non-verbal behaviours such as eye contact can be disturbed (Mauk et al. 1997). Children with Asperger syndrome might simply have rigid thinking which does not disturb them unduly, while others experience anxiety and sensory sensitivity problems (Quill 1995). Some of the latter respond to medications that reduce anxiety, either taken singly or in a 'cocktail' of various drugs, designed specifically for their particular constellation of disturbed perception and thinking.

About two-thirds of parents report that their children who are later diagnosed as autistic were aloof during infancy (Howard et al. 2001), with the other characteristics of the condition subsequently appearing in place of the usual developmental milestones. However, some children have a normal developmental pattern until 12–24 months, following which their skills regress (Quill 1995). This subgroup of children are more likely than others with autism to have seizures (Howard et al. 2001; Quill 1995).

Attention deficit disorders

Attention deficit hyperactivity disorder (ADHD) comprises predominantly vocal or motoric hyperactivity; ADD involves inattentiveness; and a combined form comprises both. The terms are relatively new labels for a condition that was first identified almost 100 years ago and has variously been described as hyperactivity, minimal brain dysfunction and hyperkinesis (Anastopoulos & Barkley 1992).

Most estimates say that around 3–5% of children and adolescents have ADHD (Wodrich 1994), with little variation across socioeconomic groups and with more boys than girls being recognised. Most children show their first signs of the condition between 3 and 4 years of age, and to be diagnosed must have evidenced the condition prior to the age of 7 years (Anastopoulos & Barkley 1992).

In the early childhood years in particular, it is difficult to distinguish normal childhood exuberance from ADD and ADHD, making accurate diagnosis difficult. Diagnosis is also complicated by the fact that the children's behaviour varies according to the circumstances and that their attention skills can be deficient in different ways (see chapter 10).

Some writers believe that impulsivity is at the heart of the attention deficit disorders. Although not yet certain, a possible neurological explanation for the behaviours is that arousal pathways in the brain fail to activate brain regions involved in decision making, while inhibitory pathways fail to suppress impulsivity and distractability—and that these mechanisms are differently affected in different children (Riccio et al. 1993).

As well as the cluster of primary symptoms, children with ADD or ADHD often show other, secondary symptoms that can complicate management. These include behavioural problems, emotional outbursts, relationship difficulties, learning disabilities (despite having average intellectual abilities overall), and a higher than normal rate of health problems such as incoordination, sleep disturbances, middle ear and upper respiratory infections, asthma and allergies (Anastopoulos & Barkley 1992).

Whereas negative parental discipline was earlier accused of causing ADHD, most practitioners now believe that such parenting styles are instead the *result* of having a child with ADHD in the family. This view is supported by research showing that parents' style becomes more positive when the children's behaviour improves—say, in response to medication (Anastopoulos & Barkley 1992; Wodrich 1994). It also stands to reason that the parents are not the cause in families where one child has the condition and the siblings do not.

Many children outgrow the condition within a year of its diagnosis. For those who do not, the longer-term outcome is still mostly unknown, although the severity of childhood symptoms is probably unrelated to adult outcome (Hart et al. 1995). Throughout childhood and adolescence, the inattentive symptoms remain relatively stable but then improve substantially during early adulthood, while the hyperactive-impulsive behaviour progressively improves throughout childhood (Barkley 1988; Hart et al. 1995).

CHRONIC ILLNESS

With the exception of certain metabolic disorders and AIDS which can cause sensory impairment, changes in muscle tone and central nervous system disturbances (Bruder 1995), most chronic childhood illnesses do not have a direct effect on the brain's capacity to learn. Nevertheless, some medical treatments such as radiotherapy or chemotherapy can themselves cause disabilities in children such as growth retardation, neurocognitive deficits and immune system suppression (Tyler & Colson 1994).

Even without these treatment side-effects, long-term health problems can compromise children's development through interruptions to their education and relationships with parents and peers. The children's early exploration can be restricted by the reduced stimulation that is available to them in hospital, by a lack of energy caused by their illness, and by the children's need to be protected from infection (McCarthy 1987). If the illness is terminal and the children are aware of this, their motivation to explore and learn can be reduced.

Socially, children's misunderstandings of their condition and its treatment, their early encounters with pain and the prospect of death can lead to fears that surpass those of healthy children (McCarthy 1987). Ongoing relationships with medical personnel can cause children to direct their social interactions to adults rather than peers. Meanwhile, the requirements of their management can increase children's dependency on adults. Their family circumstances are likely to be stressed, particularly with conditions such as AIDS, which were transmitted from the mother and which impair the mothers' own health and impede their ability to oversee their children's treatment (Bruder 1995).

Thus, while children with disabilities in general do not require medical interventions, those with chronic health problems obviously require treatment that not only improves their health but also optimises their participation in education. To promote continuity, any medication and dietary regimens will need to be integrated into the children's education program, while centre activities can be supplied for children to complete during absences.

After an absence, children's re-entry to their education program needs to be planned carefully, with opportunities for them to debrief about their experiences and chances for their peers to be informed about the reason for their absence and present needs (McCarthy 1987; Tyler & Colson 1994). The children's and families' privacy must be preserved, however, and disclosure cannot result in stigmatising the child or family; at the same time, others must be protected from cross-infection (Bruder 1995). So that you do not confuse the children themselves or undermine their parents, you will also need to find out what they have been told about their condition, particularly if they are dying (McCarthy 1987). In such circumstances you will need also to take care of yourself, allow yourself to grieve, and channel your grief into responding positively to the children's present needs (Bruder 1995).

GIFTEDNESS

Children can have the potential for significantly advanced development in a single or many developmental domains. Gardner (1983) lists the following skill domains: verbal, logical/mathematical, visual/spatial, music, body/movement, interpersonal relationships, and intrapersonal skills (that is, self-knowledge). The neurological basis of high ability in any of these domains is not entirely understood. Some researchers have gathered evidence that accurate transmission and storage of information in the brain account for gifted children's advanced abilities

Table AI.1 Summary of common disabilities

Condition	Prevalence	Characteristics
Fetal alcohol syndrome Fetal alcohol effects	1–2 per 1000 3–5 per 1000	Delayed speech, language and motor skills. Behavioural difficulties. Below-average height but normal weight. Abnormal facial features: small head, short, upturned nose, thin upper lips and flattened philtrum, wide-set eyes, flat mid face epicanthic folds over the eyes. Malformations of outer and middle ear. Cardiac, vision and hearing problems.
Fragile X syndrome	1/1500 (males) 1/2500 (females)	80% of boys and 30% of girls have intellectual disabilities. Autistic-like social behaviours. Impaired/disordered speech and language: echolalia, cluttered and perseverative speech and word-finding problems. Hyperactivity. Attention deficits. Emotional difficulties. Information processing weaknesses: especially in mathematics, grammar, sequential processing, short-term memory and problem solving. Strengths in daily living and visual skills. Some physical malformations: long face, protruding ears, prominent jaw and forehead, high-arched palate, short stature, hyperextensible joints, flat feet and enlarged testicles in males (from adolescence).
Down syndrome	1/700–1/1000	Physical signs: small head, recessed nose, eyes slanted upwards with epicanthal folds at inner corners, small ears, mouth, hands and feet, short fingers, broad neck.

Condition	Prevalence	Characteristics
		Mild to severe intellectual disability. Delayed motor skills. Speech and language delays. Medical problems: cardiac, respiratory, depressed immunity, hypothyroidism, orthopedic abnormalities, premature ageing. Hearing impairments. Vision impairments. Behavioural difficulties.
Duchenne muscular dystrophy	1/3500 (males)	Muscle wasting leading to deteriorating physical skills and death (usually in late adolescence or early adulthood).
PKU	1/14 000	Profound intellectual disability and death if untreated.
Cerebral palsy	1.5–2.7 per 1000	Movement and posture disturbances (100%). Intellectual disabilities (75%). Epilepsy (approximately 30%).
Brain injury		Emotional and family difficulties if injuries caused by child abuse. Developmental disabilities, depending on location and severity of injury.
Myelomeningocoele	0.6 in US 1.8–2.4 in Wales and Ireland < 0.6 in Africa per 1000	Paralysis and impaired sensation in lower limbs. Incontinence, constipation for lumbar lesions. Hydrocephalus (80%). Learning difficulties (75%). Intellectual disability (25%). Epilepsy (15–25%). Strabismus (20%). Spinal cord compression.
Prematurity and low birth weight	72 (low birth weight) 13 (very low birth weight) per 1000	Vision impairment. Cerebral palsy (spastic). Intellectual disability. Hearing impairment. Epilepsy.
Autism spectrum disorders	1 per 1000	Communication impairments. Social impairments. Behavioural disorders.

(Eysenck 1986; Jausovec 1997). Others speculate that, in addition, gifted children have more efficient links between the limbic system (the seat of emotions in the brain) and the prefrontal lobes, which are responsible for overseeing learning (Geake 1997). The first of these explanations accounts for an increase in the *quantity* of knowledge gifted children can acquire; the second relates to a *qualitatively* different learning style whereby, compared with average learners, gifted children are said to be more sensitive, intense and responsive emotionally, and more invested in learning (Miller et al. 1994). Thus, some regard gifted children's learning as quantitatively different from average learners', some see it as qualitatively different and others believe it to be both (see Porter 1999).

Although still debated, it seems evident that giftedness runs in families, although the exact genetic mechanism is not yet determined. Meanwhile, an optimal environment—and one that responds to children's changing needs throughout childhood—is required for this potential to be translated into sophisticated (i.e. talented) performances (Horowitz 1987). This does not mean that children require a *perfect* environment, however, as action is stimulated by some experience with overcoming challenges and some awareness of a wrong to be righted.

This brief discussion of giftedness cannot overlook the fact that children might have advanced abilities in one domain and at the same time experience a disability in another. Clearly, children can have physical or sensory impairments and still possess extraordinary information processing skills; less intuitively obvious, perhaps, are those gifted children who also have learning disabilities such as dyslexia. The disability will result in restricted input in the affected mode, but when information is given in a different channel, children who are also gifted can manipulate it in sophisticated ways. Similarly, children from educationally disadvantaging backgrounds might not display talents compared to advantaged children but are nevertheless learning more efficiently than those who are similarly disadvantaged. These children with dual exceptionalities are a challenge to identify and generally require a two-pronged program: one that offers remediation of their disability, alongside the equally important promotion of their gifted skills (Porter 1999).

ADDITIONAL RESOURCES

If you would like detailed information on various disabilities, I recommend:
Batshaw, M.L. (ed) 1997 *Children with disabilities* 4th edn, MacLennan & Petty, Sydney
Howard, V.F., Williams, B.F., Port, P.D. and Lepper, C. 2001 *Very young children with special needs: a formative approach for the 21st century* 2nd edn, Merrill Prentice Hall, Upper Saddle River, NJ

For information on giftedness, see:
Porter, L. 1999 *Gifted young children: a guide for teachers and parents* Allen & Unwin, Sydney (also Open University Press, Buckingham, UK)

Appendix II

TYPICAL DEVELOPMENTAL MILESTONES

LOUISE PORTER, BERNICE BURNIP, ZARA SODEN, MARGARET SULLIVAN

Children's skills are generally acquired in a predictable order. To follow are some commonly cited milestones for development during the early years. It is important to keep in mind, however, that children naturally differ in the rate at which they acquire the skills listed, with their pattern of skills reflecting the values of their culture and their opportunities to gain particular experiences and skills. Furthermore, although the skills listed below are separated into the various developmental domains, it is essential to realise that all are actually interwoven and that apparent delays in one developmental domain do not necessarily signal a difficulty in that skill area but can be a secondary outcome of impairments in another—for example, when children's vision or physical disabilities affect their environmental exploration and thus their development of cognitive concepts.

Qualitative aspects of skills	Typical behaviours
Birth to 3 months	
Gross motor	
The neonate has little control against gravity.	Holds head up momentarily while in prone position.
Movements and postures appear lopsided or asymmetrical.	Lifts head when supported at adult's shoulder.
Reflexes (which are innate responses to stimulation) become integrated in these early months, permitting subsequent development of purposeful movement.	Kicks reciprocally.
	Rolls or falls from side to supine position.
	Repeats satisfying actions.
Fine motor	
Grasp and release are dominated by reflexes.	Grasps with hand tightly fisted.
Arm movements are random.	Release starts as an avoiding reaction in response to touch on the back of the hand.
	By 3 months, arms move to midline spontaneously and simultaneously.

Qualitative aspects of skills	Typical behaviours

Language (comprehension)
Baby listens to pitch, intonation, and intensity of others' language.

Responds to voices.
Locates sounds by moving eyes.

Speech (expressive language)
Baby vocalises reflexively but adults respond as if speech were deliberate. By the end of this period, babies' sounds become social, in that they are made in response to adults' speech and they capture adult attention.

Cries when uncomfortable or hungry.
Uses different types of cries to signal different needs.
Coos and gurgles with pleasure.
Uses some vowels and consonants.
Repeats satisfying sounds.

Cognitive
Exploration of the environment is unplanned.

Inspects surroundings.
Inspects own hands.

Self-help
Feeding skills are initially reflexive but come under voluntary control throughout this stage.

Opens mouth in response to food.
Coordinates sucking, swallowing and breathing.
Clutches and pulls clothing.

Social-emotional
Object permanence has not yet developed and so infants are equally contented with various caregivers. Conversational turn-taking builds attachment.
Experiences joy (from 6 weeks) and distress.
Will cry contagiously when peers are upset.

Regards caregivers' face.
Enjoys physical contact, snuggles in.
Makes eye contact.
Communicates distress.
At 4–10 weeks, begins social smiling—that is, smiles spontaneously to caregiver's face, voice or smile.

4–6 months
Gross motor
Control against gravity of head and upper trunk and some limb movement is emerging in lying.
Control of side-to-side and supported rotational movement is beginning.

Head, eyes, hands and feet can be aligned with body midline in lying and while sitting with support.
Able to still self in lying and sitting.
Bears weight on hands in prone position.
At 4 months, rolls from supine to side and prone to side.
Bears some weight in supported standing.

Fine motor
Increasing voluntary control of grasp.
Grasp becomes more functional and can accommodate different sized objects.
Release is still accidental.
There is more control over arm movements and posture.
Forearm has voluntary supination (the thumb side·of the forearm faces up), allowing objects to be viewed more easily.
At this age, infants use vision to guide

Scratches surfaces.
Clutches at bedclothes and caregivers' clothing.
Reaches towards objects with both hands.
Rakes objects towards self.
Grasps feet.
Holds out objects but does not release.
Transfers object from hand to hand.
Uses ulnar grasp (fingers closed against palm).

Qualitative aspects of skills	*Typical behaviours*
their reaching. Play is predominantly tactile and increasingly visual.	Holds an object in each hand at same time. Pokes fingers into holes and at objects. Reaches objects on opposite side of body. Uses both hands in coordinated exploration.

Language (comprehension)

Comprehension is developing at a faster rate than speech.	Responds to own name.

Speech (expressive language)

Begins to respond to opportunities at turn taking in 'conversation' with caregivers.	Babbles using vowel sounds such as 'ee' and 'uh' which are produced before consonants such as /m/ and /b/. Imitates vocalisations that are within repertoire.

Cognitive

Object permanence will develop during this stage. Attachment to others is facilitated by memory advances. Infants' ability to point, grasp, explore and exchange socially with carers promotes cognitive mastery of the environment. They learn that actions and manipulations affect objects.	Explores objects through mouthing. Looks for partially hidden objects. Anticipates trajectory of an object. Shows anticipatory excitement. Begins rattle play. Repeats a familiar activity. Shakes or bangs toys to make different sounds.

Self-help

Feeding is no longer driven by reflexes. Infants can now inhibit the rooting reflex. Early reaching signals the beginning of eye–hand coordination. Passive during dressing.	Feeds self a biscuit. Swallows pureed foods. Uses tongue to move food. Drinks from an adapted cup. Reaches for an object that attracts interest. By 6 months, pulls off hat.

Social-emotional

Infants are learning to trust their primary caregiver and to feel safe that their needs will be responded to sensitively and in a timely fashion. Experiences anger (at 4 months) and sadness (at around 5–7 months).	Shows a preference for familiar others. Smiles at people, objects and own actions. Cries, smiles, kicks, coos and laughs to attract attention. Is soothed by being picked up. Responds gaily to social play. Lifts arms to primary caregiver. Cries if another child cries.

6–9 months

Gross motor

Control of rotational body movements is strengthening (that is, movements around the body's long axis), allowing one body	Rolls over and over. Sits solo. Moves in and out of sitting.

Qualitative aspects of skills	*Typical behaviours*
segment to twist on another (e.g. trunk over pelvis). Uses movement for locomotor exploration. The use of baby walkers may delay development of transitional movement sequences.	Creeps, crawls—backwards first. Pulls to stand. Stands while holding on.

Fine motor

| Reach is more accurate, aided by increasing forearm supination. Development of hand control is facilitated by gains in postural control, particularly being able to sit. Mouthing reduces and tactile exploration through fingering increases. By the end of this stage release is voluntary. | Uses a radial palmar grasp: an object is held in the palm with the thumb and radial fingers pressing the object into the palm. Release begins during mouthing or bimanual play when one hand pulls an object from the other hand. Release can occur against a surface. Extends arms protectively. |

Language (comprehension)

| By this age, infants listen to the vocalisations of others. They recognise some words and different tones of voice. Already they respond to a few words. | Looks at pictures briefly. Recognises names of family members or pets. Understands some words such as 'bye-bye', 'no' or own name. Responds to simple requests with gesture. |

Speech (expressive language)

| Infants practise sound production and will play sound games with parents, repeating some sounds, simple words such as 'da-da' or an emphasised syllable. They produce intonation patterns. They use social gestures. | Speech sounds start to be limited to those of the infant's own language. Babbling incorporates reduplicated sounds such as /bababa/ and contains phonemes that will be heard later in first word approximations. Demands by pointing and vocalising. Imitates coughs and other sounds. Vocalises loudly to get attention. |

Cognitive

| Intentionality is being developed in response to infants' ability to explore physically and visually. Curiosity develops. Attention is drawn to a dominant stimulus and infants are easily distracted by another. | Finds object after watching it being hidden. Works to reach objects. Plays for 2–3 minutes with a single toy. Repeats actions in order to repeat a consequence. |

Self-help

| Infants are developing increasing awareness of their clothing as separate from themselves. | Holds and drinks from bottles or spout cups with lids. Mouths and gums solid food. Bites voluntarily. Feeds self finger foods with whole hand grasp. Pulls off booties. |

Qualitative aspects of skills	Typical behaviours

Social-emotional
Separation anxiety will appear in this phase as a result of infants' attainment of object permanence, which is now applied to familiar adults as well as objects. Experiences enjoyment, fear, humour and shyness.

Shows anxiety when separated from primary caregiver.
Smiles at self in mirror.
Infant-to-infant interactions increase.
Enjoys teasing.
Will protest when dissatisfied.
Fights for disputed toy.

9–12 months
Gross motor
When first walking solo, toddlers have a wide base, short stride and no arm swing.

Climbs horizontally over low obstacles in crawling.
Cruises furniture.
Stands solo briefly at 10–11 months.
Walks solo briefly at 11–14 months.
Arms held in 'high guard' for trunk control.
At 11–14 months, stoops and recovers.

Fine motor
Movement about on all fours supplies sensory input to the hands and arms.
Arm strength is enhanced.
Infants can grasp using fingertips and distal (end) portions of fingers.
The thumb side of the hand is developing as the skill side.
Cognitive development and improved accuracy of reach encourage experimentation with new objects.
Vision is less necessary to guide reaching and grasping.

Can pick up increasingly small objects.
At 9 months, uses an inferior pincer grasp.
By 12 months, uses a superior grasp.
Uses both hands freely.
Tries to imitate scribble.
Puts objects into and out of containers.

Language (comprehension)
Recognises words as symbols for objects.
Understands simple directives or commands.

Understands 'no'.
Listens selectively to familiar words.
Enjoys looking at books.
Responds to simple verbal requests.

Speech (expressive language)
May produce one or more word utterances.
Imitates familiar words.

Babbles single vowel-consonant syllables (e.g. 'ba').
Uses behaviours and vocalisations to express desires.
Imitates sounds gestures not previously in repertoire.

Cognitive
Intentionality is now established.
Cause-and-effect understanding is developing.

Begins to see the connection between actions and consequences (e.g. putting lids on).

Qualitative aspects of skills	Typical behaviours
Cognitive development is highly dependent at this stage on early physical exploration and thus on infants' motor skills.	Performs an action to attain a desired result.

Self-help

Infants understand the functional use of objects. They increasingly cooperate with dressing.	Insists on doing things independently. Finger feeds a variety of foods using a pincer grasp. Grasps spoon in fist. Chews by munching. Holds arm out to assist with dressing upper body. Pulls off socks.

Social-emotional

Children are beginning to be able to use imitation in play. They like to be in constant sight and hearing of an adult. They are learning to cooperate and will show guilt at misdeeds. They recognise that they are separate individuals from parent. They are developing a sense of humour. Emotional repertoire now includes anxiety, fear, affection, protest, elation, surprise, frustration, shame, wariness and negativism.	Enjoys turn-taking games. Shows preferences for people, objects and situations. Demonstrates affection to adults. Shows but does not yield toys to others. Displays separation anxiety. Will attempt to change adults' intent using persuasion or protest.

12–18 months

Gross motor

Walking continues with 'bow legs'. Will throw large balls underarm (with a two-handed toss) unless taught otherwise. Vertical climbing is beginning, first onto parents' lap and, later still, up playground equipment.	Pulls toy while walking. At 15 months, crawls up stairs. Crawls down stairs or goes down on bottom. At 15–18 months, trots (walks quickly with no airborne phase). At 13–16 months, throws a ball underarm in sitting position (with no aim). At 15–18 months, throws a ball forward while standing (with no aim). Walks into a large ball while trying to kick it. Picks up toy from floor without falling. Carries large toy while walking. Moves to music.

Fine motor

Precision grips on small objects is established. The toddler refines learned manipulation patterns to combine them into more complex and longer play sequences. There is further differentiation of the two	Holds two objects in the hand at once. Builds a three-block tower. Holds a crayon and scribbles. Rotates and examines three-dimensional objects. Turns pages two or three at a time.

Qualitative aspects of skills	Typical behaviours
sides of the hand.	Paints with whole arm movement,
Has controlled release.	changing hands.
Is interested in 'tool' use.	Deliberately throws or drops objects to
The grip is static, with movement coming	watch them fall.
from the shoulder, elbow and wrist.	
In play, the toddler increasingly acquires	
bilateral (two-hand) skills with one hand	
stabilising and the other manipulating.	

Language (comprehension)
Multiword comprehension is beginning, whereby children can understand three or more words out of context.
They can point to some objects when named.

Can respond to simple and often-repeated commands such as 'Give me your bottle'.
Understands 50 words (nouns, verbs and adjectives).
Understands 'where' questions when these are accompanied by gesture.
Enjoys looking at a book.
Identifies at least one body part.

Speech (expressive language)
Children aged 12–18 months are beginning to use words purposefully, expressing a variety of communicative functions.
They have a vocabulary of about 20 words.
They sing spontaneously.

Will repeat familiar words on request and in imitation of a model.
By 18 months, can use a few words appropriately.
Words are approximations of their adult equivalent (e.g. 'bobo' for 'bottle').
Communicates by pointing accompanied with a word (e.g. 'Wassat?').
Uses exclamations: 'Oh-oh!'.
Says 'no' meaningfully.
Refers to self by name.

Cognitive
Cause-and-effect and object permanence are now well established.
Learns primarily through exploration.
Trial-and-error learning is beginning to be informed by insight.
Shows some understanding of categories.
Shows pleasure at achievement of self-selected goal.
Can concentrate for some time on a task of their choosing but attention span is limited on adult-directed activities.
Focus is rigid as competing stimuli must be ignored, resulting in apparently obstinate behaviour.

Toys with hinges, switches, push buttons and pop-ups are increasingly enjoyed.
Matches similar objects.
Simple pretend play directed towards self (e.g. eating, sleeping).
Immediate imitation of a model.
Uses a 'tool' to obtain a desired object.
Can place round, and later, square pieces in formboard puzzles.
May become angry if interrupted.

Self-help
At this age, children can anticipate self-help activities.
Their developing trunk stability allows for

Finger feeds part of a meal.
Can use a spoon to self-feed, with some spilling.

Qualitative aspects of skills	*Typical behaviours*
more participation in dressing. Grasp is now delicate, with ability to use appropriate force. Release now deliberate and purposeful.	Takes bite-sized pieces from plate. Independently drinks with cup, with some tipping. Indicates when wet or soiled. Tries to push off soiled pants. Takes off shoes, socks, hat, mittens, coat. Puts on hat. Tries to put on shoes. Undoes bows and snap fasteners. Holds head in position for hair brushing. Brings brush to head.

Social-emotional

The use of routines supplies toddlers with some predictability. They use their primary caregiver for 'emotional refuelling' while moving away briefly but repeatedly. Begin to prefer interactions with peers. They display extremes of emotions. Play is becoming more experimental but still ritualised.	Pulls adult to show or help. Hugs and kisses adults. Can play in parallel with two other children. Plays simple object-centred games. Recognises difference between 'you' and 'me'. Laughs at incongruous events.

18–24 months
Gross motor

Legs are now straight in walking (i.e. no longer bow legged). Rotational changes in alignment of lower limb bones continue. The development of ball skills depends heavily on exposure to ball play.	Climbs onto an adult chair, holds on for support, turns and sits. Walks up then down stairs with hand held, two feet per step. Brief airborne phase begins in running. Rises on tip-toes with hand support. Squats. Moves on ride-on toys without pedals.

Fine motor

Significant changes in hand skills occur during this period. Cognitive gains allow more complex movement patterns to be used. Pencil grasp becomes more controlled. Eye–hand coordination is beginning in ball play. Development of perceptual-motor ability allows for refinements of earlier hand skills.	Can use isolated finger movements. Builds a six-block tower. Uses a fingertip grasp for precision tasks. Uses a palmar grasp for power tasks. Can hold objects with appropriate pressure (e.g. so that a biscuit is not crushed). Can place and release accurately. Imitates vertical and circular strokes. Manipulates objects into small openings.

Language (comprehension)

Receptive vocabulary growth continues to be much more rapid than expressive vocabulary.	By 2 years, understands more than 1000 words. Begins to understand temporal words

Qualitative aspects of skills	*Typical behaviours*
Children can now understand some words out of context. Comprehension of personal pronouns begins to develop.	such as 'soon' and 'later'. Begins to distinguish between common objects, such as cat and dog; milk and juice. Follows a series of two simple but related directives. Identifies three to six body parts. Enjoys nursery rhymes.
Speech (expressive language) This is a normal echolalic stage, when young children repeat part of what they hear. Most grow out of this by approximately 2½ years of age. Turn taking is beginning to occur in primitive conversations.	Uses speech to gain attention. Uses words with, or instead of, gestures. Once 50 words are acquired, can combine these into two-word sentences (e.g. 'Want bikky'). May use jargon (syllable strings that sound like language). Attempts to sing songs with words. Imitates three to four word phrases. Makes sounds to animals.
Cognitive Cause-and-effect understanding is developing. Attention span is lengthening but is not discretionary: children cannot give equally long concentration to adult-selected activities. Deferred imitation is now made possible by memory storage and representational thought. Children can now use some foresight before acting.	Completes simple puzzles. Varies creatively own imitation of a model. Finds object not observed being hidden. Sorts and matches objects. Recalls recent events. Remembers where things belong. Constructive play emerges. Play becomes symbolic, first directed at the self and then at objects (e.g. putting a doll to bed). Increased use of non-realistic objects in pretend play. Activates mechanical toys.
Self-help Can integrate sensory experiences and make accurate motor responses to allow for tasks such as dressing and threading. Has distinct food preferences.	Unwraps food. Rotary chews solid foods. Scoops food, feeds self with spoon. Indicates wet pants. Lifts foot for shoes or pants when dressing. Removes loose shoes, pushes down shorts, removes socks on request. Opens mouth for teeth to be brushed. Holds toothbrush and approximates brushing. Allows wiping of nose. Washes and dries hands partially. Tries to wash body. Helps with simple household tasks.

Qualitative aspects of skills	*Typical behaviours*
Social-emotional Children are learning that they can exercise some autonomy. This, plus their fixed attention skills can make it difficult to redirect them once they are fixed on an idea or action. Their egocentrism at this age is characterised by their assumption that what upsets them is the cause of another's distress. They may show fear at departure of primary caregiver and cry in relief at his or her return. They now experience guilt, pride, affection, jealousy and defiance. Symbolic play begins to emerge. Children are beginning to initiate their own play.	Reveals sense of ownership: defends possessions. Shows affection to other children. Imitates adult behaviours in play. Plays by self, initiating own games. Plays in parallel and associatively. Attempts to comfort others in distress. Laughs at incongruous events and play with words. Plays house. Imitates adult behaviours in play.

24–36 months (2–3 years)

Gross motor Walks with arms at sides, with a narrower base, longer stride, but little push off with toes. Is flat-footed. Has little body rotation in walking. Airborne phase in running lengthens. Legs develop 'knock knees', peaking at around 3½ years of age. This corresponds with in-toeing (or 'pigeon toes') if very flat-footed.	Can stand on one leg for 1–2 seconds. At 2 years, walks up and down stairs alone, still two feet per step. At 2½ years, walks up with support, one foot per step. May begin climbing heights, with reduced sense of danger. Climbs over, in/out with help for hand placement and weight shift. Begins to jump, usually with one foot leading. Can jump from a bottom step. Kicks a ball and retains balance. Needs to be shown how to position arms to catch.
Fine motor Ability to make manipulative movements within the hand improves. For the majority of children, handedness is present.	Strings four large beads. Turns book pages singly. Imitates a drawing of a face. Imitates directional movements for writing tasks: vertical, horizontal and circular strokes. Uses scissors to snip paper. Manipulates play dough. Turns knobs.
Language (comprehension) Has a 2500-word receptive vocabulary comprising nouns, verbs, prepositions and adjectives.	Understands two or three prepositions (e.g. under, in, on). Responds correctly to common multiword

Qualitative aspects of skills	*Typical behaviours*
Can follow two-step commands. Understand simple time concepts such as 'tomorrow'. Enjoys hearing stories repeated.	sentences (e.g. 'Put your cup on the table'). Cannot understand compound commands (e.g. 'Take your coat off and put your slippers on'). Understands negatives: no, don't, can't. Understands 'what' and 'where' questions. Points to pictures of common objects when these are named. Begins to understand 'long' and 'short'. Enjoys simple stories and requests repetition.

Speech (expressive language)

| Can now participate in conversations and sustain these for two to three turns. Around 70% of speech is intelligible but children express frustration at not being understood. | Expressive vocabulary of 1000 words. An average of three to four words per sentence. Asks for wants. Uses pronouns 'I', 'me', 'you', 'mine'. Will ask 'what' and 'where' questions (e.g. 'Where's Mummy?'). Uses plurals of nouns. Tells simple stories about recent experiences. Identifies some colours. Can use most vowel and consonant sounds correctly. Makes negative statements (e.g. 'Can't do it'). |

Cognitive

| One-to-one number correspondence is developing. Children are now able to amuse themselves for extended periods. Can transfer their attention when bid, unless engrossed already. Learning is through exploration and adult mediation. Can self-correct to meet adult standards. Can follow adults' directives to attend to particular stimuli. | Can plan actions mentally without acting them out. Can relate an experience to another using 'if . . . then' logic. Matches and uses associated objects (e.g. sock and shoe). Can sort objects by size. Can count by rote from 1 to 5. Can count two or three objects. Can complete three to four piece puzzles. Identifies body parts with function. Knows two to three primary colours. |

Self-help

| Children of this age take particular pride in their own achievements, particularly in the self-help domain, and they resist assistance. They understand and stay away from common dangers. | Holds cup or glass with one hand, with the other poised to help. Pours liquids. Uses spoon well with minimal spilling. Spears food with fork. Opens jars. Unzips clothes. Pulls pants down. |

Qualitative aspects of skills	*Typical behaviours*
	Pulls pants up from ankles.
	Removes coat, jumpers, T-shirts.
	Puts on coat with assistance.
	Puts on socks and shoes.
	Unties and removes shoes.
	Is interested in lacing.
	Identifies clothing appropriate to different occasions.
	Combs and brushes hair.
	Washes and brushes teeth (not thoroughly).
	Wipes nose on request.
	Independent daytime toileting control when adult regulates toilet trips.
	Can anticipate the need to urinate.

Social-emotional

Children at this stage are distinguishing themselves as separate individuals.	Plays near other children.
Frustration tantrums peak.	Joins in briefly with other children's play.
Sometimes shy with strangers.	Defends possessions, using 'mine'.
Make constant demands for parents' attention.	Begins to play house.
Cooperation is facilitated by language development which assists reasoning skills.	Participates in simple group activities (e.g. sings, claps, dances).
By the end of the third year, some children make a special friend.	Knows own gender.
They are easily roused to anger when frustrated.	Acts to help others in distress.
Numbers of emotions and finer discriminations between them continue to increase with age but at this age children experience emotions one at a time and completely (for the moment).	

36–48 months (3–4 years)
Gross motor

By this age, motor skill depends largely on practice.	Can run around obstacles.
Stop-start and turning are more efficient while walking and running.	Stands on one leg for 3–5 seconds.
	Some can hop on one foot.
There is a longer airborne phase during running, with arm swing, longer stride, increased speed, stop-start and cornering abilities.	Can walk on toes.
	Can walk on heels.
	Jumps with two feet together, 4–5 jumps in a sequence.
Is more aware of danger during climbing but still needs supervision.	Can walk up stairs alone, one foot per step.
	Walks or jumps down stairs, two feet per step.
	Scoops ball to chest when catching.
	May catch a bounced ball more easily than one that has been thrown.
	Rides a tricycle.

Qualitative aspects of skills	Typical behaviours

Fine motor

Precision grasps of tools are established but will be refined over the next 3–5 years with practice.
In-hand manipulation skill of moving small objects from the fingertips and thumb to the palm and back again (translation) is developing. After 36 months this movement can occur even when other small objects remain in the hand. (This is called stabilisation.)

Uses a fingertip grasp on pencil.
Able to hold a small object in the fingertips while storing one or more in palm.
Draws a circle.
Draws face of a person.
Imitates a cross.
Draws a somewhat recognisable picture that is meaningful to self.
Cuts along a line and around a circle.
Can roll a ball and mould a biscuit shape with playdough.

Language (comprehension)

At this age, children display a relatively large growth in vocabulary.

Understands children's stories.
Understands concepts such as smaller, more, less, same.
Can state some opposites (e.g. 'Hot and. . .?').
Can carry out a series of two to four related directives.
Understands when told 'Let's pretend'.

Speech (expressive language)

Talks a lot and rapidly. Sentences are longer and more varied.
Children may repeat the initial sound in words (e.g. 'b-b-b-baby').
This is a normal developmental stage and does not mean that they are beginning to stutter. They have many ideas to get across with language that does not yet come automatically to them, so they build in pauses as they find the words to express themselves.
They use new words meaningfully.

Will make requests, tell jokes, protest and agree.
Asks many questions for information: why and how questions.
May substitute some sound for others (e.g. 'baf' for 'bath').
Tells about past experiences.
Uses 'ed' on some verbs to indicate past tense.
Refers to self using pronouns 'I' or 'me'.
Speech is understandable to strangers, although there are still some articulation errors.

Cognitive

Concentration span is now longer on self-selected activities but it cannot alternate its focus.
Learns through observing and imitation by testing predictions and via adult explanations.
Has increased understanding of concepts, functions and grouping of objects.

Plans out pretend play in advance.
Acts out sequences with toys.
Can put graduated sizes in order.
Recognises and matches six colours.
Names basic shapes and colours.
Counts up to five objects, touching each one (rational counting).
Completes simple picture puzzles.
Knows the sequence of routine events.

Self-help

3–4 year olds are now able to perform many self-care tasks with diminishing supervision.

Can hold a cup by its handle.
Drinks securely, with one hand holding vessel.

Qualitative aspects of skills	*Typical behaviours*
	Pours well from small pitcher.
	Wipes up spills.
	Can dress and undress without help, except for difficult fastenings and shoe laces.
	Buttons and unbuttons large buttons.
	Uses toilet independently, except for thorough wiping.
	Washes hands unassisted.
	Washes body well in bath.
	Wipes nose without request.

Social-emotional

Children are beginning to show clear preferences for particular playmates. Many children of this age enjoy imaginary companions.

They are interested in others' emotions.

They begin to express their own emotions verbally.

They are eager to please, although often self-willed and uncooperative.

They can accept the absence of their primary caregiver if in a supportive environment.

Beginning to tolerate frustration as emotions begin to come under self-control, albeit inconsistently.

Joins in play with other children in an associative fashion, commenting on each other's actions and exchanging toys.
Takes turns with assistance.
Shares with assistance.
Begins acting out whole scenes in dramatic play.
Has one or two preferred friends.

48–60 months (4–5 years)

Gross motor

When walking, legs are almost straight again at knee, ankle and mid-foot (knock-knees have corrected).

Physical growth slows, so food requirements reduce.

Runs on toes.
Can walk a straight line, but still with some wobbles at 48 months.
Can take a standing jump over a rope held stationary at 15 cm height, with feet parallel on take-off and landing and synchronised (30 cm height by 5 years).
Jumps up to 20 sequential jumps forward.
Walks up and down stairs with no hands, one foot per step (although may use a handrail in crowds).
Catches a 20–24 cm ball with an efficient and secure catch in forearms with elbows bent.
Can kick a basketball into a box 1 metre away.
Turns somersaults.

Fine motor

Two sides of the hand—the skill (thumb) side and stability (little finger) side—are well established.

Draws stick figure.
Copies square (4 years).
Prints a few capital letters.

Qualitative aspects of skills	Typical behaviours
In the majority of children, the arches of their hand are well established, giving greater control and endurance with hand use. The two hands are able to perform different movements simultaneously and proficiently to carry out an activity. Their preferred hand becomes increasingly specialised.	Cuts around a circle. Draws, names and describes a recognisable picture. Able to fold paper with reasonable accuracy. Can place paper clips on paper.

Language (comprehension)

At this stage, children can listen for extended periods to stories although they might misinterpret the events. Their vocabulary and concept knowledge continue to grow. They can now use these skills to express ideas, solve problems and plan ahead.	Can follow three unrelated commands in correct sequence. Understands comparatives (e.g. big, bigger, biggest). Understands concept of zero. Can put three pictures in a sequence to tell a story. Understands first, middle, last. Understands sequences of events when these are explained to them.

Speech (expressive language)

Children's more extensive vocabulary allows them more routinely to use words in social play to solve problems rather than being aggressive. They can use language to describe imaginary situations. They use language to find out about their world. Swearing and chanting emerge as children play with the rhythms and patterns (and prohibitions) of language.	Expressive vocabulary of 1500 words. Average sentence length of five words. Asks questions using 'who' and 'how'. Can define words such as 'carrot' and 'fire fighter'. Adapts language use for listeners: uses more complex sentences when talking to an adult compared with a baby. Now uses other conjunctions in addition to 'and' (e.g. 'because', 'when', 'if'). Can sing songs and recite poems from memory. May still have some difficulty with consonants such as /s/ and /t/ and consonant blends such as 'str' and 'gl'.

Cognitive

Can now integrate spatial, cause-and-effect and representational thinking into problem solving. Close to their fifth birthday, can divide attention and pay selective attention reasonably automatically. Increased understanding of concepts.	Counts objects in sequence with one-to-one correspondence. Matches pictures of familiar object pairs. Can describe what will happen next. Understands sophisticated time concepts such as yesterday and last week.

Self-help

Children of this age are able to perform many self-care tasks independently with	Cuts easy foods with a knife. Uses spoon and fork competently.

Qualitative aspects of skills	*Typical behaviours*
verbal prompts only, although they commonly prevaricate.	Serves self and helps set table. Dresses with supervision. Places shoes on correct feet. Night-time toileting reliable. Knows front from back of clothing.

Social-emotional

Children are now able to negotiate during social play and conform to group decisions. Family membership is a strong source of self-esteem. They can share and take turns more reliably (although this occurs sooner in children with early experience of group care settings).

Plays cooperatively: children engage together to achieve a common goal. Dramatic play more closely mirrors reality, with attention to detail. Shows interest in exploring gender differences. Shows concerns and sympathy for others.

60–72 months (5–6 years)

Gross motor

Running and jumping are now more rhythmical and efficient, with help from arm movements.

Reciprocal arm-swing when walking. Uses an adult pattern for climbing and descending stairs. By 6 years, hops on the spot 10 or more times. Can run and kick a ball. By 5 years can catch in hands a 20–24 cm ball thrown in midline. Hits a ball with a bat or stick. Skips with alternating feet.

Fine motor

Hand movements continue to improve in efficiency and control.

Can hold several small objects in the hand while picking up or releasing one in thumb and fingertips. Draws triangle, diamond. Adds trunk and arms to drawing of a person. Draws identifiable objects without a model. Copies own name in large, irregular letters. Copies numbers unevenly. Cuts around objects.

Language (comprehension)

Language continues to develop after the age of five, although at a slower rate than previously. They now have a receptive vocabulary of at least 20 000 words.

Demonstrates preacademic skills: letter word, and number recognition. Laughs at multiple meanings of words.

Speech (expressive language)

By this age, most children use complex forms of the language. There are few obvious differences between their grammar and that of adults.

Expressive vocabulary of over 2000 words. A few consonant sounds (e.g. 'ch and 'j') will not be fully mastered until age 7 or 8. Gives and receives information.

Qualitative aspects of skills	*Typical behaviours*

They still need to learn subject–verb agreement and irregular forms of past tense verbs.
They can take appropriate turns in conversation.
They communicate well with family, friends or strangers.

Cognitive

Attention span has increased; children can direct their attention at adult command; they can select what to pay attention to, and divide their attention between tasks.

Can retell a story from a book with reasonable accuracy.
Names some letters and numerals.
Is beginning to use time concepts accurately (e.g. tomorrow).

Self-help

Efficiency of performance improves. Dawdling over self-care tasks lessens with the children's increased awareness of time and the consequences of being late.
Level of supervision needed for self-care tasks continues to decrease.

Spreads soft sandwich toppings with a knife.
Dresses self completely (except for shoe laces).
Brushes teeth unassisted.
Carries liquid in open container without spilling.
Washes hands at appropriate times (e.g. before meals).
Independent grooming.

Social-emotional

Children are able to delay gratification—that is, sacrifice an immediate outcome for a longer term outcome—and so can withdraw from disputes.
They can now accurately interpret the source of a friend's distress.
They generally have one or two close friends of the same sex.
Quarrels are frequent but of short duration and soon forgotten.
They can feel more than one emotion at a time, as long as it is of the same category.
Their ability to understand others' emotions has a direct effect on their social competence.

Chooses own friends.
Plays simple competitive games that are not too highly organised.
Can negotiate and direct roles, rules and tasks during social play.
Comforts playmates in distress.
Protects other children and animals.
Offers help to others voluntarily.
Judges behaviour as right or wrong.

72 months + (6–7 years +)

Gross motor

By 6 to 7 years, children display a mature running pattern.
Further refinement throughout childhood depends on training and practice with new movement challenges.

Anticipates and prepares to catch.
Catches 15–24 cm ball in hands easily and repetitively, with elbows bending to absorb impact.
Catches to the side of body space.

Qualitative aspects of skills	Typical behaviours
By 7 years, leg and foot alignment is similar to adults' (i.e. there is slight out-toeing).	Catches 5 cm (tennis) ball. Throws a ball in the air and catches it.

Fine motor

As dynamic eye skills (e.g. tracking) have developed, children's eye–hand coordination continues to improve. The majority have a well established dynamic tripod pencil grip. They have proficient in-hand manipulation skills and use gravity to assist.	Uses a dynamic tripod pencil grip, with pencil moved by moving fingertips. Copies rectangle. Writes letters and numbers with some accuracy, but still has errors. Letter size decreases, with letter formation more consistent.

Language (comprehension)

Vocabulary continues to grow.	Understands jokes, word puns and figurative language. Can understand more complex stories.

Speech (expressive language)

Pragmatic skills improve. Conversational skills are refined. Sentence structure becomes more complex.	Most English speech sounds acquired including t̲h̲in and trea̲s̲ure.

Cognitive

Children now have the ability to focus on several attributes of an object simultaneously (termed decentration). They begin to use logic to solve problems, reverse steps in a problem-solving sequence. They are able to discern differences between appearance and reality. They are lively intellectually.	Accepts that matter is conserved, even though the container shape alters. Loves exploration.

Self-help

Children are able independently to perform most necessary self-care tasks although will continue at times to seek adult support.	Cuts and spreads with knife. Grooming independent. Selects appropriate clothing. Turns clothing right side out. Buttons back buttons. Ties shoe laces. Blows and wipes nose independently.

Social-emotional

Play continues to be the main vehicle driving development in all domains. Around the age of seven years, sex discrimination emerges.	Plays games with rules increasingly. Sensitive to criticism. Wants to be best and first at everything.

Sources: Allen and Schwartz 2001; Burns 1992; Case-Smith 1995; Cook et al. 2000; Furuno et al. 1985; Henderson 1995; Howard et al. 2001; Jones 1992; Kostelnik et al. 1998;

Lerner et al. 1998; Linder 1990; Nixon and Aldwinckle 1997; Nixon and Gould 1999; Owens 2001; Raver 1999; Sheridan et al. 1999; Tachdjian 1997; Talay-Ongan 2000.

ADDITIONAL RESOURCES

Berk, L. 2000 *Child development* 5th edn, Allyn & Bacon, Boston, MA

Nixon, D. and Aldwinckle, M. 1997 *Exploring: child development from three to six years* Social Science Press, Katoomba, NSW

Nixon, D. and Gould, K. 1999 *Emerging: child development in the first three years* 2nd edn, Social Science Press, Katoomba, NSW

Vialle, W., Lysaught, P. and Verenikina, I. 2000 *Handbook on child development* Social Science Press, Katoomba, NSW

Appendix III

INDICATORS OF ADVANCED DEVELOPMENT IN YOUNG CHILDREN

LOUISE PORTER

The following characteristics and behaviours can indicate advances in children's development during the early childhood years. However, it must be said that some of these signs can be due to reasons other than giftedness—and that no gifted child will display all of the signs. Furthermore, it is not clear which behaviours are essential for giftedness and which are unnecessary, and we have insufficient knowledge to allow us to give extra weight to the most important features (Perleth et al. 2000).

Nevertheless, the fundamental criterion for defining giftedness is that the children's development (in at least one developmental domain) is proceeding around one-third faster than expected at that age—such that a 3-year-old more closely resembles at least a 4-year-old's development and a 6-year-old behaves and achieves more like an 8-year-old (or older).

Cognitive (thinking) skills

Children who are developing significantly ahead of age in their intellectual abilities may show an array of the following behaviours. They:

- achieve developmental milestones early (around one-third sooner than expected);
- learn quickly;
- observe the environment keenly;
- are active in eliciting stimulation from the environment—sometimes leading to reliance on parents to act as 'input' for them;
- may read, write or use numbers in advanced ways (although this is not very common: if the children are reading during the preschool years, they are likely to be highly gifted; if they are not reading early, that may not be significant);
- show advanced preferences for books and films, unless too sensitive to older themes;

- have quick and accurate recall (although this is necessary, having a good memory is not sufficient on its own to indicate giftedness);
- can recall skills and information introduced some time ago;
- possess deeper knowledge than other children (have information on more topics, and know more about those topics);
- have an ability to teach other children (although they might become irritated if others appear not to be learning, and may have difficulty describing the steps of tasks as they themselves did not need to learn them in a stepwise fashion but were competent almost immediately);
- understand abstract concepts (e.g. death or time) early;
- are imaginative or creative (not just with artistic pursuits but in their problem solving as well);
- have an advanced sense of humour (because they understand incongruity, which is the basis of humour).

Learning style

As well as *what* they are able to achieve, young children who are learning at a faster pace than usual typically go about tasks in sophisticated ways—that is, *how* they achieve is exceptional. They:

- are motivated, curious and seek to understand;
- will focus intensely on an area of interest, as long as there is sufficient challenge;
- have wide-ranging interests;
- are alert (sometimes resulting in poor sleeping patterns and sometimes in sound sleep as a result of expending their energy all day);
- respond to novel stimuli and get used quickly to repetitive activities;
- have a longer than usual concentration span on challenging topics of interest (but may 'flit' from one activity to another if activities are not challenging enough);
- use metacognitive skills early to manage their own thinking processes;
- have a clear understanding of cause and effect;
- possess good planning skills;
- have an internal locus of control;
- are less impulsive than usual for their age (and so have fewer injuries than usual);
- can be independent when working at challenging, non-routine tasks but highly dependent when bored;
- can think logically.

Speech and language skills

Children whose advances fall within the verbal domain tend to show the following characteristics. They:

- comprehend language early;
- use advanced speech, in terms of vocabulary, grammar and clear articulation;
- will use metaphors and analogies (e.g. when hanging upside-down on a jungle gym will announce that they are a bat);
- will make up songs or stories spontaneously;
- can modify their language to suit less mature children;
- use language for a real exchange of ideas and information at an early age;
- can carry out instructions to do several things in succession.

Motor abilities

Children with advanced physical skills may display the following characteristics. They:

- have early motor development, particularly in skills that are under cognitive control (e.g. balance), in contrast with those (e.g. stamina) which are purely physical;
- can locate themselves within the environment;
- have an early awareness of left and right (without necessarily being able to name these accurately);
- may have average fine motor skills, which means that these lag behind their other developmental skills, leading to some children's reluctance to draw or write and later to untidy handwriting through lack of practice and reduced motivation;
- can put together new or difficult puzzles (particularly if visually advanced, in contrast with children who prefer to learn auditorally);
- can take apart and reassemble objects with unusual skill;
- can make interesting shapes or patterns with objects;
- have high levels of physical energy (sometimes leading to queries about motoric or vocal ADHD).

Social skills

Some gifted children are particularly adept at relationships and are tuned in to other people and their feelings. These children often:

- have highly developed empathy for others;
- are less egocentric than usual—that is, can interpret accurately what is bothering others;
- have advanced play interests;
- can play games with rules earlier than usual;
- may form close, reciprocal friendships from a young age (as long as intellectual peers are available);
- seek out older children or adults for companionship if intellectual peers are not available;
- might withdraw to solitary play if intellectual peers are not available;

- are often sought out by other children—that is, others feel drawn to them although the gifted children themselves might not feel so warmly disposed to others who are not 'soulmates';
- can display leadership skills, although in their early years they might not have the maturity to exercise tact with those whom they are leading;
- develop moral reasoning and judgment early (although might not act accordingly unless circumstances facilitate this);
- take an early interest in social issues involving injustices (sometimes leading to the need for media blackouts in times of wars and other world crises).

Emotional and behavioural characteristics

Finally, some children whose development is advanced have been described as showing the following emotional features. They:

- can be emotionally sensitive, intense and responsive. (As this can be a response to frustration at their uneven developmental levels across a range of skill domains, any children with atypical development may be similarly emotional.);
- develop fears early;
- develop their self-concept early and so are aware from a young age of being different from others (from perhaps as young as 2 years old);
- are self-confident in their strong domains but less confident in their less advanced domains;
- might be perfectionist, in the sense of seeking to achieve at high levels;
- can be oversensitive to criticism;
- may become frustrated at their lesser skills, which can lead to emotional or behavioural outbursts;
- may accept responsibility usually given only to older children (which is important not to exploit, as the children may not be free to develop fully while taking care of others' business);
- are non-conformist, and so do not take kindly to authoritarian forms of discipline whereby they are expected to do as they are told without an explanation.

Source: adapted from Porter (1999:74–6).

BIBLIOGRAPHY

1 Fundamentals of early education

Alberto, P.A. and Troutman, A.C. 1999 *Applied behaviour analysis for teachers* 5th edn, Merrill, Upper Saddle River, NJ

Andersson, B.E. 1989 'Effects of public day-care—a longitudinal study' *Child Development* vol. 60, no. 4, pp. 857–66

——1992 'Effects of day care on cognitive and socioemotional competence of thirteen-year-old Swedish schoolchildren' *Child Development* vol. 63, no. 1, pp. 20–36

Athey, I. 1984 'Contributions of play to development' in *Child's play: developmental and applied* eds T.D. Yawkey & A.D. Pellegrini (pp. 9–27) Lawrence Erlbaum, Hillsdale, NJ

Australian Early Childhood Association 1991 'Australian Early Childhood Association code of ethics' *Australian Journal of Early Childhood* vol. 16, no. 1, pp. 3–6

Bailey, D.B. Jr and McWilliam, R.A. 1990 'Normalizing early intervention' *Topics in Early Childhood Special Education* vol. 10, no. 2, pp. 33–47

Bailey, D.B. Jr, McWilliam, R.A., Buysse, V. and Wesley, P.W. 1998 'Inclusion in the context of competing values in early childhood education' *Early Childhood Research Quarterly* vol. 13, no. 1, pp. 27–47

Bailey, D.B. and Wolery, M. 1992 *Teaching infants and preschoolers with handicaps* 2nd edn, Merrill, Columbus, OH

Bennett, T., DeLuca, D. and Bruns, B. 1997 'Putting inclusion into practice: perspectives of teachers and parents' *Exceptional Children* vol. 64, no. 1, pp. 115–31

Berk, L. 2000 *Child development* 5th edn, Allyn & Bacon, Boston, MA

Bondurant-Utz, J.A. 1994 'The team process' in *A practical guide to infant and preschool assessment in special education* eds J.A. Bondurant-Utz & L.B. Luciano (pp. 59–71) Allyn & Bacon, Boston, MA

Bowman, B.T. and Stott, F.M. 1994 'Understanding development in a cultural context' in *Diversity and developmental appropriate practices: challenges for early childhood education* eds B.L. Mallory & R.S. New (pp. 119–33) Teachers College Press, New York

Braggett, E.J. 1994 *Developing programs for gifted students* Hawker Brownlow, Melbourne

Bredekamp, S. 1993 'The relationship between early childhood education and early childhood special education: healthy marriage or family feud?' *Topics in Early Childhood Special Education* vol. 13, no. 3, pp. 258–73

Bredekamp, S. and Copple, C. (eds) 1997 *Developmentally appropriate practice in early childhood programs* revised edn, National Association for the Education of Young Children, Washington, DC

Brotherson, M.J., Cunconan-Lahr, R. and Cook, C.C. 1995 'Policy supporting self-determination in the environments of children with disabilities' *Education and Training in Mental Retardation and Developmental Disabilities* vol. 30, no. 1, pp. 3–14

Bruder, M.B. and Staff, I. 1998 'A comparison of the effects of type of classroom and service characteristics on toddlers with disabilities' *Topics in Early Childhood Special Education* vol. 18, no. 1, pp. 26–37

Burchinal, M.R., Roberts, J.E., Nabors, L.A. and Bryant, D.M. 1996 'Quality of center child care and infant cognitive and language development' *Child Development* vol. 67, no. 2, pp. 606–20

Buysse, V. and Bailey, D.B. Jr 1993 'Behavioral and developmental outcomes in young children with disabilities in integrated and segregated settings: a review of comparative studies' *The Journal of Special Education* vol. 26, no. 4, pp. 434–61

Buysse, V., Wesley, P.W. and Keyes, L. 1998 'Implementing early childhood inclusion: barrier and support factors' *Early Childhood Research Quarterly* vol. 13, no. 1, pp. 169–84

Casto, G. and Mastropieri, M.A. 1986 'The efficacy of early intervention programs: a meta-analysis' *Exceptional Children* vol. 52, no. 5, pp. 417–24

Clyde, M. 1995 'Concluding the debate: mind games—what DAP means to me' in *DAPcentrism: challenging developmentally appropriate practice* ed. M. Fleer (pp. 109–16) Australian Early Childhood Association, Watson, ACT

Coady, M. 1994 'Ethical and legal issues for early childhood practitioners' in *Issues in early childhood services: Australian perspectives* eds E.J. Mellor & K.M. Coombe (pp. 1–10) William C. Brown, Dubuque, IO

Cole, K.N., Mills, P.E., Dale, P.S. and Jenkins, J.R. 1991 'Effects of preschool integration for children with disabilities' *Exceptional Children* vol. 58, no. 1, pp. 36–45

Cook, R.E., Tessier, A. and Klein, M.D. 2000 *Adapting early childhood curricula for children in inclusive settings* 5th edn, Merrill, Englewood Cliffs, NJ

Cooke, T.P., Ruskus, J.A., Apolloni, T. and Peck, C.A. 1981 'Handicapped preschool children in the mainstream: background, outcomes, and clinical suggestions' *Topics in Early Childhood Special Education* vol. 1, no. 1, pp. 73–83

Copland, I. 1995 'Developmentally appropriate practice and early childhood special education' *Australian Journal of Early Childhood* vol. 20, no. 4, pp. 1–4

Dahlberg, G., Moss, P. and Pence, A. 1999 *Beyond quality in early childhood education and care: postmodern perspectives* Routledge Falmer, London

Dau, E. (ed.) 1999 *Child's play revisiting play in early childhood settings* MacLennan & Petty, Sydney

David, T. 1999 'Valuing young children' in *Early education transformed* eds L. Abbott & H. Moylett (pp. 82–92) Falmer, London

Diamond, K.E., Hestenes, L.L. and O'Connor, C.E. 1994 'Integrating young children with disabilities in preschool: problems and promise' *Young Children* vol. 49, no. 2, pp. 68–75

Diamond, K.E., Hestenes, L.L., Carpenter, E.S. and Innes, F.K. 1997 'Relationships between enrollment in an inclusive class and preschool children's ideas about people with disabilities' *Topics in Early Childhood Special Education* vol. 17, no. 4, pp. 520–36

Dinnebeil, L.A., McInerney, W., Fox, C. and Juchartz-Pendry, K. 1998 'An analysis of the perceptions and characteristics of childcare personnel regarding inclusion of young children with special needs in community-based programs' *Topics in Early Childhood Special Education* vol. 18, no. 2, pp. 118–28

Dockett, S. and Fleer, M. 1999 *Play and pedagogy in early childhood: bending the rules* Harcourt Brace, Sydney

Dunst, C.J. 2000 'Revisiting "Rethinking early intervention"' *Topics in Early Childhood Special Education* vol. 20, no. 2, pp. 95–104

Elkind, D. 1986 'Formal education and early childhood education: an essential difference' *Phi Delta Kappan* vol. 67, no. 9, pp. 631–6

Favazza, P.D. and Odom, S.L. 1997 'Promoting positive attitudes of kindergarten-age children toward people with disabilities' *Exceptional Children* vol. 63, no. 3, pp. 405–18

Fewell, R.R. and Oelwein, P.L. 1990 'The relationship between time in integrated environments and developmental gains in young children with special needs' *Topics in Early Childhood Special Education* vol. 10, no. 2, pp. 104–16

Field, T. 1991 'Quality infant day-care and grade school behavior and performance' *Child Development* vol. 62, no. 4, pp. 863–70

Field, T., Masi, W., Goldestein, S., Perry, S. and Parl, S. 1988 'Infant day care facilitates preschool social behavior' *Early Childhood Research Quarterly* vol. 3, no. 4, pp. 341–59

Fleer, M. 1995 'Does cognition lead development, or does development lead cognition?' in

DAPcentrism: challenging developmentally appropriate practice ed. M. Fleer (pp. 11–22) Australian Early Childhood Association, Watson, ACT

Gagné, F. 1991 'Toward a differentiated model of giftedness and talent' in *Handbook of gifted education* eds N. Colangelo & G.A. Davis (pp. 65–80) Allyn & Bacon, Boston, MA

Glover, A. 1999 'The role of play in development and learning' in *Child's play: revisiting play in early childhood settings* ed. E. Dau (pp. 5–15) MacLennan & Petty, Sydney

Gow, L. 1990 'Integration in Australia: overview' in *The exceptional child: an introduction to special education* ed. S. Butler (pp. 31–55) Harcourt Brace Jovanovich, Sydney

Green, A.L. and Stoneman, Z. 1989 'Attitudes of mothers and fathers of nonhandicapped children' *Journal of Early Intervention* vol. 13, no. 4, pp. 292–304

Guralnick, M.J. 1981 'The social behavior of preschool children at different developmental levels: effects of group composition' *Journal of Experimental Child Psychology* vol. 31, no. 1, pp. 115–30

——1991 'The next decade of research on the effectiveness of early intervention' *Exceptional Children* vol. 58, no. 2, pp. 174–83

——1994 'Mothers' perceptions of the benefits and drawbacks of early childhood mainstreaming' *Journal of Early Intervention* vol. 18, no. 2, pp. 168–83

——1997 'Second-generation research in the field of early intervention' in *The effectiveness of early intervention* ed. M.J. Guralnick (pp. 3–20) Paul H. Brookes, Baltimore, MD

——1999 'The nature and meaning of social integration for young children with mild developmental delays in inclusive settings' *Journal of Early Intervention* vol. 22, no. 1, pp. 70–86

——2000 'An agenda for change in early childhood inclusion' *Journal of Early Intervention* vol. 23, no. 4, pp. 213–22

Guralnick, M.J., Connor, R.T., Hammons, M., Gottman, J.M. and Kinnish, K. 1995 'Immediate effects of mainstreamed settings on the social interactions and social integration of preschool children' *American Journal on Mental Retardation* vol. 100, no. 4, pp. 359–77

Guralnick, M.J. and Groom, J.M. 1987 'The peer relations of mildly delayed and nonhandicapped preschool children in mainstreamed playgroups' *Child Development* vol. 58, no. 6, pp. 1556–72

——1988 'Peer interactions in mainstreamed and specialized classrooms: a comparative analysis' *Exceptional Children* vol. 54, no. 5, pp. 415–25

Hanline, M.F. and Fox, L. 1993 'Learning within the context of play: providing typical early childhood experiences for children with severe disabilities' *Journal of the Association for Persons with Severe Handicaps* vol. 18, no. 2, pp. 121–9

Hanson, M.J., Wolfberg, P., Zercher, C., Morgan, M., Gutierrez, S., Barnwell, D. and Beckman, P. 1998 'The culture of inclusion: recognizing diversity at multiple levels' *Early Childhood Research Quarterly* vol. 13, no. 1, pp. 185–209

Harris, S.L., Handleman, J.S., Krostoff, B., Bass, L. and Gordon, R. 1990 'Changes in language development among autistic and peer children in segregated and integrated settings' *Journal of Autism and Developmental Disorders* vol. 20, no. 1, pp. 23–31

Hauser-Cram, P., Bronson, M.B. and Upshur, C.C. 1993 'The effects of classroom environment on the social and mastery behavior of preschool children with disabilities' *Early Childhood Research Quarterly* vol. 8, no. 4, pp. 479–97

Holahan, A. and Costenbader, V. 2000 'A comparison of developmental gains for preschool children with disabilities in inclusive and self-contained classrooms' *Topics in Early Childhood Special Education* vol. 20, no. 4, pp. 224–35

Horowitz, F.D. 1987 'A developmental view of giftedness' *Gifted Child Quarterly* vol. 31, no. 4, pp. 165–8

Hundert, J., Mahoney, B., Mundy, F. and Vernon, M.L. 1998 'A descriptive analysis of developmental and social gains of children with severe disabilities in segregated and inclusive preschools in southern Ontario' *Early Childhood Research Quarterly* vol. 13, no. 1, pp. 49–65

Janney, R.E., Snell, M.E., Beers, M.K. and Raynes, M. 1995 'Integrating students with moderate and severe disabilities into general education classes' *Exceptional Children* vol. 61, no. 5, pp. 425–39

Katz, L. 1995 *Talks with teachers of young children* Ablex, Norwood, NJ

Kemp, C. and Carter, M. 1993 'Efficacy research in early intervention: an elusive quest?' *Australasian Journal of Special Education* vol. 17, no. 2, pp. 3–15

Lieber, J., Capell, K., Sandall, S.R., Wolfberg, P., Horn, E. and Beckman, P. 1998 'Inclusive preschool programs: teachers' beliefs and practices' *Early Childhood Research Quarterly* vol. 13, no. 1, pp. 87–105

Long, P. 1996 'Special educational needs' in *Education in early childhood: first things first* eds S. Robson & S. Smedley (pp. 123–35) David Fulton, London

Ludlow, B.L. and Berkeley, T.R. 1994 'Expanding the perceptions of developmentally appropriate practice: changing theoretical perspectives' in *Diversity and developmental appropriate practices: challenges for early childhood education* eds B.L. Mallory & R.S. New (pp. 107–18) Teachers College Press, New York

McDonnell, A.P., Brownell, K. and Wolery, M. 1997 'Teaching experience and specialist support: a survey of preschool teachers employed in programs accredited by NAEYC' *Topics in Early Childhood Special Education* vol. 17, no. 3, pp. 263–85

McLean, M., Bailey, D.B. Jr and Wolery, M. (eds) 1996 *Assessing infants and preschoolers with special needs* 2nd edn, Merrill, Englewood Cliffs, NJ

Macintyre, C. 2001 *Enhancing learning through play: a developmental perspective for early years settings* David Fulton, London

Mahoney, G., Robinson, C. and Powell, A. 1992 'Focusing on parent–child interaction: the bridge to developmentally appropriate practice' *Topics in Early Childhood Special Education* vol. 12, no. 1, pp. 105–20

Malouf, D.B. and Schiller, E.P. 1995 'Research and practice in special education' *Exceptional Children* vol. 61, no. 5, pp. 414–24

Maris, P. and Brown, R. 2000 'Effects of different forms of school contact on children's attitudes toward disabled and non-disabled peers' *British Journal of Educational Psychology* vol. 70, no. 3, pp. 337–51

Martin, G. and Pear, J. 1999 *Behavior modification: what it is and how to do it* 6th edn, Prentice Hall, Upper Saddle River, NJ

Meisels, S.J. 1991 'Dimensions of early identification' *Journal of Early Intervention* vol. 15, no. 1, pp. 26–35

Mills, P.E., Cole, K.N., Jenkins, J.R. and Dale, P.S. 1998 'Effects of differing levels of inclusion on preschoolers with disabilities' *Exceptional Children* vol. 65, no. 1, pp. 79–90

Moss, E. 1992 'Early interactions and metacognitive development of gifted preschoolers' in *To be young and gifted* eds P.S. Klein & A.J. Tannenbaum (pp. 278–318) Ablex, Norwood, NJ

Moss, P. 1999 'Early childhood institutions as a democratic and emancipatory project' in *Early education transformed* eds L. Abbott & H. Moylett (pp. 142–52) Falmer, London

National Association for the Education of Young Children (NAEYC) 1986 'Position statement on developmentally appropriate practice in early childhood programs serving children from birth through age 8' *Young Children* vol. 41, no. 6, pp. 3–19

——1989 'Code of ethical conduct' *Young Children* vol. 45, no. 1, pp. 25–9

New, R.S. and Mallory, B.L. 1994 'Introduction: the ethic of inclusion' in *Diversity and developmental appropriate practices: challenges for early childhood education* eds B.L. Mallory & R.S. New (pp. 1–13) Teachers College Press, New York

Norris, C. and Closs, A. 1999 'Child and parent relationships with teachers in schools responsible for the education of children with serious medical conditions' *British Journal of Special Education* vol. 26, no. 1, pp. 29–33

Ochiltree, G. 1994 *Effects of child care on young children: forty years of research* Australian Institute of Family Studies, Melbourne

Odom, S.L. 2000 'Preschool inclusion: what we know and where we go from here' *Topics in Early Childhood Special Education* vol. 20, no. 1, pp. 20–7

Peck, C.A., Carlson, P. and Helmstetter, E. 1992 'Parent and teacher perceptions of outcomes for typically developing children enrolled in integrated early childhood programs: a statewide survey' *Journal of Early Intervention* vol. 16, no. 1, pp. 53–63

Phillips, D.A. and Howes, C. 1987 'Indicators of quality child care: review of research' in *Quality in child care: what does research tell us?* ed. D. Phillips (pp. 1–19) National Association for the Education of Young Children, Washington, DC

Pope, A.M. 1992 'Preventing secondary conditions' *Mental Retardation* vol. 30, no. 6, pp. 347–54

Porter, L. 1999 *Gifted young children: a guide for teachers and parents* Allen & Unwin, Sydney (also Open University Press, Buckingham, UK)

Porter, L. & McKenzie, S. 2000 *Professional collaboration with parents of children with disabilities* Whurr, London (also MacLennan & Petty, Sydney)

Rekers, G.A. 1984 'Ethical issues in child behavioral assessment' in *Child behavioral assessment* eds T.H. Ollendick & M. Hersen (pp. 244–62) Pergamon, New York

Richarz, S. 1993 'Innovations in early childhood education: models that support the integration of children with varied developmental levels' in *Integrating young children with disabilities into community programs: ecological perspectives on research and implementation* eds C.A. Peck, S.L. Odom and D.D. Bricker (pp. 83–107) Paul H. Brookes, Baltimore, MD

Robson, S. 1996 'The physical environment' in *Education in early childhood: first things first* eds S. Robson & S. Smedley (pp. 153–71) David Fulton, London

Roffey, S. 1999 *Special needs in the early years: collaboration, communication and coordination* David Fulton, London

Rubenstein, J.L., Howes, C. and Boyle, P. 1981 'A two-year follow-up of infants in community-based day care' *Journal of Child Psychology and Psychiatry* vol. 22, no. 3, pp. 209–18

Salisbury, C.L. 1991 'Mainstreaming during the early childhood years' *Exceptional Children* vol. 58, no. 2, pp. 146–55

Sameroff, A.J. 1990 'Neo-environmental perspectives on developmental theory' in *Issues in the developmental approach to mental retardation* eds R.M. Hodapp, J.A. Burack & E. Zigler (pp. 93–113) Cambridge University Press, Cambridge, UK

Sandall, S.R. 1993 'Curricula for early intervention' in *Family-centered early intervention with infants and toddlers: innovative cross-disciplinary approaches* eds W. Brown, S.K. Thurman & L.F. Pearl (pp. 129–51) Paul H. Brookes, Baltimore, MD

Sheridan, M.D., Harding, J. and Meldon-Smith, L. 1999 *Play in early childhood: from birth to six years* ACER Press, Melbourne

Shonkoff, J.P. and Meisels, S.J. (eds) 2000 *Handbook of early intervention* 2nd edn, Cambridge University Press, Cambridge, UK

Simeonsson, R.J., Cooper, D.H. and Scheiner, A.P. 1982 'A review and analysis of the effectiveness of early intervention programs' *Pediatrics* vol. 69, no. 5, pp. 635–41

Stoiber, K.C., Gettinger, M. and Goetz, D. 1998 'Exploring factors influencing parents' and early childhood practitioners' beliefs about inclusion' *Early Childhood Research Quarterly* vol. 13, no. 1, pp. 107–24

Stonehouse, A. 1991 *Our code of ethics at work* Australian Early Childhood Association, Watson, ACT

——1994 *Not just nice ladies: a book of readings on early childhood care and education* Pademelon, Sydney

Stoneman, Z. 1993 'The effects of attitude on preschool integration' in *Integrating young children with disabilities into community programs: ecological perspectives on research and implementation* eds C.A. Peck, S.L. Odom & D.D. Bricker (pp. 223–48) Paul H. Brookes, Baltimore, MD

Turnbull, A.P. and Turnbull, H.R. III 1997 *Families, professionals and exceptionality: a special partnership* 3rd edn, Merrill, Upper Saddle River, NJ

Vandell, D.L., Henderson, V.K. and Wilson, K.S. 1988 'A longitudinal study of children with day-care experiences of varying quality' *Child Development* vol. 59, no. 5, pp. 1286–92

Williams, P. 1996 'The law and students with learning difficulties: some recent developments' *Australian Journal of Learning Disabilities* vol. 1, no. 2, pp. 4–13

Winter, S.M., Bell, M.J. and Dempsey, J.D. 1994 'Creating play environments for children with special needs' *Childhood Education* vol. 71, no. 1, pp. 28–32

Wolery, M., Holcombe, A., Venn, M.L., Brookfield, J., Huffman, K., Schroeder, C., Martin, C.G. and

Fleming, L.A. 1993 'Mainstreaming in early childhood programs: current status and relevant issues' *Young Children* vol. 49, no. 1, pp. 78–84

Wolery, M., Venn, M.L., Holcombe, A., Brookfield, J., Martin, C.G., Huffman, K., Schroeder, C. and Fleming, L.A. 1994a 'Employment of related service personnel in preschool programs: a survey of general educators' *Exceptional Children* vol. 61, no. 1, pp. 25–39

Wolery, M., Werts, M.G. and Holcombe, A. 1994b 'Current practices with young children who have disabilities: placement, assessment, and instruction issues' *Focus on Exceptional Children* vol. 26, no. 6, pp. 1–12

Wolery, M., Werts, M.G., Caldwell, N.K., Snyder, E.D. and Lisowski, L. 1995 'Experienced teachers' perceptions of resources and supports for inclusion' *Education and Training in Mental Retardation and Developmental Disabilities* vol. 30, no. 1, pp. 15–26

2 Collaborating with parents

a'Beckett, C. 1988 'Parent/staff relationships' in *Trusting toddlers: programming for one to three year olds in child care centres* ed. A. Stonehouse (pp. 140–53) Australian Early Childhood Association, Watson, ACT

Abbott, C.F. and Gold, S. 1991 'Conferring with parents when you're concerned that their child needs special services' *Young Children* vol. 46, no. 4, pp. 10–14

Arthur, L., Beecher, B., Dockett, S., Farmer, S. and Death, E. 1996 *Programming and planning in early childhood settings* 2nd edn, Harcourt Brace, Sydney

Bailey, D.B. Jr 1987 'Collaborative goal-setting with families: resolving differences in values and priorities for services' *Topics in Early Childhood Special Education* vol. 7, no. 2, pp. 59–71

Beckman, P.J., Barnwell, D., Horn, E., Hanson, M.J., Gutierrez, S. and Lieber, J. 1998 'Communities, families, and inclusion' *Early Childhood Research Quarterly* vol. 13, no. 1, pp. 125–50

Bennett, T., DeLuca, D. and Bruns, B. 1997 'Putting inclusion into practice: perspectives of teachers and parents' *Exceptional Children* vol. 64, no. 1, pp. 115–31

Bentley-Williams, R. and Butterfield, N. 1996 'Transition from early intervention to school: a family focussed view of the issues involved' *Australasian Journal of Special Education* vol. 20, no. 2, pp. 17–28

Botuck, S. and Winsberg, B.G. 1991 'Effects of respite on mothers of school age and adult children with severe disabilities' *Mental Retardation* vol. 29, no. 1, pp. 43–7

Chandler, P.A. 1994 *A place for me: including children with special needs in early care and education settings* National Association for the Education of Young Children, Washington, DC

Colangelo, N. and Dettman, D.F. 1983 'A review of research on parents and families of gifted children' *Exceptional Children* vol. 50, no. 1, pp. 20–7

Cook, R.E., Tessier, A. and Klein, M.D. 2000 *Adapting early childhood curricula for children in inclusive settings* 5th edn, Merrill, Englewood Cliffs, NJ

Cornell, D.G. and Grossberg, I.N. 1986 'Siblings of children in gifted programs' *Journal for the Education of the Gifted* vol. 9, no. 4, pp. 253–64

Daka-Mulwanda, V., Thornburg, K.R. and Klein, T. 1995 'Collaboration of services for children and families: a synthesis of recent research and recommendations' *Family Relations* vol. 44, no. 2, pp. 219–23

Dale, N. 1996 *Working with families of children with special needs: partnership and practice* Routledge, London

Dinnebeil, L.A., Hale, L. and Rule, S. 1996 'A qualitative analysis of parents' and service coordinators' descriptions of variables that influence collaborative relationships' *Topics in Early Childhood Special Education* vol. 16, no. 3, pp. 322–47

——1999 'Early intervention program practices that support collaboration' *Topics in Early Childhood Special Education* vol. 19, no. 4, pp. 225–35

Dunst, C.J. 2000 'Revisiting "Rethinking early intervention"' *Topics in Early Childhood Special Education* vol. 20, no. 2, pp. 95–104

Dunst, C.J., Trivette, C. and Deal, A. 1988 *Enabling and empowering families: principles and guide-lines for practice* Brookline Books, Cambridge, MA

——1994 *Supporting and strengthening families: volume 1: methods, strategies, and practices* Brookline Books, Cambridge, MA

Foster, M., Berger, M. and McLean, M. 1981 'Rethinking a good idea: a reassessment of parent involvement' *Topics in Early Childhood Special Education* vol. 1, no. 3, pp. 55–65

Fowler, S.A., Schwartz, I. and Atwater, J. 1991 'Perspectives on the transition from preschool to kindergarten for children with disabilities and their families' *Exceptional Children* vol. 58, no. 2, pp. 136–45

Freeman, S.F.N., Alkin, M.C. and Kasari, C.L. 1999 'Satisfaction and desire for change in edu-cational placement for children with Down Syndrome' *Remedial and Special Education* vol. 20, no. 3, pp. 143–51

Geldard, D. 1998 *Basic personal counselling* 3rd edn, Prentice Hall, Sydney

Grant, G., Ramcharan, P., McGrath, M., Nolan, M. and Keady, J. 1998 'Rewards and gratifi-cations among family caregivers' *Journal of Intellectual Disability Research* vol. 42, no. 1, pp. 58–71

Greenberg, J.S., Seltzer, M.M., Krauss, M.W. and Kim, H-W. 1997 'The differential effects of social support on the psychological well-being of aging mothers of adults with mental illness or mental retardation' *Family Relations* vol. 46, no. 4, pp. 383–93

Guralnick, M.J. 1991 'The next decade of research on the effectiveness of early intervention' *Exceptional Children* vol. 58, no. 2, 174–83

Guralnick, M.J., Connor, R.T. and Hammond, M. 1995 'Parent perspectives of peer relationships and friendships in integrated and specialized programs' *American Journal on Mental Retardation* vol. 99, no. 5, pp. 457–76

Hadden, S. and Fowler, S.A. 1997 'Preschool: a new beginning for children and parents' *Teaching Exceptional Children* vol. 30, no. 1, pp. 36–9

Hanline, M.F. 1993 'Facilitating integrated preschool service delivery for transitions for children, families and professionals' in *Integrating young children with disabilities into community programs: ecological perspectives on research and implementation* eds C.A. Peck, S.L. Odom & D.D. Bricker (pp. 133–46) Paul H. Brookes, Baltimore, MD

Hanline, M.F. and Halvorsen, A. 1989 'Parent perceptions of the integration transition process: over-coming artificial barriers' *Exceptional Children* vol. 55, no. 6, pp. 487–92

Hanson, M.J., Wolfberg, P., Zercher, C., Morgan, M., Gutierrez, S., Barnwell, D. and Beckman, P. 1998 'The culture of inclusion: recognizing diversity at multiple levels' *Early Childhood Research Quarterly* vol. 13, no. 1, pp. 185–209

Harry, B. 1992 'Making sense of disability: low-income, Puerto Rican parents' theories of the problem' *Exceptional Children* vol. 59, no. 1, pp. 27–40

Hayes, A. 1998 'Families and disabilities: another facet of inclusion' in *Educating children with special needs* 3rd edn, eds A. Ashman & J. Elkins (pp. 39–66) Prentice Hall, Sydney

Heath, H.E. 1994 'Dealing with difficult behaviors: teachers plan with parents' *Young Children* vol. 49, no. 5, pp. 20–4

Hickson, J. 1992 'A framework for guidance and counseling of the gifted in a school setting' *Gifted Education International* vol. 8, no. 2, pp. 93–103

Hodapp, R.M., Freeman, S.F.N. and Kasari, C.L. 1998 'Parental educational preferences for students with mental retardation: effects of etiology and current placement' *Education and Training in Mental Retardation and Developmental Disabilities* vol. 33, no. 4, pp. 342–9

Hutchins, M.P. and Renzaglia, A. 1998 'Interviewing families for effective transition to employment' *Teaching Exceptional Children* vol. 30, no. 4, pp. 72–8

Jakubowski, P. and Lange, A. 1978 *The assertive option: your rights and responsibilities* Research Press, Champaign, IL

Jones, V.F. and Jones, L.S. 1998 *Comprehensive classroom management: creating communities of support and solving problems* 5th edn, Allyn & Bacon, Boston, MA

Ketelaar, M., Vermeer, A., Helders, P.J.M. and Hart, H. 1998 'Parental participation in intervention programs for children with cerebral palsy: a review of research' *Topics in Early Childhood Special Education* vol. 18, no. 2, pp. 108–17

Lopez, A. 1996 'Creation is ongoing: developing a relationship with non-English speaking parents' *Child Care Information Exchange* vol. 107, pp. 56–9

Lynch, E.W. and Hanson, M.J. 1996 'Ensuring cultural competence in assessment' in *Assessing infants and preschoolers with special needs* 2nd edn, eds M. McLean, D.B. Bailey Jr and M. Wolery (pp. 69–95) Merrill, Englewood Cliffs, NJ

Lynch, E.W. and Stein, R.C. 1987 'Parent participation by ethnicity: a comparison of Hispanic, Black and Anglo families' *Exceptional Children* vol. 54, no. 2, pp. 105–11

McBride, N. 1992 'Early identification of the gifted and talented students: where do teachers stand?' *Gifted Education International* vol. 8, no. 1, pp. 19–22

McKenzie, S. 1993 'Consultation with parents of young children with disabilities regarding their perception of children's services and service professionals and their needs associated with access and participation in generic children's services' unpublished Masters Dissertation, Flinders University of South Australia, Adelaide

McWilliam, R.A., Lang, L., Vandiviere, P., Angell, R., Collins, L. and Underdown, G. 1995 'Satisfaction and struggles: family perceptions of early intervention services' *Journal of Early Intervention* vol. 19, no. 1, pp. 43–60

McWilliam, R.A., Tocci, L. and Harbin, G.L. 1998 'Family-centered services: service providers' discourse and behavior' *Topics in Early Childhood Special Education* vol. 18, no. 4, pp. 206–21

McWilliam, R.A., Young, H.J. and Harville, K. 1996 'Therapy services in early intervention: current status, barriers and recommendations' *Topics in Early Childhood Special Education* vol. 16, no. 3, pp. 348–74

Mahoney, G. and Bella, J.M. 1998 'An examination of the effects of family-centered early intervention on child and family outcomes' *Topics in Early Childhood Special Education* vol. 18, no. 2, pp. 83–94

Mahoney, G. and Filer, J. 1996 'How responsive is early intervention to the priorities and needs of families?' *Topics in Early Childhood Special Education* vol. 16, no. 4, pp. 437–57

Marion, R.L. 1980 'Communicating with parents of culturally diverse exceptional children' *Exceptional Children* vol. 46, no. 8, pp. 616–23

Nelson-Jones, R. 1988 *Practical counseling and helping skills* Holt, Rinehart & Winston, New York

Palmer, D.S., Borthwick-Duffy, S.A. and Widaman, K. 1998a 'Parent perceptions of inclusive practices for their children with significant cognitive disabilities' *Exceptional Children* vol. 64, no. 2, pp. 271–82

Palmer, D.S., Borthwick-Duffy, S.A., Widaman, K. and Best, S.J. 1998b 'Influences on parent perceptions of inclusive practices for their children with mental retardation' *American Journal on Mental Retardation* vol. 103, no. 3, pp. 272–87

Porter, L. 1999 *Gifted young children: a guide for teachers and parents* Allen & Unwin, Sydney (also Open University Press, Buckingham, UK)

Porter, L. and McKenzie, S. 2000 *Professional collaboration with parents of children with disabilities* Whurr, London (also MacLennan & Petty, Sydney)

Powell, D.R. 1994 'Parents, pluralism, and the NAEYC statement on developmentally appropriate practice' in *Diversity and developmental appropriate practices: challenges for early childhood education* eds B.L. Mallory & R.S. New (pp. 166–82) Teachers College Press, New York

Powell, D.S., Batsche, C.J., Ferro, J., Fox, L. and Dunlap, G. 1997 'A strength-based approach in support of multi-risk families: principles and issues' *Topics in Early Childhood Special Education* vol. 17, no. 1, pp. 1–26

Ramey, C.T. and Ramey, S.L. 1992 'Effective early intervention' *Mental Retardation* vol. 30, no. 6, pp. 337–45

Rimmerman, A., Kramer, R. and Levy, J.M. 1989 'Who benefits most from respite care?' *International Journal of Rehabilitation Research* vol. 12, no. 1, pp. 41–7

Rosin, P. 1996 'The diverse American family' in *Partnerships in family-centred care: a guide to collaborative early intervention* eds P. Rosin, A.D. Whitehead, L.I. Tuchman, G.S. Jesien, A.L. Begun & L. Irwin (pp. 3–28) Paul H. Brookes, Baltimore, MD

Ryndak, D.L., Downing, J.E., Morrison, A.P. and Williams, L.J. 1996 'Parents' perceptions of educational settings and services for children with moderate or severe disabilities' *Remedial and Special Education* vol. 17, no. 2, pp. 106–18

Salend, S.J. and Taylor, L. 1993 'Working with families: a cross-cultural perspective' *Remedial and Special Education* vol. 14, no. 5, pp. 25–32

Sandler, A.G. and Mistretta, L.A. 1998 'Positive adaptation in parents of adults with disabilities' *Education and Training in Mental Retardation and Developmental Disabilities* vol. 33, no. 2, pp. 123–30

Sebastian, P. 1989 *Handle with care: a guide to early childhood administration* 2nd edn, Jacaranda Press, Brisbane, QLD

Seligman, M. and Darling, R.B. 1997 *Ordinary families; special children* 2nd edn, Guilford, New York

Silverman, L.K. 1997 'Family counseling' in *Handbook of gifted education* 2nd edn, eds N. Colangelo & G.A. Davis (pp. 382–97) Allyn & Bacon, Boston, MA

Sokoly, M.M. and Dokecki, P.R. 1995 'Ethical perspectives on family-centred early intervention' in *Working with families in early intervention* ed. J.A. Blackman (pp. 186–98) Aspen, Gaithersburg, MD

Stainton, T. and Besser, H. 1998 'The positive impact of children with an intellectual disability on the family' *Journal of Intellectual and Developmental Disability* vol. 23, no. 1, pp. 57–70

Summers, J.A., Dell'Oliver, C., Turnbull, A.P., Benson, H.A., Santelli, E., Campbell, M. and Siegal-Causey, E. 1990 'Examining the individualised family service plan process: what are family and practitioner preferences?' *Topics in Early Childhood Special Education* vol. 10, no. 1, pp. 78–99

Turnbull, A.P. and Turnbull, H.R. 1997 *Families, professionals and exceptionality: a special partnership* 3rd edn, Merrill, Upper Saddle River, NJ

Warfield, M.E. and Hauser-Cram, P. 1996 'Child care needs, arrangements, and satisfaction of mothers of children with developmental disabilities' *Mental Retardation* vol. 34, no. 5, pp. 294–302

Washington, K., Schwartz, I.S. and Swinth, Y. 1994 'Physical and occupational therapists in naturalistic early childhood settings: challenges and strategies for training' *Topics in Early Childhood Special Education* vol. 14, no. 3, pp. 333–49

Westling, D.L. 1996 'What do parents of children with moderate and severe mental disabilities want?' *Education and Training in Mental Retardation and Developmental Disabilities* vol. 31, no. 2, pp. 86–114

Westling, D.L. and Plaute, W. 1999 'Views of Austrian parents about special education services for their children with mental disabilities' *Education and Training in Mental Retardation and Developmental Disabilities* vol. 34 , no. 1, pp. 43–57

White, K.R., Taylor, M.J. and Moss, V.D. 1992 'Does research support claims about the benefits of involving parents in early intervention programs?' *Review of Educational Research* vol. 62, no. 1, pp. 91–125

Winton, P. 1993 'Providing family support in integrated settings: research and recommendations' in *Integrating young children with disabilities into community programs: ecological perspectives on research and implementation* eds C.A. Peck, S.L. Odom & D.D. Bricker (pp. 65–80) Paul H. Brookes, Baltimore, MD

Wolery, M. 1989 'Transition in early childhood special education: issues and procedures' *Focus on Exceptional Children* vol. 22, no. 2, pp. 1–16

3 Identification and assessment

Anastasi, A. and Urbina. S. 1997 *Psychological testing* 7th edn, Prentice Hall, Upper Saddle River, NJ

Bondurant-Utz, J.A. and Luciano, L.B. 1994 'Norm-based assessment: determination of eligibility' in *A practical guide to infant and preschool assessment in special education* eds J.A. Bondurant-Utz & L.B. Luciano (pp. 151–9) Allyn & Bacon, Boston, MA

Borland, J.H. and Wright, L. 1994 'Identifying young, potentially gifted economically disadvantaged students' *Gifted Child Quarterly* vol. 38, no. 4, pp. 164–71

Brambring, M. and Tröster, H. 1994 'The assessment of cognitive development in blind infants and preschoolers, *Journal of Visual Impairment and Blindness* vol. 88, no. 1, pp. 9–18

Cahan, S. and Gejman, A. 1993 'Constancy of IQ scores among gifted children' *Roeper Review* vol. 15, no. 3, pp. 140–3

Chitwood, D.G. 1986 'Guiding parents seeking testing' *Roeper Review* vol. 8, no. 3, pp. 177–9

Ciha, T.E., Harris, B., Hoffman, C. and Porter, M.W. 1974 'Parents as identifiers of giftedness: ignored but accurate' *Gifted Child Quarterly* vol. 18, no. 3, pp. 191–5

Cook, R.E., Tessier, A. and Klein, M.D. 2000 *Adapting early childhood curricula for children in inclusive settings* 5th edn, Merrill, Englewood Cliffs, NJ

Fallen, N.H. 1985 'Assessment: techniques, processes, and issues' in *Young children with special needs* 2nd edn, eds N.H. Fallen & W. Umansky (pp. 61–131) Merrill, Columbus, OH

Figueroa, R.A. 1989 'Psychological testing of linguistic-minority students: knowledge gaps and regulations' *Exceptional Children* vol. 56, no. 2, pp. 145–52

Fuchs, D. and Fuchs, L.S. 1986 'Test procedure bias: a meta-analysis of examiner familiarity effects' *Review of Educational Research* vol. 56, no. 2, pp. 243–62

Fuchs, D., Fuchs, L.S., Power, M.H. and Dailey, A.M. 1985 'Bias in the assessment of handicapped children' *American Educational Research Journal* vol. 22, no. 2, pp. 185–98

Gallagher, J.J. and Moss, J.W. 1963 'New concepts of intelligence and their effect on exceptional children' *Exceptional Children* vol. 30, no. 1, pp. 1–5

Gonzalez, G. 1974 'Language, culture and exceptional children' *Exceptional Children* vol. 40, no. 8, pp. 565–70

Hansen, J.B. and Linden, K.W. 1990 'Selecting instruments for identifying gifted and talented students' *Roeper Review* vol. 13, no. 1, pp. 10–15

Helm, J.H., Beneke, S. and Steinheimer, K. 1998 *Windows on learning: documenting young children's work* Teachers College Press, New York

Heward, W.L. 2000 *Exceptional children: an introduction to special education* 6th edn, Merrill, Upper Saddle River, NJ

Hooper, S.R. and Edmondson, R. 1998 'Assessment of young children: standards, stages and approaches' in *Young children with special needs* 3rd edn, eds W. Umansky & S.R. Hooper (pp. 340–71) Merrill, Upper Saddle River, NJ

Hundert, J., Morrison, L., Mahoney, W., Mundy, F. and Vernon, M.L. 1997 'Parent and teacher assessments of the developmental status of children with severe, mild/moderate, or no developmental disabilities' *Topics in Early Childhood Special Education* vol. 17, no. 4, pp. 419–34

Jacobs, J.C. 1971 'Effectiveness of teacher and parent identification of gifted children as a function of school level' *Psychology in the Schools* vol. 8, no. 2, pp. 140–2

Kaufman, A.S. 1990 'The WPPSI-R: you can't judge a test by its colors' *Journal of School Psychology* vol. 28, pp. 387–94

Kaufman, A.S. and Harrison, P.L. 1986 'Intelligence tests and gifted assessment: what are the positives?' *Roeper Review* vol. 8, no. 3, pp. 154–9

Lynch, E.W. and Hanson, M.J. 1996 'Ensuring cultural competence in assessment' in *Assessing infants and preschoolers with special needs* 2nd edn, eds M. McLean, D.B. Bailey Jr & M. Wolery (pp. 69–95) Merrill, Englewood Cliffs, NJ

McConnell, S.R. 2000 'Assessment in early intervention and early childhood special education: building on the past to project into our future' *Topics in Early Childhood Special Education* vol. 20, no. 1, pp. 43–8

McCormick, L. and Schiefelbusch, R. 1984 *Early language intervention: an introduction* Merrill, Columbus, OH

McLean, M., Bailey, D.B. Jr and Wolery, M. (eds) 1996 *Assessing infants and preschoolers with special needs* 2nd edn, Merrill, Englewood Cliffs, NJ

McLoughlin, J.A. and Lewis, R.B. 2001 *Assessing students with special needs* 4th edn, Merrill Prentice Hall, Upper Saddle River, NJ

Marion, R.L. 1980 'Communicating with parents of culturally diverse children' *Exceptional Children* vol. 46, no. 8, pp. 616–23

Meisels, S.J. and Atkins-Burnett, S. 2000 'The elements of early childhood assessment' in *Handbook of early intervention* 2nd edn, eds J.P. Shonkoff and S.J. Meisels (pp. 231–57) Cambridge University Press, Cambridge, UK

Miller-Jones, D. 1989 'Culture and testing' *American Psychologist* vol. 44, no. 2, pp. 360–6

National Association for the Education of Young Children 1988 'NAEYC position statement on standardized testing of young children 3 through 8 years of age' *Young Children* vol. 43, no. 3, pp. 42–7

Neisworth, J.T. and Bagnato, S.J. 1988 'Assessment in early childhood special education' in *Early intervention for infants and children with handicaps: an empirical base* eds S.L. Odom & M.B. Karnes (pp. 23–49) Paul H. Brookes, Baltimore, MD

——1992 'The case against intelligence testing in early intervention' *Topics in Early Childhood Special Education* vol. 12, no. 1, pp. 1–20

Pendarvis, E. and Howley, A. 1996 'Playing fair: the possibilities of gifted education' *Journal for the Education of the Gifted* vol. 19, no. 2, pp. 215–33

Pyryt, M.C. 1996 'IQ: easy to bash, hard to replace' *Roeper Review* vol. 18, no. 4, pp. 255–8

Rowe, H. 1990 'Testing and evaluation of persons with handicap' in *The exceptional child: an introduction to special education* ed. S. Butler (pp. 543–68) Harcourt Brace Jovanovich, Sydney

Sattler, J.M. 1992 *Assessment of children* rev. 3rd edn, Jerome M. Sattler Publishing, San Diego, CA

Shaklee, B.D. 1992 'Identification of young gifted students' *Journal for the Education of the Gifted* vol. 15, no. 2, pp. 134–44

Silverman, L.K., Chitwood, D.G. and Waters, J.L. 1986 'Young gifted children: can parents identify giftedness?' *Topics in Early Childhood Special Education* vol. 6, no. 1, pp. 23–38

Spangler, R.S. and Sabatino, D.A. 1995 'Temporal stability of gifted children's intelligence' *Roeper Review* vol. 17, no. 3, pp. 207–10

Sternberg, R.J. 1982 'Lies we live by: misapplication of tests in identifying the gifted' *Gifted Child Quarterly* vol. 26, no. 4, pp. 157–61

Tannenbaum A.J. 1983 *Gifted children: psychological and educational perspectives* Macmillan, New York

——1992 'Early signs of giftedness: research and commentary' in *To be young and gifted* eds P.S. Klein & A.J. Tannenbaum (pp. 3–32) Ablex, Norwood, NJ

Taylor, R.L. 2000 *Assessment of exceptional students: educational and psychological procedures* 5th edn, Allyn & Bacon, Boston, MA

Wechsler, D. 1958 *The measurement and appraisal of adult intelligence* 4th edn, Williams & Wilkins, Baltimore, MD

Wolery, M. 1996a 'Using assessment information to plan intervention programs' in *Assessing infants and preschoolers with special needs* 2nd edn, eds M. McLean, D.B. Bailey Jr & M. Wolery (pp. 491–518) Merrill, Englewood Cliffs, NJ

——1996b 'Monitoring child progress' in *Assessing infants and preschoolers with special needs* 2nd edn, eds M. McLean, D.B. Bailey Jr & M. Wolery (pp. 519–60) Merrill, Englewood Cliffs, NJ

Worthen, B.R. and Spandel, V. 1991 'Putting the standardized test debate in perspective' *Educational Leadership* vol. 48, no. 5, pp. 65–9

4 Principles of program individualisation

Atwater, J.B., Carta, J.J., Schwartz, I.S. and McConnell, S.R. 1994 'Blending developmentally appropriate practice and early childhood special education: redefining best practice to meet the needs of all children' in *Diversity and developmental appropriate practices: challenges for early childhood education* eds B.L. Mallory & R.S. New (pp. 185–201) Teachers College Press, New York

Bailey, D.B. and McWilliam, R.A. 1990 'Normalizing early intervention' *Topics in Early Childhood Special Education* vol. 10, no. 2, pp. 33–47

Bailey, D.B. and Wolery, M. 1992 *Teaching infants and preschoolers with handicaps* 2nd edn, Merrill, Columbus, OH

Bailey, D.B. Jr, Burchinal, M.R. and McWilliam, R.A. 1993 'Age of peers and early childhood development' *Child Development* vol. 64, no. 3, pp. 848–63

Bailey, S. 1997 'Acceleration as an option for talented students' in *Parents as lifelong teachers of the gifted* eds B.A. Knight & S. Bailey (pp. 43–50) Hawker Brownlow Education, Melbourne

Barbour, N.B. 1992 'Early childhood gifted education: a collaborative perspective' *Journal for the Education of the Gifted* vol. 15, no. 2, pp. 145–62

Barclay, K. and Benelli, C. 1994 'Are labels determining practice?: programming for preschool gifted childen' *Childhood Education* vol. 70, no. 3, pp. 133–6

Belgrad, S.F. 1998 'Creating the most enabling environment for young gifted children' in *The young gifted child: potential and promise, an anthology* ed. J.F. Smutny (pp. 369–79) Hampton Press, Cresskill, NJ

Benbow, C.P. 1991 'Meeting the needs of gifted students through use of acceleration' in *Handbook of special education: research and practice: volume 4: emerging programs eds M.C. Wang, M.C. Reynolds & H.J. Walberg (pp. 23–36) Pergaman Press, Oxford, UK

Borland, J.H. 1989 *Planning and implementing programs for the gifted* Teachers College, Columbia University, New York

Bouchard, L.L. 1991 'Mixed age groupings for gifted students' *Gifted Child Today* vol. 14, no. 5, pp. 30–5

Bragett, E.J. 1992 *Pathways for accelerated learners* Hawker Brownlow Education, Melbourne

——1993 'Acceleration: what, why, how and when?' *Gifted children need help?: a guide for parents and teachers* ed. D. Farmer (pp. 120–6) New South Wales Association for Gifted and Talented Children Inc, Sydney

Bredekamp, S. 1997 'NAEYC issues revised position statement on developmentally appropriate practice in early childhood programs' *Young Children* vol. 52, no. 2, pp. 34–40

Bredekamp, S. and Copple, C. (eds) 1997 *Developmentally appropriate practice in early childhood programs* revised edn, National Association for the Education of Young Children, Washington, DC

Carta, J.J., Schwartz, I.S., Atwater, J.B. and McConnell, S.R. 1991 'Developmentally appropriate practice: appraising its usefulness for young children with disabilities' *Topics in Early Childhood Special Education* vol. 11, no. 1, pp. 1–20

Cavallaro, C.C., Haney, M. and Cabello, B. 1993 'Developmentally appropriate strategies for promoting full participation in early childhood settings' *Topics in Early Childhood Special Education* vol. 13, no. 3, pp. 293–307

Cohen, L.M. 1989 'Understanding the interests and themes of the very young gifted child' *Gifted Child Today* vol. 12, no. 4, pp. 6–9

——1998 'Facilitating the interest themes of young bright children' in *The young gifted child: potential and promise, an anthology* ed. J.F. Smutny (pp. 317–39) Hampton Press, Cresskill, NJ

Cook, R.E., Tessier, A. and Klein, M.D. 2000 *Adapting early childhood curricula for children in inclusive settings* 5th edn, Merrill, Englewood Cliffs, NJ

Dahlberg, G., Moss, P. and Pence, A. 1999 *Beyond quality in early childhood education and care: postmodern perspectives* Routledge Falmer, London

Diamond, K.E., Hestenes, L.L. and O'Connor, C.E. 1994 'Integrating young children with disabilities in preschool: problems and promise' *Young Children* vol. 49, no. 2, pp. 68–75

Diezmann, C.M. and Watters, J.J. 1997 'Bright but bored: optimising the environment for gifted children' *Australian Journal of Early Childhood* vol. 22, no. 2, pp. 17–21

Dunn, L. and Kontos, S. 1997 'What have we learned about developmentally appropriate practice?' *Young Children* vol. 52, no. 5, pp. 4–13

Erwin, E.J. 1993 'Social participation by young children with visual impairments in specialized and integrated environments' *Journal of Visual Impairment and Blindness* vol. 87, no. 5, pp. 138–42

Eyre, D. 1997 *Able children in ordinary schools* David Fulton, London

Feldhusen, J.G., van Winkle, L. and Ehle, D.A. 1996 'Is it acceleration or simply appropriate instruction for precocious youth?' *Teaching Exceptional Children* vol. 28, no. 3, pp. 48–51

Fraser, S. and Gestwicki, C. 2002 *Authentic childhood: exploring Reggio Emilia in the classroom* Delmar, Albany, NY

Guralnick, M.J., Paul-Brown, D., Groom, J.M., Booth, C.L., Hammond, M.A., Tupper, D.B. and Gelenter, A. 1998 'Conflict resolution patterns of preschool children with and without developmental delays in heterogeneous playgroups' *Early Education and Development* vol. 9, no. 1, pp. 49–77

Hanline, M.F. 1993 'Facilitating integrated preschool service delivery for transitions for children, families and professionals' in *Integrating young children with disabilities into community programs: ecological perspectives on research and implementation* eds C.A. Peck, S.L. Odom & D.D. Bricker (pp. 133–46) Paul H. Brookes, Baltimore, MD

Hanson, M.J., Beckman, P.J., Horn, E., Marquart, J., Sandall, S.R., Greig, D. and Brennan, E. 2000 'Entering preschool: family and professional experiences in this transition process' *Journal of Early Intervention* vol. 23, no. 4, pp. 279–93

Harrison, C. 1999 *Giftedness in early childhood* 2nd edn, Gerric, Sydney

Hauser-Cram, P., Bronson, M.B. and Upshur, C.C. 1993 'The effects of classroom environment on the social and mastery behavior of preschool children with disabilities' *Early Childhood Research Quarterly* vol. 8, no. 4, pp. 479–97

Helm, J.H., Beneke, S. and Steinheimer, K. 1998 *Windows on learning: documenting young childen's work* Teachers College Press, New York

Holden, B. 1996 'Educational provisions: Early childhood' in *Gifted and talented: New Zealand perspectives* eds D. McAlpine & R. Moltzen (pp. 139–58) ERDC Press, Palmerston North, NZ

Ivory, J.J. and McCollum J.A. 1999 'Effects of social and isolate toys on social play in an inclusive setting' *The Journal of Special Education* vol. 32, no. 4, pp. 238–43

Johnson, J.E. and Johnson, K.M. 1992 'Clarifying the developmental perspective in response to Carta, Schwartz, Atwater, and McConnell' *Topics in Early Childhood Special Education* vol. 12, no. 4, pp. 439–57

Kanevsky, L. 1994 'A comparative study of children's learning in the zone of proximal development' *European Journal for High Ability* vol. 5, pp. 163–75

Katz, L. 1988 'What should children be doing?' *Rattler* Spring 1988, pp. 4–6

Katz, L.G. and Chard, S.C. 1989 *Engaging children's minds: the project approach* Ablex, Norwood, NJ

Katz, L.G., Evangelou, D. and Hartman, J.A. 1990 *The case for mixed-age grouping in early education* National Association for the Education of Young Children, Washington, DC

Kessler, S.A. 1991 'Alternative perspectives on early childhood education' *Early Childhood Research Quarterly* vol. 6, no. 2, pp. 183–97

Klein, P.S. 1992 'Mediating the cognitive, social, and aesthetic development of precocious young children' in *To be young and gifted* eds P.S. Klein & A.J. Tannenbaum (pp. 245–77) Ablex, Norwood, NJ

Kontos, S., Moore, D. and Giorgetti, K. 1998 'The ecology of inclusion' *Topics in Early Childhood Special Education* vol. 18, no. 1, pp. 38–48

Kostelnick, M.J. 1992 'Myths associated with developmentally appropriate programs' *Young Children* vol. 47, no. 4, pp. 17–23

Kulik, J.A. and Kulik, C.-L.C. 1997 'Ability grouping' in *Handbook of gifted education* 2nd edn, eds N. Colangelo & G.A. Davis (pp. 230–42) Allyn & Bacon, Boston, MA

Lambert, E.B. and Clyde, M. 2000 *Re-thinking early childhood theory and practice* Social Science Press, Katoomba, NSW

Lewis, C. and Taylor, H. 1997 'The learning environment' in *Visual impairment: access to education for children and young people* eds H. Mason, S. McCall, C. Arter, M. McLinden & J. Stone (pp. 196–204) David Fulton, London

Lloyd, L. 1997 'Multi-age classes: an option for all students?' *The Australasian Journal of Gifted Education* vol. 6, no. 1, pp. 11–20

Losardo, A. and Bricker, D. 1994 'Activity-based instruction and direct instruction: a comparison study' *American Journal on Mental Retardation* vol. 98, no. 6, pp. 744–65

MacNaughton, G. and Williams, G. 1998 *Techniques for teaching young children: choices in theory and practice* Longman, Sydney

McCollum, J.A. and Bair, H. 1994 'Research in parent-child interaction: guidance to developmentally appropriate practice for young children with disabilities' in *Diversity and developmental appropriate practices: challenges for early childhood education* eds B.L. Mallory & R.S. New (pp. 84–106) Teachers College Press, New York

Mahoney, G. and Wheedon, C.A. 1999 'The effect of teacher style on interactive engagement of preschool-aged children with special learning needs' *Early Childhood Research Quarterly* vol. 14, no. 1, pp. 51–68

Mason, D.A. and Burns, R.B. 1996 ' "Simply no worse and simply no better" may simply be wrong: a critique of Veenman's conclusion about multigrade classes' *Review of Educational Research* vol. 66, no. 3, pp. 307–22

Maxwell, S. 1996 'Meaningful interaction' In *Education in early childhood: first things first* eds S. Robson & S. Smedley (pp. 87–104) David Fulton, London

Mirenda, P. and Donnellan, A. 1987 'Issues in curriculum development' in *Handbook of autism and pervasive developmental disorders* eds D. Cohen & A. Donnellan (pp. 211–26) John Wiley & Sons, New York

Montgomery, D. 1996 *Educating the able* Cassell, London

Morelock, M.J. and Morrison, K. 1996 *Gifted children have talents too: multidimensional programmes for the gifted in early childhood* Hawker Brownlow Education, Melbourne

Moss, P. 1999 'Early childhood institutions as a democratic and emancipatory project' in *Early education transformed* eds L. Abbott & H. Moylett (pp. 142–52) Falmer, London

Mosteller, F., Light, R.J. and Sachs, J.A. 1996 'Sustained inquiry in education: lessons from skill grouping and class size' *Harvard Educational Review* vol. 66, no. 4, 797–842

National Association for the Education of Young Children (NAEYC) 1986 'Position statement on developmentally appropriate practice in early childhood programs serving children from birth through age 8' *Young Children* vol. 41, no. 6, pp. 3–19

NAEYC and the National Association of Early Childhood Specialists in State Departments of Education 1991 'Guidelines for appropriate curriculum content and assessment in programs serving children ages 3 through 8' *Young Children* vol. 46, no. 3, pp. 21–38

National Childcare Accreditation Council (NCAC) 1993 *Putting children first: quality improvement and accreditation system handbook* NCAC, Sydney

New, R.S. and Mallory, B.L. 1994 'Introduction: the ethic of inclusion' in *Diversity and developmental appropriate practices: challenges for early childhood education* eds B.L. Mallory & R.S. New (pp. 1–13) Teachers College Press, New York

Nidiffer, L.G. and Moon, S.M. 1994 'Serving the gifted dyslexic and gifted at risk: using differentiated-integrated curricula and enrichment' *Our Gifted Children* vol. 2, no. 8, pp. 39–43

Patton, M.M. and Kokoski, T.M. 1996 'How good is your early childhood science, mathematics, and technology program?: strategies for extending your curriculum' *Young Children* vol. 51, no. 5, pp. 38–44

Perkins, D.N., Jay, E. and Tishman, S. 1993 'Beyond abilities: a dispositional theory of thinking' *Merrill Palmer Quarterly* vol. 39, no. 1, pp. 1–21

Piirto, J. 1999 *Talented children and adults* 2nd edn, Merrill, Upper Saddle River, NJ

Porter, L. 1999 *Gifted young children: a guide for teachers and parents* Allen & Unwin, Sydney (also Open University Press, Buckingham, UK)

Richarz, .S. 1993 'Innovations in early childhood education: models that support the integration of children with varied developmental levels' in *Integrating young children with disabilities into community programs: ecological perspectives on research and implementation* eds C.A. Peck, S.L. Odom and D.D. Bricker (pp. 83–107) Paul H. Brookes, Baltimore, MD

Roberts, J.E., Burchinal, M.R. and Bailey, D.B. 1994 'Communication among preschoolers with and without disabilities in same-age and mixed-age classes' *American Journal on Mental Retardation* vol. 99, no. 3, pp. 231–49

Robson, S. 1996 'The physical environment' in *Education in early childhood: first things first* eds
    S. Robson & S. Smedley (pp. 153–71) David Fulton, London
Rodger, R. 1999 *Planning an appropriate curriculum for the under fives* David Fulton, London
Rogers, K.B. and Kimpston, R.D. 1992 'Acceleration: what we do vs what we do not know'
    Educational Leadership vol. 50, no. 2, pp. 58–61
Rule, S., Fiechtl, B.J. and Innocenti, M.S. 1990 'Preparation for transition to mainstreamed post-
    preschool environments: development of a survival skills curriculum' *Topics in Early
    Childhood Special Education* vol. 9, no. 4, pp. 78–90
Rule, S., Losardo, A., Dinnebeil, L., Kaiser, A. and Rowland, C. 1998 'Translating research on nat-
    uralistic instruction into practice' *Journal of Early Intervention* vol. 21, no. 4, pp. 283–93
Salisbury, C.L. and Vincent, L.J. 1990 'Criterion of the next environment and best practices: main-
    streaming and integration ten years later' *Topics in Early Childhood Special Education* vol. 10,
    no. 2, pp. 78–89
Sandall, S.R. 1993 'Curricula for early intervention' in *Family-centered early intervention with
    infants and toddlers: innovative cross-disciplinary approaches* eds W. Brown, S.K. Thurman &
    L.F. Pearl (pp. 129–51) Paul H. Brookes, Baltimore, MD
Smidt, S. 1998 *Guide to early years practice* Routledge, London
Smutny, J.F., Walker, S.Y. and Meckstroth, E.A. 1997 *Teaching young gifted children in the regular
    classroom: identifying, nurturing, and challenging ages 4–9* Free Spirit Publishing, Minneapolis,
    MN
Stonehouse, A. 1988 'Characteristics of toddlers' in *Trusting toddlers: programming for one to three
    year olds in child care centres* ed. A. Stonehouse (pp. 1–13) Australian Early Childhood Associ-
    ation, Watson, ACT
——1999 'Play, a way of being for babies and toddlers' in *Child's play: revisiting play in early child-
    hood settings* ed. E. Dau (pp. 152–63) MacLennan & Petty, Sydney
Theilheimer, R. 1993 'Something for everyone: benefits of mixed-age grouping for children, parents,
    and teachers' *Young Children* vol. 48, no. 5, pp. 82–7
Tomlinson, C.A. 1996 'Good teaching for one and all: does gifted education have an instructional
    identity?' *Journal for the Education of the Gifted* vol. 20, no. 2, pp. 155–74
Van Tassel-Baska, J. 1997 'What matters in curriculum for gifted learners: reflections on theory,
    research and practice' in *Handbook of gifted education* 2nd edn, eds N. Colangelo & G.A. Davis
    (pp. 126–35) Allyn & Bacon, Boston, MA
Veenman, S. 1995 'Cognitive and noncognitive effects of multigrade and multi-age classes: a best-
    evidence synthesis' *Review of Educational Research* vol. 65, no. 4, pp. 319–81
——1996 'Effects of multigrade and multi-age classes reconsidered' *Review of Educational Research*
    vol. 66. no. 3, pp. 323–40
Ward, C.D. 1996 'Adult intervention: appropriate strategies for enriching the quality of children's
    play' *Young Children* vol. 51, no. 3, pp. 20–5
Wolery, M. 1989 'Transition in early childhood special education: issues and procedures' *Focus on
    Exceptional Children* vol. 22, no. 2, pp. 1–16
——1991 'Instruction in early childhood special education: "seeing through a glass darkly . . .
    knowing in part"' *Exceptional Children* vol. 58, no. 2, pp. 127–34
——1996 'Monitoring child progress' in *Assessing infants and preschoolers with special needs*
    2nd edn, eds M. McLean, D.B. Bailey Jr & M. Wolery (pp. 519–60) Merrill, Englewood
    Cliffs, NJ
Wolery, M. and Bredekamp, S. 1994 'Developmentally appropriate practices and young children
    with disabilities: contextual issues in the discussion' *Journal of Early Intervention* vol. 18,
    no. 4, pp. 331–41
Wolery, M. and Fleming, L.A. 1993 'Implementing individualized curricula in integrated settings' in
    *Integrating young children with disabilities into community programs: ecological perspectives
    on research and implementation* eds C.A. Peck, S.L. Odom & D.D. Bricker (pp. 109–32) Paul
    H. Brookes, Baltimore, MD
Wolery, M., Werts, M.G. and Holcombe, A. 1994 'Current practices with young children who have

disabilities: placement, assessment, and instruction issues' *Focus on Exceptional Children* vol. 26, no. 6, pp. 1–12

Wright, L. and Coulianos, C. 1991 'A model program for precocious children: Hollingworth preschool' *Gifted Child Today* vol. 14, no. 5, pp. 24–9

5 Vision

Artre, C. 1997 'Listening skills' in *Visual impairment: access to education for children and young people* eds H. Mason, S. McCall, C. Arter, M. McLinden & J. Stone (pp. 143–8) David Fulton, London

Artre, C., Mason, H.L., McCall, S., McLinden, M. and Stone, J. 1999 *Children with visual impairments in mainstream settings* David Fulton, London

Bernbaum, J.C. and Batshaw, M.L. 1997 'Born too soon, born too small' in *Children with disabilities* 4th edn, ed. M.L. Batshaw (pp. 115–39) MacLennan & Petty, Sydney

Caloroso, E.E. and Rouse, M.W. 1993 *Clinical management of strabismus* Butterworth-Heinemann, Boston, MA

Duckman, R. 1987 'Vision therapy for the child with cerebral palsy' *Journal of the American Optometric Association* vol. 58, no. 1, pp. 28–35

Getman, G.N. 1993 *How to develop your child's intelligence* 2nd edn, Optometric Extension Program Foundation, Santa Ana, CA

Hallahan, D.P. and Kauffman, J.M. 2000 *Exceptional learners: introduction to special education* 8th edn, Allyn & Bacon, Boston, MA

Heward, W.L. 2000 *Exceptional children: an introduction to special education* 6th edn, Merrill, Upper Saddle River, NJ

Howard, V.F., Williams, B.F., Port, P.D. and Lepper, C. 2001 *Very young children with special needs: a formative approach for the 21st century* 2nd edn, Merrill Prentice Hall, Upper Saddle River, NJ

Howell, E.R. and Peachey, G.T. 1990 'Visual dysfunction and learning' in *The exceptional child: an introduction to special education* ed. S.R. Butler (pp. 223–57) Harcourt Brace Jovanovich, Sydney

Kavner, R.S. 1985 *Your child's vision* Simon & Schuster, New York

Kingsley, M. 1997 'The effects of a visual loss' in *Visual impairment: access to education for children and young people* eds H. Mason, S. McCall, C. Arter, M. McLinden & J. Stone (pp. 23–9) David Fulton, London

Leat, S.J., Shute, R.H. and Westall C.A. 1999 *Assessing children's vision: a handbook* Butterworth-Heinemann, Boston, MA

Lewis, C. and Taylor, H. 1998 'The learning environment' in *Visual impairment: access to education for children and young people* eds H. Mason, S. McCall, C. Arter, M. McLinden & J. Stone (pp. 196–204) David Fulton, London

Lowe, D. 1990 'Overview' in *The exceptional child: an introduction to special education* ed. S.R. Butler (pp. 207–22) Harcourt Brace Jovanovich, Sydney

Mason, H., McCall, S., Arter, C., McLinden, M. and Stone, J. (eds) 1997 *Visual impairment: access to education for children and young people* David Fulton, London

Menacker, S.J. and Batshaw, M.L. 1997 'Vision: our window to the world' in *Children with disabilities* 4th edn, ed M.L. Batshaw (pp. 211–39) MacLennan & Petty, Sydney

Pagliano, P. 1998 'Students with vision impairment' in *Educating children with special needs* 3rd edn, eds A. Ashman & J. Elkins (pp. 383–416) Prentice Hall, Sydney

Pellegrino, L. 1997 'Cerebral palsy' in *Children with disabilities* 4th edn, ed. M.L. Batshaw (pp. 499–528) MacLennan & Petty, Sydney

Roizen, N.J. 1997 'Down syndrome' in *Children with disabilities* 4th edn, ed. M.L. Batshaw (pp. 361–76) MacLennan & Petty, Sydney

Shaw, S. 2001 'Screenings and the economic cost: are we kidding ourselves?' *Australian Optometry Newspaper* vol. 22, no. 1, p. 5

Strickling, C. 1998 *Impact of vision loss on motor development: information for occupational and physical therapists working with students with visual impairments* Texas School for the Blind and Visually Impaired, Austin, TX

Wesson, M.D. and Maino, D.M. 1995 'Oculovisual findings in children with Down syndrome, cerebral palsy and mental retardation without specific etiology' in *Diagnosis and management of special populations* ed. D.M. Maino (pp. 30–6) Mosby-Year Book, St Louis, MO

White, G. and Telec, F. 1998 'Birth to school' in *Towards excellence: effective education for students with vision impairments* eds P. Kelley and G. Gale (pp. 103–17) Royal Institute for Deaf and Blind Children, Sydney

6 Motor skills

Alexander, R., Boehme R. and Cupps, B. 1993 *Normal development of functional motor skills: the first year of life* Therapy Skill Builders, Tucson, AZ

American Psychiatric Association 1994 *Diagnostic and statistical manual of mental disorders, fourth edition (DSM- IV)* APA, Washington, DC

Bower, E., McLellan, D.L., Arney, J. and Campbell, M.J. 1996 'A randomised controlled trial of different intensities of physiotherapy and different goal-setting procedures in 44 children with cerebral palsy' *Developmental Medicine and Child Neurology* vol. 38, no. 3, pp. 226–37

Box, J. and Lancaster, A. 1997 *From cuddles to coordination* Royal Blind Society, Sydney

Burns, Y. 1992 *NSMDA Physiotherapy assessment for infants and young children* CopyRight, Brisbane

Burns Y. and MacDonald, J. (eds) 1996 *Physiotherapy and the growing child* Saunders, London

Creger, P.J. (ed.) 1995 *Developmental interventions for preterm and high-risk infants* Therapy Skill Builders, Tucson, AZ

Cusick, B.D. 1990 *Progressive casting and splinting for lower extremity deformities in children with neuromotor dysfunction* Therapy Skill Builders, Tucson, AZ

Eckersley, P.M. (ed.) 1993 *Elements of paediatric physiotherapy* Churchill Livingstone, Edinburgh

Finnie N. 1997 *Handling the young cerebral palsied child at home* 3rd edn, Butterworth-Heinemann, Oxford, UK

Foudriat, B.A., Di Fabio, R.P. and Anderson, J.H. 1993 'Sensory organization of balance responses in children 3–6 years of age: a normative study with diagnostic implications' *International Journal of Pediatric Otorhinolaryngology* vol. 27, no. 3, pp. 255–71

Fox, A.M. and Polatajko, H.J. (eds) 1994 'The London Consensus' from *Children and clumsiness: an international consensus meeting* London (Ontario) October 1994

Freeman, P. 1993 'Sensory disorders: the deaf and blind child' in *Elements of paediatric physiotherapy* ed. P.M. Eckersley (pp. 247–65) Churchill Livingstone, Edinburgh

Gentile, A.M. 1987 'Skill acquisition: action, movement, and neuromotor processes' in *Foundations for physical therapy in rehabilitation movement science* eds J.H. Carr, R.B. Shepherd, J. Gordon, A.M. Gentile & J.M. Held (pp. 93–154) Heinemann, London

Gillberg, I.C. and Gillberg, C. 1989 'Children with preschool minor neurodevelopmental disorders. IV: Behaviour and school achievement at age 13' *Developmental Medicine and Child Neurology* vol. 31, no. 1, pp. 3–13

Horak, F. 1987 'Clinical measurement of postural control in adults' *Physical Therapy* vol. 67, no. 12, pp. 1881–5

Klein, M.D. and Morris, S.E. 2000 *Pre-feeding skills* 2nd edn, Therapy Skill Builders, Tucson, AZ

Losse, A., Henderson, S.E., Elliman, D., Hall, D., Knight, E. and Jongmans, M. 1991 'Clumsiness in children—do they grow out of it?: a ten-year follow-up study' *Developmental Medicine and Child Neurology* vol. 33, no. 1, pp. 55–68

Lundy-Ekman, L., Ivry, R., Keele, S. and Woollacott, M. 1991 'Timing and force control deficits in clumsy children' *Journal of Cognitive Neuroscience* vol. 3, no. 4, pp. 367–76

Nixon, D. and Gould, K. 1999 *Emerging: child development in the first three years* 2nd edn, Social Science Press, Katoomba, NSW

Moltzen, R. 1996 'Characteristics of gifted children' in *Gifted and talented: New Zealand perspec-*

tives eds D. McAlpine & R. Moltzen (pp. 43–61) ERDC Press, Palmerston North, NZ

Papalia, D.E. and Olds, S.W. 1992 *Human development* 5th edn, McGraw Hill, New York

Porter, L. 1999 *Gifted young children: a guide for teachers and parents* Allen & Unwin, Sydney (also Open University Press, Buckingham, UK)

Rang, M. 1993 'Other feet' in *The art and practice of children's orthopedics* eds D.R. Wenger & M. Rang (pp. 168–200) Raven Press, New York

Roedell, W.C., Jackson, N.E. and Robinson, H.B. 1980 *Gifted young children* Teachers College, Columbia University, New York

Shepherd, R.B. 1995 *Physiotherapy in paediatrics*, 3rd edn, Butterworth Heinemann, Oxford, UK

Shumway-Cook, A. and Woollacott, M.H. 1985 'The growth of stability: postural control from a developmental perspective' *Journal of Motor Behavior* vol. 17, no. 2, pp. 131–47

—— 2001 *Motor control: theory and practical applications* 2nd edn, Lippincott Williams & Wilkins, Baltimore, MD

Stanley, F.J. 1994 'The aetiology of cerebral palsy' *Early Human Development* vol. 36, no. 2, pp. 81–8

Tachdjian, M.O. 1997 *Clinical pediatric orthopedics: the art of diagnosis and principles of management* Appleton & Lange, Stamford, CT

Van Sant, A. and Goldberg, C. 1999 'Normal motor development' in *Pediatric Physical Therapy* 3rd edn, ed J.S. Tecklin (pp. 1–27) Lippincott, Philadelphia, PA

Watter, P. 1996 'Physiotherapy management of children ñ minor co-ordination dysfunction' in *Physiotherapy and the growing child* eds Y.R. Burns & J. MacDonald (pp. 415–32) Saunders, London

Wilson-Howle, J.M. 1999 'Cerebral palsy' in *Decision making in pediatric neurologic physical therapy* ed. S.K. Campbell (pp. 23–83) Churchill Livingstone, Philadelphia, PA

Wolff, P.H., Gunnoe, C.E. and Cohen C. 1983 'Associated movements as a measure of developmental age' *Developmental Medicine and Child Neurology* vol. 25, no. 4, pp. 417–29

7 Daily living skills

Anderson, J.M. 1997 *Sensory motor issues in autism* Therapy Skill Builders, Tucson, AZ

Ayres, J. 1981 *Sensory integration and the child* Western Psychological Services, Los Angeles, CA

Birch, L.L., Johnson, S.L. and Fischer, J.A. 1995 'Children's eating: the development of food-acceptance patterns' *Young Children* vol. 50, no. 2, pp. 71–8

Burton, A.W. and Dancisak, M.J. 2000 'Grip form and graphomotor control in preschool children' *The American Journal of Occupational Therapy* vol. 54, no. 1, pp. 9–19

Case-Smith, J. 1996 'Fine motor outcomes in preschool children who receive occupational therapy services' *The American Journal of Occupational Therapy* vol. 50, no. 1, pp. 52–61

Chapparo, C. 1998 'Sensory integration theory course' Unpublished paper, Adelaide, South Australia

Dunn, W. and Westman, K. 1997 'The sensory profile: the performance of a national sample of children without disabilities' *The American Journal of Occupational Therapy* vol. 51, no. 1, pp. 25–34

Exner, C.E. 1989 'Development of hand functions' in *Occupational therapy for children* eds P.N. Pratt & A.S. Allen (pp. 235–59) Mosby, St Louis, MO

——1997 'Clinical interpretation of "In-hand manipulation in young children: translation movements"' *The American Journal of Occupational Therapy* vol. 51, no. 9, pp. 729–32

Heins, T. and Ritchie, K. 1988 'Beating sneaky poo—ideas for faecal soiling' Unpublished booklet, location not stated

Henderson, A. 1995 'Self care and hand skill' in *Hand function in the child: foundations for remediation* eds A. Henderson & C. Pehoski (pp. 164–83) Mosby, St Louis, MO

Henderson, A. and Pehoski, C. (eds) 1995 *Hand function in the child: foundations for remediation* Mosby Year-Book, St Louis, MO

Klein, M.D. 1983 *Pre-dressing skills* rev. edn, Therapy Skill Builders, Tucson, AZ

—— 1990 *Pre-writing skills* rev. edn, Therapy Skill Builders, Tucson, AZ

—— 1999 *Pre-scissor skills* 3rd edn, Therapy Skill Builders, Tucson, AZ

Klein, M.D. and Morris, S.E. 2000 *Pre-feeding skills* 2nd edn, Therapy Skill Builders, Tucson, AZ

Levine, K.J. 1998, *Fine motor dysfunction: therapeutic strategies for the classroom* Therapy Skill Builders, Tucson, AZ

Murray, E. 1995 'Hand preference and its development' in *Hand function in the child: foundations for remediation* eds A. Henderson & C. Pehoski (pp. 154–63) Mosby, St Louis, MO

Myers, C.A. 1992 'Therapeutic fine-motor activities for preschoolers' in *Development of hand skills in the child* eds J. Case-Smith & C. Pehoski (pp. 47–61) The American Occupational Therapy Association, Rockville, MD

Pehoski, C., Henderson, A. and Tickle-Deagan, L. 1997 'In-hand manipulation in young children: rotation of an object in the fingers' *The American Journal of Occupational Therapy* vol. 51, no. 7, pp. 544–52

——1997 'In-hand manipulation in young children: translation movements' *The American Journal of Occupational Therapy* vol. 51, no. 7, pp. 719–28

Schneck, C.M. and Henderson, A. 1990 'Descriptive analysis of the developmental progression of grip position for pencil and crayon control in nondysfunctional children' *The American Journal of Occupational Therapy* vol. 44, no. 10, pp. 894–900

Schneck, C. and Battaglia, C. 1992 'Developing scissor skills in young children' in *Development of Hand Skills in the Child* eds J. Case-Smith and C. Pehoski (pp. 79–89) The American Occupational Therapy Association, Rockville, MD

Shellenger S. and Williams, M.S. 1995 *The Alert program with songs for self regulation* Therapy Works, Inc, Albuquerque, NM

Spitzer, S., Roley, S.S., Clark, F. and Parham, D. 1996 'Sensory integration: current trends in the United States' *Scandinavian Journal of Occupational Therapy* vol. 3, pp. 123–38

Steer, V. 1999 'Identifying and meeting sensory needs' presentation to National Toy Library Conference, Adelaide, September, 1999

Tannenbaum, A.J. 1983 *Gifted children: psychological and educational perspectives* Macmillan, New York

White, M. 1984 'Pseudo-encopresis: from avalanche to victory, from vicious to virtuous cycles' *Family Systems Medicine* vol. 2, no. 2, pp. 156–60

Wilbarger J. and Wilbarger P. 1991 *Sensory defensiveness in children aged 2–12* Avanti Education Programs, Santa Barbara, CA

Washington K., Schwartz I. and Swinth Y. 1994 'Physical and occupational therapists in naturalistic early childhood settings: challenges and strategies for training' *Topics in Early Childhood Special Education* vol. 14, no. 3, pp. 333–49

8 Hearing

Abbasi, K. 1997 'Neonatal screening recommended for hearing impairment'. *British Medical Journal* vol. 315, 1327–32. Retrieved 7 August 2000 from the Academic ASAP database on the World Wide Web: http://web6.infotrac.galegroup.com

Amarjit, A. and Scott, J. 1999 'The Darwin child care ear project' *Taralye Bulletin* vol. 17, no. 2, pp. 19 –22

ASHA 1991 'The use of FM amplification instruments for infants and preschool children with hearing impairment' *American Speech-Language-Hearing Association* vol. 33, suppl. 5, pp. 1–2.

Bamford, J. and Saunders, E. 1991 *Hearing impairment, auditory perception and language disability* 2nd edn, Whurr, London

Bamiou, D.E., Macardle, B., Bitner-Glindzicz, M. and Sirimanna, T. 1999 'Aetiological investigations of hearing loss in childhood: a review' *Clinical Otolaryngology* vol. 25, no. 87, pp. 98–106

Bess, F.H., Dodd-Murphy, J. and Parker, R.A. 1998 'Children with minimal sensorineural hearing loss: prevalence, educational performance, and functional status' *Ear and Hearing* vol. 19, no. 5, pp. 339–54

Bluestone, C.D. and Klein, J.O. 1988 *Otitis media in infants and children* W.B. Saunders, Philadelphia, PA

Brown, M. and Remine, M. 1996 'Partner preferences and acceptability into play for preschoolers with and without normal hearing' *Australian Journal of Education of the Deaf* vol. 2, no. 1, pp. 30–5

Brown, R. 1973 *A first language: the early stages* Harvard University Press, Cambridge, MA

Clark, J.G. and Jaindl, M. 1996 'Conductive hearing loss in children: etiology and pathology' in *Hearing care for children* eds F.N. Martin & J.G. Clark (pp. 45–72) Allyn & Bacon, Boston, MA

CNN 2000 'Study links ear infections to pacifier use' *CNN news service, staff and wire reports* Retrieved 20 February 2001 from the World Wide Web: http://www.cnn.com/2000/HEALTH/children/09/05/ear.infections/idex.html

Department of Human Services 1998 *The health of young Victorians* Victorian Government Department of Human Services, Melbourne. Retrieved 7 August 2000 from the World Wide Web: http://hna.dhs.vic.gov.au/phd/9709090/9709090.pdf/

Deslandes, S. and Burnip, L.G. 1995 'Choosing an early intervention program for hearing impaired children' *Australasian Journal of Special Education* vol. 19, no. 2, pp. 54–61

Diefendorf, A.O. 1996 'Hearing loss and its effects' in *Hearing care for children* eds F.N. Martin & J. G. Clark (pp. 3–19) Allyn & Bacon, Boston, MA

Downs, M.P. and Yoshinaga-Itano, C. 1999 'The efficacy of early identification and intervention for children with hearing impairment' *Paediatric Clinics of North America* vol. 46, no. 1, pp. 79–87

Edwards, C. 1996 'Auditory intervention for children with mild auditory deficits' in *Amplification for children with auditory deficits* eds F.H. Bess, J.S. Gravel & A.M. Tharpe (pp. 383–98) Bill Walkerson Center Press, Nashville, TN

English, K. and Church, G. 1999 'Unilateral hearing loss in children: an update for the 1990s' *Language, Speech and Hearing Services in School* vol. 30, no. 1, pp. 26–33. Retrieved 22 February 2001, from ProQuest database on the World Wide Web: http://www.umi.com/globalauto/

Finitzo, T. (Chair) 2000 'Year 2000 position statement: principles and guidelines for early hearing detection and intervention programs' *American Academy of Pediatrics* vol. 106, no. 4, pp. 798–817. Retrieved 22 February 2001, from Ovid database on the World Wide Web: http://gateway2.ovid.com/ /

Flexer, C. (ed.) 1994 *Facilitating hearing and listening in young children* Singular Press, San Diego, CA

Jamieson, J.R. 1994 'Teaching as transaction: Vygotskian perspectives on deafness and mother-child interaction' *Exceptional Children* vol. 60, no. 5, pp. 434–49

Kennedy, C.R. 2000 'Neonatal screening for hearing impairment' *Archives of Disease in Childhood* vol. 83, no. 5, pp. 377–82. Retrieved 22 February 2001, from Ovid database on the World Wide Web: http://gateway2.ovid.com/

Lane, S., Bell, L. and Parson-Tylka, T. 1997 *My turn to learn: a communication guide for parents of deaf or hard of hearing children* Elks Family Hearing Resource Center, Burnaby, BC, Canada

McAnally, P.L., Rose, S. and Quigley, S.P. 1987 *Language learning practices with deaf children* Taylor & Francis, London

McPherson, B. 1990 'Hearing loss in Australian Aborigines: a critical evaluation' *Australian Journal of Audiology* vol. 12, no. 1, pp. 67–78

McShane, D. and Mitchell, J. 1979 'Middle ear disease, hearing loss and educational problems of American Indian children' *Journal of American Indian Education* vol. 19, no. 1, pp. 7–11

Medley, L.P., Roberts, J.E. and Zeise, S.A. 1995 'At-risk children and otitis media with effusion: management issues for the early childhood educator' *Topics in Early Childhood Special Education* vol. 15, p. 44. Retrieved 22 February 2001 from the Electric Library of Australasia database on the World Wide Web: http://www.elibrary.com

Mitka, M. 1999 'New laser target: otitis media' *The Journal of the American Medical Association* vol. 282, no. 19, p. 1803. Retrieved 22 February 2001 from Ovid database on the World Wide Web: http://gateway2.ovid.com/

Paul, P. and Quigley, S. 1990, *Education and deafness* Longman, New York

Roberts, J.E., Wallace, I.F. and Henderson, F.W. 1997 *Otitis media in young children: medical, developmental, and educational considerations* Paul H. Brookes, Sydney

Roizen, N.J. 1998. 'Why universal newborn hearing screening' *Seminars in Hearing* vol. 19, no. 3, pp. 235–46

Ross, M. 1991 'Hearing aids and systems' in *When your child is deaf: a guide for parents* eds D.M. Luterman & M. Ross (pp. 105–36) York, Parkton, MD

Sass-Lehrer, M. 1999 'Techniques for infants and toddlers with hearing loss' in *Intervention strategies for infants and toddlers with special needs: a team approach* ed. S.A. Raver (pp. 259–97) Merrill, Upper Saddle River, NJ

Steel, K.P. 2000 'New interventions in hearing impairment' *British Medical Journal* vol. 320, no. 7235, pp. 622–5. Retrieved 22 February 2001, from Ovid database on the World Wide Web: http://gateway2.ovid.com/

Tharpe, A.M. and Bess, F.H. 1999 'Minimal, progressive, and fluctuating hearing losses in children: characteristics, identification and management' *Paediatric Clinics of North America* vol. 46, no. 1, pp. 65–78

Tye-Murray, N. 1992 *Cochlear implants and children: a handbook for parents, teachers and speech hearing professionals* Alexander Graham Bell Association for the Deaf, Washington, DC

van Naarden, K. and Decouflé, P. 1999 'Relative and attributable risks for moderate to profound bilateral sensorineural hearing impairment associated with lower birth weight in children 3 to 10 years old' *American Academy of Pediatrics* vol. 104, no. 4, pp. 905–10. Retrieved 22 February 2001, from Ovid database on the World Wide Web: http://gateway2.ovid.com/

Webster, A. 1986 *Deafness, development and literacy* Methuen, London

Wilks, J., Maw, R., Peters, T.J., Harvey, I. and Golding, J. 1999 'Randomised controlled trial of early surgery versus watchful waiting for glue ear: the effect on behavioral problems in pre-school children' *Clinical Otolaryngology* vol. 25, pp. 209–14. Retrieved 21 February 2001 from the Academic ASAP database on the World Wide Web: http://web6.infotrac.galegroup.com

Winton, A., Smyth, V., Kei, J., McPherson, B., Latham, S. and Loscher, J. 1998 'Infant hearing screening: a comparison of two techniques' *Australia and New Zealand Journal of Public Health* vol. 22, no. 1, pp. 261–5

Wood, D., Wood, H., Griffith, S. and Howarth, I. 1986 *Teaching and talking with deaf children* Wiley & Sons, New York

Yonowitz, L., Yonowitz, A., Nienhuys, T. and Boswell, J. 1995 'MLD evidence of auditory processing factors as a possible barrier to literacy for Australian Aboriginal children' *Australian Journal of Education of the Deaf* vol. 1, no. 1, pp. 34–42

9 Communication skills

American Speech-Language-Hearing Association (ASHA) 1982 'Definitions: communication disorders and variations' *ASHA* vol. 24, pp. 949–50

Aram, D.M. and Nation, J.E. 1980 'Preschool language disorders and subsequent language and academic difficulties' *Journal of Communication Disorders* vol. 13, pp. 159–70

Banbury, M.M. and Herbert, C.R. 1992 'Do you see what I mean?' *Teaching Exceptional Children* vol. 48, no. 5, pp. 82–7

Benedict, H. 1977 'Early lexical development: comprehension and production' *Journal of Child Language* vol. 6, pp. 183–200

Bloom, L. and Lahey, M. 1978 *Language development and language disorders* Wiley, New York

Bruner, J.S. 1975 'The otogenesis of speech acts' *Journal of Child Language* vol. 2, pp. 1–19

Bryant, P. and Bradley, L. 1990 *Children's reading problems* Basil Blackwell, Oxford, UK

Cantwell, D.P. and Baker, L. 1987 'Prevalence and types of psychiatric disorders in three speech and language groups' *Journal of Communication Disorders* vol. 20, pp. 151–60

Cartwright, G.P., Cartwright, C.A. and Ward, M.E. 1995 *Educating special learners* Wadsworth, Belmont, CA

Chomsky, N. 1957 *Syntactic structures* Mouton, The Hague

Cook, R.E., Tessier, A. and Klein, M.D. 2000 *Adapting early childhood curricula for children in inclusive settings* 5th edn, Merrill, Englewood Cliffs, NJ

Dore, J. 1986 'The development of conversational competence' in *Language competence: assessment and intervention* ed. R. Schiefelbusch (pp. 3–60) College-Hill Press, San Diego, CA

Fiese, B.H. 1990 'Playful relationships: a contextual analysis of mother-toddler interaction and symbolic play' *Child Development* vol. 61, no. 5, 1648–56

Gleason, J.B. 1985 *The development of language* Charles E. Merrill, Columbus, OH

Greenberg, M.T. and Kusche, C.A. 1993 *Promoting social and emotional development in deaf children: the PATHS project* University of Washington Press, Seattle, WA

Heward, W.L. 2000 *Exceptional children: an introduction to special* 6th edn, Merrill, Upper Saddle River, NJ

Kilminster, M. and Laird, E. 1978 'Articulation development in children aged 3 to 9 years' *Australian Journal of Human Communication Disorders* vol. 6, pp. 23–30

Kretschmer, R. and Kretschmer, L. 1999 'Communication and language development' *Australian Journal of Education of the Deaf* vol. 5, pp. 17–26

Leonard, L.B. 1990 'Language disorders in preschool children' in *Human communication disorders* 3rd edn, eds G.H. Shames & E.H. Wigg (pp. 159–92) Merrill/Macmillan, New York

Lerner, J.W., Lowenthal, B. and Egan, R. 1998 *Preschool children with special needs: children at-risk, children with disabilities* Allyn & Bacon, Boston, MA

Lewis, M. and Louis, B. 1991 'Young gifted children' in *Handbook of gifted education* eds N. Colangelo & G.A. Davis (pp. 365–81) Allyn & Bacon, Boston, MA

Martin, D. 2000 *Teaching language and language difficulties* David Fulton, London

McCormick, L. 1994 'Communication disorders' in *Exceptional children and youth* eds N.G. Haring, L. McCormick & T.G. Haring (pp. 342–77) Merrill, Englewood Cliffs, NJ

McCormick, L. and Schiefelbusch, R.L. 1990 *Early language intervention: an introduction* 2nd edn, Merrill/Macmillan, New York

McLean, J. and Snyder-McLean, L.K. 1999 *How children learn language* Singular Publishing, San Diego, CA

Miller, L. 2000 'Play as a foundation for learning' in *Looking at early years education and care* eds R. Drury, L. Miller & R. Campbell (pp. 7-16) David Fulton, London

Nelson, K. 1973 'Structure and strategy in learning to talk' *Monograph of the Society for Research in Child Development* vol. 38, pp. 1–2

Owens, R.E. 1999 *Language disorders: a functional approach to assessment and intervention* 3rd edn, Allyn & Bacon, Boston, MA

—— 2001 *Language development: an introduction* Allyn & Bacon, Needham Heights, MA

Palmer, C. 1998 'Social skills' in *Towards excellence: effective education for students with vision impairments* eds P. Kelley & G. Gale (pp. 208–17) Royal Institute for Deaf and Blind Children, Sydney

Perleth, C., Lehwald, G. and Browder, C.S. 1993 'Indicators of high ability in young children' in *International handbook of research and development of giftedness and talent* eds K.A. Heller, F.J. Mönks & A.H. Passow (pp. 283–310) Pergamon, Oxford, UK

Porter, L. 1999 *Gifted young children: a guide for teachers and parents* Allen & Unwin, Sydney (also Open University Press, Buckingham, UK)

Quigley, S. and Kretschmer, R.E. 1982 *The education of deaf children: issues, theory, and practice* University Park Press, Baltimore, MD

Rescorla, L. and Goossens, M. 1992 'Symbolic play development in toddlers with expressive specific language impairment (SLI-E)' *Journal of Speech and Hearing Research* vol. 35, pp. 1290–302

Rinaldi, W. 2000 *Language difficulties in an educational context* Whurr, London

Shames, G.H., Wiig, E.H. and Secord, W.A. 1998 *Human communication disorders* Allyn & Bacon, Needham Heights, MA

Slobin, D. 1966 'The acquisition of Russian as a native language' in *The genesis of language: a psycholinguistic approach* eds F. Smith & D.A. Miller (pp. 129–48) MIT Press, Cambridge, MA

Stanovich, K.E. 1986 'Matthew effects in reading: some consequences of individual differences in the acquisition of literacy' *Reading Research Quarterly* vol. 21, pp. 360–407

Vaughn, S., Bos, C.S. and Schumm, J.S. 2000 *Teaching exceptional, diverse, and at-risk students in the general education classroom* Allyn & Bacon, Needham Heights, MA

Warren, S.F. 2000 'The future of early communication and language' *Topics in Early Childhood Special Education* vol. 20, no. 1, pp. 33–7

Wetherby, A.M. 1998 'Communication and language disorders in infants, toddlers, and preschool children' in *Human communication disorders: an introduction* eds G.H. Shames, E.H. Wiig & W.A. Secord (pp. 155–84) Allyn & Bacon, Needham Heights, MA

White, G. and Telec, F. 1998 'Birth to school' in *Towards excellence: effective education for students with vision impairments* eds P. Kelley & G. Gale (pp. 103–17) Royal Institute for Deaf and Blind Children, Sydney

Yoder, P.J., Warren, S.F., McCathren, R.B. and Leew, S. 1998 'Does adult responsivity to child behavior facilitate communication development?' in *Transitions in prelinguistic communication* eds A.M. Wetherby, S.F. Warren & J. Reichle (pp. 39–58) Brookes, Baltimore, MD

10 Cognitive skills

Alberto, P.A. and Troutman, A.C. 1999 *Applied behaviour analysis for teachers* 5th edn, Merrill, Upper Saddle River, NJ

Allen, K.E. and Schwartz, I.S. 2001 *The exceptional child: inclusion in early childhood education* 4th edn, Delmar, Albany, NY

Ashman, A. and Conway, R.N.F. 1989 *Cognitive strategies for special education* Routledge, London

——1993 *Using cognitive methods in the classroom* Routledge, London

——1997 *An introduction to cognitive education: theory and applications* Routledge, London

Bandura, A. 1986 *Social foundations of thought and action* Prentice Hall, Englewood Cliffs, NJ

Ben Ari, R. and Rich, Y. 1992 'Meeting the educational needs of all students in the heterogeneous class' in *To be young and gifted* eds P.S. Klein & A.J. Tannenbaum (pp. 348–78) Ablex, Norwood, NJ

Bogie, C.E. and Buckhalt, J.A. 1987 'Reactions to failure and success among gifted, average, and EMR students' *Gifted Child Quarterly* vol. 31, no. 2, pp. 70–2

Borkowski, J.G. and Peck, V.A. 1986 'Causes and consequences of metamemory in gifted children' in *Conceptions of giftedness* eds R.J. Sternberg & J.E. Davidson (pp. 182–200) Cambridge University Press, Cambridge, UK

Brody, L.E. and Benbow, C.P. 1986 'Social and emotional adjustment of adolescents extremely talented in verbal or mathematical reasoning' *Journal of Youth and Adolescence* vol. 15, no. 6, pp. 1–18

Burstein, M.D. 1986 'The effects of classroom organization on mainstreamed preschool children' *Exceptional Children* vol. 52, no. 5, pp. 425–34

Carr, M., Alexander, J. and Schwanenflugel, P. 1996 'Where gifted children do and do not excel on metacognitive tasks' *Roeper Review* vol. 18, no. 3, pp. 212–17

Chan, L.K.S. 1996 'Motivational orientations and metacognitive abilities of intellectually gifted students' *Gifted Child Quarterly* vol. 40, no. 4, pp. 184–94

Chen, Z. and Siegler, R.S. 2000 'Intellectual development in childhood' in *Handbook of intelligence* ed. R.J. Sternberg (pp. 92–116) Cambridge University Press, Cambridge, UK

Clark, B. 1997 *Growing up gifted: developing the potential of children at home and at school* 5th edn, Merrill, New York

Cole, P.G. and Chan, L.K.S. 1990 *Methods and strategies for special education* Prentice Hall, New York

——1994 *Teaching principles and practice* 2nd edn, Prentice Hall, New York

Cook, R.E., Tessier, A. and Klein, M.D. 2000 *Adapting early childhood curricula for children in inclusive settings* 5th edn, Merrill, Englewood Cliffs, NJ

Damiani, V.B. 1997 'Young gifted children in research and practice: the need for early childhood programs' *Gifted Child Today* vol. 20, no. 3, pp. 18–23

DiCintio, M.J. and Gee, S. 1999 'Control is the key: unlocking the motivation of at-risk students' *Psychology in the Schools* vol. 36, no. 3, pp. 231–7

Ellis, N.R. 1970 'Memory processes in retardates and normals' in *International review of research in mental retardation vol. 4* ed. N.R. Ellis (pp. 1–32) Academic Press, New York

Eysenck, H.J. 1986 'The biological basis of intelligence' in *Giftedness: a continuing worldwide challenge* eds K.K. Urban, H. Wagner & W. Wieczerkowski (pp. 97–114) Trillium Press, New York

Gardner, H. 1983 *Frames of mind: the theory of multiple intelligences* Basic Books, New York

Glasser, W. 1998 *The quality school: managing students without coercion* rev. edn, Harper Perennial, New York

Haensly, P.A. and Reynolds, C.R. 1989 'Creativity and intelligence' in *Handbook of creativity* eds J.A. Glover, R.R. Ronning & C.R. Reynolds (pp. 111–32) Plenum Press, New York

Hauser-Cram, P. 1996 'Mastery motivation in toddlers with developmental disabilities' *Child Development* vol. 67, no. 1, pp. 236–48

Horowitz, F.D. 1992 'A developmental view on the early identification of the gifted' in *To be young and gifted* eds P.S. Klein & A.J. Tannenbaum (pp. 73–93) Ablex, Norwood, NJ

Jones, H.A. and Warren, S.F. 1991 'Enhancing engagement in early language teaching' *Teaching Exceptional Children* vol. 23, no. 4, pp. 48–50

Jones, V.F. and Jones, L.S. 1998 *Comprehensive classroom management: creating communities of support and solving problems* 5th edn, Allyn & Bacon, Boston, MA

Kaplan, J.S. and Carter, J. 1995 *Beyond behavior modification: a cognitive-behavioral approach to behavior management in the school* 3rd edn, Pro-Ed, Austin, TX

Kitano, M. 1990 'A developmental model for identifying and serving young gifted children' *Early Child Development and Care* vol. 63, pp. 19–31

Knight, B.A. 1995 'The influence of locus of control on gifted and talented students' *Gifted Education International* vol. 11, no. 1, pp. 31–3

Krakow, J.B. and Kopp, C.B. 1983 'The effects of developmental delay on sustained attention in young children' *Child Development* vol. 54, pp. 1143–55

Linn, M.I., Goodman, J.F. and Lender, W.L. 2000 'Played out?: passive behavior by children with Down syndrome during unstructured play' *Journal of Early Intervention* vol. 23, no. 4, pp. 264–78

Lutz, D.J. and Sternberg, R.J. 1999 'Cognitive development' in *Developmental psychology: an advanced textbook* 4th edn, eds M.H. Bornstein & M.E. Lamb (pp. 275–311) Lawrence Erlbaum, Mahwah, NJ

McCormick, L., Noonan, M.J. and Heck, R. 1998 'Variables affecting engagement in inclusive preschool classrooms' *Journal of Early Intervention* vol. 21, no. 2, pp. 160–76

McDade, H.L. and Adler, S. 1980 'Down syndrome and short-term memory impairment: a storage or retrieval deficit?' *American Journal of Mental Deficiency* vol. 84, no. 6, pp. 561–7

McGee, G.G., Daly, T., Izeman, S.G., Mann, L.H. and Risley, T.R. 1991 'Use of classroom materials to promote preschool engagement' *Teaching Exceptional Children* vol. 23, no. 4, pp. 44–7

McWilliam, R.A. 1991 'Targeting teaching at children's use of time: perspectives on preschoolers' engagement' *Teaching Exceptional Children* vol. 23, no. 4, pp. 42–3

McWilliam, R.A. and Bailey, D.B. Jr 1992 'Promoting engagement and mastery' in *Teaching infants and preschoolers with disabilities* 2nd edn, eds D.B. Bailey Jr & M. Wolery (pp. 229–55) Merrill, New York

——1995 'Effects of classroom social structure and disability on engagement' *Topics in Early Childhood Special Education* vol. 15, no. 2, pp. 123–47

Malone, D.M. and Stoneman, Z. 1990 'Cognitive play of mentally retarded preschoolers: observations in the home and school' *American Journal of Mental Deficiency* vol. 94, no. 5, pp. 475–87

Meichenbaum, D. 1977 *Cognitive behavior modification: an integrative approach* Plenum Press, New York

Meyers, A.W., Cohen, R. and Schleser, R. 1989 'A cognitive-behavioral approach to education: adopting a broad-based perspective' in *Cognitive-behavioral psychology in the schools* eds J.N. Hughes & R.J. Hall (pp. 62–84) Guilford, New York

Morelock, M.J. and Morrison, K. 1996 *Gifted children have talents too: multi-dimensional programmes for the gifted in early childhood* Hawker Brownlow Education, Melbourne

Moss, E. 1990 'Social interaction and metacognitive development in gifted preschoolers' *Gifted Child Quarterly* vol. 34, no. 1, pp. 16–20

——1992 'Early interactions and metacognitive development of gifted preschoolers' in *To be young and gifted* eds P.S. Klein & A.J. Tannenbaum (pp. 278–318) Ablex, Norwood, NJ

Perkins, D.N., Jay, E. and Tishman, S. 1993 'Beyond abilities: a dispositional theory of thinking' *Merrill Palmer Quarterly* vol. 39, no. 1, pp. 1–21

Perleth, C., Schatz, T. and Mönks, F.J. 2000 'Early identification of high ability' in *International handbook of giftedness and talent* 2nd edn, eds K.A. Heller, F.J. Mönks, R.J. Sternberg & R.F. Subotnik (pp. 297–316) Pergamon, Oxford, UK

Porter, L. 1999 'Behaviour management practices in child care centres' unpublished doctoral dissertation, University of South Australia, Adelaide

Rabinowitz, M. and Glaser, R. 1985 'Cognitive structure and process in highly competent performance' in *The gifted and talented: developmental perspectives* eds F.D. Horowitz & M. O'Brien (pp. 75–98) American Psychological Association, Washington, DC

Risemberg, R. and Zimmerman, B.J. 1992 'Self-regulated learning in gifted students' *Roeper Review* vol. 15, no. 2, pp. 98–101

Rynders, J.E., Behlen, K.L. and Horrobin, J.M. 1979 'Performance characteristics of preschool Down's syndrome children receiving augmented or repetitive verbal instruction' *American Journal on Mental Deficiency* vol. 84, no. 1, pp. 67–73

Schraw, G. and Graham. T. 1997 'Helping gifted students develop metacognitive awareness' *Roeper Review* vol. 20, no. 1, pp. 4–8

Schwanenflugel, P.J., Stevens, T.P.M. and Carr, M. 1997 'Metacognitive knowledge of gifted children and nonidentified children in early elementary school' *Gifted Child Quarterly* vol. 41, no. 2, pp. 25–35

Seligman, M.E.P. 1975 *Helplessness: on depression, development and death* W.H. Freeman & Co, San Francisco, CA

——1995 *The optimistic child* Random House, Sydney

Shore, B.M. and Kanevsky, L.S. 1993 'Thinking processes: being and becoming gifted' in *International handbook of research and development of giftedness and talent* eds K.A. Heller, F.J. Mönks & A.H. Passow (pp. 133–48) Pergamon, Oxford, UK

Sternberg, R.J. 1999 *Cognitive psychology* 2nd edn, Harcourt Brace College, Fort Worth, TX

Umansky, W. 1998 'Cognitive development' in *Young children with special needs* 3rd edn, eds W. Umansky & S.R. Hooper (pp. 188–229) Merrill, Upper Saddle River, NJ

Vallerand, R.J., Gagné, F., Senécal, C. and Pelletier, L.G. 1994 'A comparison of the school intrinsic motivation and perceived competence of gifted and regular students' *Gifted Child Quarterly* vol. 38, no. 4, pp. 172–5

Whaley, K.T. and Bennett, T.C. 1991 'Promoting engagement in early childhood special education' *Teaching Exceptional Children* vol. 23, no. 4, pp. 51–4

Whitman, T.L., Scherzinger, M.L. and Sommer, K.S. 1991 'Cognitive instruction and mental retardation' in *Child and adolescent therapy: cognitive-behavioral procedures* ed. P.C. Kendall (pp. 276–315) Guilford, New York

Wolery, M. and Wolery, R.A. 1992 'Promoting functional cognitive skills' in *Teaching infants and preschoolers with disabilities* 2nd edn, eds D.B. Bailey Jr & M. Wolery (pp. 521–72) Merrill, New York

Zentall, S.S. 1989 'Self-control training with hyperactive and impulsive children' in *Cognitive-behavioral psychology in the schools* eds J.N. Hughes & R.J. Hall (pp. 305–46) Guilford, New York

Zirpoli, T.J. and Melloy, K.J. 1997 *Behavior management: applications for teachers and parents* 2nd edn, Merrill, Upper Saddle River, NJ

11 Emotional and social needs

Adler, R.B., Rosenfeld, L.B. and Proctor, R.F. II 2001 *Interplay: the process of interpersonal communication* 8th edn, Harcourt College, Fort Worth, TX

Antia, S.D., Kreimeyer, K.N. and Eldredge, N. 1993 'Promoting social interaction between young children with hearing impairments and their peers' *Exceptional Children* vol. 60, no. 3, pp. 262–75

Arnold, D.H., Homrok, S., Ortiz, C. and Stowe, R.M. 1999 'Direct observation of peer rejection acts and their temporal relation with aggressive acts' *Early Childhood Research Quarterly* vol. 14, no. 2, pp. 183–96

Asher, S.R. 1983 'Social competence and peer status: recent advances and future directions' *Child Development* vol. 54, pp. 1427–34

Bay-Hinitz, A.K., Peterson, R.F. and Quilitch, R. 1994 'Cooperative games: a way to modify aggressive and cooperative behaviors in young children' *Journal of Applied Behavior Analysis* vol. 27, no. 3, pp. 435–46

Bevill, A.R. and Gast, D.L. 1998 'Social safety for young children: a review of the literature on safety skills instruction' *Topics in Early Childhood Special Education* vol. 18, no. 4, pp. 222–34

Bonner, B.L., Kaufman, K.L., Harbeck, C. and Brassard, M.R. 1992 'Child maltreatment' in *Handbook of clinical child psychology* 2nd edn, eds C.E. Walker & M.C. Roberts (pp. 967–1008) John Wiley & Sons, New York

Briggs, F. and McVeity, M. 2000 *Teaching children to protect themselves* Allen & Unwin, Sydney

Brown, P.M., Remine, M.D., Prescott, S.J. and Rickards, F.W. 2000 'Social interactions of preschoolers with and without impaired hearing in integrated kindergarten' *Journal of Early Intervention* vol. 23, no. 3, pp. 200–11

Brown, W.H., Odom, S.L., Li, S. and Zercher, C. 1999 'Ecobehavioral assessment in early childhood programs: a portrait of preschool inclusion' *The Journal of Special Education* vol. 33, no. 3, pp. 138–53

Burns, R.B. 1982 *Self-concept development and education* Holt, Rhinehart & Winston, London

Cartledge, G. and Milburn, J.F. (eds) 1995 *Teaching social skills to children: innovative approaches* 3rd edn, Allyn & Bacon, Boston, MA

Cole-Detke, H. and Kobak, R. 1998 'The effects of multiple abuse in interpersonal relationships: an attachment perspective' in *Multiple victimization of children: conceptual, developmental, research and treatment issues* eds B.B.R. Rossman & M.S. Rosenberg (pp. 189–205) Haworth Press, New York

Crary, E. 1992 'Talking about differences children notice' in *Alike and different: exploring our humanity with young children* rev. edn, ed. B. Neugebauer (pp. 11–15) National Association for the Education of Young Children, Washington, DC

Curry, N.E. and Johnson, C.N. 1990 *Beyond self-esteem: developing a genuine sense of human value* National Association for the Education of Young Children, Washington, DC

DeKlyen, M. and Odom, S.L. 1989 'Activity structure and social interactions with peers in developmentally integrated play groups' *Journal of Early Intervention* vol. 13, no. 4, pp. 342–52

Derman-Sparks, L. 1992 ' "It isn't fair!": antibias curriculum for young children' in *Alike and different: exploring our humanity with young children* rev. edn, ed. B. Neugebauer (pp. 2–10) National Association for the Education of Young Children, Washington, DC

Dodge, K.A. 1983 'Behavioral antecedents of peer social status' *Child Development* vol. 54, pp. 1386–99

English, K., Goldstein, H., Shafer, K. and Kaczmarek, L. 1997 'Promoting interactions among preschoolers with and without disabilities: effects of a buddy skills-training program' *Exceptional Children* vol. 63, no. 2, pp. 229–43

Farver, J.M. 1996 'Aggressive behavior in preschoolers' social networks: do birds of a feather flock together?' *Early Childhood Research Quarterly* vol. 11, no. 3, pp. 333–50

Freeman, S.F.N. and Kasari, C. 1998 'Friendships in children with developmental disabilities' *Early Education and Development* vol. 9, no. 4, pp. 341–55

George, C. and Main, M. 1979 'Social interactions of young abused children: approach, avoidance, and aggression' *Child Development* vol. 50, no. 2, pp. 306–18

Glasser, W. 1998 *Choice theory: a new psychology of personal freedom* Harper Perennial, New York

Gootman, M.E. 1993 'Reaching and teaching abused children' *Childhood Education* vol. 70, no. 1, pp. 15–19

Guralnick, M.J., Connor, R.T., Hammond, M., Gottman, J.M. and Kinnish, K. 1995 'Immediate effects of mainstreamed settings on the social interactions and social integration of preschool children' *American Journal on Mental Retardation* vol. 100, no. 4, pp. 359–77

Guralnick, M.J. and Groom, J.M. 1987 'The peer relations of mildly delayed and nonhandicapped preschool children in mainstreamed playgroups' *Child Development* vol. 58, no. 6, pp. 1556–72

Hanline, M.F. 1993 'Inclusion of preschoolers with profound disabilities: an analysis of children's interactions' *Journal of the Association for Persons with Severe Handicaps* vol. 18, no. 1, pp. 28–35

Hanson, M.J. and Carta, J.J. 1995 'Addressing the challenges of families with multiple risks' *Exceptional Children* vol. 62, no. 3, pp. 201–12

Harrison, C. and Tegel, K. 1999 'Play and the gifted child' in *Child's play: revisiting play in early childhood settings* ed. E. Dau (pp. 97–110) MacLennan & Petty, Sydney

Harter, S. 1998 'The effects of child abuse on the self-esteem' in *Multiple victimization of children: conceptual, developmental, research and treatment issues* eds B.B.R. Rossman & M.S. Rosenberg (pp. 147–69) Haworth Press, New York

Hartup, W.W. 1989 'Social relationships and their developmental significance' *American Psychologist* vol. 44, no. 2, pp. 120–6

Hartup, W.W. and Moore, S.G. 1990 'Early peer relations: developmental significance and prognostic implications' *Early Childhood Research Quarterly* vol. 5, no. 1, pp. 1–17

Hestenes, L.L. and Carroll, D.E. 2000 'The play interactions of young children with and without disabilities: individual and environmental influences' *Early Childhood Research Quarterly* vol. 15, no. 2, pp. 229–46

Hill, S. and Reed, K. 1989 'Promoting social competence at preschool: the implementation of a cooperative games programme' *Australian Journal of Early Childhood* vol. 14, no. 4, pp. 25–31

Hoffman-Plotkin, D. and Twentyman, C.T. 1984 'A multimodal assessment of behavioral and cognitive deficits in abused and neglected preschoolers' *Child Development* vol. 55, no. 3, pp. 794–802

Howes, C. 1983 'Patterns of friendship' *Child Development* vol. 54, no. 4, pp. 1041–53

Hughes, J.N., Cavell, T.A. and Willson, V. 2001 'Further support for the developmental significance of the quality of the teacher-student relationship' *Journal of School Psychology* vol. 39, no. 4, pp. 289–301

Ivory, J.J. and McCollum J.A. 1999 'Effects of social and isolate toys on social play in an inclusive setting' *The Journal of Special Education* vol. 32, no. 4, pp. 238–43

Jordan, N.H. 1993 'Sexual abuse prevention programs in early childhood education: a caveat' *Young Children* vol. 48, no. 6, pp. 76–9

Katsurada, E. and Sugawara, A.I. 1998 'The relationship between hostile attributional bias and aggressive behavior in preschoolers' *Early Childhood Research Quarterly* vol. 13, no. 4, pp. 623–36

Katz, L. 1995 *Talks with teachers of young children* Ablex, Norwood, NJ

Katz, L.G. and McClellan, D.E. 1997 *Fostering children's social competence: the teacher's role* National Association for the Education of Young Children, Washington, DC

Kelly, B. 1996 'The ecology of peer relations' *Early Child Development and Care* vol. 115, no. 1, pp. 99–114

Klimes-Dougan, B. and Kistner, J. 1990 'Physically abused preschoolers' responses to peers' distress' *Developmental Psychology* vol. 26, no. 4, pp. 599–602

Ko, S.F. and Cosden, M.A. 2001 'Do elementary-school based child abuse prevention programs work: a high school follow-up' *Psychology in the Schools* vol. 38, no. 1, pp. 57–66

Kohler, F.W. and Strain, P.S. 1999 'Maximizing peer-mediated resources in integrated preschool classrooms' *Topics in Early Childhood Special Education* vol. 19, no. 2, pp. 92–102

Kontos, S. and Wilcox-Herzog, A. 1997 'Teachers' interactions with children: why are they so important?' *Young Children* vol. 52, no. 2, pp. 4–12

Kostelnick, M.J., Stein, L.C., Whiren, A.P. and Soderman, A.K. 1998 *Guiding children's social development* 3rd edn, Delmar, Albany, NY

Luthar, S.S. and Zigler, E. 1991 'Vulnerability and competence: a review of the research on resilience in childhood' *American Journal of Orthopsychiatry* vol. 6, pp. 6–22

McConnell, S.R., Sisson, L.A., Cort, C.A. and Strain, P.S. 1991 'Effects of social skills training and contingency management on reciprocal interactions of preschool children with behavioral handicaps' *The Journal of Special Education* vol. 24, no. 4, pp. 473–95

McGrath, H. 1997 *Dirty tricks: classroom games for teaching social skills* Longman, Melbourne

McGrath, H. and Francey, S. 1991 *Friendly kids; friendly classrooms* Longman Cheshire, Melbourne

Mize, J. 1995 'Coaching preschool children in social skills: a cognitive-social learning curriculum' in *Teaching social skills to children and youth: innovative approaches* 3rd edn, eds G. Cartledge & J.F. Milburn (pp. 237–61) Allyn & Bacon, Boston, MA

National Childcare Accreditation Council (NCAC) 1993 *Putting children first: quality improvement and accreditation system handbook* NCAC, Sydney

Odom, S.L., McConnell, S.R. and McEvoy, M.A. (eds) 1992 *Social competence of young children with disabilities: issues and strategies for intervention* Paul H. Brookes, Baltimore, MD

Odom, S.L., McConnell, S.R., McEvoy, M.A., Peterson, C., Ostrosky, M., Chandler, L.K., Spicuzza, R.J., Skellenger, A., Creighton, M. and Favazza, P.C. 1999 'Relative effects of interventions supporting the social competence of young children with disabilities' *Topics in Early Childhood Special Education* vol. 19, no. 2, pp. 75–91

Okagaki, L., Diamond, K.E., Kontos, S.J. and Hestenes, L.L. 1998 'Correlates of young children's interactions with classmates with disabilities' *Early Childhood Research Quarterly* vol. 13, no. 1, pp. 67–86

Orlick, T. 1982 *The second cooperative sports and games book* Pantheon, New York

Peterson, C. 1996 *Looking forward through the life span: developmental psychology* 3rd edn, Prentice Hall, Sydney

Pope, A.W., McHale, S.M. and Craighead, E.W. 1988 *Self-esteem enhancement with children and adolescents* Pergamon, New York

Putallaz, M. and Gottman, J.M. 1981 'An interactional model of children's entry into peer groups' *Child Development* vol. 52, no. 3, pp. 986–94

Putallaz, M. and Wasserman, A. 1990 'Children's entry behavior' in *Peer rejection in childhood* eds S.R. Asher & J.D. Coie (pp. 60–89) Cambridge University Press, Cambridge, UK

Reynolds, M.A. and Holdgrafer, G. 1998 'Social-communicative interactions of preschool children with developmental delays in integrated settings: an exploratory study' *Topics in Early Childhood Special Education* vol. 18, no. 4, pp. 235–42

Rodd, J. 1996 *Understanding young children's behaviour* Allen & Unwin, Sydney

Rose, S.R. 1983 'Promoting social competence in children: a classroom approach to social and cognitive skill training' in *Social skills training for children and youth* ed. C.W. LeCroy (pp. 43–59) Haworth Press, New York

Rubin, Z. 1980 *Children's friendships* Harvard University Press, Boston, MA

Rutter, M. 1985 'Resilience in the face of adversity: protective factors and resistance to psychiatric disorder' *British Journal of Psychiatry* vol. 147, pp. 598–611

Sainato, D.M. and Carta, J.J. 1992 'Classroom influences on the development of social competence in young children with disabilities' in *Social competence of young children with disabilities: issues and strategies for intervention* eds S.L. Odom, S.R. McConnell & M.A. McEvoy (pp. 93–109) Paul H. Brookes, Baltimore, MD

Sapon-Shevin, M. 1986 'Teaching cooperation' in *Teaching social skills to children: innovative approaches* 2nd edn, eds G. Cartledge & J.F. Milburn, Pergamon, New York

——1999 *Because we can change the world: a practical guide to building cooperative, inclusive classroom communities* Allyn & Bacon, Boston, MA

Seligman, M.E.P. 1975 *Helplessness: on depression, development and death* W.H. Freeman & Co, San Francisco, CA

——1995 *The optimistic child* Random House, Sydney

Steele, B.F. 1986 'Notes on the lasting effects of early child abuse throughout the life cycle' *Child Abuse and Neglect*, vol. 10, pp. 281–91

Strain, P.S. and Hoyson, M. 2000 'The need for longitudinal, intensive social skill intervention: LEAP follow-up outcomes for children with autism' *Topics in Early Childhood Special Education* vol. 20, no. 2, pp. 116–22

Swetnam, L., Peterson, C.R. and Clark, H.B. 1983 'Social skills development in young children: preventive and therapeutic approaches' in *Social skills training for children and youth* ed. C.W. LeCroy (pp. 5–27) Haworth Press, New York

Trawick-Smith, J. 1988 ' "Let's say you're the baby, OK?": play leadership and following behavior of young children' *Young Children* vol. 43, no. 5, pp. 51–9

Trickett, P.K. 1998 'Multiple maltreatment and the development of self and emotion regulation' in *Multiple victimization of children: conceptual, developmental, research and treatment issues* eds B.B.R. Rossman & M.S. Rosenberg (pp. 171–87) Haworth Press, New York

12 Guiding children's behaviour

Alberto, P.A. and Troutman, A.C. 1999 *Applied behaviour analysis for teachers* 5th edn, Merrill, Upper Saddle River, NJ

Amatea, E.S. 1989 *Brief strategic intervention for school behavior problems* Jossey-Bass, San Francisco, CA

Atwater, J.B. and Morris, E.K. 1988 'Teachers' instructions and children's compliance in preschool classrooms: a descriptive analysis' *Journal of Applied Behavior Analysis* vol. 21, no. 2, pp. 157–67

Baumrind, D. 1967 'Child care practices anteceding three patterns of preschool behavior' *Genetic Psychology Monographs* vol. 75, pp. 43–88

——1971 'Current patterns of parental authority' *Developmental Psychology Monograph* vol. 4, no. 1, pp. 1–103

Birch, L.L., Johnson, S.L. and Fischer, J.A. 1995 'Children's eating: the development of food-acceptance patterns' *Young Children* vol. 50, no. 2, pp. 71–8

Briggs, F. and McVeity, M. 2000 *Teaching children to protect themselves* Allen & Unwin, Sydney

Brophy, J. 1981 'Teacher praise: a functional analysis' *Review of Educational Research* vol. 51, no. 1, pp. 5–32

Conway, R. 1998 'Meeting the needs of students with behavioural and emotional problems' in *Educating children with special needs* 3rd edn, eds A. Ashman & J. Elkins (pp. 177–228) Prentice Hall, Sydney

Crockenberg, S. and Litman, C. 1990 'Autonomy as competence in 2–year-olds: maternal correlates of child defiance, compliance, and self-assertion' *Developmental Psychology* vol. 26, no. 6, pp. 961–71

de Shazer, S., Berg, I.K., Lipchik, E., Nunnally, E., Molnar, A., Gingerich, W. and Weiner-Davis, M. 1986 'Brief therapy: focused solution development' *Family Process* vol. 25, no. 2, pp. 207–22

Durrant, M. 1995 *Creative strategies for school problems* Eastwood Family Therapy Centre, Sydney (also W.W. Norton, New York)

Fisch, R., Weakland, J.H. and Segal, L. 1982 *The tactics of change: doing therapy briefly* Jossey-Bass, San Francisco, CA

Gartrell, D. 1987 'Punishment or guidance?' *Young Children* vol. 42, no. 3, pp. 55–61

——1998 *A guidance approach for the encouraging classroom* Delmar, Albany, NY

Glasser, W. 1998 *The quality school: managing students without coercion* rev. edn, Harper Perennial, New York

Gordon, T. 1974 *Teacher effectiveness training* Peter H. Wyden, New York

——1991 *Teaching children self-discipline at home and at school* Random House, Sydney

Herbert, M. 1987 *Behavioural treatment of children with problems: a practice manual* 2nd edn, Academic Press, London

Jakubowski, P. and Lange, A. 1978 *The assertive option: your rights and responsibilities* Research Press, Champaign, IL

Johnson, B., Whittington, V. and Oswald, M 1994 'Teachers' views on school discipline: a theoretical framework' *Cambridge Journal of Education* vol. 24, no. 2, pp. 261–76

Kaplan, J.S. and Carter, J. 1995 *Beyond behavior modification: a cognitive-behavioral approach to behavior management in the school* 3rd edn, Pro-Ed, Austin, TX

Kohn, A. 1996 *Beyond discipline: from compliance to community* Association for Supervision and Curriculum Development, Alexandria, VA

——1999 *Punished by rewards: the trouble with gold stars, incentive plans, A's, praise, and other bribes* 2nd edn, Houghton Mifflin, Boston, MA

Lieber, J., Capell, K., Sandall, S.R., Wolfberg, P., Horn, E. and Beckman, P. 1998 'Inclusive preschool programs: teachers' beliefs and practices' *Early Childhood Research Quarterly* vol. 13, no. 1, pp. 87–105

McCaslin, M. and Good, T.L. 1992 'Compliant cognition: the misalliance of management and instructional goals in current school reform' *Educational Researcher* vol. 21, no. 3, pp. 4–17

Molnar, A. and Lindquist, B. 1989 *Changing problem behaviour in schools* Jossey-Bass, San Francisco, CA

Parpal, M. and Maccoby, E.E. 1985 'Maternal responsiveness and subsequent child compliance' *Child Development* vol. 56, no. 5, pp. 1326–34

Porter, L. 1999a *Young children's behaviour: practical approaches for caregivers and teachers* MacLennan & Petty, Sydney

——1999b 'Behaviour management practices in child care centres' unpublished doctoral dissertation, University of South Australia, Adelaide

——2000a *Student behaviour: theory and practice for teachers* 2nd edn, Allen & Unwin, Sydney

——2000b *Behaviour in schools: theory and practice for teachers* Open University Press, Buckingham, UK

——2001 *Children are people too: a parent's guide to young children's behaviour* 3rd edn, Small Poppies SA, Adelaide

Rogers, B. 1998 *'You know the fair rule' and much more: strategies for making the hard job of discipline and behaviour management in school easier* ACER, Melbourne

Rogers, C. 1951 *Client-centred therapy* Constable, London

Rogers, C.R. and Freiberg, H. 1994 *Freedom to learn* 3rd edn, Merrill, New York

Ryan, R.M. and Deci, E.L. 1996 'When paradigms clash: comments on Cameron and Pierce's claim that rewards do not undermine intrinsic motivation' *Review of Educational Research* vol. 66, no. 1, pp. 33–8

Sapon-Shevin, M. 1996 'Beyond gifted education: building a shared agenda for school reform' *Journal for the Education of the Gifted* vol. 19, no. 2, pp. 194–214

Smith, M.A., Schloss, P.J. and Hunt, F.M. 1987 'Differences in social and emotional development' in *The young exceptional child: early development and education* eds J.T. Neisworth & S.J. Bagnato (pp. 350–86) Macmillan, New York

Appendix I: Common causes of atypical development

Anastopoulos, A.D. and Barkley, R.A. 1992 'Attention deficit-hyperactivity disorder' in *Handbook of clinical child psychology* 2nd edn, eds C.E. Walker & M.C. Roberts (pp. 413–30) John Wiley & Sons, New York

Ashman, A. 1998 'Students with intellectual disabilities' in *Educating children with special needs* 3rd edn, eds A. Ashman & J. Elkins (pp. 417–61) Prentice Hall, Sydney

Barkley, R.A. 1988 'Attention deficit disorder with hyperactivity' in *Behavioral assessment of childhood disorders* 2nd edn, eds E.J. Mash & L.G. Terdal (pp. 69–104) Guilford, New York

Batshaw, M.L. 1997 'Fragile X syndrome' in *Children with disabilities* 4th edn, ed. M.L. Batshaw (pp. 377–88) MacLennan & Petty, Sydney

Batshaw, M.L. and Conlon, C.J. 1997 'Substance abuse: a preventable threat to development' in *Children with disabilities* 4th edn, ed. M.L. Batshaw (pp. 143–62) MacLennan & Petty, Sydney

Bernbaum, J.C. and Batshaw, M.L. 1997 'Born too soon, born too small' in *Children with disabilities* 4th edn, ed. M.L. Batshaw (pp. 115–39) MacLennan & Petty, Sydney

Bruder, M.B. 1995 'The challenge of pediatric AIDS: a framework for early childhood special education' *Topics in Early Childhood Special Education* vol. 15, no. 1, pp. 83–99

Eysenck, H.J. 1986 'The biological basis of intelligence' in *Giftedness: a continuing worldwide challenge* eds K.K. Urban, H. Wagner & W. Wieczerkowski (pp. 97–114) Trillium Press, New York

Fishler, K. and Koch, R. 1991 'Mental development in Down syndrome mosaicism' *American Journal on Mental Retardation* vol. 96, no. 3, pp. 345–51

Garber, J.B. 1991 'Myelodysplasia' in *Pediatric neurologic physical therapy* 2nd edn, ed. S.K. Campbell (pp. 169–212) Churchill Livingston, New York

Gardner, H. 1983 *Frames of mind: the theory of multiple intelligences* Basic Books, New York

Geake, J. 1997 'Thinking as evolution in the brain: implications for giftedness' *The Australasian Journal of Gifted Education* vol. 6, no. 1, pp. 27–33

Hart, E.L., Lahey, B.B., Loeber, R., Applegate, B. and Frick, P.J. 1995 'Developmental change in attention-deficit hyperactivity in boys: a four-year longitudinal study' *Journal of Abnormal Child Psychology* vol. 23, no. 6, pp. 729–49

Hatton, D.D., Bailey, D.B. Jr, Roberts, J.P., Skinner, M., Mayhew, L., Clark R.D., Waring, E. and Roberts, J.E. 2000 'Early intervention services for young boys with Fragile X syndrome' *Journal of Early Intervention* vol. 23, no. 4, pp. 235–51

Hauser-Cram, P., Bronson, M.B. and Upshur, C.C. 1993 'The effects of classroom environment on the social and mastery behavior of preschool children with disabilities' *Early Childhood Research Quarterly* vol. 8, no. 4, pp. 479–97

Horowitz, F.D. 1987 'A developmental view of giftedness' *Gifted Child Quarterly* vol. 31, no. 4, pp. 165–8

Howard, V.F., Williams, B.F., Port, P.D. and Lepper, C. 2001 *Very young children with special needs: a formative approach for the 21st century* 2nd edn, Merrill Prentice Hall, Upper Saddle River, NJ

Jausovec, N. 1997 'Differences in EEG alpha activity between gifted and non-identified individuals: insights into problem solving' *Gifted Child Quarterly* vol. 41, no. 1, pp. 26–31

Liptak, G.S. 1997 'Neural tube defects' in *Children with disabilities* 4th edn, ed. M.L. Batshaw (pp. 529–52) MacLennan & Petty, Sydney

Mauk, J.E., Reber, M. and Batshaw, M.L. 1997 'Autism and other pervasive developmental disorders' in *Children with disabilities* 4th edn, ed. M.L. Batshaw (pp. 425–47) MacLennan & Petty, Sydney

Mazzocco, M.M.M. and O'Connor, R. 1993 'Fragile X syndrome: a guide for teachers of young children' *Young Children* vol. 49, no. 1, pp. 73–7

McCarthy, M. 1987 'Chronic illness and hospitalization' in *The young exceptional child: early development and education* eds J.T. Neisworth & S.J. Bagnato (pp. 231–59) Macmillan, New York

Miller, N.B., Silverman, L.K. and Falk, R.F. 1994 'Emotional development, intellectual ability, and gender' *Journal for the Education of the Gifted* vol. 18, no. 1, pp. 20–38

Pellegrino, L. 1997 'Cerebral palsy' in *Children with disabilities* 4th edn, ed. M.L. Batshaw (pp. 499–528) MacLennan & Petty, Sydney

Porter, L. 1999 *Gifted young children: a guide for teachers and parents* Allen & Unwin, Sydney (simultaneously published by Open University Press, Buckingham, UK)

Quill, K.A. 1995 *Teaching children with autism: strategies to enhance communication and socialization* Delmar, New York

Riccio, C.A., Hynd, G.W., Cohen, M.J. and Gonzalez, J.J. 1993 'Neurological basis of attention deficit hyperactivity disorder' *Exceptional Children* vol. 60, no. 2, pp. 118–24

Roizen, N.J. 1997 'Down syndrome' in *Children with disabilities* 4th edn, ed. M.L. Batshaw (pp. 361–76) MacLennan & Petty, Sydney

Sameroff, A.J. 1982 'The environmental context of developmental disabilities' in *Intervention with at-risk and handicapped infants: from research to application* ed. D. Bricker (pp. 141–52) University Park Press, Baltimore, MD

——1990 'Neo-environmental perspectives on developmental theory' in *Issues in the developmental approach to mental retardation* eds R.M. Hodapp, J.A. Burack & E. Zigler (pp. 93–113) Cambridge University Press, Cambridge, UK

Shepherd, R.B. 1995 *Physiotherapy in paediatrics* Butterworth Heinemann, Oxford, UK
Shonkoff, J.P. and Marshall, P.C. 2000 'The biology of developmental vulnerability' in *Handbook of early intervention* 2nd edn, eds J.P. Shonkoff and S.J. Meisels (pp. 35–53) Cambridge University Press, Cambridge, UK
Tyler, J.S. and Colson, S. 1994 'Common pediatric disabilities: medical aspects and educational implications' *Focus on Exceptional Children* vol. 27, no. 4, pp. 1–16
Wodrich, D.L. 1994 *Attention deficit hyperactivity disorder: what every parent wants to know* Paul H. Brookes, Baltimore, MD

Appendix II: Typical developmental milestones

Allen, K.E. and Schwartz, I.S. 2001 *The exceptional child: inclusion in early childhood education* 4th edn, Delmar, Albany, NY
Burns, Y. 1992 *NSMDA physiotherapy assessment for infants and young children* CopyRight Publishing, Brisbane
Case-Smith, J. 1995 'Grasp, release and bimanual skills in the first two years of life' in *Hand function in the child: foundations for remediation* eds A. Henderson & C. Pehoski (pp. 113–35) Mosby Year Books, St. Louis, MO
Cook, R.E., Tessier, A. and Klein, M.D. 2000 *Adapting early childhood curricula for children in inclusive settings* 5th edn, Merrill, Englewood Cliffs, NJ
Furuno, S., O'Reilly, K.A., Hosaka, C.M., Inatsuke, T.T., Allman, T.L. and Zeisloft, B. 1985 *Hawaii early learning profile (HELP) activity guide* VORT Corporation, Palo Alto, CA
Henderson, A. 1995 'Self care and hand skill' in *Hand function in the child: foundations for remediation* eds A. Henderson & C. Pehoski (pp. 164–83) Mosby, St Louis, MO
Howard, V.F., Williams, B.F., Port, P.D. and Lepper, C. 2001 *Very young children with special needs: a formative approach for the 21st century* 2nd edn, Merrill Prentice Hall, Upper Saddle River, NJ
Jones, C.J. 1992 *Social and emotional development of exceptional students: handicapped and gifted* Charles C. Thomas, Springfield, IL
Kostelnick, M.J., Stein, L.C., Whiren, A.P. and Soderman, A.K. 1998 *Guiding children's social development* 3rd edn, Delmar, Albany, NY
Lerner, J.W., Lowenthal, B. and Egan, R. 1998 *Preschool children with special needs: children at-risk, children with disabilities* Allyn & Bacon, Boston, MA
Linder, T. 1990 *Transdisciplinary play-based assessment* Paul H. Brookes, Baltimore, MD
Nixon, D. and Aldwinckle, M. 1997 *Exploring: child development from three to six years* Social Science Press, Katoomba, NSW
Nixon, D. and Gould, K. 1999 *Emerging: child development in the first three years* 2nd edn, Social Science Press, Katoomba, NSW
Owens, R.E. 2001 *Language development: an introduction* Allyn & Bacon, Needham Heights, MA
Raver, S.A. (ed.) 1999 *Intervention strategies for infants and toddlers with special needs: a team approach* 2nd edn, Merrill, Upper Saddle River, NJ
Sheridan, M.D., Harding, J. and Meldon-Smith, L. 1999 *Play in early childhood: from birth to six years* ACER Press, Melbourne
Tachdjian, M.O. 1997 *Clinical pediatric orthopedics: the art of diagnosis and principles of management* Appleton & Lange, Stamford, CT
Talay-Ongan, A. 2000 *Typical and atypical development in early childhood* Memo Press, Sydney

Appendix III: Indicators of advanced development

Perleth, C., Schatz, T. and Mönks, F.J. 2000 'Early identification of high ability' in *International handbook of giftedness and talent* 2nd edn, eds K.A. Heller, F.J. Mönks, R.J. Sternberg & R.F. Subotnik (pp. 297–316) Pergamon, Oxford, UK
Porter, L. 1999 *Gifted young children: a guide for teachers and parents* Allen & Unwin, Sydney (also Open University Press, Buckingham, UK)

INDEX

Aboriginal children 145
absences 74, 202, 237
abstract learning 5, 71, 164, 172, 177
abuse of children 8, 14, 163, **193–5**, 214, 215, 226, 232–3
academics 57, 64, 163
acceleration 64
acceptance 16, 191, 195, 198, 200, 202
access 11, 13, 22, 31, 97, 206
accessibility of information 26
accountability 20, 22, 38
acknowledgment 198, **218–9**
acquisition of skills 58
    see also knowledge acquisition
activity-based instruction 67
    see also naturalistic instruction
ADD/ADHD 54, 101, 229, 230, **235–6**
adult-directed teaching 8, 13, 68
    see also direct instruction
adults-in-waiting 8
advocacy 7, 24, 29–30, 31, 38–9
aggression 102, 148, 150, 168, 193, 201–2, **207–8**, 220, 230
AIDS 236–7
aids, hearing 151–2
aims of programs 58–9
alcohol 228
    see also fetal alcohol effects/syndrome
alerting activities 122
alertness 98, 118, 119–21, 124, 126
    see also arousal
alignment of joints/bones 99, 104
altruism 12
amblyopia 85, 86
Angelman syndrome 231
anxiety 48, 119, 123, 194, 213, 235
Apgar scale 41
apologies 220
applied behaviour analysis (ABA) 211, 215
apprenticeship 15
Achilles tendon 104, 110
arousal 47, 103, 106, 119, 177
arthritis 107, 126

articulation 158–9, 164, 165, 167
Asperger syndrome 158, 235
aspirations, of parents 20, 25
assertiveness 32, 192, 207, 220–1
assessment 1, 28, **36–55**
    of hearing impairment 147–9
    of language skills 166–7
    principles of 38–40
    purposes of 37–8
asthma 108, 236
astigmatism 87, 92
at risk 41, 52
ataxia 92, 100, 232
athetoid 100
atlantoaxial instability 103
    see also neck instability
attachment 119, 192, 200, 201, 207
    see also bonding
attention deficit disorders 54, 101, 229, 230, **235–6**
attention seeking 224
attentiveness 47, 54, 68, 102, 121, 148, 174, **177–8**, 184
    see also concentration span
attitude 16, 20
attribution training 189, 199
audiogram 142–3
audiologist 143, 151, 152
auditory sense 102, 117, 125
    see also hearing
augmentive communication systems 69, 164
    see also sign languages
autism spectrum disorders 103, 104, 167, **234–5**, 239
    see also Asperger syndrome
autonomy 15, 191, **199–200**, 207
average 51–2

baby talk 141
    see also motherese, parentese
background movement 104, 106, 109
balance 99, 102, 103, 104, 106–7, 109, 110, **112–3**, 115, 118, 135, 136

ball skills 86, 109, 110, 114–5
  see also milestones
bathing 99, 136
behavioural
    difficulties 13, 31, 47, 90, 102, 119, 145,
    155, 169, 186, 194, 200, 201, **210–27**, 232,
    235
        causes of 215–6
behavioural optometrists 91, 94, 95
behaviourist methods 8, 211
    see also applied behaviour analysis
belonging 191
bias of assessment 40, 43, 45
bilateral hand skills 127, 129
bilingualism 39, 145, 166
binocular vision 85, 89, 91, 92
bionic ear 152
birth weight, low 145, 163, 228, 231–2, 234,
  239
biting 210, 235
bladder control 101, 136
    see also toileting
blindness 63, 83, 91–2
    definition 81
body language 34
    see also nonverbal communication
body speed 93, 133
boisterous 105, 196, 201
bonding 113–9
    see also attachment
bottom–up model 57, 70–1
bottom shuffle 99
bowel control 101, 136
    see also toileting
Braille 94
brain injury 83, 98, 232–3, 239
breathiness 156, 159
bright children 52
    see also gifted
brushes 128
bullying 196, 215
    see also exclusion
bunny hopping 100
burnout 25

calm, state of 119, 124, 125
calming activities 122
cancer 104
cardiac 54, 92, 108, 114
case manager 31–2
casting 110
castor carts 101, 108
cause-effect understanding 175–6, 182

cerebral palsy 92, **97–101**, 103,
    104, 107, 109, 110, 164, 231–2, 239
    classification of 100
chain
    of events 224–5
    of hearing 142
checklists 43
chemotherapy 236
cheerleaders 197
child abuse *see* abuse
child-oriented approach 13
choice 7, 8, 27, 31, 62, 123, 179, 199, 217
    of school 30
classification 38, 40
cleft palate 148, 165
climate 60, 188, 194
climbing 99, 108, 109, 110, **111–2**, 123, 124,
    128
    see also milestones
clothing 161
    see also dressing, milestones
clowning 102
clumsiness 89, 98
coaches 197
cochlea 142, 152
    see also ear, inner
cochlear implant 152
cognitive skills 15, 174–90, 218
    see also milestones
collaboration 59
    with parents *see* parents
collaborative problem solving 32, 33, 192,
    221
colour
    naming 44–5
    perception 85, 88
communication 32–5, 74, 142, **154–73**
    components of 155–9
    disorders 164–6
    see also language
community 59
compassion fatigue 25
competitiveness 105, 203
comprehension 47
    see also language
comprehensive assessment 40, 51
computers 69, 125
concentration span 49, 62, 92, 122, 148, 177,
    232
    see also attentiveness
concept development 82
concrete learning 5, 71
conductive hearing loss 143–4, 148

cones 88
confidence 15, 59, 62, 63, 96, 103, 108, 123,
    179, 188, 192, 196, 200, 213, 217
    of parents 23, 24, 33
confidentiality 8
conformity 9
consent 7–8
consequences 218
    see also rewards, punishment
consequential thinking 183
consistency 218, **225–6**
consonants 159, 160
    see also milestones
constipation 136
consumers 22, 56
content
    differentiation 69–73
    of language 156, 158, 165, 168
    of programs 13, 59, 60, 73, 171, 174
continence 101
    see also toileting
contingency 141, 142
    see also joint referencing
cooperation 34, 59, 197, 201, 213, 215
cooperative efforts/play 42, 73, 203
coordination
    motor 102
    of services 13, 31–2
cortical vision impairment 83
counselling 31, 150
courtesy 33
crawling 100, 125
creativity 15, 59, 62
creeping 100
critical period 155
cross-eyed 85
culture 9, 10, 13, 33–5, 39, 45, 59, 98, 126,
    135, 155, 159, 190, 197

daily living skills **117–39**
deafness 140–1, 143, 152
decision making (by parents) 21
defensibility 39, 45
defensiveness 121
demand-based model 22
dependence 25
    see also independence
depression 194
depth perception 89, 90, 92
dermatitis 126
developmental delay 4, 103, 167
    see also intellectual disability

developmental
    coordination disorder (DCD) **101–3**, 104,
        105, 109, 110
    emergency 82
    model 8–9, 69–70
developmentally appropriate practice 13–14
diagnosis 37, 48, 51, 54, 228
    see also labels
dietitian 137
differentiation of programs 59–74
diplegia **99–101**, 109, 110
direct instruction 14, 171
    see also adult-directed teaching
directives 66
disability, defined 5
discipline 211
discrimination 7, 33, 192
    skills 82, 84, 94, 167
disease
    of joints 104
    of ear 144
    of eye 87, 90–1, 93
disengagement 119
    of parents 33–4
    see also engagement
dispositions 10, 15, 57, **58–9**, 65, 66, 70, 73,
    172, 176, **185–90**
distance, from speaker 148
distractability 90, 178
    see also attentiveness
diversity 9, 11, 59, 65
doctor *see* medical practitioner
double vision 86
Down syndrome 54, 92–3, 103, 108, **230**, 231,
    238–9
drawing 90
dressing 90, 99, **135**, 190
    see also milestones
drinking 97, 103, 105
    see also feeding
drugs
    illicit 163, 193, 228, 229
    treatment *see* medication
dual exceptionalities 240
Duchenne muscular dystrophy 104, 231, 239
dummy *see* pacifier
dyslexia 4, 240
dyspraxia 102

ear
    drum 146
    canal 151
    inner 107, 118, 143, 152

middle 141, 144, 146, 236
outer 144
wax 151
early intervention 4, 70
effects of 6, 19, 30
for hearing impairment 147, 152
for language impairments 167
timing of 6
eating 97, 103, 105, 118, 121, 138, 230
see also feeding
echolalia 163, 168, 234
ecological perspective 8–9, 16
effectiveness 216
efficacy 15, 188–9
efficiency of assessment 51
eligibility 30, 31, 32, 45, 48
emmetropia 84, 87
empathy 25, 150, 193, 207
emotional blackmail 8
emotional needs 15, **191–200**
employers, parents as 22
empowerment 20, 23, 51, 65, 68
empty vessels 8
endurance 102, 104, 109, 113, 114
engagement 11, 58, 67, 68, 70, 72, 142, 178, **186–7**
English as a second language 39, 145, 206
enlargement of text 86
enrichment 64
entry skills 204–5, 207
environment 12, 13, 59
differentiation 60–5, 93–4
epilepsy 92, 97, **232**, 235
see also seizures
equity 39, 46
esotropia 85
ethics **7–8**, 36, 211, 216
eustachian tube 146
evaluation 37, **75–6**
exclusion 192, 206–7
exhaustion 90
see also fatigue
exotropia 86
experts 21, 34, 213
exploration 14, 59, 65, 67, 68, 69, 108, 121, 175, 176, 237
expressive language 156, 158–9, 166, 190
see also milestones, speech
extended family 34
extensor muscles 106
extracurricular activities 105
see also leisure activities
eye-hand coordination 82–3, 86, 90, 92, 95

eye
contact/gaze 34, 83, 158, 197, 235
dominance/preference 90, 91
exercises 86, 94
movements 84–5, 91, 105, 118
sight 57

factory model of education 8
failure 189
falls 96, 99, 124, 232
false negatives 40
family-centred style 22–6
fatigue 130, 131, 132, 133
see also exhaustion, tiredness
fears 194
feedback 66, 68, 163, 171, 179–80, 183, 184, 189, 194, 198, 199, **218–9**
physical 97, 107, 110
proprioceptive 124
sensory 138
vestibular 123
feedforward 97, 107
feeding 97, 136–8, 164, 231, 232
see also eating, drinking, food, milestones
fetal alcohol effects/syndrome 229, 238
fidgeting 90
fine motor 64, 101
see also eye-hand coordination
first words 159, 161
fitness 58, 96, 98, 103, 105, 108, 111, 114
flexor muscles 106, 110
floor of tests 48
fluency
of skill use 58
of speech 156, 165
follow up 192–3
food 122, 138, 160, 161, 211
see also eating, feeding
form of language 156, 157, 158, 165, 168
fragile bones 101
fragile-X syndrome 229–30, 238
friendliness 23, 25–6
friendships 12, 26, 28, 196. 197, **200–2**
frustration 33, 102, 150, 170, 189
fun 191–2, 196, 225
functions of families 23–4

gaps in services 31
generalisation 13, 29, 58, 67, 70, 75, 103, 106, 107, 178, 184, **185**, 204
gifted children 1, 4, 5, 16, 24–5, 42, 45, 48, 52, 54 60, 63, **237**, **240**
behaviour of 263

characteristics of 260–3
cognitive skills of 177, 180, 181, 182–3, 260–61
emotional characteristics of 263
hand skills of 133
independence of 189
language skills of 164, 170, 172, 182, 261–2
learning style of 261
locus of control 189
motor skills of 104–5, 262
perfectionism 189, 198
social skills of 201, 262–3
vision skills of 93
glare 89, 149
glasses *see* lenses
glue ear 144
goal-directed movement 97, 107, 110
goals of discipline 213–5
God's will 34
goodness of fit 9, 11
Gower's sign 104
grammar 157, 169
grasp
development 126–7
pencil 91, 130–3
strength 129
gravity 103, 105, 118, 123, 138
grief 24
grip *see* grasp
grooming 136
see also milestones
group
composition 63, 65
size 62, 187, 217
story time 62, 63, 75, 109, 119, 168, 170, 202
gross motor *see* motor
guidelines 218

hand-eye coordination 82–3
see also eye-hand coordination
hand
dominance/preference 90, 132, **134–5**
grasp/grip 112, 124
skills 99, 125–35
handicap, defined 5
handling techniques 101, 108, 110
harm 7, 8
head
aches 89
banging 210, 235
control 97, 118

health 58, 97, 145, 236
see also illness
hearing 118
impairments 83, 92, 97, **140–53**, 165, 167
effects of 144, 163
heart *see* cardiac
helplessness 188, 199
hemiplegia 92, **99–100**, 108–9
heterogeneous grouping 63, 65
higher-order skills 58, 67, 68
highly able *see* gifted
hopping 110, **113–4**
see also milestones
horizontal relevance 75
hospitalisation 47
humanism 211, 213, 215, 221
humiliation 220
hydrocephalus 233–4
hygiene 136
see also milestones
hypertonia 100
hyperopia 84, 87, 89, 92
hypotonia 100, 232

ideal self 195, **198–9**
identification *see* assessment
ignoring behaviour 225
illness 74, 106, 234, 236–7
illumination *see* lighting
imagination 15
imitation, deferred 176
impairments 5, 228
impulsivity 54, 90, 102, 109, 115, 169, 222, 236
inclusion 10, **11–13**, 17
inclusive settings 28–9
independence 7, 62, 68, 74, 127, 169, 189–90, 197, 213
individualisation of programs 28, 29, **56–77**
individualised education plan (IEP) 21, 60
individualised family service plan (IFSP) 60
individually appropriate practice **13–14**
infections 82, 83, 91, 97, 144, 145, 148, 163, 232, 236, 237
information, parents' need for 26–7, 31
information processing 174, 232, 240
initiative 15
integration 10
intellectual delay/disability
and blindness 92
and cognitive skills 177, 180, 182
and generalisaiton 185
and independence 189

and language skills 164, 166, 171
and locus of control 188
and physical disabilities 103, 106, 109, 110
and social skills 12, 201, 204
causes of 228–235
definition 4, 26
see also learning difficulty/disability
intellectual development 126
intelligence tests 43–5
intentionality 175
interaction 12
interdisciplinary 16–17, 32, 97, 101–2, 167
    see also multidisciplinary
interests 60, 67, 70, 179, 187
integration 71
intelligibility 150
intensity of voice 156, 159
interpreters 27
    see also translators
interrelated development 10, 71
intimacy 10, 66
intimidation 33, 216
intonation 34, 150, 156, 159, 165, 234
irritability 102, 109
isolated children 12, 201–2
    parents 29
IQ tests 43–5

jargon 27, 34
jaw lifting 138
    opening 109
    see also mouth opening
joint
    alignment 104
    movement 107
    referencing 163
    see also contingency
judgment–based assessment 43
jumping 109, 110, **113–4**, 123
justice 7, 38, 45, 216

knowledge acquisition skills 174, 176,
    177–82

labels 26, 39, **54–5**, 228
language 156
    delay 166
    disability/impairment 74, 83, 101, 141,
        154–5, 166
        signs of 168–9
    skills 15, 47, 58, 94, 190
    see also comprehension
lazy eye 85–6

learned helplessness 188
learning difficulty/disability 4–5, 101, 155,
    181, 184
    see also intellectual disability
learning style 13, 190, 199, 261
    see also dispositions
legislation 3
leisure activities 32
lenses, corrective 81, 82, 86, 92
ligaments 103, 230
lighting 63, 93, 149, 150
limits on professional relationship 26
limps 99, **104**
lip reading 151
listening 22, 32, 66, 220
    training 94
    with eyes 219
literacy 58, 94, 104, 159, 171–2
locus of control 188–9, 211, 213
loneliness 12, 201
long-sightedness 57, 84, 87, 92
low vision clinic 91

macula 84, 86, 93
magnification 86
mainstreaming 10
maintenance of skills 58
    see also generalisation
manipulation skills 130
marionette 231
massage 122, 123
mean 51–2
means–end analysis 176, 184
mediation of
    learning 14, 17, **67–8**, 187, 190
    social skills 204–6
medical 97, 104
    practitioner 91, 101, 108, 136, 148
    see also health, illness
medication 47, 97, 110, 232, 235, 236
meetings 21, 27, 29–30
melting pot 9
memory 68, 102, 156, 164, 174, 178 180–2,
    185, 190
mental retardation 5
    see also intellectual disability
metacognitive skills 14, 15, 174, 176, 179,
    182–5, 190
methods of teaching 13
    see also process
midline 109, 114, 134
milestones 16, 39, 41, 43, 52, 70
    in each developmental domain 241–58

mistakes 180, 188, 189, 192–3, 194, 197, 198–9, 216, 219–20
mobility training 94, 101
mode of learning 179
monitoring 38, 52, **75–6**
morphemes 157, 171
morphology 156, 157, 169
motherese 162
    see also baby talk, parentese
motivation 77, 83, 103, 106, 135, 175, **187–8**
motor
    control 85
    development 126
    learning 97–8, 107–16
    planning 102, 103, 112, 126
    skills 89, 96–116
mouth–opening 104
    see also jaw opening
mouthing objects 63, 121, 123
movement
    dysfunctional reactions to 123–4
    sequencing 106
    speed 99
    strength 99
    see also motor
multidisciplinary team 16, 29–30, 136
    see also interdisciplinary team
muscle
    length/balance 97, 103, 106, 110
    strength 97, 103, 104, 107, 110, 124
    tone 97, 98, 100, 102, 103, 107, 118, 128, 137, 138, 164, 231
muscular dystrophy 104, 231, 239
musculoskeletal 97, 107, 108, 111
mutual gaze 141–2
myelomeningocoele 101, 233–4, 239
myopia 87, 89, 92, 94

nasality 156, 165
natural consequences 67, 219, 226
naturalistic learning/teaching 14, 29, **66–8,** 170–1, 187
near body senses 118
neck instability 108
    see also atlantoaxial instability
needs of families 26–32
neglect 163, **193–5,** 201, 206
negotiated curriculum plan (NCP) 60
nervous system 83, 97, 107, 118, 121, 236
neural pathways 57
neural tube defects 233–4
    see also spina bifida
noise 145, 148

non-verbal communication 150, 155, 156, 157, 158, 163, 164, 204, 235
    see also body language
normalisation 10, 11
normed tests 38, 43–6
numeracy 58
nystagmus 85, 86, 92

obedience 195, 215
obesity 231
    see also weight
object permanence 176
observation 41–2, 88
occipital lobe 83
occupational therapy 29, 43, 117, 136, 137
one size fits all 13
optic nerve 83
optometrists 90–1, 92, 94, 95
opthalmologists 91, 92
options 11, 30
opposite response 225
oral-motor skills 164
orientation 105
    training 94
orthoptists 91
orthotics 104, 110
oscillation of eyes 86
osteoporotic bones 101
otitis media 144, 146, 147
outsourcing 31
overtesting 49

pace 59, 68, 124, 178, 184
pacifier 122, 145
pain, awareness of 121, 234
parent-professional relationship 21–2
parentese 162, 170
    see also baby talk
parents 13, 226
    as teachers 19, 21, 24
    collaboration with 1, 16, **19–35,** 41–2
    involvement in assessment 50–1
    with a disability 23
parents' reactions to
    disability 24, 150
    giftedness 24–5
partner, communication 149–50, 170
passivity 13–14, 66, 155, 175
patching of eyes 86
pattern interruption 224
percentile rank 52–3
perception 175, 235
perfectionism 189, 194, 198

peripheral vision 85, 90
permanence, of objects 176
persistence 15, 59, 66, 67, 188, 189, 213
phenlyketonuria (PKU) 4, 231, 239
phonemes 156, 158
phonological awareness 171, 172
phonology 156, 157, 168–9
photophobia 89, 94
physical disabilities 47, 82, **96–116**, 178, 240
   and social inclusion 201
physical skills 15, 58
   see also motor skills
physiotherapy 14, 29, 97, 101, 104, 109, 112,
   137
Piaget 14
pigeon–toed 111, 115
   see also milestones
pitch of voice *see* intonation
pity 25
PKU (phenlyketonuria) 4, 231, 239
placement 10, 28, 38, 40, 41, 48, 63, 64, 170,
   202, 203
planning, by parents 27
plateaus of development 49–50, 173
play 12, **14–15**, 57, 68–9, 155, 169–70, 201
   stereotypical 234
   themes of 71
pluralism 9–10, 25, 215
policy 3
popularity 12
portfolios 41, 73
positioning 108, 137, 178
positiveness 23
postmodern perspective 8–9, 16
posture 89, 231
postural control 98, 103, 106–7
   see also balance
potency 15, 215
poverty 23, 33, 228, 229
practice effects 49
Prader-Willi syndrome 164, **231**
pragmatics 156, 157, 158, 168–9
pragmatism 40
praise 198, 218–9
   see also rewards
pregnancy 234
prematurity 92, 145, 229, 231–2, 234, 239
   see also birth weight
prevention 4
primary
   behaviours 211
   service provider 17
priorities 21, 33, 34, 53–4

privatisation 31
problem solving **183–4**
   skills 58, 66, 67, 175, 181
   with parents 33
   see also collaborative problem solving
processes, learning 10, 59, 60, 73, 74, 171,
   174, 187, 198
   differentiation 65–9
products 59, 60
   differentiation 73–4
prognosis 54
program
   aims 58
   differentiation 59–74
   individualisation 28, 29, **56–77**
projects 73
prompts 67, 68, 109, 112, 171, 184, 204
proprioception 102, 107, 112, 113, 118, 122,
   124
   dysfunctional reactions 124–5
propulsion 113, 115
prosody 159, 165
protection 191, 192–5
protectiveness training 194–5
pseudohypertrophy 104
psychologist 136, 167
punishment 211, 215, 216, 217, 225
   disadvantages of 214
pupil size 89
purposes
   of assessment 37–8
   of early childhood education 56–7
pushy (parents) 24
put-downs 198

quadriplegia 100
quality
   of learning 59, 240
   of life 54, 167
   of voice 151, 159, 165
questions 67

racial differences 47
   see also culture, discrimination
radio 144
rapport 23, 47
ratios of adults to children 12, 62, 217
readiness 69–70, 155
reading 64, 86, 89, 93, 95, 144, 155, 171–2
realism 23
receptive language 156, 158, 166, 190
   see also comprehension, milestones
recreation 23, 96

referral 32, 90, 91, 148
reflexes 85, 100, 164, 231, 232
refractive errors 82, 85, 86, **87**, 89, 91, 92
reframing 224
rehearsal 182, 185
reinforcement *see* rewards
relationships 10, 15, 59, 217
    see also friendships
release 128
relevance 75, 188
reliability of tests 44–5, 48
remedial training 14
reports, assessment 36, 40
resonance 156, 159
respect 198, 200
respiratory problems 108, 231, 236
respite care 31
responsiveness 23, 25
retardation 5
    see also intellectual disability
reticence 201, 204
retina 83, 84, 88
retinitis pigmentosa 93–4
retinopathy 92
Rett syndrome 231
reverberation 148
reversal 225
rewards 8, 211, 215, 216, 217, 219, 225, 226
    disadvantages of 212
rhythm 109, 114, 165
rights 13, 211, 215, 221
    of parents 20, 21
risk taking 124, 180, 196, 198–9
rods 88
rotation 105–6, 109, 111, 130
rote learning 70, 235
Rousseau 8
routines 75, 187, 217, 235
rules 218
running 100, 113–4
    see also milestones

saccadic eye movements 85, 91
safety 28–9, 62, 83, 96, 109, 112, 118, 123,
    124, 191, **192–5**, 199, 207, 217
safety programs 194–5
saving face 219–20
scaffolding 14, 67, 141, 190
    see also mediation of learning
school, choice of 30
scissors 125, 126, 132, 133–4
screening 37, 40, 88, 230, 233
secondary

behaviours 211
    disabling conditions 69, 94
    prevention 4
second opinion 51
segregated settings 28–9
seizures 83, 97, 231, 232, 233
    see also epilepsy
self-actualisation 192
self-care tasks 129, 135–8
    see also self-help skills, milestones
self-concept 194, 195, 218
self-control 59, 182–3, 195, 197, 213, 219,
    221–3
self-discipline 213–4
self-efficacy *see* efficacy, locus of control
self-esteem 59, 95, 101, 102, 191, 194, **195–9**
self-help skills 94
self-instruction 183, 190, 197
self-regulation *see* self–control
self-talk 169
    see also self–instruction
semantics 156, 159, 161, 168–9
sensitivity 10, 23–5, 217
sensorineural hearing loss 143, 145
sensory
    defensiveness 121
    disabilities/impairments 47, 63, 96, 106,
        166, 167, 171, 233, 240
    integration 118–25, 126
    modulation 121
    processing 104, 109, 118–25
    sensitivity 235
separation
    difficulties 196
    marital 23
sequencing
    movements 106, 109
    sounds 166
short-sightedness 87, 89, 92, 94
shunt 233–4
sign languages 142, 151, 155, 164
    see also augmentive communication
        systems
size of groups 62, 187, 217
skill fingers/side 128, 132
smell 118, 125
smoking 145
social
    justice 38, 45
    play 68–9
    skill interventions 150, 193, **202–8**
    skills 83, 94, 142
socialisation 15, 23, 59, 114

sole parents 23
somatosensation *see* proprioception
space 34, 60
spanking 211
spastic 99, 100, 231
spatial awareness/perception 82, 102
   see also visuospatial
specialists 13, 16, 69, 73, 97, 173
specific
   developmental language disorder 166
   language impairment 166
   learning disabilities
   see also learning disabilities
speech 83, 103, 156, 158–9
   disorders 165
   see also milestones
speech/language pathologists 14, 29, 43, 137,
   165, 167
spina bifida 101, 233–4
   see also myelomeningocoele
splinter skills 75
spurts of growth/development 49–50, 101
squint 89
   see also strabismus
stamina 136, 233
   see also endurance
standard deviation 52, 53
standing frame 101, 108
statistics 51–3
status 8, 21
stepfamilies 23
stigma 5, 54, 237
story time 62, 63, 75, 109, 119, 168, 170, 172,
   202
strabismus **85–6**, 92
strength 113
   see also muscle strength
stress 74, 119, 199, **200**, 223
stretching of muscles 104, 110, 111
stuttering 165
style of learning 13, 190, 261
   see also dispositions
sucking 118, 160
surgery 86, 97, 103, 110, 232, 233
survival 23, 187, 191, 193, 222
sway back 104
symbolic play 176
sympathy 25
syntax 156, 157, 161, 168–9

tactile *see* touch
tactile defensive 121
tailored activities 71

talented children *see* gifted
tantrums 221–3, 225, 235
taste 118, 125
teacher-directed instruction *see* adult-directed
   teaching
team 16–17
technological adaptations 69
television 125
tendons 104, 110
tertiary prevention 4
testing 36–55
   defined 37
themes of play 71
therapy 29, 74
tiered
   activities 72
   products 74
time away 223–4
time out 211, 223
tiptoes 114
tiredness 102, 109, 119, 150
   see also fatigue
toe
   standing 99, 100, 109
   walking 100, 102, **103–4**, 110, 235
toileting 136
   see also bladder, bowel
tone *see* muscle tone
tongue movements 138, 160
top-down model 57, 70
topic 58, 150, 157, 161, 168
touch 34, 102, 118, 168
   activities to integrate 123
   reactions to 121
   sensitivity 103
toys 67, 72, 82, 161, 203
tracking (of eyes) 57, 93, 118
traffic 62
training of staff 13
trampoline 103, 112, 113, 123, 124
transdisciplinary team 17
transitions 24, 30–1, 35, 43, 68, **74–5**, 186–7,
   197
translators 34
trauma 145, 163, 232–3
   see also brain injury
tunnel vision 81, 94

underachievement 54, 196
undressing 135
   see also dressing, milestones
unilateral hearing impairment 144
use of language 156, 157, 158, 165

validity of tests 44–5, 48
values 1, 6, **7–10**, 11, 25, 35, 59
vehicular crashes 145, 232
vertical
   relevance 75
   surfaces 89, 132
vestibular sense 107, 118, 123
views of childhood 8, 56, 213
vision 101, 117, 118, 125, 126, 140, 141, 148,
   152
vision impairment **81–95**, 97, 98, 107, 114,
   163–4
   signs of 88–90
visuospatial 111, 113
   see spatial perception
vocabulary 167, 168, 171, 172
   see also first words, milestones
volume 144, 156, 159, 165
Vygotsky 14

waiting time 62, 187
walking 97
   see also motor skills
web space 132
weight 230
   bearing 99, 103, 108–9, 125, 128
   birth, low 145, 163, 228, 231–2, 234,
     239
   shift 105–6, 108–9, 112
   see also prematurity
wheelchairs 63, 101, 108
withdrawal 102, 148, 193, 200, 213
World Health Organisation 6
wrist 128
writing 114, 125, 126, 131, 132, 133, 144, 155

X–chromosome 88, 229–30, 238

zone of proximal development 14